APPLEWOOD'S
AMERICAN CITIES
SERIES

A History of Boston

*The metropolis of Massachusetts from Its
origin to the present period*

Caleb Hopkins Snow

D1207712

APPLEWOOD BOOKS
Carlisle, Massachusetts

A History of Boston
was originally published in
1825

ISBN: 978-1-4290-2191-3

APPLEWOOD'S
AMERICAN CITIES
SERIES

Thank you for purchasing an Applewood book.
Applewood reprints America's lively classics—books from the past
that are still of interest to modern readers.

Our mission is to build a picture of the past through primary sources.
We do not change a word of the editions we reissue, believing that it is
important to present the past without editing it. Sometimes words, thoughts,
images or ideas from the past may seem inappropriate to the
modern reader. We apologize for any discomfort this may bring.
We believe in the value of bringing the past back, just as it was,
for the purposes of informing the present and future.

This facsimile was printed using many new technologies together
to bring our tradition-bound mission to you. Applewood's facsimile
edition of this work may include library stamps, scribbles, and margin notes
as they exist in the original book. These interesting historical artifacts
celebrate the place the book was read or the person who read the book.
In addition to these artifacts, the work may have additional errors
that were either in the original, in the digital scans,
or introduced as we prepared the book for printing. If you believe the work has such
errors, please let us know by writing to us at the address below.

For a free copy of our current print catalog featuring our bestselling books, write to:

APPLEWOOD BOOKS
P.O. Box 27
Carlisle, MA 01741

For more complete listings, visit us on the web at www.awb.com

PREPARED FOR PRINTING BY HP

J. Kidder del.

Entered according to Act of Congress, by A. Bowen.

A. Bowen Sc.

SOUTH EAST VIEW OF BOSTON.

A

HISTORY OF BOSTON,

THE

Metropolis of Massachusetts,

FROM ITS

ORIGIN TO THE PRESENT PERIOD;

WITH SOME

ACCOUNT OF THE ENVIRONS.

BY CALEB H. SNOW, M. D.

Mons Idæus ubi et gentis cunabula n   ''*·rgil.*

EMBELLISHED WITH ENGRAVINGS.

BOSTON :

PUBLISHED BY ABEL BOWEN, No. 2, CONGRESS-SQUARE,
CONGRESS-STREET.

PRINTED BY MUNROE AND FRANCIS,
128 WASHINGTON-STREET.
1825.

DISTRICT OF MASSACHUSETTS, TO WIT:

District Clerk's Office.

BE it remembered, that on the twenty eighth day of November, A. D. 1825, in the fifti-
eth year of the Independence of the *United States of America*, ABEL BOWEN, of the
said District, has deposited in this Office the title of a book, the right whereof he claims
as Proprietor, in the words following, *to wit :*

A HISTORY of BOSTON, the Metropolis of Massachusetts ; from its origin to the present period. With some account of the Environs. By CALEB H. SNOW, M. D. Mons
Idæus ubi et gentis cunabula nostræ.—*Virgil.* Embellished with Engravings,

In conformity to the act of the Congress of the United States, entitled, "An act for
the encouragement of learning, by securing the copies of maps, charts and books, to the
authors and proprietors of such copies, during the times therein mentioned:" and also
to an act, entitled, "An act supplementary to an act, entitled an act for the encouragement of learning, by securing the copies of maps, charts, and books, to the authors and
proprietors of such copies during the times therein mentioned ; and extending the benefits
thereof to the arts of designing, engraving and etching, historical and other prints."

JOHN W. DAVIS, *Clerk of the District of Massachusetts.*

PREFACE.

THE reader may expect to find in this book some account of the persecutions, which drove the first settlers of New England from their native country, and some brief notices of the settlements, that were made or attempted to be made, in various parts of the United States, before the arrival of Governour Winthrop and the company under him, which laid the foundation of Boston. There taking up our history, I have endeavoured to select from the mass of records, which numerous hands have left to us, those facts which appear to have excited any great or general interest among the inhabitants of this metropolis.

To those who are aware of the disadvantages under which I have composed this work, I need offer no apology for the imperfections they may discover in the execution of it. To others it may be proper to mention, that Mr. Bowen, the publisher, was disappointed in his expectation of the assistance of other gentlemen, and that my engagements with him commenced at least four weeks after his proposals of the 17th April, 1824, had been issued. To enable him to fulfil the terms of those proposals, I was obliged to let the first number appear, on the first of July, before I could possibly know what the succeeding number should contain. The case has been similar with all the other numbers. I have consequently found it necessary to put my notes to the press, almost in the same form in which I had taken them, at the hazard of being compelled afterwards to exclude other matter, perhaps more important. These circumstances, indeed, do not derogate from the correctness of the work, or from its usefulness as a book of reference, so far as it extends, yet they may account for some peculiarities, which might otherwise have been amended ; and the same circumstances will, I trust, sufficiently apologize for any disproportion between the importance of some of the subjects and the attention I seem to have bestowed upon them. It has been my aim to be accurately minute and scrupulously correct : some errours are marked in the errata, (into which also has crept the mistake of *Barton's* for *Purton's* ;) and I am requested to rectify another, which occurs on page 356, attributing to Mr. Wallcut an agency in the formation of the Historical Society, to which he makes no claim.

As Mr. Bowen is the proprietor of Shaw's Description of Boston, I have, sometimes without the formality of marks of quotation, made such use of that book as suited the purposes of mine ; how much I have depended on it may be ascertained, if any have the curiosity to compare the two. It is right, however, to state, that this volume contains three times the quantity of matter contained in Mr. Shaw's, and thirty-two pages more than were originally promised, besides several extra plates.

While engaged in this pursuit, I have been particularly indebted to the libraries of the Historical Society and the Athenæum : the records in the offices of the secretary of the commonwealth and clerks of the city have been of much service to me : every facility has been afforded at each of these places for the accomplishment of my object ; and I have great reason to acknowledge my obligations to the gentlemen who have those invaluable archives and collections in charge, and no less to many private gentlemen, for the patience and politeness with which they have attended to my frequent calls for information and assistance.

CALEB H. SNOW.

Boston, October 20, 1825.

Plan of BOSTON in 1824

NAMES

OF THE

STREETS, LANES, PUBLICK EDIFICES, &c.

IN THE CITY OF BOSTON, JULY, 1824.

N. B. To find any street on the plan, search for the number annexed, in the square given by the letters following the name; thus, for School-street look in square F h, and you find the number 123. Publick edifices, &c. not numbered, are located within the squares referred to. The wards are designated by large figures, and the dotted lines show the boundaries of each. The ancient high-water mark is shown by the shading on the new plan.

Allen st. N.	-	-	-	C d	52	Causeway st.	-	-	E c	30
Allen st. S.	-	-	-	C e	53	Central st.	-	-	H h	96
Ann st.	-	-	-	I e	24	Central court	-	-	E j	
Arch st.	-	-	-	F j	138	Centre st. N.	-	-	H f	28
Ash st.	-	-	-	D n	162	Centre st.	-	-	B g	69
Atkinson st.	-	-	-	H j	110	Chamber st.	-	-	C f	60
Bangs alley	-	-	-	H h		Charlestown st.	-	-	G d	34
Bath st.	-	-	-	H i	93	Chardon st.	-	-	E f	64
Battery alley	-	-	-	J c	10	Charles st.	-	-	A h	129
Battery-march st.	-	-	H h	95		Charter st.	-	-	H b	3
Beach st.	-	-	-	E l	150	Chauncy place	-	-	F j	139
Beacon st.	-	-	-	E h	124	Chesnut st.	-	-	B i	131
Bedford st.	-	-	-	E k	142	Clark st.	-	-	I d	14
Bedford place	-	-	-	F k		Columbia st.	-	-	F k	147
Belknap st.	-	-	-	C g	73	Common st.	-	-	E i	134
Bennet st. S.	-	-	-	F n	156	Congress st.	-	-	G h	91
Bennet st. N.	-	-	-	I d	9	Cooks court	-	-	F b	
Berry st.	-	-	-	H j	111	Copeland lane	-	-	F f	
Blossom st.	-	-	-	C f	58	Cornhill court	-	-	G h	
Bowdoin st.	-	-	-	D g	77	Court st.	-	-	F h	92
Bowdoin place	-	-	D h			Court square	-	-	F h	
Bowdoin square	-	-	E f	65		Crab alley	-	-	H h	
Boylston st.	-	-	-	D l	151	Crescent court	-	-	E e	
Boylston court	-	-	D l			Cross st.	-	-	H e	27
Boylston square	-	-	D l			Custom house st.	-	I h	98	
Brattle st.	-	-	-	F g	83	Custom house	-	-	I h	98
Brattle sq.	-	-	-	G g	198	Deacon st.	-	-	F e	180
Bread st.	-	-	-	I h	99	Derne st.	-	-	D g	181
Bridge st.	-	-	-	B f	57	Devonshire st.	-	-	G h	89
Brighton st.	-	-	-	B c	47	Distill-house square	-	F e	41	
Broad st.	-	-	-	I h	102	Doane st.	-	-	H h	
Bromfield lane	-	-	F i	122		Dock square	-	-	H g	
Bulfinch st.	-	-	-	E g	78	East st.	-	-	G l	182
Bulfinch place	-	-	E g			Eaton st.	-	-	C e	56
Bumstead place	-	-	E i			Elliot st.	-	-	D m	152
Butolph st.	-	-	-	C g	71	Elm st.	-	-	G f	81
Butlers row	-	-	-	H g		Essex st.	-	-	E l	146
Cambridge st.	-	-	-	C f	66	Exchange st.	-	-	G g	86
Carnes court	-	-	-	F f		Federal st.	-	-	G j	126
Carver st.	-	-	-	C m	160	Federal court S.	-	-	G j	
Castle st.	-	-	-	D o	165	Federal court N.	-	-	G f	

PRINCIPAL WHARVES.

NOTED BLOCKS.

PUBLICK EDIFICES.

State house - -	D h	South Boston School	
Laboratory -	C l	Boylston Hall -	D l
Town house, or old State house	G h	Medical College	D k
Old Court house -	F h	Massachusetts General Hospital	B e
County Court house	F h	Province House -	F i
Municipal Court house	D d	Asylum for Indigent Boys	H e
Jail and House of Correction	D d	Female Orphan Asylum -	F l
House of Industry	South Boston	City Market and Gallery of fine arts	G g
Alms House -	C c	Parkman's Market -	B f
Faneuil Hall -	H g	Columbian Museum -	F h
Ward Room, No. 3	G d	New England Museum -	F g
Eliot School, N. Bennet st.	G d	Atheneum -	H j
Hancock School, Hanover st.	G e	Theatre - -	J j
Mayhew School, Hawkins st.	F e	Concert Hall -	F g
Bowdoin School, Derne st.	D g	Exchange Coffee House	G h
High school, Pinckney st. -	B g	Green Dragon -	G f
Latin School, School st. -	F h	Washington Gardens -	E j
Adams School, Mason st. -	E j	Pantheon Hall -	D l
Franklin School, Nassau st.	D m	Marlboro' Hotel -	F i
Boylston School, Fort Hill	I j	Custom House -	I h

CHURCHES.

CONGREGATIONAL.

First, Chauncy place -	F j	Eighth, Hollis st. -	D m
Second, Hanover st.	H e	Ninth, Lynde st. -	D f
Third, Old South -	F i	Tenth, Park st. -	E i
Fourth, Brattle st. -	32 G g	Eleventh, Essex st. -	E k
Fifth, Clark st. -	I d	Twelfth, N. Allen st. -	C e
Sixth, Summer st. -	G k	Thirteenth -	South Boston
Seventh, Federal st. -	G j		

BAPTIST.

First, Stillman st.	H d	Third, Charles st. -	A h
Second, Salem st. -	H d	African, Belknap st. -	C g

EPISCOPALIAN.

King's Chapel, Common st.	F h	St. Paul's, Common st. -	D i
Christ's ch. Salem st. -	H c	St. Matthew's, South Boston -	
Trinity ch. Summer st.	F j		

QUAKER.

Congress st. - -	G h

UNIVERSALIST.

First, North Bennet st. -	I d	Third, Bulfinch st. -	E g
Second, School st. -	F i		

METHODIST.

First, Methodist alley -	J c	Second, Bromfield lane -	E i

ROMAN CATHOLICK.

Church of the Holy Cross, Franklin st. F j   St. Augustine's Chapel, South Boston.

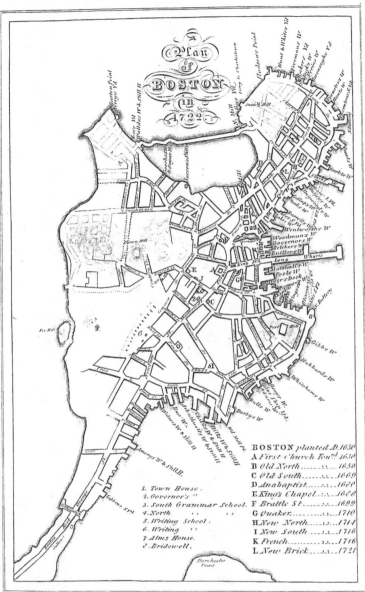

A Plan of BOSTON in 1722.

BOSTON planted A.D. 1630
A First Church En^d 1630
B Old North 1650
C Old South 1669
D Anabaptist 1660
E King's Chapel 1688
F Brattle St 1699
G Quaker 1710
H New North 1714
I New South 1716
K French 1716
L New Brick 1721

1. Town House.
2. Governor's "
3. South Grammar School.
4. North " "
5. Writing School.
6. Writing "
7. Alms House.
8. Bridewell.

Dorchester Point

Entered according to Act &c   by Bowen   A. Bowen Sc.

HISTORY OF BOSTON.

INTRODUCTION.

The City of Boston owes its origin to a spirit of civil and religious liberty, which was excited to action by the persecutions that prevailed in England, during the reigns of Queen Elizabeth, and Kings James and Charles the First. Most of those who can properly be considered as *first settlers* arrived here, and in other parts of New-England, prior to the year sixteen hundred and forty-three. By that time, it is computed, the number of emigrants amounted to twenty-one thousand two hundred souls, or thereabouts.*

Had this multitude been composed of barbarian hordes, who, in their wanderings for sustenance, might have chanced to light upon this fair theatre in its wild and savage state, we should have had no interest in tracing their history. The wilderness they found, would have remained a wilderness still, and their descendants have been dancing yet to the orgies of Woonand and Mannit, or listening to the powaws of Hobbamoc and Kiehtan. Not so with us : the hand of refinement has beautified the charms of nature ; monuments of art in our own habitations and in the temples of our God, a thousand endearments and ten thousand privileges enjoyed, invite us on every side to inquire into the character of the men that have preceded us, and to review the steps in which our fathers and ourselves have been led from infancy to our present state. To do this is the object we have now set before us ; and we are animated to the work by the persuasion,

---

* *Neal*, N. E. ch. V. states the number at 4000, and thinks the above computation very extravagant, on the ground that only 298 transports were employed. A little calculation, however, would have shown that if each of those had brought 72 persons, the number would be accounted for : whereas some of them were ships of good burthen that carried about two

2

that a familiar acquaintance with the story of our early times
will tend to generate in the reader ' a love of country of the
best complexion, and of the highest order ; a love of country
chastened and improved by elevated sentiments and dignified
examples ;' while the recapitulation of events more recent
may serve to gratify the pride, which springs from a consciousness of having borne a part in transactions worthy to be
recorded.

---

hundred passengers apiece. Besides, if any confidence is to be placed in the following
estimate, which Neal cites without any doubts, the matter is almost certainly decided.

Johnson, in his Wonder-Working Providence, published in London, 1654, has thus stated
the costs of the expedition. Chap. 13, 14.

The passage of the persons - - - - - - - - - - - - - - - -	95,000*l.*
The transportation of swine, goats, sheep, neate and horse, exclusive of their cost -	12,000
Getting food for all the persons until they could get the wood to tillage -	45,000
Nayles, glasse, and other iron worke for their meeting-houses, and other dwelling houses, before they could raise any other meanes in the country to purchase them - - - - - - - - - - - - - - - - - - -	18,000
Armes, powder, bullet, and match, with great artillery - - - - - - -	22,000
	192,000*l.*

"The whole sum amounts unto 192,000*l.* beside that which the adventurers laid out in
England—neither let any man think the sum above expressed did defray the whole charge
of this army."

The charge for a passage was 5 pounds for a person ;—nursing children not to be reckoned ; those under four years old, three for one; under eight years, two for one ; under twelve
years, three for two.—*Prince,* Dec. 1. 1629.—*Judge Davis'* Disc.

CHAPTER I.

From smoking racks and burning flame,
Through seas of their own blood, they came.

Ver. Lau.

THE fathers of Boston entered upon the stage of life while
Elizabeth enjoyed the throne, and they learnt in the nursery,
the tale of former persecution and of deaths for conscience
sake. It would have been happy for them, if her reign had
afforded no occasion to recollect the relation she bore to her
tyrannical father and more cruel sister. She indeed discountenanced popery, but established a church herself, to whose
rites and ceremonies it was most unpardonable heresy not to
conform. ' My masters and ye ministers of London,' was
the word, ' the Council's pleasure is, that ye strictly keep the
unity of apparel, like this man who stands here, canonically
habited, with a square cap, a scholar's gown, priest-like,
with a tippet, and in the church a linen surplice. Ye that
will subscribe, write *Volo* ; those that will not subscribe, write
Nolo ; be brief ; make no words.' The consequence of a
refusal was immediate suspension, with threats of deprivation
in case of not conforming within three months. Many were
accordingly suspended and deprived, and rules were enacted
which forbid printers and booksellers to publish any appeal
the sufferers might desire to make.

The weight of this harsh treatment fell in the first instance
upon ministers. Great numbers of the laity, however, sympathized with them ; they abhorred the habits, and would not
frequent the churches where they were used. Several of the
deprived ministers, therefore, and their friends, associated
and resolved to break off from the public churches, and to
assemble for worship in private houses, or elsewhere as they
had opportunity ; this step was the era or date of the *Separation*, 1566. Such a procedure could not fail to heighten the
displeasure of the Queen and her bishops. The commissioners were enjoined to be still more severe ; and thereupon
twenty-four men and seven women were seized and cast into
prison, for attending a sermon and communion service in a
private hall, and having the boldness to defend their conduct
before the bishop of London and other magistrates. But
neither their arguments nor their sufferings had any influence
to effect the deliverance of the puritans. As we approach

nearer to the period of our particular history, we find them
exposed to impositions less and less tolerable ; and as a natural result of persecution, more and more convinced, both of
the correctness of their own principles, and of the errors of
their persecutors.   Most of their objections had hitherto been
made to the *ceremonies* of the church :   to these they came
by degrees to add doubts concerning her doctrines.   This
widened the extent of their criminality, and the more certainly to convict them, they were compelled to answer upon oath
against themselves.

In the midst of so much wrong, it is gratifying to discover
that there was a spirit in the parliament which convened in
1571, to attempt something in favour of the puritans.   An act
was passed with that view, but no material benefit ever accrued from it.   The commissioners went on rigorously executing
the old laws against all opponents of the established church.
Among others, two anabaptists suffered under the act for burning of hereticks, in Smithfield, July 1575.   The narrowness
of the terms of conformity reduced the number of able
preachers : most of the incumbents were disguised papists, or
such conformists as were incapable of performing the ministerial duties.   A fourth part at least of all the preachers in
England were under suspension, and so many parishes were
vacated that persons who wished to hear a sermon must go
five, seven, twelve, and even twenty miles, and that too under
the penalty of a fine for being absent from their parish church,
where no service was performed.   More effectually to distress
both people and ministers, the former were forbidden to employ any of the latter as instructers of their children.

The people of London and Cornwall petitioned parliament
for relief : the whole country exclaimed against the bishops
for their high proceedings, but all to little purpose.   Some
slight appearances of milder measures were now and then to
be seen, but the next day would dissipate all hope, and the
dissenters would be called to witness the public execution of
their friends on the gallows.   The Queen continued resolutely
bent on perfect obedience to her requirements, and in 1583
established a *court of high commission*, with powers to inquire
into misdemeanors by every way and means they could devise, and to punish by fine or imprisonment according to their
discretion.   The proceedings of this tribunal were as merciless as its powers were boundless :   and when the Commons
inclined to remedy some of the evils that arose from this and
other measures of the Queen, they found out the iniquity of
the act of supremacy, which vested the whole power of re-
forming the policy of the church in the single person of her
Majesty, who would permit no infringement on her prerogative from any quarter whatsoever.

Under these circumstances the puritans could expect no
amelioration of their condition during her reign : they therefore looked forward with anxious hopes, to the probable accession of King James, who, having been bred a puritan,
they anticipated would redress their wrongs. Elizabeth died
on the 24th of March, 1603, and James came to the throne
only to disappoint these hopes. He had hardly been king a
year before a proclamation was issued, in which he ordered
the puritan ministers either to conform by a given day, or
dispose of themselves and families some other way. He was
determined to be rid of them, and to sanction his own will,
procured the opinion of several judges, that it was lawful to
deprive such ministers as would not conform, that it was not
necessary to furnish one accused, with a copy of his charge,
and that it was treasonable to frame petitions and collect numerous signatures to the same, as the puritans had done. After these determinations, the Archbishop, Bancroft, resumed
fresh courage and pursued the nonconformists without the
least compassion. The most trifling causes furnished ground
for the prosecution of the laity, and three hundred of the
clergy were either silenced, or deprived, or excommunicated,
or cast into prison, or forced to leave their country, by the
end of the year 1604.

A considerable number of religious people had left England, in the time of Mary's persecutions, and some of them
returned on Elizabeth's accession. We have detailed sufficiently the reception they met, and we behold them now
reduced to the alternatives of stifling their consciences or
quitting their homes. Among those who preferred the latter,
we perceive a company, to whose unwavering attachment to
pure and undefiled religion we are indebted for the settlement
of our country. In the spring of 1608, the persecution growing still hotter, the Rev. John Robinson with a church under
his care removed into Holland and settled at Leyden.* They
had not long been there, before they found themselves encountered with many inconveniences : they felt that they
were neither for health, nor purse, nor language, well accommodated, but the concern which they most of all had, was for
their posterity. They could not, with ten years' endeavours,
bring their neighbours to any suitable observance of the
Lord's day, without which they knew that all practical religion must wither miserably : their children left them, some becoming soldiers, and others sailors; in a few years more their

* Their first attempt to escape was made at Boston, in Lincolnshire, where they were seized and searched, rifled of their money, books, &c. and then committed to prison. After a
month's confinement the greatest part were dismissed, but seven of the principal men were
detained and bound over to the assizes.—*Hutch.* ii. app. No. 1.

descendants would be Dutch, and their church extinct. These
and other reasons they considered deeply, and after much deliberation took up the resolution, under the conduct of Heav-
en, to remove into AMERICA.*

CHAPTER II.

The world was all before them, where to choose
Their place of rest, and Providence their guide.

                                        Milton.

AT the time when that resolution was taken, very little was
known of the state of this part of America. Columbus, who
was a Genoese, had discovered the West Indies in 1492, under Spanish patronage. In the spring of 1497. John Cabot,
a Venetian, obtained a commission from Henry VII. under
which he made a voyage from England, and discovered the
continent of North America, in the latitude of forty-five degrees. He proceeded first northerly to the sixty-seventh degree, and then returning coasted to the south as far as Florida.
The southern continent was found by Columbus in 1498.
The first voyage from France to America was made in 1524, by
Verrazano, a Florentine. By these voyages and discoveries, the princes of the several states, which authorized them,
fancied themselves to have acquired the rights of territory
and jurisdiction. The Spanish and French made various
settlements in the course of a century. On the part of the
English little or nothing seems to have been done, until Sir
Walter Raleigh attempted the colonization of Virginia, between 1584 and 1607, when Jamestown was established. An
effort was made to plant a colony near the mouth of the river
Kennebeck, under the auspices of some very able persons,
about the year 1607, but the severity of the winter and the
loss of their storehouse by fire disheartened them, and the
men took advantage of the first shipping to return to England,
the next year. A settlement was commenced at Newfoundland in 1610, and in 1614 some Dutch adventurers built a
fort at Albany, and laid the foundation of that city, and of
New-York.

Massachusetts Bay, the bottom of which forms the harbour
of Boston, had not been much explored previous to that time.
Twelve years before, Bartholomew Gosnold, the first Englishman who came in a direct course to this part of America,

----

* Magnalia.

sailed from Falmouth in March, and made some part of the eastern coast on the 14th of May. Before this, the usual route had been by the Canaries and the West Indies. He did not enter the bay, but steered directly from Cape Ann to the opposite headland, to which he gave the name of Cape Cod, from the multitude of that sort of fish, which abounded there.

In the year 1614, the celebrated traveller and navigator, Capt. John Smith, sailed from England with two ships under his command. He explored the coast from Manhegan, an island near Penobscot river, to Cape Cod. This trip he made in a boat with eight men, for the purpose of bartering with the natives, and making such discoveries as might be of future advantage to his employers, and his country.

Speaking of these parts, he says, I have seen at least forty several habitations upon the sea coast, and sounded about five-and-twenty excellent good harbours. Of all the four parts of the world, I have yet seen uninhabited, could I have but means to transplant a colony, I would rather live here than any where ; and if it did not maintain itself, were we but once indifferently well fitted, let us starve. Here are many isles planted with corn, groves, mulberries, savage gardens and good harbours. The sea coasts, as you pass them, show you all along large cornfields and great troops of well proportioned people.—Massachusetts, in particular, he calls the paradise of these parts, notices its high mountain, and its river which doth pierce many days' journey into the entrails of that country. But (adds he) the French having remained here near six weeks left nothing for us to examine. On his return to England, he formed a map from his rough draught and observations, which he presented to Prince Charles; who was so well pleased with his description of this new discovered region, that he gave it the name of New-England. In this map, Smith gave names to the most remarkable places on the coast, none of which are retained— among others he gave the name of Boston to Agamenticus.

This voyage was completed within the period of six months, and produced a clear profit of fifteen hundred pounds to the principals. Doubtless the spirit of commercial enterprise was more powerfully excited by this substantial result, than by the high coloured and wonderful description which the Captain gave of the country.

When Smith embarked for London, he left his largest ship under the command of Thomas Hunt, to load her with fish for Spain. Hunt, when he was ready to sail, enticed into the ship twenty-seven Indians from Patuxet and Nauset (since Plymouth and Eastham) under pretence of trading with them. Immediately he seized upon the poor innocent creatures and stowing them under his hatches, carried them off to Malaga, where he sold a number of them for twenty pounds a man. This atrocious act enraged the Indians, but was eventually of some service to the settlers, as we shall have occasion to mention.

During a number of years after this, the coast was annually visited by vessels, mostly fitted out by merchants, for taking fish, and trading with the Indians for furs. Of these voyages we have little information. No attempt was made to establish a plantation within the bay till 1620, when a permanent settlement was made at Plymouth.

The company which we left in Leyden, at the close of our last chapter, furnished the interesting band that made this settlement. With mutual embraces and many tears, they took leave of their pastor and sailed for Southampton, in England, where they were to meet another vessel prepared for the same expedition. On Wednesday the 6th of September, 1620, they loosed from Plymouth, and after many difficulties, in boisterous storms, upon the ninth of November, by break of day, they espied land, which proved to be Cape Cod. It was not their intention to have come so far to the northward. They therefore made some attempts to proceed towards the Hudson, but the wind proving contrary, were compelled to stop. Being thus thrown upon a coast where their patent gave them no right or power, and some strangers, who had joined them from London, disputing the authority of the Governour and assistants, they did, as the light of nature itself directed them, forthwith form themselves into a body politic, by a solemn contract to which they subscribed their names.

This first of American constitutions was in the following form :—" In the name of God, Amen. We whose names are underwritten, the loyal subjects of our dread sovereign lord king James, by the grace of God, of G. B. France and Ireland king, defender of the faith, &c. having undertaken for the glory of God and the advancement of the christian faith, and honour of our king and country, a voyage to plant the first colony in the northern parts of Virginia, do by these presents solemnly and mutually in the presence of God and one of another, covenant and combine ourselves together in a civil body politick, for our better ordering and preservation, and furtherance of the end aforesaid—and BY VIRTUE HEREOF, to enact, constitute, and frame such just and equal laws, ordinances, acts, constitutions and offices, from time to time as shall be thought most meet and convenient for the general good of the colony. In witness whereof, we have hereunder subscribed our names. Cape Cod, eleventh of November, in the year of the reign of our sovereign lord K. James of England, France and Ireland, the eighteenth and of Scotland the fifty-fourth, A.D. 1620."

Having adopted this measure, they proceeded to the choice of Mr. John Carver for their Governour, and on the same day sent ashore fifteen or sixteen men well armed, to look for a convenient spot for their intended residence. Their first and second search was unsatisfactory ; and it was not till the 16th of December, that the ship arrived and anchored in the harbour of Patuxet, where the pilgrims at length took up their abode, and named the place New-Plymouth.*

CHAPTER III.

" Welcome, welcome, Euglishmen !"
Samoset.

THE winter, which lay before these pilgrims, though not severely cold, proved a doleful one, on account of the sickness and deaths among their number ; but the spring favourably advanced more early than usual. They had seen only very few of the natives, and met with no one near enough to hold any communication, until, on the 16th of March 1621, they were suddenly alarmed by the appearance of an Indian, who presented himself fearlessly, and in broken English, gave them a friendly salutation. His name was Samoset ; a sagamore, or lord of Moratiggon he. ' He had a bow and two arrows : he was a tall straight man : the hair of his head was black, long behind, only short before, none on his face at all. He asked some beer, but we gave him strong water, and biscuit, and butter, and cheese, and pudding, and a piece of mallard, (roast duck,) all which he liked very well.' Their visitor gave the party much useful information, and they sent him, the next day, on a message to their Indian neighbours. Through him they had frequent intercourse with small parties of the savages, and at last he brought and introduced to them Squanto, Squantum or Tisquantum, the only surviving native of the place they had taken possession of. Squanto was one of the twenty, that Hunt had carried to Spain, and had found his way into England, where he received kindness, which he was now disposed to requite. Our new comers found him very faithful to them, on most occasions, as long as he lived, serving them in their expeditions as a guide, mediator and interpreter.

Before the expiration of a year from the time of their landing, the people at Plymouth had, by kind dealing and prudent

management, induced nine of the Indian sachems to sign a
treaty with them, and acknowledge submission to king James.
This gave them sufficient confidence in the peaceable disposition of the natives, to justify their undertaking to explore the
country, farther than had before been done.   One of the first
excursions for this purpose was a voyage to the Massachusetts,*
in which they discovered the harbour of Boston.   The following relation gives us the fullest account of that voyage,
and being written by one of the party, deserves a place in
his own words, as a specimen of the minuteness with which
they recorded all occurrences.†

'It seemed good to the company in general, that though
the Massachusetts had often threatened us, (as we were informed) yet we should go amongst them, partly to see the
country, partly to make peace with them, and partly to procure their truck.   For these ends the governours chose ten
men, fit for the purpose, and sent Tisquantum, and two other
savages, to bring us to speech with the people, and interpret
for us.

'[On the 18th September 1621, being Tuesday] we set out
about midnight, the tide then serving for us ; we, supposing it
to be nearer than it is, thought to be there the next morning
betimes : but it proved well near twenty leagues from New-
Plymouth.   We came into the bottom of the bay, but being
late we anchored and lay in the shallop, not having seen
any of the people.   The next morning we put in for the shore.
There we found many lobsters, that had been gathered together by the savages, which we made ready under a cliff.‡
The captain sent two sentinels behind the cliff, to the landward, to secure the shallop, and taking a guide with him, and
four of our company went to seek the inhabitants, where they
met a woman coming for her lobsters ; they told her of them
and contented her for them.   She told them where the people
were : Tisquantum went to them :   the rest returned, having
direction which way to bring the shallop to them.

'The sachem, or governour of this place, is called Obba-
tinewat, and though he live in the bottom of the Massachuset
Bay, yet he is under Massasoyt.   He used us very kindly ;
he told us he durst not remain in any settled place, for fear of
the Tarentines.   Also the squaw sachem or Massachusets
queen was an enemy to him.   We told him of divers sachems
that had acknowledged themselves to be king James his men,
and if he also would submit himself, we would be his safe-
guard from his enemies ; which he did, and went along with us
to bring us to the squaw sachem.

* Originally the name of the Indian nation inhabiting Boston and its vicinity,
† Mass. Hist. Coll 2. ix. 57.   ‡ Supposed to have been Copp's hill.

' Again we crossed the bay, which is very large and hath at least fifty islands in it, but the certain number is not known to the inhabitants. Night it was before we came to that side of the bay where this people were,————that night also we rid at anchor aboard the shallop. On the morrow we went ashore all but two men, and marched in arms up the country. Having gone three miles, we came to a place where corn had been newly gathered, a house pulled down, and the people gone. A mile from hence, Nanepashemet their king *in his life time* had lived. His house was not like others, but a scaffold was largely built, with poles and planks some six foot from ground, and the house upon that, being situated on the top of a hill.

' Not far from hence, in a bottom, we came to a fort built by their deceased king, the manner thus : there were poles some thirty or forty foot long, stuck in the ground as thick as they could be set one by another, and with these they enclosed a ring some forty or fifty foot over. A trench breast high was digged on each side : one way there was to go into it with a bridge. In the midst of this palisado stood the frame of an house, wherein *being dead* he lay buried.

' About a mile from hence we came to such another, but seated on the top of an hill ; here Nanepashemet was killed, none dwelling in it since the time of his death. At this place we staid, and sent two savages to look the inhabitants, and to inform them of our ends in coming, that they might not be fearful of us. Within a mile of this place they found the women of the place together, with their corn on heaps, whither we supposed them to be fled for fear of us, and the more, because in divers places they had newly pulled down their houses, and for haste in one place had left some of their corn, covered with a mat, and nobody with it.

' With much fear they entertained us at first, but seeing our gentle carriage towards them, they took heart and entertained us in the best manner they could, boiling cod and such other things as they had for us. At length with much sending for, came one of their men, shaking and trembling for fear. But when he saw that we intended them no hurt, but came to truck, he promised us with his skins also. Of him we inquired for their queen ; but it seemed she was far from thence, at least we could not see her. Here Tisquantum would have had us rifled the savage women, and taken their skins, and all such things as might be serviceable for us : for, (said he) they are a bad people, and have oft threatened you : but our answer was, were they never so bad, we would not wrong them, or give them any just occasion against us ; for their words, we little weighed them, but if they once attempted any thing against us, then we would deal far worse than he desired. Having well spent the day, we returned to the shallop, almost all the women accompanying us to the shore.   We promised them to come again to them, and they us, to keep their skins.

'Within this bay, the savages say there are two rivers ; the one whereof we saw, having a fair entrance, but we had no time to discover it.   Better harbours for shipping cannot be than here are.   At the entrance of the bay are many rocks ; and in all likelihood good fishing ground.   Many, yea, most of the islands have been inhabited, some being cleared from end to end, but the people are all dead or removed.   Our victual growing scarce, the wind coming fair, and having a light moon, we set out at evening, and through the goodness of God, came safely home before noon the day following,' with a considerable quantity of beaver and a good report of the place, *wishing we had been seated there.*

In the spring of 1622, another voyage was made from Plymouth to the Massachusetts, but from the accounts we have of it, we gain no particular description of the places visited.   The fisheries in these parts soon increased greatly, thirty to sixty vessels sometimes coming in the course of a season.

In May, 1622, Mr. Thomas Weston, who was one of the adventurers at first engaged in the foundation of Plymouth colony, but afterwards deserted it, sent over two ships with 50 or 60 men, at his own charge, to settle a plantation for him. They resorted to the place afterwards called Weymouth, but the dissolute conduct of the people soon reduced them to poverty and distress, and the company was broken up, the following year.   Another attempt by Captain Gorges to settle a plantation at the same place also failed.   Early in 1624, Mr. David Thompson, Gent. a Scotchman who the year before had begun a plantation about Pascataqua (near Portsmouth N. H.) on account of a mercantile concern, either disliking his place or his employers, removed down into the Massachusetts Bay.   There he possessed himself of a fruitful island (now Thompson's island, belonging to Dorchester,) and a very desirable neck of land, which were afterwards confirmed to him by the General Court.   Not long after this, several of the Plymouth people, among whom was Mr. Roger Conant, removed and settled themselves at Nantasket, (Hull) at the entrance of the Massachusetts bay, where a building had before been set up, to accommodate those that traded with the natives.

The only remaining party, which it seems necessary to mention, is that which was brought in 1625, by Captain Wolaston, and left at a place not far from Weston's, in what is now called Braintree, but was for some years considered a part of Boston.   He located them in the northerly mountainous part of the place, which he named Mount Wolaston. This enterprise was a speculation of his and three or four partners, who brought with them a number of servants, with suitable provisions, and other requisites to raise a plantation : and they might have effected their purpose well enough, had it not been for one Thomas Morton, a master of misrule, that some time had been a pettifogger of Furnival's Inn, (a law-school in Holborn, London,) and possibly might have brought some small adventure of his own or other men's, with the rest. The Captain and his chief partner, having gone with part of the company, to Virginia, Morton in their absence made the remainder merry one night, and persuaded them to turn out the lieutenant, who had been left in command. This counsel was easy to be taken, as suiting well the genius of the young men, and so, with Morton at their head, they spent their time in eating, drinking and dancing right merrily about a may-pole : and as if they had found a mine or spring of plenty, they changed the name of the place to Merry-Mount.* This school of profaneness was broken up, soon after a regular government became established in Massachusetts.

Having thus glanced at most, if not all of the prior settlements and attempts to settle in these parts, we are now prepared to speak of the origin and proceedings of the company of the Massachusetts Bay.

CHAPTER IV.

Religion stands on tiptoe in our land,
Ready to pass to the 'Merican strand.
Herbert in Gookin.

THE death of King James took place on the twenty-seventh day of March, 1625, and he was succeeded in the throne, by his son Charles the First, who committed the government of the church to men of arbitrary principles, passionately fond of the established rites and ceremonies, and disposed to press the observance of them with rigid exactness. Neither learning, nor piety, nor diligence and success in his profession, nor any other qualification could save a man from ruin, that scrupled conformity to the injunctions of the bishops. The king had put the reins into their hands, and they drove on so furiously, that the whole nation groaned under their tyranny, till, at last, the very name of bishop grew odious to the people : and when they could get rid of their tyranny no other way, they were forced to draw their swords in defence of their liberties, whereby the kingdom was involved in a civil war.†

Hubbard's Hist. of N. E. p. 108.   † *Neal.*

This being the melancholy state of affairs, the Rev. John White, minister of Dorchester, England, encouraged by the success of the Plymouth colony, projected a new settlement in the Massachusetts bay. He had prevailed with Roger Conant, a most religious, prudent, worthy gentleman, to make a beginning as early as the year 1625. He removed from Nantasket, first to Cape Ann, and thence in the course of the fall of 1626, to Naumkeag, Salem. Mr. Conant's companions were soon disheartened, and mostly quitted the place ; but he was urged by Mr. White to remain, with assurances, that if he and three honest men more would yet stay upon the spot, he would procure a patent for them, and send them over friends, goods and provisions. ' Well,' says the Magnalia, ' it was not long before the Council of Plymouth, in England, had by a deed bearing date March 19th, 1627-8, sold unto some six knights and gentlemen about Dorchester, that part of New-England, which lies between a great river called Merrimack and a certain other river there called Charles. But shortly after this, Mr. White brought the said honourable persons into an acquaintance with several other persons of quality, about London ; who associated with them, and jointly petitioned the king to confirm their right by a new patent, which he did on the 4th of March, in the fourth year of his reign.' This patent, or charter, constituted the associates and all others who should be admitted free of the association, one corporate body politick, by the name of the Governour and company of the Massachusetts bay in New-England, whose jurisdiction was to extend in breadth, from three miles north of any and every part of the Merrimack, to three miles south of any and every part of the Charles river, including all lands within the space of three miles to the southward of the southernmost part of the Massachusetts bay, and to reach in length from the Atlantic ocean to the South sea. Their general business was to be disposed and ordered by a court composed of a Governour, Deputy Governour, and eighteen Assistants.*

---

* See the charter at length in *Hutch.* Coll. of papers, p. 1.

The following were the patentees, who are named in the order in which they are numbered. Those marked‡ were the six original associates :

20. Thomas Adams	19. Thomas Goffe	3. Sir Richard Saltonstall
9. Samuel Aldersey	12. George Harwood	4. Sir Thomas Southcot‡
15. Richard Bellingham	5. John Humphrey ‡	17. Samuel Vassall
21. John Brown	23. Thomas Hutchins	24. William Vassall
22. Samuel Brown	8. Isaac Johnson	10. John Ven
11. Matthew Craddock	13. Increase Nowell	7. Simon Whetcomb ‡
18. Theophilus Eaton	14. Richard Perry	16. Nathaniel Wright
6. John Endicott ‡	25. William Pincheon	2. Sir John Young ‡
26. George Foxcroft	1. Sir Henry Rosewell ‡	

Soon after the first purchase abovementioned, and previous to the procuring of this charter, Mr. John Endicott, who was one of the company, was sent over with a few men (in June, 1628) and uniting his own men with those formerly in the country, they made up in all not much above fifty or sixty persons. Another supply was sent over in the spring of 1629, which consisted of three hundred and eighty-six men, women, maids and children. They arrived in June. The Rev. Francis Higginson was a principal member of this last company. They found but six houses built, besides that of Mr. Endicott, at which Mr. Higginson was kindly entertained.*

About a hundred of this party, under the conduct of Mr. Thomas Graves, soon removed to Charlestown, where a small settlement was already made. By Mr. Endicott's permission, three brothers, of the name of Ralph, Richard, and William Sprague, had started from Salem, in the preceding summer, with three or four more, to explore the country westward; and after travelling above twelve miles through the woods, they light on a neck of land, called by the Indians, Mishawum. Their old sachem being dead, his eldest son John Sagamore was chief in power. He is described as a man of gentle and good disposition, and freely consented to their settling there. Probably he was the more readily induced to this, by the good conduct, and the advantages he derived from the skill of Thomas Walford, a blacksmith, who had previously taken up his residence, and built himself a house, which he had thatched and palisadoed, at the south end of the west hill, not far from the river. Both the town and river received their name in honour of the king.

The success, which now attended the plantation, encouraged the company to persevere : and several of the principal members entered into an agreement† to remove with themselves and families, provided the whole government, together with the patent, might first be legally transferred and established, to remain with them and others who should be inhabitants therein. The proposal of this measure occasioned considerable debate; and it was finally adopted, both for the sake of avoiding the inconveniences attending the administration of the government, at such a distance, and also for the sake of inducing gentlemen of wealth and quality to embark in the expedition, with their property and families. This was an act of great political importance. Neither the advocates, nor the opposers of it, could have truly estimated its magnitude,

---

* In 1628, the Plymouth people, having obtained a patent for Kennebeck, where they had traded for two years in conjunction with David Thompson, erected a house up the river in a convenient place for business.—*Prince.*

† *Hutch.* Coll. p. 25.

or have foreseen the great events, which it ultimately produced.

This alteration in the management of the company affairs, was made in August 1629, and on the 20th of October following, a special court was held for the purpose of electing a new Governour, deputy and assistants, who should be willing to remove. Mr. John Winthrop was chosen for the Governour, and Mr. Humphrey for the deputy, to hold their places for a year ; but Mr. Humphrey, not being likely to be ready to sail, when the rest expected to be, Mr. Thomas Dudley was afterwards chosen in his stead.

Preparations then began to be made with vigour, for the embarkation of a great colony. The Company appointed ten persons,* as undertakers, who after much intreaty, accepted the charge of the management of the stock, and were ordered to provide a sufficient number of vessels, for the transportation of passengers and goods. Accordingly, by the end of February, 1630, a fleet of fourteen sail was furnished with men, women, children, all necessaries, men of handicrafts, and others of good condition, wealth and quality, to make a firm Plantation.†

In this fleet were congregated our fathers, with their wives and their little ones, about to quit forever their native country, kindred, friends and acquaintance. Let us pause a moment, and mingle our sympathy with their sorrows, ' as hand in hand we see them lead each other to the sandy banks of the brinish ocean.'

' They were about to leave the land of their fathers' sepulchres, perhaps forever ; to break asunder those cords of affection, which so powerfully bind a good man to his native soil ; and to dissolve those tender associations which constitute the bliss of civil society. In ordinary cases, the pain of separation is lessened by the promises of hope—the pleasure of another interview ; but here adieu, to most of them at least, was to be the last, like the final farewell to a departing spirit.'

---

* Of whom five were to remain in England, and five to go with the colony.   Messrs. Winthrop, Dudley, Johnson, Saltonstall and John Revel were the five that came over.—*Eliot.* Biog. Dict. Johnson.   † *Prince.*

CHAPTER V.

" Westward the star of empire rolls its way."

THE fleet above mentioned all sailed before the end of May, and reached America in safety. The first vessel that arrived was the Mary-John, which brought over the Rev. Messrs. John Warham and John Maverick, with many godly families and people, under their care, from Devonshire, Dorsetshire, and Somersetshire, together with Messrs. Edward Rossiter and Roger Ludlow, two of the assistants, and Roger Clap, who was afterwards captain of the castle in Boston harbour. They had some difficulty on the passage, with the master of the vessel, Capt. Squibb, who, like a merciless man, put them and their goods ashore on Nantasket point, notwithstanding his engagement was to bring them up Charles river. They succeeded, however, in obtaining a boat from some of the old planters ; and having laden her with goods, and manned her with some able men well armed, (not more than ten, under Captain Southcot, a brave low country soldier) they went up towards Charlestown. There they found some wigwams, a few English people, and one English house. They continued their course up the river till it became narrow and shallow, which is at Watertown, where they landed their goods with much labour on a steep bank. At evening they were much alarmed with information, that there was a body of three hundred savages encamped near by them. Fortunately they had been accompanied from Charlestown by an old planter, who knew enough of the Indian tongue and Indian disposition, to succeed in persuading them not to molest the party during the night. In the morning, some of the savages made their appearance, but stood awhile at a distance : at last one of them held out a bass, and the English sent a man with a biscuit, to exchange for it ; and thus commenced a friendly intercourse. A shelter for their goods was erected at the place, but they did not long remain there, for their companions discovered a neck of land* fit to keep cattle upon, adjoining Mattapan, (Dorchester,) and these were ordered to join them.

This all took place before the fourteenth of June, on which day the admiral of the New England fleet arrived in Salem

* This neck of land included what is now called South Boston.

harbour. In the vessel which bore that distinction, Gov.
Winthrop and Mr. Isaac Johnson came passengers, and the
Governour has left us, in his journal, a circumstantial account
of the voyage, from which we select the following particulars.

On Monday, March 29, 1630, they were riding at the
Cowes, near the Isle of Wight, in the Arabella (for so they
called the Eagle, in honour of the Lady Arabella, wife of Mr.
Johnson) a ship of three hundred and fifty tons, Capt. Peter
Milbourne, manned with fifty-two seamen, and carrying
twenty-eight guns. The Ambrose, Jewel, and Talbot were
riding by their side. On that day it was agreed, that, forasmuch as it was uncertain when the rest of the fleet would be
ready, these four ships should consort together, the Arabella
to be admiral, Talbot vice admiral, Ambrose rear admiral,
and the Jewel a captain.

By head winds and other causes they were detained a
week, during which they improved one day as a fast. On
the 8th of April, about six in the morning, the wind being E.
and by N. and fair weather, we weighed anchor and set sail.
By daylight on the 9th we were come to Portland, but the
other ships not being able to hold up with us, we were forced
to spare our mainsail, and went on with a merry gale. In the
morning we descried, from the top, eight sail astern of us,
and supposing they might be Dunkirkers,* our captain caused the gun room and gun deck to be cleared, all the ham-
mocks taken down, our ordnance loaded, powder chests and
fire works made ready, and our landsmen were quartered
among the seamen, twenty-five appointed musketeers, and
every man assigned to his post. The wind continued N. with
fair weather, and after noon it calmed, and we still saw those
eight ships to stand towards us. Having more wind than we,
they came up again, so that our captain and the masters of
our consorts were more occasioned to think they might be
Dunkirkers ! for we were told at Yarmouth there were ten
sail of them waiting for us ! Whereupon we all prepared to
fight with them ; took down some cabins which were in the
way of our guns, threw out of every ship such bed matters as
were subject to fire, hove out our long boat, and put up our
waste cloths, and drew forth our men, and armed them with
muskets and other weapons, and instruments for fireworks ;
and for an experiment, our captain shot a ball of wildfire, fastened to an arrow, out of a cross-bow, which burnt in the
water a good time. The Lady Arabella, and the other

---

* Dunkirk was then a part of the Spanish Netherlands, and war existed between Great
Britain and Spain.

women and children, were removed into the lower deck, that they might be out of danger.

All things being thus fitted, we went to prayer. It was much to see how cheerful and comfortable all the company appeared ; not a woman or child that showed fear, though all did apprehend the danger to be great ; for there had been eight against four, and the least of the enemy's ships was reputed to carry thirty brass pieces : but our trust was in the Lord of hosts : and the courage of our captain, and his care and diligence, did much encourage us.

It was now about one of the clock, and the fleet seemed to be within a league of us ; therefore the captain, because he would show he was not afraid of them, and that he might see the issue before night, tacked about and stood to meet them, and when we came within hail, we perceived them to be our friends : and so, God be praised, our fear and danger was turned into mirth and friendly entertainment.

The weather during the remainder of the voyage was variable, sometimes mild, and sometimes boisterous. The passengers, as may well be supposed, suffered from sea-sickness, and that contributed to the amusement of the hardy sailors. ' Our children and others that were sick, and lay groaning in the cabins, we fetched out, and having a rope stretched from the steerage to the mainmast, we made them stand, some on one side and some on the other, and swing it up and down till they were weary, and by this means they soon grew well and merry. The captain set our children and grown men to some other harmless exercises, which the seamen were very active in, and which did our people much good, though the sailors would sometimes play the wag with them.'

Very strict attention to religious duties was observed, and the most rigid discipline enforced. On one occasion, two of the landsmen were laid in the bolts all night, for piercing a rundlet of strong water, and stealing some of the same ; and the next morning, the principal was openly whipped, and both were kept on bread and water all day. Two young men falling at odds, and fighting, contrary to orders which were set up in the ship, were sentenced to walk upon deck till night, with their hands tied behind them : and another man, ' for using contemptuous speech *in our presence*,' was laid in bolts, till he made open confession of his offence. A servant of one of the company had made a bargain with a child, to sell him a trinket box worth three pence, for three biscuits a day all the voyage, and the rogue had received about forty, and sold them to his comrades, before he was found out. ' We caused his hands to be tied up to a bar, and hung a basket full of stones about his neck, and so he stood for two hours.'

Thus they commenced their state, with the maintenance of dignity, sobriety, good order, and honesty.

No accident of any moment occurred on board the Arabella. They saw one or two whales (one with a bunch on his back, about a yard above water!) and all the way were birds flying and swimming, when they had no land near, by two hundred leagues.

On the third of June, they approached near enough to the coast, to get soundings in eighty fathoms, and on the seventh, in thirty fathoms, they were regaling themselves with fresh fish of their own catching. On the eighth, they had sight of land, which they supposed Manhegan, but it proved to be Mount Desert. So pleasant a scene here they had, as did much refresh them, and there came a smell off the shore, like the smell of a garden : and Noah could hardly have been more gratified to behold his dove, with the olive leaf in her mouth, than they must have been delighted, to receive a visit from a wild pigeon, and another small bird from the land.

All day on the eleventh, they stood to and again, within sight of Cape Ann. On Saturday the twelfth, at four in the morning, they gave notice of their approach, from two pieces of ordnance, and sent their skiff ashore. In the course of the day, passing through the narrow strait between Baker's isle and another little island, they came to an anchor, a short distance from Salem harbour.

Mr. Endicott and others went on board ; and we that were assistants, and some other gentlemen, and some of the women and our captain, returned with him to Salem, where we supped on a good venison pasty and good beer. Next morning, many of the rest of the people went on shore, upon the other side of the harbour, and feasted themselves with strawberries, which they found in such abundance that they named the place Strawberry bank.

Early in the morning of Monday the fourteenth, ' we weighed anchor, and the wind being against us, and the channel so narrow that we could not well turn, we warped in our ship, and came to an anchor in the inward harbour. In the afternoon, we went with the most of our company on shore, and our captain gave us a salute of five guns.'

The other ships of the fleet fell in daily, and by the sixth of July, thirteen out of the fourteen had arrived safe in New-England, without the loss of more than fifteen lives by sickness or accident. A day of publick thanksgiving was therefore kept, on the eighth of that month, through all the plantations.

CHAPTER VI.

Whate'er in life may be my varied lot,
Boston, dear Boston, ne'er shall be forgot.

R. T. Paine.

It appears to have been the original design, that the principal part of this colony of fifteen hundred persons should
have settled in one place, which they intended to call by the
name of Boston. This design was frustrated by such circumstances as the following.*

They found the colony at Salem in a sad and unexpected
condition. Above eighty deaths had occurred the winter before, and of those that remained alive, many were weak
and sickly. All the corn and bread, amongst them all, was
hardly sufficient to feed them a fortnight ; so that when the
remainder of the great company of servants, sent over two
years before, applied for sustenance. they found themselves
wholly unable to afford it, ' by reason that the provisions
shipped for them were taken out of the ship they were put in,
and they who were trusted to ship them in another, failed us
and left them behind. Whereupon necessity forced us, to
our extreme loss, to give them all liberty, who had cost us
about sixteen or twenty pound a person, furnishing and sending over.'

' But bearing these things as we might, we began to consult
about a place for our sitting down: for Salem, where we landed, pleased us not. So some were sent to the bay, to search
up the rivers for a convenient place, who upon their return
reported to have found a good place upon Mystick : but some
others of us seconding these, to approve or dislike of their
judgement, we found a place liked us better, three leagues up
Charles river. Thereupon we unshipped our goods into
other vessels, with much cost and labour, and brought them in
July to Charlestown. But there receiving information (by
some of the ships lately arrived) of some French preparations
against us, we were forced to change our counsel ; for many
of our people were sick of fevers and the scurvy, and we
were thereby weakened and unable to carry our baggage and
ordnance so far up the river as we proposed. For our present shelter, therefore, we were obliged to plant dispersedly,
(in various directions from Saugus to Dorchester.) This dis-

---

* From Dudley's letter to the Countess of Lincoln. Mass. H. C. 1. viii. 38.

persion troubled some of us, but help it we could not, wanting ability to remove to any place fit to build a town upon,
and the time being too short to deliberate any longer, lest the
winter should surprize us before we had erected our houses.
So ceasing to consult further, for that time, they who had
health to labour fell to building.'

Governour Winthrop was among those who stopped at
Charlestown. He and other publick officers were accommodated in a building, called *the great house*, on the westerly
side of the present market square. The remainder resided
in cottages, booths, and tents, where their lodgings were so
cold and moist, as to cause a continued prevalence of disease
among them, to such an extent as that there were not enough of
the well, to take care of the sick. Dr. Samuel Fuller, a deacon
of the church of Plymouth, appears to have spent several
weeks in the neighbourhood in attendance upon them, but
without doing much good (as he complained) for the want of
drugs and things fitting to work with. Deaths spread around
them, and almost every family was filled with lamentation for
the loss of some of its members.

In consequence of this affliction, the Governour proposed
to Mr. Johnson, that a day should be set apart for fasting and
prayer. Accordingly, Friday, the 30th of July, was agreed
upon, and devoted for that purpose. After the services of
the day,* it had been proposed, that such godly persons
among them, as knew each other, should enter into a church
covenant. Conformably to this arrangement, Governour Winthrop, Deputy Governour Dudley, Mr. Johnson, and the Rev.
Mr. Wilson, on that day signed the following covenant :

" In the name of our Lord Jesus Christ, and in obedience
to his holy will and divine ordinance,

" We, whose names are here underwritten, being by his
most wise and good providence brought together into this part
of America, in the Bay of Massachusetts, and desirous to
unite into one congregation or church, under the Lord Jesus
Christ, our head, in such sort, as becometh all those, whom he
hath redeemed, and sanctified to himself, do hereby solemnly
and religiously, as in his most holy presence, promise and
bind ourselves to walk in all our ways according to the rule
of the gospel, and in all sincere conformity to his holy ordinances, and in mutual love and respect to each other so near,
as God shall give us grace."

---

* The first meetings of the congregation were held in the open air, under the shade of
an oak tree, and probably continued to be so for some time ; for here, says *Roger Clap*,
I have heard Mr. Wilson and Mr. Phillips preach many a good sermon——they afterwards
met in the *great house*.

On the Lord's day following, five more were added to the church, namely, Increase Nowell, Thomas Sharp, Simon Bradstreet, assistants, William Gager, a surgeon, and William Colburn.

At this time they had no other intention than that of making Charlestown the place of their permanent abode, and the Governour had ordered timber to be cut, and a house framed for himself there. But the sickness increasing, and the weather being hot, the people grew uneasy and discontented for the want of water. Strange as it may seem to those who now know that Charlestown abounds with good water, yet they could then only find one brackish spring, and that upon the beach, on the west side of the northwest field, (near the present site of the state prison) which was not to be come at, but when the tide was down.* This spring could not supply half the necessities of the multitude, and the death of many was thought to be owing to the want of wholesome drink. Several persons were therefore induced to make excursions, for the discovery of some more heathful spot.

Besides the English who were located at Charlestown, when the Governour and his colony arrived, there lived on Noddle's island, one Mr. Samuel Maverick, a man of very loving and courteous behaviour, very ready to entertain strangers. The Governour lay a night at his house, while on the first exploring party. He had thrown up a small fort on the island, by the aid of Mr. Thompson, and had four cannon mounted in it to protect him from the Indians. Mr. Maverick was a man that made some figure in the history of after times, and had a grant or confirmation of the island from the general court.†

On the south side of the mouth of Charles river there also resided, in a small cottage, one Mr. William Blackstone. The spot upon which he had pitched, was near a point on the western side of a peninsula, which, at high water, appeared in those days like two islands, the north and south parts being connected only by a narrow isthmus. The Indian name of the place was *Shawmut*, and the English at Charlestown called it TRIMOUNTAIN.

Mr. Blackstone's self interest did not stifle his feelings of humanity, and though he might claim the peninsula for his property, as having been the first Englishman, that slept upon it, he communicated to the Governour the information that he had found an excellent spring on his side of the river, and urged him with pressing invitations to remove thither. This incident, and the fact of their being much pleased with the

---

* Johnson's W. W. P. ch. 17. and Dr. Bartlett's hist. sketch of Charlestown in M. H. Coll. 2. ii. 88. 165.

† August 20. The Gift, being the fourteenth and last vessel of the N. E. fleet, arrives with the loss of but one passenger, though she had been twelve weeks at sea.

plain neck (which then bore the name of Blackstone's neck,) at the south end of the peninsula, induced Mr. Johnson, who was a very influential and leading man, to remove with several others and begin a settlement.   This took place in August.

On Monday the 23d of August, the first Court of Assistants, under the authority of the patent, was holden on board the Arabella, at Charlestown.   The first question propounded, was, *How shall the ministers be maintained ?*—and it was ordered that houses be built for them at the public charge, and their salaries were established.   The minister at Watertown, Rev. George Phillips, was to have thirty pounds a year, and Mr. Wilson twenty pounds a year till his wife came over, beginning from the tenth of July preceding.   All this was at the common charge, excepting that the people at Dorchester and Salem were not to be taxed for this object.   Governour Winthrop undertook to see the above orders carried into effect, at his plantation, which embraced Charlestown and Boston.

On Friday, the 27th of the same month, the congregation kept a fast, and chose Mr. Wilson for their teacher, Mr. Increase Nowel an elder, and Dr. Gager and Mr. William Aspinwall for deacons.   These were all installed by the imposition of hands, with a solemn protest, that it was only by way of election and confirmation, and not designed to invalidate, or disparage Mr. Wilson's previous ordination in England.

At the second court of Assistants, which was also holden at Charlestown, an order was passed, that no person plant in any place within the limits of the patent, without leave from the Governour and Assistants, or a major part of them.   At this court it was also ordered, that the town at Mattapan be called Dorchester, that upon Charles River, Watertown, and that Trimountain be called BOSTON.   This was on the 7th day of September, 1630, and from that day we date the foundation of our city.

Whence originated the two latter of these three names, Shawmut, Trimountain and Boston, is matter of historical record.   In regard to the signification of Shawmut we can only state conjecture.   It seems to have been a universal custom, derived from the first fathers of mankind, to denominate places, from some peculiar excellences discovered in them : and the names appropriated were generally drawn from fancied resemblances, in these peculiarities, to parts of the human body. Before the art of sinking wells was known, fountains or springs of water were of infinite value ; and the practice of giving names to places from them, was prevalent among the aborigines of Massachusetts. It was very common with the Jews and other Eastern nations, to call such springs by the terms appropriated in their languages to the eye, whose piercing brilliancy sparkles in the visage, as the gurgling fountain does upon the grassy plain. Those that believe, with many who are not altogether unwise, that the native American tribes were descendants of the ten tribes of Israel, will have little difficulty to discover in Shauimut the radicals of the two eyes, that shoot forth on either side of the ridge of high land between Charles and Congress streets, and the termination, *ut*, which is a particle of place, equivalent to *at*. Such will readily coincide in the ingenious conclusion lately drawn, that Shawmut signified *living fountains*, to which the natives were probably in the daily habit of crossing over, in their canoes, from the opposite peninsula, to procure fresh water when the great spring there was overflowed by the tide.*

The etymology of the word Trimountain leads us directly to the origin of that name. Shawmut presented to those who viewed it from Charlestown, the appearance only of three large hills ; one on the north, one far to the east, and another forming the whole western extremity of the place. On the last were three lofty and majestic eminences, and on the brow of the easternmost of these, three little rising hillocks appeared in a contiguous range. The combination of these circumstances doubtless gave rise to the name of Trimountain.

No reason is assigned on the records of the court for changing the name of Trimountain for that of Boston. It is however universally agreed, that the name itself had been selected in compliment to the Rev. John Cotton, who at that time was a preacher at Boston, in Lincolnshire, and whom they expected very soon to come over and take part in the establishment of their colony. Boston, moreover, had been a place of note in the annals of the persecuted puritans, and several of those who first settled here were born there : and

---

* Mass. H. C. 2. x. 174. To the examples there adduced, may be added Moshawsick the name of Providence, where is still shown a venerated spring, which induced Roger Williams to stop his canoe and land at that place.

Our Shawmut is still remarkable for the great number of its productive springs of excellent water. A well has recently been dug for the accommodation of a house, building at the head of School street, opposite the Stone Chapel. When the workmen had reached the depth of about sixtyfive feet, a spring burst into the well several feet from the bottom, and flowed with such rapidity as to fill it to the height of forty feet in twenty-five minutes. Next morning they undertook to draw out the water by means of a whip tackle. In the course of seven hours, during which time several men with two horses raised at the rate of five barrels of water in two minutes, making in all more than a thousand barrels, they succeeded in exhausting the water so far as to admit of laying the wall. In a few days the water assumed the usual level of that in other wells.

it is also not improbable, that the sagacity of Winthrop and
Johnson seeing ‘ the prognosticks of its future greatness written on the face of nature, too legibly and too indelibly to be
mistaken,’ they may have claimed for the place of their choice,
the name originally intended for their chief city.

Boston, in Lincolnshire, is a borough town, seated on both
sides of the river Witham, near its mouth. It is a hundred
and seventeen miles north of London. In 1811, it contained
8113 inhabitants. It is governed by a mayor and sends two
members to parliament. It is famous for the tower of its
Gothick church, which is two hundred and eighty-two feet
high, being one of the most lofty and elegant of the kind, and
a noted sea-mark. The English name, Boston, appears to
have been a contraction of Botolph's town, which name
the place bore in old time, in honour of Botolph, a pious
Saxon, who had a monastery there. It is worthy of notice,
however, that Iccan-hoe, which was a more ancient Saxon
appellation, signifies Oxen-town, between which and the mean-
ing of Boston there is a fancied resemblance.

CHAPTER VII.

Better to sit in Freedom's hall,
With a cold damp floor and mouldering wall,
Than to bend the neck, and to bow the knee
In the proudest palace of slavery.

German Epigram.

THE third court of Assistants sat at Charlestown, September 28th, 1630. The first General Court of the colony was
holden at Boston, not by representatives, but by every one
that was free of the corporation, in person, on the 19th of October following. Between these two dates, Gov. Winthrop
and most of the people had removed from Charlestown,
where there remained but seventeen male inhabitants. The
rank which the several towns held in point of population and
wealth combined, may be discovered from the apportionment
of a tax of fifty pounds, levied for some military purposes.

1. Charlestown was to pay £. 7		6. Medford .	£. 3
2. Boston 11		7. Salem . . .	3
3. Dorchester 7		8. (Weymouth)	2
4. Roxbury 5		9. Nantasket . .	1
5. Watertown 11			
			£. 50

The publick object of most importance which first engaged the attention of those in office, was the selection of a proper place for a fortified town, of which they supposed there would be great necessity, to secure them from the natives. Several places were proposed. At one meeting, December 6th, they resolved to build upon the neck between Roxbury and Boston, and appointed a committee to attend to the business. The committee met, and growing wiser by deliberation, concluded that the location was not a suitable one for the purpose, and agreed to meet again at Watertown to consider farther on the subject. There, on the 21st, they made up their minds to erect their fortifications at a spot a mile below, where they thought was a fit place for a fortified town ; but at last on the 28th. they finally decided on building about three miles above Charlestown, on the northwest side of the river. They called the place Newtown (at present Cambridge) and the Governour and Deputy, with all the assistants, except Messrs. Sharp and Endicott obliged themselves to build houses there, in the following spring. But before much was done in compliance with this obligation, Chicatabot, the chief of the Indians near Boston, came to visit the Governour, and made such high professions of friendship as to diminish the apprehensions of danger, so that the necessity of having a fortified town gradually appeared less and less, until the plan was wholly laid aside. This result must have been doubly gratifying to the people of Boston, who would have regarded the formal establishment of the seat of government at Newtown as fatal to their own prosperity.

About a year had now elapsed since the colony had left their native land. Many of them had there enjoyed the best of society. Their family connexions were honourable : their professions and occupations in life had been reputable and profitable, and every comfort, which the possession of ' fruitful lands, stately buildings, goodly orchards and gardens' could afford, had been at their command. Here they could expect to find nothing but a desert, without any worldly allurement to recommend it ; but they calculated on the free enjoyment of religious privileges, and that sufficed to counterbalance every other consideration. On that they relied with confidence that it would encourage them to sustain affliction and hardship of every description, that the imagination could anticipate. The tenour of every memorial which our first settlers have left behind them, proves this to have been their predominant feeling. Questionless there were some among them whose object was merchandize, and who devoted themselves to commercial pursuits with the hope of gain : doubtless, too, says Foxcroft, in his observations on the rise and primitive state of New-England, ' They had a mixture of false profes-

sors among them, but let me speak it freely, without offence
to any, the first beginners of this plantation, as to the body of
them, were an excellent set of real and living Christians.'
And their religion exhibited itself pure and undefiled in the
scenes of distress which they witnessed, and the firmness of
their faith was manifested by the patience with which they
submitted to privation, and the perseverance with which they
pursued their object.

We have mentioned the prevalence of a mortal sickness
among them previous to the removal from Charlestown. Its
ravages did not abate immediately in consequence of that
change of residence, but continued till December, by which
time two hundred at least had fallen its victims.* With char-
acteristick impartiality death swept away the wealthy and
the poor, the bondman and his master. Besides others of
note they had to mourn over the ladies of Messrs. Coddington and Pincheon, two of the Assistants, and the Lady Arabella. The death of the last named personage excited a very
general interest. She was the pride of the colony. There
were several other women of distinction, who encountered the
fatigue and perils of the day with laudable resolution, but the
devotedness of the lady Arabella shone peculiarly conspicuous. She was a daughter of the Earl of Lincoln, and her
union with Mr. Johnson was a very happy one. The language of her soul to him was such as is ascribed to an ancient
Spanish lady—' whithersoever your fatall destinie shall dryve
you, eyther by the furious waves of the great ocean, or by
the many-folde and horrible dangers of the lande, I wyl surely beare you company. There can no peryll chaunce to me
so terrible, nor any kinde of death so cruell, that shall not be
much easier for me to abyde, than to live so farre separate
from you.' Pattern of fidelity! her desire was gratified : she
left the paradise of peace and plenty which she enjoyed in
the family of her noble father, and came into a wilderness of
wants, that proved too severe a trial for her. The virtues of
her mind could not protect her body from the tide of adversi-
ties, which overwhelmed her soon after her arrival:

> ' O'er her soft form diseases sternly crept,
> And gave the lovely victim to the tomb.'

She died and was buried at Salem in the month of August.

The tears which this event occasioned had scarcely ceased
to flow, when the people of Boston were called to weep for
the loss of Mr. Johnson himself. The death of such a man
spread a melancholy paleness on every countenance. All

---

* When the fleet returned this fall, about 200 of the people either returned home or left
Massachusetts for various reasons.—*Dudley's Letter.*

JOHNSON HALL, COURT-SQUARE.

J.Bowen del et Sc.

considered him as their principal patron. He might be called the father of Boston, as it was he that persuaded Governour Winthrop and the rest of the company to cross the river. He was the richest man of all the planters, and had early bent himself with pious zeal to advance the interests of the colony. He assisted many good people with means to come over, bequeathed a portion of his property to the company, and ordered his executors to carry on his share or part in it.

He was the son of Abraham Johnson, Esq. of Clipsham, in the county of Rutland, and his estates lay in Rutland, Northamptonshire, and Lincolnshire. The first mention made of him, in connexion with the Massachusetts company, is that he was chosen one of the Assistants on the thirteenth of May, sixteen hundred and twenty-nine. The confidence which the corporation had in him is evident, from their soon after electing him as a referee, in a case of dispute which arose between Mr. Endicott and John and Samuel Brown at Salem. He was one of those that signed the agreement to remove, in case the government and patent might be transferred, and one of the argumentators appointed to discuss the expediency of that measure. After the decision in favour of that step, he was nominated at the same time with Winthrop, Saltonstall and Humphrey, as a candidate for the office of first Governour. On his arrival here, he was clothed with the powers of a Justice of the peace, and in that capacity presided with Winthrop at a jury of inquest on the 18th of September. This is the last of his official acts recorded. The weight of publick cares, added to the burden of his grief for the loss of his wife, overpowered the strength of his constitution, and he yielded up his life, ' in sweet peace,' on the 30th of that month.

Mr. Johnson had chosen for his lot the square which lies between Court Street, Washington, School and Common Streets. Tradition locates his house about the centre of the Northeast side, that is, near the present site of the old Court-House. According to his particular desire expressed on his death bed, he was buried at the Southwest corner of the lot, and the people exhibited their attachment to him, by ordering their bodies to be buried near him. This was the origin of the first burying place, at present the Chapel burial ground.

There is a mournful pleasure in marking the terms of affection and respect, in which the early writers uniformly speak of Mr. Johnson's character. Governour Winthrop says ' he was a holy man and wise.' Dudley, that ' he was a prime man among us, zealous for religion, and made a most godly end, dying willingly and professing his life better spent in promoting this plantation, than it could have been any other way ; he left to us a loss greater than the most conceived.' His namesake, the author of the Wonder Working Providence,

speaks of him as ' endued with many precious gifts, and a
chief pillar to support this new erected building; so that at
his departure there were not only many weeping eyes, but
some fainting hearts, fearing the failure of the undertaking :'
and Cotton Mather comprehends all in the report, that he
was a perfect and upright man.

In the midst of these afflictions Dr. Gager died. He
was their principal, if not their only physician and surgeon. He is represented as a man of skill in his profession,
and we have seen that the soundness of his faith, and the purity of his life had promoted him to the office of a deacon in
the infant church. He was considered a publick servant, and
the same court, which provided for the salaries of the ministers, ordered that a house should be built for him against the
coming spring, that he should be furnished with a cow, and
be paid twenty pounds for his first year, and afterwards have
thirty pounds per annum at the common charge.*

Several other deaths are recorded which added to the
grief of the people; among them that of Mr. Robert Welden,
who had been chosen to be a military captain, but died at
Charlestown, before having an opportunity to act in that capacity. He was a young gentleman of high promise, and
considerable experience as a soldier. His remains were
brought to Boston, and interred with military honours, ' three
volleys of shot' being then, as at present, the customary tribute of respect.

There was yet one other distress to be endured, and that
was the danger of famine. We know they arrived too late
in the season to plant, and brought too small a stock of provisions with them, and the extreme drought of the summer
had threatened a total consumption of the fruits of the earth.
When the winter set in, which was on the 24th of December,
the cold came on with violence. Till that day the weather
had been for the most part fair, and open, with gentle frosts
at night; but, by the 26th, the river was so frozen over that
they of Charlestown could not come to the sermon at Boston,
till afternoon at high water. From that time their chief care
was to keep themselves warm, and as comfortable in other
respects as their scanty means would permit. They were so
short of provisions that many were obliged to live upon mus-
cles, clams and other shell fish, with groundnuts and acorns
instead of bread. ' Oh,' says Roger Clap, ' the hunger that
many suffered, and saw no hope in the eye of reason to be
relieved. Flesh of all kinds was a rare thing, and bread so
very scarce that sometimes I thought the very crumbs of my

---

* *Douglass*, in his way, says, ' Winthrop was very charitable particularly in distributing
his medicinal Van Helmont nostrums among the poor.'

father's table would have been sweet to me; and when I could have meal and water and salt boiled together' (the elements of a favourite New England dish) 'who could wish better !'

Being thus situated, they beheld with much joy the return of Captain William Pierce on the 5th of February 1631, in the ship Lion, laden with provisions, according to a contract which he had made previous to his sailing away in the fall.

We close this chapter of calamities with an account of the FIRST FIRE which is recorded to have happened in Boston. About noon on the 16th of March, 1631, the chimney of Mr. Thomas Sharp's house caught fire, the splinters not being clayed at the top, and taking the thatch burnt it down. The wind being Northwest drove the fire to Mr. Colburn's house* which was some rods off, and burnt that down also. Both of these gentlemen's houses were as good and as well furnished as the most in the plantation. Much of their own furniture was destroyed, together with the goods of some other families, which occupied parts of their houses.

Captain Pierce was soon ready to return, and Mr. Wilson had made arrangements to go with him. On the 29th of March he had an affectionate meeting at the Governour's, with a number of his people. He recommended to them the strict observance of religious duties during his absence, and designated Messrs. Winthrop, Dudley and Nowell, as the persons in his opinion best qualified to lead the devotions of the congregation. He sailed from Salem on the first of April, and the Boston church was thus left destitute of a preacher, until the arrival of Mr. John Eliot in the November following.

CHRONOLOGICAL ITEMS.

With a view to exhibit some traces of the early progress in trade, and of the customs of the times, we introduce a few miscellaneous articles, in this place.

1630. Aug. 23. Ordered that carpenters, joiners, bricklayers, sawyers and thatchers take no more than two shillings a day under pain of ten shillings to giver and taker.—Orders similar to this were frequently made, regulating and altering the prices of labour and of commodities. Six years after, it was left to towns to agree upon prices among themselves.

---

* Mr. Colburn was chosen deacon after the death of Dr. Gager, but is always called by his title of Mr. which in those days was used as the term Esquire is at present. Church member were invariably distinguished as 'our brother' or 'our sister.' Goodman and Goodwife were common appellations.

Oct. 25. The Governour began to discourage the practice of drinking toasts at table : so it grew by little and little to be disused.

The Ambrose was new masted at Charlestown.

Messrs. Winthrop and Dudley joined with S. Maverick in sending out a pinnace to trade for corn. She went as far as Rhode Island and procured a hundred bushels.

Nov. 9. Proposals are issued to have a ferry set up between Boston and Charlestown.

30. One man is to be whipped for stealing a loaf of bread and another for shooting a fowl on the sabbath day.

1631. March 4. Nicholas Knopp was fined five pounds for taking upon him to cure the scurvy by a water of no value, which he sold at a very dear rate ; to be imprisoned till he pay his fine, or give security for it, or else be whipped, and be liable to any man's action, of whom he had received money for the said water.

22. All who have cards, dice or gaming tables in their houses shall make way with them before the next court.

May 18. Election day at Boston ; Winthrop and Dudley are rechosen by general consent.

William Cheeseborough's house burnt at Boston, all the people being present.

Thomas Williams undertakes to set up the first ferry : has four pence a person from Winnesimet to Boston.

June 14. Edward Convers sets up another ferry.

July 4. The Governour built a bark at Mystick, which was launched this day, and called the Blessing of the Bay. In the course of the season this vessel made several coasting trips.

26. A night watch of six persons is established at Boston. Charlestown and Roxbury were to furnish two men each, and Boston the other two.

Monthly trainings are ordered.

Aug. 16. Four men fined for drinking too much.

Sept. 27. Mr. Josias is fined for stealing from the Indians and condemned to forfeit his title and henceforth to be called Josias.

Oct. 25. Gov. Winthrop notes 'a plentiful crop.'

30. A stone house which the Governour was erecting at Mystick was washed down to the ground, in a violent storm. the walls being laid in clay instead of lime.

CHAPTER VIII.

Some are, and must be, greater than the rest.

Pope.

On the second of November, 1631, the Lion arrived again from England, and brought the Governour's wife and some of his children, together with the Rev. John Eliot and about sixty others. This event afforded the Bostonians an opportunity to exhibit their attachment to Mr. Winthrop by one of those publick demonstrations, in which they have always delighted. The vessel was detained below the town two days, and in that time preparation was made for the reception of the honourable passengers. When the Governour and his family left the ship, the Captain gave them a salute of six or seven guns, and at the landing, the military officers received them with a guard, and welcomed them with divers volleys of shot and three artillery pieces. Several of the assistants and most of the people of the neighbourhood assembled to witness the scene and to enhance the joyfulness of the occasion, marvellous store of kids, venison, poultry, geese and partridges, and other luxuries were brought and sent as presents. The like manifestation of love had never been seen in New England. It is hardly necessary to add that on the 11th of November they kept a day of thanksgiving at Boston.

The succeeding winter passed away without any material occurrences. At the General Court, in Boston, on the 8th of May, 1632, the same Governour and Deputy were elected, and it was then thought expedient to pass an order that two men should be chosen from each town, to confer with the Court of Assistants about raising a publick stock. This order was the first step towards a house of representatives.*

---

* More of form was given to this branch of the government in April 1634, when it was determined, that the freemen of each plantation should choose two or three before every general court, and that such persons so deputed should have full power to deal in all the affairs of the commonwealth, wherein the freemen have to do, excepting only the election of magistrates, at which every man was still to give his own voice. In 1636 the number of representatives was apportioned according to the number of inhabitants, no town to have more than three, and persons might send their written votes, endorsed by the name of the voter, instead of attending in person at the court on Election day.

The delegates were at that time called deputies or committees, and Messrs. William Colburn and William Cheeseborough had the honour to be the first from Boston.

Mr. Wilson returned from London, bringing his wife with him, on the 26th of May, and the congregation began in August to build a house for publick worship, and one for the residence of their pastor. Towards these purposes they made a voluntary contribution of a hundred and twenty pounds. The meeting house was erected on the south side of State Street, opposite the new building now erecting at the head of Wilson's lane, for the accommodation of the United States' Branch Bank. Its roof was thatched and its walls were of mud. It would be pleasant to be able to point to the very ground whereon this first temple stood. Mr. Emerson, in his historical sketch of the church, fixes it not far from the spot on which the Exchange Coffee House had been newly reared. But our search for that edifice is equally unavailing: literally, not one stone of that enormous structure is left upon another. A writer in seventeen hundred ninety-five says it was on the ground on which the Branch bank then stood : we trust it will never be so difficult to direct the future inquirer to the new office of the present Branch.*

As the season grew late and the weather severe, those members of the church who belonged to Charlestown, found it inconvenient to attend worship in Boston. They therefore signified their desire to constitute a new society on the other side of the river. The eleventh of October was set apart for seeking the direction of Heaven, and on the fourteenth, eighteen men and fifteen women were peaceably dismissed from their relation to the church. These afterwards elected Mr. Thomas James for their teacher, and formed the first congregational church in Charlestown.

Up to that period one hundred and fifty one members, of whom one hundred and thirty were brethren, had joined the Boston church in full communion. In those days they had a distinction of offices in the church which does not prevail among us. Mr. Wilson was at first ordained as teacher, and on the 22d of November he was chosen pastor. Mr. Thomas Oliver was also chosen ruling elder. They were both ordained in form; the two deacons first imposing hands upon the elder, and then the elder and two deacons upon the pastor. The church made considerable effort to retain Mr. Eliot with them in the capacity of teacher, but were disappointed by his fixed resolution to settle at Roxbury.

Boston was now gradually assuming preeminence over the other towns. The court had resolved by general consent, in

* The Dorchester people had built a meeting house prior to March 1632.

October, that it was the fittest place for publick meetings of
any in the bay, and ordered a house of correction to be built
here, and also a house for the beadle, which was a corporation officer, something similar to a sheriff. Considerable
progress had been made towards the fortification of the
town, by works on Fort Hill, which was then called Corn
Hill, and the people had increased so rapidly that the land
within the peninsula was not sufficient for their use. The
right of improving several places, in the neighbourhood, for
their cattle and the procuring of wood, had therefore been
granted them. Another ferry had also become necessary between this and Charlestown, and the wind mill had been
brought from Watertown. The latter was a source of profit.

It would seem that Dudley did not witness this advance of
Boston with perfect satisfaction. According to the agreement
before mentioned, he with Mr. Secretary Bradstreet and other gentlemen of note, went forward in the spring of sixteen
hundred thirty-one, with their design to build at Newtown. The
Deputy finished his house in a style which the Governour
thought too expensive and showy, both on account of the hard-
ness of the times, and of the example, which might lead others
to undue extravagance. A wainscoting of clapboards constituted this offensive peculiarity. The Governour himself
had also set up a house at Newtown, but in the course of the
fall he had it taken down and removed to Boston, where he
had resolved in future to reside. This step was no small disappointment to the rest, and occasioned some ill will between
the Governour and Deputy. The latter accused the former
of a breach of his promise to build at Newtown. The discontent became so great that their mutual friends advised
them to submit the subject to the opinion of several ministers.
The Governour's answer to the accusation against him was,
that he had fulfilled the words of his promise, having had a
house up, and servants living in it by the day appointed.
As to the removal of the house, he alleged that he perceived
the other assistants did not go forward in building : and moreover, the people of Boston having been discouraged by the
Deputy from removing to Newtown, had petitioned him, under
all their hands, not to leave them, according to the promise
he had made to them, when they first sat down with him at
Boston. On these and similar explanations, the referees
agreed that the Governour's conduct was in some degree ex-
cusable, and he acknowledged himself faulty, so far as they
declared him to be so. They awarded that he should pay
the Deputy twenty pounds towards his expenses in building,
or else provide a minister for the people at Newtown, and
contribute something towards his maintenance for a time. The
Governour wisely chose to do the former, and remitted the

money. The Deputy was not behind him in complaisance,
and returned the same with assurances that he was so well
satisfied of the Governour's good will, that he should not have
been tempted to accept it, if it had been a hundred pounds
instead of twenty. Thus this difficulty terminated, and they
afterwards kept peace and friendly correspondency together.

Fac simile of the Governour and Deputy's Signatures.

WOOD'S DESCRIPTION.

The rising importance of the Massachusetts colony early
attracted the attention of travellers as well as of statesmen, and
perhaps the fair report of some of the former may have had as
much influence in awakening the jealousy of the latter, as the
misrepresentations of some disaffected persons are supposed to
have had. William Wood, the author of New England's
Prospect, has furnished us with the result of his observations
in and about Boston in the year 1633.   His descriptions are
so accurate that they could hardly be amended, and the facts
noticed by him are mostly corroborated by other accounts.
They are therefore peculiarly entitled to a place here.
' First I will begin with the outmost plantation in the patent,
to the southward, which is called Wichaguscusset [Wey-
mouth.] This is but a small village, yet is well timbered and
hath good store of hay ground.—Three miles to the north of
this is Mount Wolaston, a very fertile soil, and a place very
convenient for farmers' houses, there being great store of
plain ground, without trees.—Six miles further to the north
lieth Dorchester, which is the greatest town in New England,
well wooded and watered, very good arable and hay grounds.
The inhabitants of this town were the first that set upon the
trade of fishing in the bay.—A mile from this town lieth Roxbury which is a fair and handsome country town ; the inhabitants of it being all very rich : a clear and fresh brook runs

through the town, and a quarter of a mile to the north is a small river called Stony River, upon which is built a water mill. Up westward it is something rocky, whence it hath the name of Roxbury. Here is no harbour for ships, because the town is seated in the bottom of a shallow bay; which is made by the neck of land on which Boston is built, so that they can transport all their goods from the ships in boats from Boston, which is the nearest harbour.

'This harbour is made by a great company of islands, whose high cliffs shoulder out the boisterous seas; yet may easily deceive any unskilful pilot; presenting many fair openings and broad sounds, which afford too shallow water for ships, though navigable for boats, and pinnaces. It is a safe and pleasant harbour within, having but one common and safe entrance, and that not very broad; there scarce being room for three ships to come in board and board at a time; but being once in, there is room for the anchorage of 500 ships. The seamen having spent their old store of wood and water, may here have fresh supplies from the adjacent islands, with good timber to repair their weather beaten ships.

'Boston is two miles N. E. of Roxbury. Its situation is very pleasant, being a peninsula hemmed in on the south side by the bay of Roxbury, and on the north side, with Charles river, the marshes on the back-side, being not half a quarter of a mile over; so that a little fencing will secure their cattle from the wolves. The greatest wants are wood and meadow ground, which never were in this place ;*. being constrained to fetch their building timber, and fire wood from the islands in boats, and their hay in loyters; it being a neck, and bare of wood, they are not troubled with these great annoyances, wolves, rattlesnakes and muspuetos. Those, that live here upon their cattle, must be constrained to take farms in the country, or else they cannot subsist; the place being too small to contain many, and fittest for such as can trade into England, for such commodities as the country wants, being the chief place for shipping and merchandize.

'This neck of land is not above four miles in compass, in form almost square, having on the south side, at one corner,

---

* *Mr. Wood* was wrong in asserting that '*wood was never in this place.*' It had doubtless been the favourite residence of the natives for many years, and a considerable portion had been cleared by burning, as was their custom for the culture of corn; hence it was sometimes called the *plain neck*, and compared with the surrounding country, covered with interminable forests, it might, with propriety be called *plain*. There were, however, many large clumps left, sufficient for fuel and timber. The growth was probably similar to that of the islands. Had the peninsula been wholly denuded of trees, even the temptation of Mr. Blackstone's spring of fresh water, could not have induced the first planters to settle at Shawmut on the approach of a rigorous winter.—*Shaw.*

a great broad hill, whereon is planted a fort, which can command any ship, as she sails into the harbour within the still bay. On the north side is another hill, equal in bigness, whereon stands a windmill. To the northwest is a high mountain, with three little rising hills on the top of it, wherefore it is called

THE TRAMOUNT.

'From the top of this mountain, a man may overlook all the islands which lie within the bay, and descry such ships as are on the sea coast.

' This town although it be neither the greatest nor the richest, yet is the most noted and frequented, being the centre of the plantations, where the monthly courts are kept. Here likewise dwells the Governour. This place hath very good land affording rich corn-fields and fruitful gardens, having likewise sweet and pleasant springs. The inhabitants of this place, for their enlargement, have taken to themselves farm houses in a place called Muddy River, [Brookline] two miles from the town, where there is good ground, large timber, and store of marsh land and meadow. In this place they keep their swine and other cattle in the summer, whilst the corn is in the ground at Boston, and bring them to town in the winter.

' Newtown [Cambridge] is one of the neatest and best compacted towns in New England, having many fair structures, with many handsome contrived streets : the inhabitants most of them are very rich.—Half a mile westward of this is Watertown, a place nothing inferior for land, wood, meadows and water to Newtown. Within half a mile of this town is a great pond which is divided between the two towns, and divides their bounds to the northward. Both towns are on the north side of the river Charles.

' On the same side of that river is Charlestown, which is another neck of land, on whose north side runs Mystick river. At this town there is kept a ferry boat to convey passengers over Charles river, which between the banks is a quarter of a mile over, being a very deep channel. Up higher is a broad

NAHANT HOTEL.

bay, being above two miles between the shores, into which run Stony river and Muddy river. Towards the southwest in the midst of this bay is a great oyster bank: towards the northeast is a great creek, upon whose shore is situated a small village [included within the bounds of Charlestown.] At the bottom of this bay, the river begins to be narrower, being but half a quarter of a mile broad.

'The next town is Mystick [Medford] which is three miles from Charlestown by land, and a league and a half by water. It is seated by the water side very pleasantly; there are not many houses as yet. On the west side of this river the Governour hath a farm, where he keeps most of his cattle. On the east side is Mr. Craddock's plantation, where he hath a park impaled and keeps his cattle, till he can store it with deer. Here likewise he is at charges of building ships. The last year one was upon the stocks of an hundred tons; that being finished they are to build one of twice her burden.

'The last town in the still bay is Winnesimet [Chelsea,] a very sweet place for situation: it is within a mile of Charlestown, the river only parting them.

'The next plantation is Saugus [including Lynn] six miles northeast from Winnesimet. This town is pleasant for situation, seated at the bottom of a bay, which is made on one side with the surrounding shore, and on the other side with a long sandy beach, which is two miles long to the end, whereon is a neck of land called NAHANT. Upon the south side of the sandy beach the sea beateth, which is a true prognostication, to presage storms and foul weather, and the breaking up of the frost: for when a storm hath been or is likely to be, it will roar like thunder, so as to be heard six miles. Upon the north side of this bay are two great marshes which are made two by a pleasant river which runs between them. At the mouth of this river runs up a great creek into that great marsh which is called Romney Marsh, and is four miles long and two miles broad, half of it being marsh ground, and half upland grass without tree or bush.'

These descriptions were sketched before the fifteenth of August, 1633, on which day Wood set sail for England, and were published the next year accompanied with a curious map, engraved on wood.

CHAPTER IX.

"Lands you may have, we value not the soil,
Accounting tillage too severe a toil."

WHILE the people of Boston depended in good measure upon the productions of their farms and gardens for subsistence, their wants could not be supplied from the land within the peninsula, which did not originally exceed seven hundred acres. They were therefore allowed to extend themselves into various parts of the adjacent territory, and many of the places described in the extract we have just finished, were under the improvement of Bostonians. Conant's Island [Governour's I.] was granted to Gov. Winthrop for a nominal rent, and thus became a part of Boston, in April sixteen hundred and thirty-two. In the same year, that part of Chelsea between Powder-horn hill and Pull-in point was assigned to Boston forever, and not a long time after, the whole of Winnesimet was annexed. Brookline or Muddy river was owned and occupied by persons considered as belonging to Boston. As early as April 1634, Long Island, Hog and Deer Islands, were granted to Boston by the court for a nominal yearly rent, and convenient enlargement at Mount Wolaston was allowed to her inhabitants. They were allowed to cut wood on Dorchester neck, but the jurisdiction was to remain with Dorchester. Romney Marsh, Spectacle Island, and Noddle's Island were added before the end of sixteen hundred and thirty-six. These grants are recorded in the colony records, and it is probable the remaining Islands were occasionally annexed afterwards. At these several places, portions were allotted to every family in Boston according to their number and necessities.

The question has been asked, *by what right* did our ancestors take and retain possession of the lands we inherit? The answer is as complete and satisfactory as such a case admits. So far as the King of England's title was concerned, the grant of the council of Plymouth to the six gentlemen and their associates, and the subsequent confirmation of the King, which empowered them and others to dispose of the lands to the best advantage, were considered sufficient to cancel his claim to property in the soil.

The Indians that formerly possessed these parts were few in number when our fathers arrived. A pestilence had not long before carried off whole tribes in a manner almost incredible. Of such as remained near Boston, the greater part were peaceably disposed, and Chicatabot, the reigning sachem, instead of repelling the settlers from his dominions by force of arms, administered to their comfort, and finally sold them this speck of his extensive territory for a valuable consideration. The evidence of the conveyance is found in a quitclaim deed of one of his grandsons : it is a very curious document, dated in March sixteen hundred eighty-five,* and we insert it for the satisfaction or amusement of the present inhabitants. At this distance of time, to be sure, there is no danger of disturbance from the descendants of Chicatabot ; still the peaceable and upright manner, in which our ancestors obtained a title to the soil, is not to be forgotten.

To understand the occasion of this and similar instruments drawn about the same period, it is necessary to anticipate the fact that the charter, or patent under which the Massachusetts colony held, was likely then to be vacated; and the people were told that in that case their title to their estates would be of no value. Besides, even if the vacating of the charter might not annihilate the rights acquired under it in legal form, it was said that the General Court had not made their grants of land under the seal of the colony. This was represented as a glaring defect, which possession and improvement could not supply. When the patent was annulled (of which official information was received July 2, 1685) and a new government established, writs of intrusion were brought against some of the principal persons in the colony, and the landholders were obliged to acknowledge the insufficiency of their title, and pay the fees for a new deed. Randolph, a notable character, petitioned for half an acre of land, to be taken out of the common in Boston, and other favourites looked with a longing eye on some of the best estates, especially where the property was in a town or company : hence it was important to have in readiness every possible proof to evidence the rightful possession of the occupants.†

---

* See a copy of this Indian Quitclaim in Appendix No. I.
† See *Hutch.* Hist. i. ch. iii. There was no registry of deeds here before 1652,

CHAPTER X.

.... A gentleman that is very singular in his behaviour,
but his singularities proceed from his good sense.—*Spectator.*

THERE was another claim beside that of the Indians and
the king of England, which the settlers at Boston were bound
to satisfy. By right of previous possession, Mr. Blackstone
had a title to proprietorship in the whole peninsula. It was
in fact for a time called Blackstone's neck. How far he considered himself the owner of the soil, and what agreement he
made with Mr. Johnson when he invited him to cross the river,
does not now appear. The records of the colony inform us
that in April 1633, the court ordered fifty acres of ground to
be set out for him, near to his house in Boston, to belong to
him forever. This quantity amounted to at least a fourteenth
part of the whole place, which shows that his rights as original possessor were not regarded altogether null. On the
Boston records under date of November 10, 1634, among
other taxes assigned to William Cheeseborough the constable,
and others for assessment and collection, we find a rate of
thirty pounds to Mr. Blackstone : for what purpose it was
levied will appear from the following

DEPOSITION.

The deposition of John Odlin, aged about Eighty two
    yeares, Robert Walker aged about Seventy Eight yeares,
    Francis Hudson aged about Sixty eight yeares, and Wil-
    liam Lytherland aged about Seventy Six yeares. These
    Deponents, being ancient dwellers and Inhabitants of the
    Town of Boston in New-England from the first planting and
    Setling thereof and continuing so at this day, do jointly
    testify and depose that in or about the yeare of our Lord
    One thousand Six hundred thirty and four the then present
    Inhabitants of said Town of Boston (of whome the Honour-
    able John Winthrop Esq. Governour of the Colony was
    chiefe) did treate and agree with Mr. William Blackstone
    for the purchase of his Estate and right in any Lands lying
    within the said neck of Land called Boston, and for said
    purchase agreed that every householder should pay Six
    Shillings, which was accordingly collected, none paying
    less, some considerably more than Six Shillings, and the
    said sume collected, was delivered and paid to Mr. Black-
    stone to his full content and Satisfaction, in consideration

whereof hee Sold unto the then Inhabitants of said Town and their heirs and assigns for ever his whole right and interest in all and every of the Lands lying within the said Neck Reserveing onely unto him selfe about Six acres of Land on the point commonly called Blackstons point on part whereof his then dwelling house stood ; after which purchase the Town laid out a place for a trayning field ; which ever since and now is used for that purpose, and for the feeding of cattell : Robert Walker, and William Lytherland farther Testify that Mr. Blackstone bought a stock of Cows with the Money he received as above, and Removed and dwelt near Providence where he liv'd till the day of his Death.

Deposed this 10th of June 1684, by John Odlin, Robert Walker, Francis Hudson, and William Lytherland according to their respective Testimonye

Before us

S. Bradstreet, *Governour.*
Sam. Sewall, *Assist.*

Precisely at what time Mr. Blackstone ceased to be an inhabitant of Boston we are not informed. His name appears once more in the colony records under date of April 7, 1635, when Nahanton was ordered to pay him two skins of beaver for damages done his swine by setting of traps. An allotment of fifteen acres at Muddy river was made to him by the allotters of Boston, in January 1638, and on the ninth of March in the same year, his name is mentioned for the last time, in describing the boundaries of certain lots of lands. It is stated by one author* that he left Boston about that time, which corresponds with the statement of another† that he lived in Boston nine or ten years.

Mr. Blackstone was a very eccentrick character. He was a man of learning, and had received episcopal ordination in England ; seems to have been of the puritan persuasion and to have left his native country for his nonconformity. Johnson says he was here before the vernal of twenty-nine, which makes him to have come over with Mr. Endicott. Hubbard adopts the authority and tells us he began to hew stones in the mountains, wherewith to build, but when he saw all sorts of stones would not suit in the building, as he supposed, he betook himself to till the ground, wherein probably he was more skilled, or at least had a better faculty ; retaining no symbol of his former profession but his canonical coat. Mather is less rude, and allows him to have been a godly

---

* *Backus* Vol. i. 58.
† *Lechford,* who wrote his 'Plain Dealing' in 1641. *Hutch.* 1. ch. i. v.

episcopalian, though he was of a particular humour, and would never join himself to any of our churches, giving this reason for it : *I came from England, because I did not like the* LORD-BISHOPS; *but I cannot join with you, because I would not be under the* LORD-BRETHREN.*

He had been admitted to take the freeman's oath in May, 1631, before the order was passed, which restricted that privilege to church members only. He cultivated with success the six acres which he retained, and soon had a garden plot and an orchard, near his cottage and spring. These we take to have been situated in the neighbourhood of the present Alms House. The point, at which Cragie's bridge commences, is called, on the ancient plans of the town, Barton's point, and is the same referred to in the foregoing deposition.

It was not very long before Mr. Blackstone found that there might be more than one kind of nonconformity, and was virtually obliged to leave the remainder of his estate here, and remove a second time into the wilderness. We have no thought that ' he was driven from Boston because he was an episcopal minister,' but a man may be very ill at ease in many a place where he may be allowed to stay by sufferance. Let the cause of his removal have been what it may, certain it is that he went and settled by the Pawtucket river, ' built a house and cultivated part of the land now comprising the Whipple farm in Cumberland,' Rhode Island.

The place to which he removed, the ' Attleborough Gore ' of history, fell within the limits of Plymouth colony, in the records of which colony we find still farther memoirs of this respectable and memorable man. His name, however, does not occur in those records until the year 1661, when mention is made of a place ' called by the natives Waweepoonseag, where one Blackstone now liveth.' This was probably the aboriginal name of a rivulet, at present known as Abbot's Run, which is tributary to the Pawtucket. At this his new plantation he lived uninterrupted for many years, and there raised an orchard, the first that ever bore apples in Rhode Island. He had the first of the sort called yellow sweetings, that were ever in the world, and is said to have planted the first orchard in Massachusetts also.

Mr. Blackstone's house was situated near the banks of the river, on a knoll which he named Study Hill. It was surrounded by a park, which was his favourite and daily walk for a series of years. Though he was far from agreeing in opinion with Roger Williams, he used frequently to go to Providence to preach the gospel; and to encourage his younger hearers, while he gratified his own benevolent dispo-

---

* *Hubbard* N.E. p. 113. *Johnson* W. W. P. ch. ix. Magnalia i. 221.

ALMS-HOUSE, LEVERET STREET.

sition, he would give them of his apples, which were the first
they ever saw. It is said that when he grew old and unable
to travel on foot, not having any horse, he used to ride on a
bull, which he had tamed and tutored to that use. He died
May 26, 1675, and lies buried on classick ground, on Study
Hill, where a flat stone marks his grave.

Concerning Mr. Blackstone's family we infer that it consisted of but three persons while he continued in Boston : he
having had a portion for three heads allotted to him at Muddy
River. His wife, whose name was Sarah, died about two
years before him. He left a son named John, for whom
guardians were appointed in 1675, and a daughter who was
married to Mr. John Stevenson.

The death of this venerable pilgrim happened at a critical
period, the beginning of an Indian war. His estate was desolated, and his house burnt by the natives. His library
which contained a hundred and eighty-six volumes, from folios
to pamphlets, shared the same fate. His family is now extinct : but we hope and trust the musing stranger will hereafter find his name on some marble tablet of historical inscriptions erected by the munificent hand of some Bostonian.*

CHAPTER XI.

For empire formed, and fit to rule the rest.

Dryden.

The long desired arrival of Mr. Cotton took place on the
fourth of September, 1633. He came in the Griffin, a ship
of three hundred tons, which brought about two hundred
other passengers. His celebrity which was great in England,
had already filled the American settlements, and prepared
him a most welcome reception. His talents were considered
common property, and it was the immediate concern of the
wise and good, where he should fix his residence and how
receive an honourable support. He might have selected any
situation in the country, and was indeed urged to accept several invitations other than what he received in Boston, but he
was somewhat compelled by the advice of the Governour and
a council of the elders in the colony, as well as the unanimous
voice of the First Church here to bestow his principal labours.
It was at first proposed that Mr. Cotton should be maintained
from the treasury, in consideration of the political as well as
ecclesiastical benefits, that were expected from his ministry ;

---

* Mass. H. C. 2. ix. 174. x. 170.

but the maturer judgment of a majority of the council quashed the proposal.

Mr. Cotton was ordained teacher of the First Church on the tenth of October ; and on the same day Mr. Thomas Leverett was chosen a ruling elder, and Mr. Giles Firmin, sen. a godly apothecary from Sudbury in England was chosen deacon.* In addition to the imposition of the hands of the elders, as in the case of Mr. Wilson, the ceremony of calling on the people to signify their election of the candidate, and on him to acknowledge his acceptance of their call, and also the presentation of the right hand of fellowship by the neighbouring ministers, was introduced on this occasion. Immediately upon his induction, Mr. Cotton entered upon the duties of his office ; and so great was his influence both in ecclesiastical and civil affairs, that the measures he recommended were forthwith adopted in the church, and his private political counsels were with equal readiness enforced by the government.†

Considerable trading had already been carried on at Boston, but there appears not to have been any regular system introduced, until March, 1634. In Gov. Winthrop's journal for that month, it is stated that by order of court a market was erected at Boston to be kept upon Thursday the fifth day of the week, being lecture day.‡ Samuel Cole set up the first house of entertainment, and John Cogan, merchant, the first shop. In July of the preceding year, a proposition had been made by the Plymouth people, to have the Bostonians join with them in trading to Connecticut, but they thought fit not to meddle with it.

The General Court this year held their session in Mr. Cotton's meeting house. It fell to his lot to preach the Election sermon, and he improved the occasion to deliver this doctrine, that a magistrate ought not to be turned into the condition of a private man, without just cause and on publick conviction, any more than a magistrate may turn a private man out of his freehold without publick trial. His sermon, however, did not have the effect he probably intended ; for the freemen proceeding forthwith to vote for a Governour and Deputy, Mr. Winthrop was left out, Mr. Dudley chosen in his place, and Mr. Roger Ludlow elected Deputy. A consequence of this change was that Newtown became the seat of government for the year ensuing.

---

* This Mr. Firmin's son Giles practised physick at Ipswich and afterwards returned to England.

† *Emerson's* Hist. First Church.

‡ This is the earliest notice of the Thursday lectures in the Journal, but an order of court, passed in October 1633, regulating the hours at which lectures should be held (1. P. M.) shows that they had been earlier established.

In the course of the fall, a little affair occurred which serves to show us somewhat of the spirit of the times. Some of the people had been abused and insulted on board a vessel in the harbour, and it was thought best not to suffer the insult to pass unnoticed. The power of the government and the advice of the ministers was put in requisition, and the supercargo of the ship being on shore was summarily seized, and committed to custody till he gave bail that the offender should be forthcoming. Upon examination, not much could be made of the matter, and the bail was discharged with advice to the master not to bring any such disorderly persons this way again.

It will hardly be credited, yet it is true that so early as the period of which we are treating, Mr. Cotton found it necessary to exert his influence to suppress superfluous and unnecessarily expensive fashions. The court in September of this year made a law, that tobacco should not be taken in company, or before strangers, and condemned to disuse a great variety of articles of dress. Gold or silver laces, girdles, or hat-bands, embroidered caps, immoderate great veils and immoderate great sleeves incurred special disapprobation. Such things were all subject to forfeiture, with an exception that some of the articles already in use might be worn out. But a sermon of Mr. Cotton's at Salem had as powerful an effect as the fear of the law. He taught the women there, that they had no occasion to wear the veil, in compliance with any scriptural direction, and they were so enlightened and convinced by his discourse, that every woman in the afternoon appeared without her veil, and ever after considered it a shame to wear one. Mr. Cotton had before urged the same doctrine at Boston ; we may safely add, with like success.*

We have now reached the date of the oldest volume of the town records, that remains extant. The first page commences with the doings of the first day of the seventh month,† 1634. This entry, and those made for a short time after, appear in the handwriting of Gov. Winthrop ; a circumstance which makes us regret the more, that the records of the four first years should have been lost. We are thus left without direct information of the course pursued in regard to the division of land among the settlers, and of other steps they must have taken to bring their affairs into so good order as we find them in, at this period.

It is apparent from this first record that the management of the affairs of the town had been committed to a select body of men. The number at this period was ten, as appears from the following extract :

* *Winthrop*, March 4, 1634. *Hubbard*, N. E. 205.
† Equivalent to September; March being considered the first month.

'Month 8th, day 6th. At a general meeting upon publick notice given the fifth day of the last week it was ordered and agreed as follows:

'*Imprimis.* Richard Bellingham, Esquire, and J. Cogan, merchant, were chosen in the place of Giles Firmin [senior] deceased, to make up the number 10, to manage the affairs of the town.'

The persons thus chosen are not distinguished by the appellation of SELECTMEN, till the year sixteen hundred and forty five: they were sometimes called Townsmen. Dorchester chose such a body in 1633, for the first time: it is probable that the measure had been previously adopted in Boston: Charlestown did not choose them till 1634. The courts of the colony had made no provision for any such form of town government. It is not till May 3d. 1636, that we find an order to the following effect:—The freemen of every town are empowered to dispose of lands, grant lots and make such orders as may concern the well ordering of their town, not repugnant to laws of court or kingdom; also to lay fines not exceeding twenty shillings, appoint officers, constables and surveyors.— It is clear that the town of Boston exercised all this authority long before the passing of this order. The course had probably been adopted by common consent, and some event may have occurred, which rendered it necessary to give the sanction of court to the procedure.

The names of the first board of Selectmen on record are

John Winthrop	Giles Firmin [sen.]
William Coddington	John Coggeshall
Capt. [John] Underhill	William Pierce
Thomas Oliver	Robert Harding
Thomas Leverett	William Brenton.

It was customary for the inhabitants to meet to transact business relative to the police of the town immediately after the Thursday lecture. On the 11th of December they met to choose seven men who should divide the town lands among them. They chose by ballot and elected all ' of the inferior sort' except one of the elders and a deacon. This was done through fear that the richer gentlemen would not give the poorer class so large a proportion of the land as they thought should be allotted to them, but would rather leave a greater part at liberty for new comers and for Common, which Gov. Winthrop had often persuaded them was best for the town. Mr. Cotton and others were offended at this proceeding. Mr. Winthrop expressed his regret that Boston should be the first to shake off her magistrates; whereupon, on motion of Mr. Cotton, who showed them that it was scriptural to have all such business committed to the elders, they all agreed to have a new election, which was deferred to the next lecture day.

The town records are silent as to the names of the first ' inferior sort :' those who were chosen at the second meeting, December 18th, 1634, were,

Mr. Winthrop,	Mr. Colburn,
Mr. Coddington,	Mr. Cotton,
Mr. Oliver,	and
Mr. Bellingham,	William Balston.

The jealousy, manifested by the people on this occasion, was natural, and the exhibition of their power may have been politick and prudent : their submission to the arguments of Mr. Cotton and Mr. Winthrop was reasonable, and evinces a character, of which their posterity may without vanity be proud.

CHAPTER XII.

These drew not for their fields the sword
Like tenants of a feudal lord.

Scott.

THIS committee was empowered ' to divide and dispose of all such lands, belonging to the town, as are not yet in the lawful possession of any particular person, according to the orders of the court, leaving such portions in common, for the use of new comers, and the further benefit of the town, as in their best discretion they shall think fit—the islands hired by the town to be also included in this order.' On the ninth of February following, ' it is agreed by general consent, that all the inhabitants shall plant only upon such ground as is already broken up, or inclosed, in the neck,* or else upon the ground at Noddle's Island from Mr. Maverick's grant, and that *every able man, fit to plant, shall have allowed to him two acres to plant on, and every able youth one acre*, to be allotted out by Mr. Hutchinson, Mr. Cogan, Mr. Sampford, and William Cheeseborough, and Mr. Brenton, or any three of them.' Neither of these, it will be perceived, were on the former committee : their duties were different, the one regarding chiefly the lands within the peninsula, the other having refer-

---

* Those who have occasion to search the early records of the town, should know, that sometimes the whole peninsula was called the *Neck* ; sometimes that part only, which connects Boston with Roxbury ; and sometimes they will meet with the expression, *within the Neck*, (and *the two Necks*, and *the inward Neck*.) These distinctions are to be particularly observed in tracing the original titles of the allotments.—*Shaw*,

8

ence to the lands at Muddy river, Pullin point, and other places assigned to Boston people for their improvement.

What special care they took to preserve themselves a peculiar people, will appear from the record of the 30th November, 1635. ' It is agreed, that no further allotments shall
be granted unto any new comers, but such as may be likely
to be received members of the congregation.—*Item*, that none
shall sell their houses or allotments to any new comers, but
with the consent and allowance of those that are appointed
allotters.—*Item*, that all such as have allotments for habitation
allotted unto them shall build thereon, before the first of the
first month next, called March, or else it shall be in the power
of the allotters to dispose of them.'   Several instances occurred in which these orders were faithfully executed: fines
were inflicted on some who ventured to bargain for lands
without permission, and sales were declared void. Those who
failed to build were compelled to offer satisfactory excuse.*

Four days after the passing of the above order, it was
further agreed ' that in regard of the unequal disposing of the
planting ground heretofore, none shall be accounted to have
any estate of inheritance in any planting ground upon the
neck save only in their house plots, gardens, and yards, until
the town shall take order for a more equal disposing thereof
by distribution.   And on the 14th of December, ten days
after the last, it is agreed by general consent, that the poorer
sort of inhabitants, such as are members, or likely so to be,
and have no cattle, shall have their proportion of allotments
for planting ground and other assigned unto them by the allotters, and laid out at Muddy river by the aforenamed five
persons, [viz. Messrs. Colburn, Aspinwall, Sampford, Balston,
and Richard Wright] or four of them—those that fall between
the foot of the hill and the water, to have but four acres upon
a head, and those that are farther off to have five acres for
every head, the plot to begin next Muddy river side.'

Conformably to the preceding orders a distribution was
declared on the 8th of January 1638.   The names of the
heads of families are recorded and the quantity of land allotted to each, with the boundaries of the same.   The number
of families of ' the poorer sort' provided for, was eighty-six,

* Town Records, June 6, 1636. 'We find that Richard Fairbank hath sold unto two
strangers the two houses in Sudbury end, that were Wm. Balston's, contrary to a former order, and therefore the sale to be wrong, and the said R. F. to forfeit for his breaking thereof
five pounds.

March 30, 1641. Notice shall be given by the constables unto such as have not built upon
their house lots, which have been set out to them above a year, that they come to the next
meeting to show cause why their lots should not be granted to others, according to the original grant ; and if they come not, that then the town will dispose of them.

and the number of heads 337. Besides these, allotments were assigned to thirty other families, such as Gov. Winthrop's, Mr. Wilson's, Mr. Cotton's, Mr. Robert Keayne's and other principal persons, some of whom had upwards of 300 acres apiece.

On the tenth of January 1642, it was found necessary to adopt the following vote. ' Notwithstanding the order made concerning the disposing of land in this neck, on the fourth of the tenth, sixteen hundred thirty-five, yet for peace sake and for avoiding of confusion in the town, many lands having been bought and sold at dear rates, the rights of all lands disposed of, shall belong to the present owners as they should have done, if the former order had never been, and the said former order is hereby repealed. *Provided*, that this order shall not concern such marsh ground as hath been let from year to year.'

Under date of March 4th ensuing we find another record on this subject, when it is ordered that the residue of the town's lands, not yet disposed of (excepting those that are laid out for commons at Boston, Braintree, and Muddy River) shall be divided amongst the present inhabitants, together with such as shall be admitted within two months now next following, and that in this manner, viz. a greater proportion to them that have had less than their due, and the less to them that have had more, and proportionally to them that have had none, and this is to be done by the Selectmen, chosen for the town's business. Finally on the 7th Sept. 1645, we have this important entry; 'whereas the several grants of house lots and other lands, recorded in this town book, are entered only as granted to the proprietors themselves, without mention of their heirs, it has been thought fit to be hereby declared and ordered, that all such grants were and shall be intended to be ESTATES IN FEE SIMPLE, with all due and usual privileges and appurtenances, and are to be so construed and taken, to all intents, except in such cases wherein any particular estate for term of years is specially expressed.'

The foregoing citations present all our direct information of the course pursued, in regard to the division of land among the settlers at Boston. All the lands in the colony had become the property of the company by their charter, and Hubbard informs us, that at a court in May 1629, it was agreed, that every adventurer who had advanced fifty pounds should have 200 acres of land allowed him ; and that 50 acres apiece should be allowed those, that went over at their own charge. This may account for some of the great lots we have mentioned. In the settlement of Salem, at first, the smallest families were entitled to ten-acre lots, with a reserve

of such common lands for pasture, as might accommodate
them, near their own houses.* Johnson, in his account of
Woburn, gives us a more particular account of ' the manner
how this people have populated their towns,' than we have
discovered elsewhere. ' This town, *as all others*,' saith he,
' had its bounds fixed by the General Court, to the contents
of four miles square : the grant is to seven men of good and
honest report, upon condition, that, within two years, they
erect houses thereon, and so go on to make a town thereof
upon the Act of Court. These seven men have power to
give and grant out lands unto any persons, who are willing to
take up their dwellings within the said precinct, and to be admitted to all common privileges of the said town, giving them
such an ample portion, both of meadow and upland, as their
present and future stock of cattle and hands were like to improve, with eye had to others, that might after come to popu-
late the said town. This they did without any respect of
persons ; yet such as were exorbitant, and of a turbulent
spirit, unfit for a civil society, they would reject : till they
come to mend their manners, such came not to enjoy any
freehold. These seven men ordered and disposed of the
streets of the town, as might be best for the improvement of
the land, and that civil and religious society maintained. To
which end, those that had land nearest the place for Sabbath
assembly, had a lesser quantity at home and more farther off,
to improve for corn of all kinds. They refused not men for
their poverty, but according to their ability were helpful to
the poorest sort, in building their houses, and distributed to
them land accordingly : *the poorest had six or seven acres of
meadow and twenty-five of upland* or thereabouts. Thus was
this town populated, and after this manner are the towns of
New England peopled.'

That the inhabitants of Boston were equally careful as to
the character of those they received among them, as were the
people of Woburn, we have already seen, and they continued
to be so for a series of years. At a Selectmen's meeting,
January, 1637, ' it was agreed that Widow Bushnell, George
Harwood, and John Low, the wheelwright, shall have house
lots and gardens *upon the usual condition of inoffensive carriage.*
In 1652, Feb. Richard Woody is admitted an inhabitant on
condition he shall not be offensive by his trade. August, 1657,
John Pierce is admitted an inhabitant upon the testimony of
James Everill and Isaac Collamore. Care was also taken,
to secure the town from charge on account of new comers,
and bonds were required to that effect, before leave to reside

* *Hubbard*, N. E. 123.—Mass. H. C. 1. vi. 262.—W. W. P. ch. xxii. See also *Hutch.* coll.
of papers, p. 88. 91.

here could be obtained. This practice commenced as early
as 1652, and the bonds are recorded in this stile, sc. 'Margaret Norris, an Irishwoman is admitted into the town, and
David Faulkoner is bound to secure the town from any charge
as respecting her, in a bond of seven pounds. Witness his hand

Mark
𝕯𝖆𝖛𝖎𝖉 D. F. 𝕱𝖆𝖚𝖑𝖐𝖔𝖚𝖊𝖗.
of.

26th, of 5th. 1658.'

One of the privileges of being admitted an inhabitant was
the right to improve the common lands, which so far as we
can learn appear to have been reserved in every town. Prior
to 1640 mention is frequently made of TOWN FIELDS, in the
Boston records, and they seem to have been inclosed by general fence. Thus, in Feb. 1635 we read, ' all the fences are
to be made sufficient by the seventh of the second month, and
they to be looked unto by our brother Grubb and Hudson
for the *new field;* brother Penniman and brother Colburn for
the field by him, and by brother Penn and brother Belcher
for the *fort-field;* brother Matson and brother Everill at the
mill-field.'

Again, March 1, 1636. All the fences belonging to the
town fields are to be overseen and looked unto thus, ' *the field
towards Roxbury* by Jacob Eliot and Jonathan Neegoose;
the fort field by James Penn and Richard Gridley; the mill
field by John Button and Edward Bendall, and the new field
by John Audley and Thomas Fairweather.' In June, ' a sufficient footway is ordered to be made from *W. Colburn's field*
and unto Samuel Wilbour's field next Roxbury, by the surveyors of high ways.'

Of the abovenamed fields that next to Roxbury* comprised
what we at present call the neck; the fort field that portion
of the town lying round about Fort hill : the mill field was at
the north part of the town, and was so called from the windmill, which stood on what is at present called Copp's hill : the
new field was that purchased of Mr. Blackstone, and included
the ground in the vicinity of the General Hospital ;* out of all
these, lots were from time to time granted to individuals.
The field by Mr. Colburn contained the greater part† of the
present Common, and probably extended at that time as far
as Beacon street.

---

* See town records Dec. 26, 1642, and Oct. 28, 1639.

† On the 6th October 1787 Wm. Foster conveyed to the town of Boston "a certain tract of
land containing two acres and one eighth of an acre situated lying and being near the Common and bounded E. on the highway, 324 ft. North on the Common 295 ft. 5 in. W. on
the new burial ground, 302 ft. 3 in. S. on Pleasant st. 281 ft. 9 inches," which makes the
Southeast corner of the present Common.

Respecting this the following vote was passed on the 30th of March 1640, ' Henceforth there shall be no land granted either for house plot or garden to any person, out of the open ground or common field, which is left between the Sentry hill and Mr. Colburn's end, except three or four lots to make up the street from brother Robert Walker's to the round marsh.' This vote was followed in May, 1646, by these, 1.—It is granted that all the inhabitants shall have equal right of commonage in the town : those who are admitted by the town are to be inhabitants. 2.—It is ordered that all who shall after the date hereof, come to be an inhabitant in the town of Boston shall not have right of commonage, unless he hire it of them that are commoners. 3.—There shall be kept out of the Common by the inhabitants of the town but seventy milch kine. 4.—No dry cattle, young cattle, or horse, shall be free to go on the common this year, but one horse of Elder Oliver. 5.—No inhabitant shall sell his right of commonage, but may only let it out to hire from year to year. 6.—No common marsh or pasture ground shall hereafter, by gift or sale, exchange or otherwise, be counted unto propriety, without consent of the major part of the inhabitants of the town.'

Thus stood the subject of the Common until May 1660, when ' upon motion of some the inhabitants of Boston, the General Court ordered, that the selectmen of the town from time to time shall, and are hereby empowered to order the improvement and feeding of their commons, within the neck of land, by such cattle as they shall deem meet, any law, usage, or custom to the contrary notwithstanding.'

It seemed expedient to throw these materials together in this place, in order that the reader might acquire some idea of the manner in which the town and individuals obtained their title to their several estates. We leave the after history of the Common to be introduced in another place.

CHRONOLOGICAL ITEMS.

Continued from p. 40.

1632. *July.* The congregation, i. e. the church at Boston wrote to the elders and brethren of the other churches for their advice on these questions, to wit, whether one person might be a civil magistrate and a ruling elder at the same time ? if not, then which should he lay down ? and whether there might be divers pastors in the same church ? The first was agreed by all negatively ; the second, doubtful ; the third, doubtful also. In consequence of this decision, Mr.

Nowell, who was then an Elder in the Boston church, relinquished that office and devoted himself to the duties of a civilian.

Aug. 20. Gov. Winthrop has a son born, who is baptized by the name of William. The Governour himself held the child, as others in the congregation did use. William (saith he) signifies a common man.*

Sept. 4. Court at Boston. Order a man to be severely whipt for cursing, swearing, justifying the same, and glorying in it.

Oct. 3. Every one shall pay a penny sterling for every time of taking tobacco in any place.

18. Capt. Camock and Mr. Vesy, a merchant from Piscataqua, bring sixteen hogsheads of corn to the windmill at Boston.

1633. *March* 4. Roxbury, Watertown, and Newtown are assessed six pounds, and Boston only five pounds, of a tax of £30.

The first notorious thief in Massachusetts is censured thus : all his estate forfeited ; out of which double restitution shall be made to those whom he hath wronged ; shall be whipt, and bound as a servant to any that will retain him for three years, and after to be disposed of by the court, as they shall think meet.

May. We had sent forth a pinnace after the pirate Dixey Bull, but when she had been gone two weeks, she came home, having not found him.

Aug. 220 persons had joined Boston church : men 130.

Sept. Every hand, except magistrates and ministers, is to assist in finishing the fort at Boston.

Mr. Cotton desired baptism for his son, born on their passage, whom he therefore named Seaborn.

Oct. 2. The bark Blessing which had been sent to the Southward returned : she had been at Long Island.

Nov. A small ship of about sixty tons was built at Medford and called the Rebecca.

Mr. Wilson, *by leave of the congregation* of Boston, went to Agawam (Ipswich) to teach the people of that plantation.

Chicatabot dies, and many of his people. This chief used frequently to come to Boston, and was on very friendly terms with Gov. Winthrop. At one time he came with his sannops and squaws, and presented the governour with a bushel of corn. After taking some refreshments, and having each a

---

* Journal. *Prince*, under date Oct. 29, 1630, says, ' The first recorded as baptized in the Boston church are said to be baptized in said church in this month, and are only three, namely, *Joy* and *Recompence*, daughters of Br. John Milles ; and *Pitie*, daughter of our brother Wm. Baulstone.

cup of sack, with a taste of tobacco, he ordered the whole party away in a thunder storm. Only himself with one squaw and sannop staid over night, and the Governour allowed him to sit at his table, where he behaved himself as soberly as an Englishman. He sometimes wore English clothes, and as his best dress had become rather the worse for age, he applied to the Governour, in honest simplicity, to sell him a suit. The Governour, assuming the dignity of his office, told him that English sagamores did not use to truck; and calling his tailor he ordered him to make a full suit for Chicatabot. They were to be ready in three days, and he engaged to come for them: but as he had no wish to be under an obligation, he left two good skins of beaver as a present for the Governour. He returned at the time appointed, and his regimentals were in readiness. They suited him finely and he was mightily pleased. The Governour complimented him farther with a collation, 'but he would not eat till the Governour had given thanks, and after meal he desired him to do the like, and so departed.' In this he exhibited more politeness than some of his brother chiefs, who while on a visit here were invited to attend a sermon; for they got weary of the service, and went out and broke into a neighbouring house, and without ceremony satisfied their hungry appetites with the best they could find.

This year a water mill was built at Roxbury.

1634. *March.* Boston and Roxbury disagree about their bounds.

4. A man that had often been punished for drunkenness, is now ordered to wear a red D about his neck for a year.

There was stirred up a spirit of jealousy between Mr. James the pastor of Charlestown and many of his people, so as Mr. Nowell, and some others who had been dismissed from Boston, began to question the fact of breaking from Boston, and it grew to such a scruple of conscience among them, that the advice of the other ministers was taken in it, who after two meetings could not agree about their continuance or return.

April 3. Gov. Winthrop went on foot to Agawam, and because the people there wanted for a minister, spent the sabbath with them, and exercised by way of prophecy.

20. John Coggeshall, gent. being dismissed from the church of Roxbury to Boston, though he were well known and approved, yet was not received but by confession of his faith.

May. By this time the fort at Boston was in defence, and divers pieces of ordnance mounted in it.

The week the court was, there arrived six ships with store of passengers and cattle.

Nov. The Rebecca came from Narraganset with 500 bushels of corn.

1635. *Jan.* 13. The church of Boston kept a day of humiliation, for the absence of their pastor and other brethren gone to England, and like to be troubled and detained there, and for that the Lord had made a breach upon them (by the drowning of two men and two boys a short time previous.) Mr. Cotton preached out of Numbers xxxv. 13, and one of the members taught from these words, *Wherefore doth a living man complain ?*

March 23. Whereas the wood upon the neck of land toward Roxbury gate, this last winter, hath been disorderly cut off and wasted, whereby the poor inhabitants are disappointed of relief they might have had there, in after and needful times, now it is generally agreed that Mr. Treasurer [Coddington], Mr. Bellingham, and Mr. Wm. Hutchinson, with the three deacons, shall consider who have been faulty herein, and set down what restitution of wood unto the poor such shall make, according to their several proportions, allotted by the major part of these six.

☞ Item. That whosoever at any publique meeting shall fall into any private conference to ye hindring of ye publique businesses, shall forfeit for every such offence twelve pence to be paid into ye constable's hand for publique uses.

May 6. A general court was held at Newtown, when John Haynes, Esq. (of Newtown) was chosen Gov. and Richard Bellingham, Esq. (of Boston) Dep. Gov. The Governour and Deputy were elected by papers wherein their names were written, but the Assistants were chosen by papers without names ; thus the Governour propounded one to the people, when they all went out, and came in at one door, and every man delivered a paper into a hat—such as voted for the party named, gave in a paper with some figure or scroll on it, others gave in a blank.

A BEACON is to be set on the Sentry hill at Boston, to give notice to the country of any danger ; to be guarded by one man stationed near, and fired as occasion may be.

Boston differs with Dorchester about their bounds at Mt. Wolaston, and with Charlestown concerning Romney Marsh. These matters are considered in General Court.

Absence from church meetings on the Lord's day is complained of, and the subject submitted to cognizance of two Assistants, who may correct offenders at discretion, by fine not to exceed 10*s.* or by imprisonment.

It is worthy of note here, that hitherto the punishments inflicted for crimes had been in most cases *ex post facto,* and some of them pretty severe, putting in jeopardy both life and

9

limb : branding with a hot iron, and clipping off the ears
were very common things. But now ' the deputies having
conceived greater danger to our state, in regard that our magistrates, for want of positive laws in many cases, might proceed according to their discretions, it was agreed that some
men should be appointed to frame a body of grounds of laws,
in resemblance to a Magna Charta, which being allowed by
some of the ministers and the General Court, should be received for fundamental laws.' Messrs. Cotton and Bellingham
were members of the commission for this important purpose,
and had the greatest share in the work.

CHAPTER XIII.

" My father was as brave a lord
As ever Europe might afford ;
My mother was a lady bright."

ON the sixth of October, 1635, there arrived at Boston
two ships, the Defence and the Abigail. Mr. Wilson the
pastor of Boston church was one of the passengers, and Mr.
Henry Vane was another. The fame acquired by the latter
in the course of his life, renders his character and history
while here peculiarly interesting. Gov. Winthrop thus introduces him : ' one Mr. Henry Vane (son and heir to Sir Henry
Vane, comptroller of the King's house,) a young gentleman
of excellent parts, who had been employed by his father,
when he was embassador, in foreign affairs, yet being called
to the obedience of the gospel, forsook the honours and pre-
ferment of the court to enjoy the ordinances of Christ in
their purity here. His father, being very averse to this way,
would hardly have consented to his coming hither ; but that
on acquainting the King with his son's disposition and desire,
he commanded him to send him hither, and gave him license
to stay three years.'

English authors represent him as a man of profound dissim-
ulation, and of quick conception : very eloquent, ready,
sharp and weighty in his expressions : of a pleasant wit, and
great understanding, piercing into and discerning the purposes of other men with wonderful sagacity, whilst he had
himself a true vultum clausum, such a singular countenance
that no man could guess from it what he intended.

At the time of his arrival here, Mr. Vane was but twenty-
three years of age : he made great professions of religion,

was enthusiastick, and conformed to the peculiar scruples of the day. The people of Boston very soon became attached to him. He was admitted into the church on the first of November, and on the 30th of that month we find his name in the following important regulation, adopted in a general town-meeting:

'None of the members of this congregation, or inhabitants amongst us, shall sue one another at the law, before that Mr. Henry Vane and the two elders, Mr. Thomas Oliver and Thomas Leverett, have had the hearing and deciding of the cause, if they can.'

It does not appear that it was found expedient to renew this order, in any future year.

The next notice we find of Mr. Vane is that he united with Hugh Peters, also a famous man afterwards, in endeavours to procure a reconciliation between the magistrates and some other 'persons of quality.' There was not indeed any publick or notorious disagreement existing, that required this interference, but there was evidently some alienation of affection, and the result of it had been that factions were beginning to rise among the people, some adhering more to Winthrop and some more to Dudley, of whom the former was thought to be too lenient and the latter too severe. At the meeting now procured by Vane and Peters, explanations were made on all sides, and harmony restored on terms which were satisfactory to all.

It is not strange that the man whom the people of Boston had thought worthy of their highest confidence, and who had shown so good a faculty at regulating magistrates themselves, should be thought worthy to be himself elected to some office. Accordingly, having been admitted a freeman on the third of March, Mr. Vane was at the next Election, in May 1636, chosen Governour of the colony.* Mr. Winthrop was at the same time chosen Dep. Governour. On this occasion Hutchinson remarks, that Gov. Haynes who seemed to stand most in the way of Mr. Winthrop had left the colony, and was settled in Connecticut; and Mr. Winthrop would have had a good prospect of recovering his former share of the people's regard, if Mr. Vane's solemn, grave deportment had not engaged almost the whole colony in his favour.

Gov. Vane had great respect shown to him at first, and took more state upon him than any Governour had ever done before. ('Because he was son and heir to a privy counsellor in England') the ships in the harbour, which were 15 in number, congratulated his election with a salute; and the next

---

* Roger Williams had previously to this received sentence of banishment, on account of his sentiments, and left this jurisdiction in January 1636.

week he invited all the masters to dinner. This was the first entertainment of the kind in Boston. Mr. Vane took advantage of the good feelings occasioned, and brought the captains to enter into some engagements respecting their trade and conduct here, which promised much utility, but which were never effectually carried into execution. His administration for several months met with much applause, but towards the end of the year the people grew discontented and he perceived it, and grew weary of the government. He received letters from his friends in London urging his return home: Messrs. Winthrop and Dudley, to whom as members with himself of the standing council he first communicated them, were agreed that the occasion would justify his compliance with the request. He therefore called a meeting of the general court, and made known to them the necessity there was for his departure, and of course for his quitting the administration. The court took time till the next morning to consider the subject, and when they met, one of the Assistants so pathetically lamented the loss of such a governour, at a period of so much danger, both from the French and the Indians, that Mr. Vane burst into tears, and avowed, that notwithstanding the occasion on which he proposed to leave the country involved the utter ruin of his estate in England, he would yet have hazarded all that, rather than have left them at such a crisis, if other things had not pressed him more. He alluded to the inevitable danger of the judgments which he feared were coming upon them, for the differences and dissensions which he saw among them, and the scandalous imputations brought upon himself, as if he were the cause of all: therefore he thought it was best for him to give place for a time. The addition of the last reasons displeased the court, but upon his acknowledgment, that the expression of them slipped from him out of passion, the court silently consented to his departure. But some of the church of Boston, being loth to part with the Governour, had a meeting and agreed that they did not apprehend the necessity of the Governour's leaving, for the reasons alleged, and sent some of their number to signify as much to the court. The Governour thereupon expressed himself to be an obedient child of the church, and therefore, notwithstanding the license of the court, he durst not go away contrary to her expressed will.

The differences and dissensions to which the Governour referred, originated in the Boston church, which it will be recollected at that time composed the great body of the people of the town. The members of the church had been accustomed to meet once a week, to repeat the sermons they had heard on the Lord's day, and to debate upon the doctrines that had been delivered. These meetings being pecu-

liar to the men, at least none of the other sex being allowed
to take part in the debates, some of the zealous women
thought it might be useful for them to have such meetings
among themselves. Accordingly, Mrs. Ann, wife of Mr.
William Hutchinson, a woman of a bold and masculine spirit,
of ready talents and great flow of speech, established one at
her house.

Mr. Hutchinson was a man of fair estate and sustained a
good reputation in England. His wife, as Mr. Cotton says,
was also highly esteemed, and people of piety cultivated her
acquaintance. After she came to Boston, which was on the
18th September 1634, she was treated with respect. Much
notice was taken of her by Mr. Cotton, and particularly by
Mr. Vane. Her husband served in the General Court on
several elections as a representative for Boston, until he was
excused at the desire of the church. So much attention
seems to have increased Mrs. Hutchinson's natural vanity,
and produced too much self-confidence.

The novelty of the thing and the fame of Mrs. H. quickly
gained her a numerous audience at her meetings. They
were kept every week, and from sixty to eighty women
would usually attend. Mrs. H. took the lead in prayer and
in the repetition of Mr. Cotton's sermons, and afterwards
made reflections of her own. She grounded her practice on
the injunction given by Paul, that the elder women should
teach the younger. At first these meetings were generally
approved, but after some time it appeared that Mrs. H. was
in the habit of making an invidious distinction between the
ministers in the colony : two or three of them she allowed to
be sound men, under the covenant of grace; the rest she condemned as under the covenant of works.

Mr. John Wheelwright, a brother-in-law to Mrs. Hutchinson, a minister of character for learning and piety, joined
with her in sentiment. To their fault of classing the clergy
under so exceptionable a distinction, as was that of grace
and works in those days, they added the propagation of two
tenets, which were deemed to be dangerous errours : 1. That
the person of the Holy Ghost dwells in a justified person. 2.
That sanctification is no proof of justification. And Mrs. H.
maintained the belief, that individuals might, as herself had
been, be favoured with immediate revelations equally infal-
lible with the scriptures.

It was not long before it was found, that the far greater
part of the Boston church, with Mr. Cotton and Gov. Vane
(whom Mr. Winthrop yet styles a wise and godly gentleman,
when he records the fact in his journal) held to the doctrine
of the indwelling of the Holy Ghost : but Mr. Vane went so
far before the rest as to maintain the idea of a personal

union. Mr. Winthrop, with Mr. Wilson the pastor, and four
or five other members, denied both. The parties discussed
their different opinions in writing, and came to this conclusion ; that they all agreed in the chief matter of substance,
namely, that the Holy Ghost is God, and doth dwell in the
believer, as the Father and Son are both said also to do ; but
as the scriptures do not declare the manner of this union, and
as the mention of the person of the Holy Ghost is not found
in them, nor in the writings of the primitive churches for the
three first centuries, it was earnestly desired, and one would
think must have been agreed, that the word person should be
forborne, as tending only to doubtful disputation.

Such were some of the notions that turned the city upside
down, as they are unintelligibly communicated to us. Had
the trouble ended here, as it ought to have done, we should
probably have known still less about it. But opinions had
been expressed too freely, and some persons retained too
much attachment to their own notions to let the matter rest.
On the contrary, affairs were so managed that the Boston
church became embroiled in its own private concerns, and
before the close of the difficulty, found herself opposed to all
the other churches in the country, and ministers and magistrates in all quarters arrayed against her.

Some members of this church were strongly inclined to
have Mr. Wheelwright settled as a colleague with Messrs. Wilson and Cotton. It was proposed on a Lord's day, and
another day appointed for deciding on the measure. When
the question was introduced, one of the members, probably
Mr. Winthrop, rose and declared that he could not give his
consent. The reason he assigned was, that he considered
the church already furnished with able ministers, with whose
sentiments and dispositions they were well acquainted, and
whose services had been highly blessed : he saw no urgent
necessity for the proposed step, and therefore doubted the
propriety of putting the welfare of the church to the least
hazard, by calling in another man who was known to hold
obnoxious sentiments. Gov. Vane expressed his surprise at
such objections, as Mr. Cotton had lately approved Mr.
Wheelwright's doctrines. Mr. C. did not precisely recollect,
and desired Mr. Wheelwright to explain some expressions
attributed to him. He did so, and in such a manner that the
first mentioned member was obliged to say he thought it quite
likely that he and Mr. Wheelwright might agree ; but still, notwithstanding he allowed him to be a very good man and very
capable minister, he could not consent to choose him for a
teacher here, for he was at best too apt to raise 'doubtful dis-
putations.' On the whole, the church concluded to give way,
with the understanding that Mr. Wheelwright might be called

to a new church about to be formed at Mount Wolaston. Thus the influence of one reasonable man, who obstinately dares to do his duty, may oftentimes prevent his friends from injuring themselves. Mr. Winthrop, however, was not forgiven for this opposition to the wishes of so many, until he offered an apology for the manner in which he made it.

The ministers in the other towns could not be inactive witnesses of what was taking place in Boston: indeed the Boston ideas had crept into some of their churches. They had repaired hither, to examine the case in a private and friendly way, soon after the obnoxious doctrines were broached. On the subject of sanctification, they could not find much difference between themselves and Messrs. Cotton and Wheelwright, but on the other subject of the personal union, they could not agree. The Court at last in a more formal way called in the aid of the clergy, and so a joint meeting of ministers and magistrates was held to exterminate heresy.

In the course of this conference Mr. Peters took occasion to tell Governour Vane that within less than two years since, the churches were in peace; and besought him to consider his short experience, and to beware of hasty and peremptory conclusions, which he perceived him to be very liable to. The bearing of these kind hints could not be misunderstood. Mr. Wilson made a very sad speech on the condition of the churches, and on the unavoidable danger of a separation, if the differences and alienations were not speedily remedied; and he laid the blame of all the trouble at the door of the new opinionists. All the magistrates except Gov. Vane and two others, (probably Messrs. Coddington & Dummer) and all the ministers except two, confirmed his declaration.

This speech of Mr. Wilson was taken so ill by Mr. Cotton and others of his church, that they called on him to obtain satisfaction. But Mr. Wilson, and some others considered that the call of the court made the case a special one, and left him at liberty, indeed made it his duty, to speak freely. In regard to any allusion to particular churches, he assured them that he meant not the Boston church or its members more than others. This explanation would not satisfy, and he was called to answer publickly for his offence, on Lord's day, Dec. 31, 1636. There Mr Vane pressed it violently against him, and so did all the church, except Mr. Winthrop and one or two others. It was strange, says the Governour's journal, 'to see how such as had known Mr. Wilson so long, and known what good he had done for that church, should fall upon him with such bitterness for justifying himself in a good cause; for he was a very holy and upright man, and for faith and love inferior to none in the country, and most dear to all men.' Mr. Cotton joined with the church in their judgment of him, not without some appearance of prejudice, yet with much wisdom and moderation. They were eager to proceed to present censure ; but Mr. Cotton dissuaded them from that, on the ground that ' it might not be done because some opposed it :' so he gave him a grave exhortation. Mr. Cotton was three years older than Mr. Wilson, and two years older than Gov. Winthrop. Notwithstanding the admonition, Mr. Wilson preached on the next Lord's day, and acquitted himself so satisfactorily that Gov. Vane himself, as was the custom in those days, ' gave publick witness to him.'

This was not the end of the church's contentions. One reputed heresy paved the way for another, till at length the sagacity of some men could discover at least eighty dangerous doctrines to prevail, either in the form of explicit avowal or of necessary inference. Partly on account of this trouble a general fast was kept in January 1637. But the observance of no rites whatever was able to abolish the existing differences or points of faith. Mr. Cotton alone of all the settled clergy was on one side ; and the very circumstance of his dissenting from his brethren was sufficient to give the dispute a wider notoriety and keener edge. The whole country was by this time divided. One party ranged itself on the side of justification, and the other on that of sanctification; and the distinction between the advocates of free grace, and the adherents to works, was as broad as that which separates protestants from papists.

The General Court which commenced its session in March upheld its interest in the controversy. It had a party in favour of Mr. Cotton and his church, but the majority was on the side of Mr. Wilson and his friends. Of course the correctness of the proceedings against him was questioned, and the church decided to have been in the wrong: his speech in the last court and the whole tenour of his conduct were adjudged not only faultless but reasonable.

Mr. Wheelwright had been so injudicious as to preach a sermon on the late fast day, which was calculated to inflame rather than to allay the irritation already existing. It was understood that he was to be called in question at this court for the seditious tendency of that sermon. Nearly all the church of Boston therefore interposed, and presented a petition or remonstrance on the subject, in which they demanded that as freemen they might be present in cases of judicature, and that the court should declare whether they had a right to deal in cases of conscience before the church. The petition was rejected as a groundless and presumptuous act. The court proceeded to adjudge Mr. Wheelwright to be guilty of sedition and also of contempt. Gov. Vane and some others offered a protest which was rejected. The church of Boston also offered another petition in which they justified Mr. Wheelwright's sermon. In conclusion, sentence was deferred till the next Court. When they were about adjourning, it was moved that the next session should be held at Newtown. Gov. Vane, considering it an undeserved reproach upon the people of Boston, refused to put the vote. The deputy, Mr. Winthrop, being also a Boston man, declined doing it, except the court required it: so the honour fell to Mr. Endicott, who put the question and it was carried in the affirmative.

We find no event in the course of the history of Boston, which appears to have excited more universal interest in the people of the town than this Antinomian controversy, as it was called. Whether their religious notions were right or wrong, it is impossible to tell; but it is evident that they felt their rights as an independent church to be encroached upon, and that they were jealous for their political privileges. The next court was held, according to vote, on the 17th of May. Soon as the meeting was organized, which was about one o'clock, a petition was offered by those from Boston. Gov. Vane would have read it; but Mr. Winthrop declared it to be out of order, as this was a court of election. Others also opposed the reading; because the petition being upon some 'pretence of liberty' (a favourite Boston notion) would spend the whole day in debate. Mr. Wilson, in his zeal, got upon the bough of a tree (it was warm weather, and the election was carried on in the field) and there made a speech, advising the people to look to their charter and proceed to the business of the day. The people applauded him and cried out *Election! Election!* the great majority was for proceeding. Gov. Vane and his friends were not contented, till the deputy told him, that if he would not go on, himself and the rest would proceed without him. Upon this he yielded, and the election resulted in a return to the original establishment, Mr. Winthrop for Governour and Mr. Dudley for Deputy. Some new assistants were chosen, and Mr. Vane, Mr. Coddington and Mr. Richard Dummer left entirely out of office. This meeting was very tumultuous; some fierce speeches were made and blows struck, but the strength being evidently on one side, the other soon grew quiet.

Boston had deferred the choice of her representatives till the election for Governour should be over. The next morning, Mr. Vane, Mr. Coddington and Mr. Atherton Hough were chosen. The court considered this selection an insult, and sent them home again, on the ground that two of the freemen of Boston had not been notified. On a new choice the next day, the town returned the same gentlemen, and 'the

10

court not finding how they might reject them, they were admitted.'

Upon the election of Mr. Winthrop, the four serjeants, who had attended the former Governour to the court, being all Boston men, laid down their halberds and went home, refusing to perform any such service in honour of Gov. Winthrop.* Mr. Vane and Mr. Coddington being discontented that the people had left them out of all office, refused to sit in the magistrates' seat in the meeting-house, and took their seats with the deacons, although Gov. W. politely invited them to sit with him.

Mr. Wheelwright appeared at this court, according to order, but as a day of fasting had been appointed for the 25th of the month, ' when it was agreed that all the churches should choose men to meet and confer about the differences,' the court gave him respite to the next session, which was appointed for the first Tuesday in August. They gave him that time to consider whether he would retract his errours and make submission, or abide the decision of the court. His answer was noble : ' if I have been guilty of sedition, let me die ; recantation is out of the question : if you proceed thus unrighteously against me, I shall appeal to the tribunal of my king.'

There was some expectation, about this time, of an arrival from England, with a party of emigrants favourable to the sentiments prevailing in Boston. This court therefore seized the opportunity of preventing such a calamity as they supposed their settlement here would be, and passed a law which prohibited all persons to entertain any stranger, who should come with intention to reside, without liberty from one of the standing council or two other assistants. This was a very severe order, and was so disliked by the people of Boston, that upon the Governour's return from court, they all refused to go out to meet him, or show him any respect.

Mr. Cotton was so dissatisfied with this law, that he was on the point of removing to New-Haven. A defence of it was published by the magistrates, and answered by Mr. Vane, who was replied to, probably by Gov. Winthrop.† But arguments served only to make each party better satisfied of their own correctness. The difference between Mr. Vane and the Governour became so great, that Vane refused an invitation to a dinner, given by the Governour in honour of Lord Leigh, a young nobleman, who was here on a visit to the

---

* The country taking notice of this, offered to send in some from the neighbouring towns to carry the halberds by course, and upon that the town of Boston offered to send some men but not the serjeants : the Governour chose rather to make use of two of his own servants.

† See *Hutch.* coll. of papers. p. 67—84.

country. His lordship and Mr. Vane prepared to return in August. At their departure (Aug. 2) Mr. Vane's friends assembled and accompanied him to the boat. A military company being under arms, gave them ' divers volleys of shot,' and five pieces of ordnance, and they had five more at the castle. The governour was absent, attending court at Newtown, ' but he had left order with the captain for their honourable dismission.'

On Mr. Vane's return to England he assumed an active part in the political affairs of the kingdom; was knighted in 1640; joined the party that was against King Charles, and after the restoration was tried for high treason and beheaded June 14, 1662.

He had lived, while in Boston, in the house which now stands on the westerly side of Common Street, (within the square *Fh* of our plan,) on one of the Tremont hillocks, next northeasterly to the mansion house of Lieut. Gov. Phillips. This is the oldest house in the city of which we have any account. It was originally small. Mr. Vane gave it to Mr. Cotton, who made an addition to it, and lived and died there. His family occupied it some time after. The building is of wood: the front part has a modern appearance, but the back exhibits marks of its antiquity.

CHAPTER XIV.

" Ah me ! outstretch'd I see,
In nameless agony,   *.*
Woman's imploring hand."

Sir Henry Vane has had the credit of being the life-blood of the party, which Mrs. Hutchinson's notions had created. However that may have been, it is very apparent that his presence here formed a powerful protection for them against the spirit of persecution, which had already been active. Roger Williams had been banished for holding opinions less dangerous, in the mind of Gov. Winthrop; and it had been declared by Mr. Vane, that the execution of the law against strangers would be followed by the banishment of such as were already here. We shall see that his forebodings were wofully prophetick.

Mrs. Hutchinson continued her lectures, and her admirers are said to have been indefatigable in spreading her sentiments : both church and state were thrown into uproar and

the affections of people strangely alienated; they were frequently quarrelsome, and upon every occasion ready to come
to blows. Both parties claimed Mr. Cotton for their own
man: the one affirmed that the doctrines they taught were
regularly deduced from his sermons, the other denied it. At
last Mr. Cotton was desired to declare himself freely from the
pulpit, which he accordingly did, and condemned most of the
new positions as false and erroneous. This brought upon him
the bitterest reproaches: he was called by some a timorous
man, that durst not abide by his own sentiments; by others a
deceiver, that taught one thing in publick and another in private. One man, more impudent if more witty than the rest,
sent him a pound of candles, bidding his servant tell him it
was because he wanted light; ' upon which the good man bestowed only a silent smile.'

The August court probably postponed the business of Mr.
Wheelwright, until they should know the result of the synod,
which was expected to meet at Newtown, in accordance with
the May vote, on the 30th of that month. The object of this
assembly having been the purification of Boston from heresy,
a particular account of it demands a place here. There were
present not only the ministers and messengers from the several churches, but also the magistrates for keeping the peace,
who were allowed both to hear, and to speak, if they had a
mind. A place was likewise appointed for the favourers of
the new opinions, and the doors were set open, for as many
as pleased to come in and hear the debates. The first day
was spent in choosing Mr. Hooker from Connecticut and Mr.
Bulkley minister of Concord, for moderators. Mr. Cotton,
though confessedly at the head of the clergy, was thought to
be too much a party to be honoured with that dignity. A list
was then read of eighty-two erroneous opinions, which had
been maintained in various parts of the country, some of
which were the most monstrous and absurd ever heard of. The
following days were spent in debating the several points. In
the morning a committee was employed in forming arguments
against the errours to be confuted that day, which in the afternoon were produced in the synod. Next day the defenders
gave in their reply, and produced their arguments for the support of their side of the question; the third day, the opponents
made the last reply. The authors of the errours were neither
mentioned nor enquired for by the synod, but the errours
themselves were confuted and condemned by reference to
particular texts of scripture, which, says Cotton Mather,
being briefly applied unto the case, did, unto reasonable men,
immediately smite the errour under the fifth rib. All the
members of the synod signed the condemnation, except Mr.
Cotton, who, though he expressed his dislike of the major part

of the doctrines, refused to condemn them in the lump : the synod endeavoured to convince him of his mistake, but in vain. Yet this did not prevent a reconciliation between him and the rest of the clergy : he agreed to unite with them in opposing what he believed to be false, and ' thereafter this reverend and worthy minister regained his former splendour, with his wonted esteem and interest in the hearts of all his friends and acquaintance.'

Numbers of the Boston church were present at this synod. They, as well as some others were offended that so many errours should be produced, and declared it a reproach laid upon the country without cause. They called for the names of persons holding this or that doctrine, and were answered, that the evidence was abundant, that such errours had advocates either in town or country, yet as the synod had no concern with persons, but with doctrines only, it was deemed inexpedient to name any individual. The minority however were too much warmed to suffer any thing to be secreted. They were urgent in their calls for names and witnesses. The moderator, called for order in vain, and the magistrates, on suggesting that if silence were not maintained they should be obliged to interpose, were told that they had no province in such an assembly. One of them retorted, that if immediate silence did not ensue, an opportunity would be given for testing the correctness of the two opinions. There was so much severity in this sort of language, that some of the Boston members withdrew from the assembly.

Among other things which this synod decreed, this was one : though some few women may meet together for prayer and mutual advice, yet such a set assembly, as is in practice at Boston, is unlawful (where sixty or more meet every week, and one woman takes upon herself the whole exercise.) Another decree was, that private members should be very sparing in their questions and observations in publick after sermon. These two decisions struck at the root of two Boston evils. Mr. Davenport delivered the decrees of the synod, and after preaching a very seasonable discourse from Philippians iii. 16. dismissed the meeting on the 22d of September.

One would have thought, says Neal, ' the unanimous voice of the synod should have quieted the minds of the people, but the heads of the faction were not to be vanquished by scripture and reason. Mr. Wheelwright continued his preaching, and Mrs. Hutchinson her meeting, and their followers were so influenced by their doctrines, that when Mr. Wilson went up into the pulpit, half the congregation would go out.' In this state of things, the people were prepared for further proceedings against those who maintained the condemned opinions. The court met on the 26th of September, when Mr. Wheelwright appeared and was dismissed till further orders. It seems that a major vote of the deputies, to execute the decrees of the late synod, could not be obtained ; therefore* the house was dissolved and a new one chosen. Eleven only out of twenty-six of the former deputies were elected into the new court, which met Nov. 2, at Newtown, because ' the town of Boston was so infected with the new opinions, that they were afraid of a riot.' The representatives from Boston were Messrs. Coddington, Aspinwall and Coggeshall.

This court, finding upon consultation that two so opposite parties could not continue in the same body without apparent hazard of ruin to the whole, agreed to send away some of the principals. For this a ' fair opportunity was offered by the remonstrance which was preferred by the Boston people in March last, and rejected by the court as presumptuous.†' The remonstrance was signed by more than sixty hands. The first step was to clear their own body from all that had any concern in it. Mr. Aspinwall was a signer and Mr. Coggeshall had defended it : they were therefore expelled, and warrant issued to the town for a new choice. The people would fain have sent the same men again, but Mr. Cotton appeared at the meeting (Nov. 6.) and with much ado dissuaded them from their resolution. They then chose William Colburn and John Oliver to be joined with Mr. Coddington.§ Oliver was in the same condemnation and he was not received. But whether the court had too much discretion to insult the town by a warrant for a third election, or whether the town had too much spirit to choose another does not appear.‖

The next business was to dispose of Mr. Wheelwright. The court summoned him to give his peremptory answer, whether he would acknowledge his offence, or abide the sentence of the court. His answer was, ' that he had been guilty of no sedition nor contempt ; that he had delivered nothing but the truth, and as for the application of his doctrine, that was made by others and not by himself,' He was then desired to leave the colony of his own accord, and upon refusal, received the following sentence : ' Mr. J. W. being formerly convicted of contempt and sedition and now justifying himself and his former practice, *being the disturbance of the civil peace,* he is by the court disfranchised and banished, having fourteen days to settle his affairs.'

Next came on the examination of the petitioners. The first who was sent for was Mr. Coggeshall, who was a deacon

---

* *Backus.*   † *Winthrop's* Journal.
‡ See this remonstrance in Appendix No. II.
§ Town records.   ‖ Mass. II. C. 2. x. 24.

of the Boston church. The court charged him with contempt for having said that if they expelled Mr. Aspinwall for signing the remonstrance, they had better make but one work of all; for though his hand was not to it, his heart was in it.' Mr. Coggeshall pleaded that his privilege as a deputy should screen him from any punishment. The court would not accede to this and he 'was disfranchised and *enjoined not to speak* any thing to disturb the publick peace upon pain of banishment.'

Mr. Aspinwall was called next. He not only had signed the remonstrance, but was himself the author of it, and had carried it about town to get signers to it. He justified himself, and was disfranchised and banished, to depart before the end of the next March.

After these, William Balston and Edward Hutchinson two of the serjeants of Boston appeared. Both their hands were to the remonstrance, and the court took a great deal of pains to make them acknowledge their offence ; but they were obstinate, and uttered a great many affronting speeches against the magistrates who were not of their opinion : so they were both 'turned out of their places, disfranchised and fined, Balston £20 and Hutchinson £40 : but H. owning his fault the next day was released of his fine, and *only* disfranchised.'

Another day, four or five more of the leading petitioners were called, and they, being obstinate too, were disfranchised. Capt. Underhill had his commission taken from him, and Thomas Marshall, the ferryman, lost his place. Ten others whose names were signed made their appearance, but the court judging that they had been drawn in, by the subtilty of a few active men, they were pardoned, upon acknowledging their offence.

As disfranchised men were not likely to be long quiet or to remain friendless, it was judged not improbable that those who had been seduced into the errours of Mr. W. and Mrs. H. might ' as others in Germany in former times, upon some revelation, make sudden irruption upon those that differ from them in judgment ; for prevention whereof it is ordered that those whose names are underwritten shall deliver in at Mr. Keayne's house, at Boston, all such guns, pistols, swords, powder, shot and match as they shall be owners of, or have in their custody—and no man who is to render his arms by this order, may buy or borrow any guns, swords or pistols, powder, shot or match, until this court shall take further order herein.' Seventy-six men are named as being disarmed by this order, only if any of them would disavow the remonstrance, they might be freed from its operation. Of these seventy-six 58 belonged to Boston. The whole number of families in town did not much exceed 120.

Mrs. Hutchinson's fate remained to be determined. She was accordingly sent for by the court. She was formally accused of the errours attributed to her, and witnesses were produced to sustain the charges. Several clergymen gave account of conferences they had held with her, which exhibited her conduct in an unfavourable light. She demanded that they should be put under oath. After much altercation that course was adopted. Messrs. Eliot, Peters and Weld were sworn, and the amount of their testimony was 'that Mrs. H. averred, that there was a broad difference between them and Mr. Cotton; that he preached a covenant of grace and they of works; that they were not able ministers of the New Testament and were not clear in their experience, because they were not sealed and were but like the apostles before the ascension.' This was the head and front of her offending. The trial lasted two days: for the most part she referred her accusers and judges to the scriptures, whose words, says Mr. Emerson, it must be confessed, as urged by the woman, often caused them some little confusion. She acknowledged her confidence in revelations, which she had received in regard to future providences, and this acknowledgment satisfied most of the court of her worthiness of banishment. She warned them to forbear, but to no purpose; the trial concludes thus:

Gov. ——If it be the mind of the court that Mrs. Hutchinson, for these things that appear before us, is unfit for our society, and if it be the mind of the court that she shall be banished out of our liberties, and imprisoned till she be sent away, let them hold up their hands:

All but three.

Those that are contrary minded, hold up yours:

Mr. Coddington and Mr. Colburn only.

Mr. Jennison. I cannot hold up my hand one way or the other, and I shall give my reason if the court require it.

Gov. Mrs. Hutchinson! the sentence of the court you hear is, that you are banished from out of our jurisdiction, as being a woman not fit for our society, and are to be imprisoned till the court shall send you away.

Mrs. H. I desire to know wherefore I am banished.

Gov. Say no more: the court know wherefore, and is satisfied.

After this sentence Mrs. H. remained in Boston and the neighbourhood, in custody of some of the clergy. The church found occasion to disapprove her conduct, and on the 22d of March 1638, she was 'cast out of the church for impenitently persisting in a manifest lie.' She received orders from the Governour to leave the jurisdiction before the close of the month, and accordingly departed on the 28th day. She went with her husband to Rhode Island. In the year 1642, after her husband's death, she removed into the Dutch country beyond New Haven, and the next year she and all her family, consisting of sixteen persons, were killed by the Indians, except one daughter, whom they carried into captivity.

In consequence of these proceedings, which the sufferers felt to be severely oppressive, however justifiable the authors may have thought themselves, a considerable number of very respectable men contemplated a removal from Boston. It was proposed by Mr. John Clarke, a learned physician, a man of ardent piety and sound understanding, sufficient knowledge and much usefulness. He with some others were chosen to select a convenient place, and after wandering up and down, in the depth of winter, they concluded upon Rhode Island, whither they removed in the spring of 1638. The court had intimations, that it was their intention to return, when the fervour of the times should be abated. To prevent this, an order of banishment was issued against a number, requiring that they should remove their families, whenever they went themselves. Mr. Coddington was included in this order. He was the principal man of the company, but for some reason had not attracted the attentions of the court heretofore, being neither disfranchised nor disarmed. He was a gentleman of family, and fortune, from Boston in Lincolnshire, and was one of the first and most eminent merchants here. His property at Mt. Wolaston was large, and he owned the first brick building which was erected in Boston.*

The jealousy entertained against Boston at this period was carried so far that an order was passed to have the courts both General and Quarter kept at Newtown, till further order. The publick stores of powder and arms were removed to Newtown and Roxbury, and the persons disarmed were excused from performing military duty. The courts returned to Boston in the latter part of the next year, but the powder was kept at Roxbury till April 1645, when seventeen barrels of it were blown up. The explosion shook the houses in Boston and Cambridge like an earthquake, and burning cinders were brought by the winds beyond the Boston meeting house.†

---

* It is difficult to say positively where this building stood. Some expert antiquary may hereafter be able to ascertain the fact by tracing out the points in the following minute.

Town records March 6. 1637. Our brother Willyam Balstone shall have the remaining swampe on the backside of Mr. Coddington's swampe unto the widdow Burton's corner payle leaving out twoe rodde and a halfe for eyther of the high wayes that are against it; the one being the way to the mylne and the other to the cove next unto Mr. Coddington's.

It appears that *bricks were made here*, from a record Dec. 26. 1636: Thomas Mount has leave to fence in a piece of the marsh before his house for the making of brick.

† Cambridge received that name at the court in May 1638, in consequence of the College being established there, and the college received the name of *Harvard* in the same year. —*Hubbard.* 237. 430.

11

CHAPTER XV.

......Emerging from a sea of dreams
Tumultuous ....   *Young.*

THE winter of 1637-8 was very severe and the inhabitants of Boston suffered extremely for the want of fuel : the snow lay four feet and a half deep, from the fourth of November to March 23d. Gov. Winthrop relates that a party of thirty men started on a fair day (Jan. 13) for the purpose of cutting wood on Spectacle Island. The next night a N. E. storm set in and was followed by two days strong N. W. winds, so that the harbour was all frozen over, except a small channel, in which twelve of the men found their way to the Governour's Garden [Ft. Warren.] Seven more were carried in the ice in a small skiff out to Broad Sound, and kept among the Brewster rocks without food or fire two days. The rest made for the main from the island, but two of them fell through the ice, and came near being drowned. Of the seven that fell among the rocks, all had their hands and feet frozen, some lost fingers and toes, and one died. On this occasion the Governour remarks in a letter to his son, that many were discouraged, and the settlement here was well nigh being broken up. It was probably in reference to the state of things, which existed at this juncture, that Boston acquired the proverbial appellation of *Lost Town.*

A voyager of some little note visited these parts about this time, and the world has been favoured with his observations, under the title of *New England's Rarities.* John Josselyn, Gent. anchored in the bay of Massachusetts before Boston, July 3d. 1638. The tenth day, says he. 'I went ashore upon Noddle's Island to Mr. Sam. Maverick, for my passage, the only hospitable man in all the country, giving entertainment to all comers, gratis. Having refreshed myself for a day or two, I crossed the bay [harbour] in a small boat to Boston, which then was rather a village than a town, there being not above twenty or thirty houses : and presenting my respects to Mr. Winthorpe the Governour, and to Mr. Cotton the teacher of Boston church, to whom I delivered from Mr. Francis Quarles the poet, the translation of the 16. 25. 51. 88. 113. 137. Psalms in English Metre for his approbation. Being civilly treated by all I had occasion to converse with, I returned in the evening to my lodgings.' Josselyn left on the twentieth of July for the eastward, where he had a brother, and returned Sep. 27th. 'Next day I went aboard of Mr. Hinderson, master of a ship of 500 tons, and Capt. Jackson in the Queen of Bohemia privateer, and from thence I went ashore to Boston where I refreshed myself at an Ordinary.' He also mentions one Long's ordinary in Charlestown. There were two such ordinaries or houses of entertainment in Boston, into which if a stranger went, he was presently followed by one appointed to that office, who would thrust himself into his company, uninvited, and if he called for more drink than the officer thought in his judgment he could soberly bear away, he would presently countermand it, and appoint the proportion beyond which he could not get one drop.

'Oct. 11. our master having been ashore upon the Governour's Island gave me half a score very fair pippins which he brought from thence, there being not one apple tree nor pear planted yet, in no part of the country, but upon that island.' Several adventures are described by our author, which would do credit to a modern English traveller in America, but convey no other useful hints, except it be one, that Mr. Maverick had in his family an African slave.

Doubts have been somewhere expressed concerning the correctness of Josselyn's statement in regard to the number of houses : but he repeats it in another part of his book, and must be understood to speak of the framed buildings then in the place, and not to have included the mud-wall cottages, of which many yet remained. The number of buildings likely to be permanent had become so great as to require such provisions as these :

1636. Oct. 4. There shall no house at all be built in this town in any of the streets or lanes, but with the advice and consent of the overseers of the town's occasions, for the avoiding of disorderly building, the inconveniences of streets and lanes, and for the more comely and commodious ordering of them, upon the forfeiture for every house built contrary to this order, of such sum as the overseers shall see fitting, under the sum of Xs.

17th. *Item.* John Gallop shall remove his pales at his yards end, within 14 days, and shall range them even with the corner of his house, for the preserving the way upon the sea bank.

Dec. 10. Not above one dwelling house may be built on any one lot, without the approbation of the town's overseers.

1637. Sept. 25. Special permission is granted to William Hudson to set his new building one foot and a half into the street, towards the sea side where he dwelleth.

1640. March 30. We find this remarkable entry: John Palmer, carpenter, is allowed to be an inhabitant here, if he can get a house, or land to set a house upon, it being not proper to allow a man an inhabitant without a habitation.

These extracts sufficiently show what many similar records corroborate, that our ancestors were not so neglectful of the appearance of their town, as we have been in the habit of supposing them to have been.

During the scenes of confusion which formed the subject of our two last chapters, the colonists had occasion to exhibit their power and courage in a short conflict with the Pequod Indians, a tribe inhabiting the parts about Connecticut River. Mr. Endicott with a party of 80 men had chastised them in the summer of 1636, but they remained quiet only while he remained about them. In 1637 the three colonies, Massachusetts, Plymouth and Connecticut, agreed to enter the Indian country with their joint forces, and attempt their entire destruction. Massachusetts sent 160 men, under the command of Capt. Israel Stoughton : of these Boston furnished 26.* Mr. Wilson, the pastor of Boston accompanied the expedition as chaplain : it fell to his part by lot, and he is represented to have gone with so much faith and joy, that he professed himself as fully satisfied that God would give the English the victory, as if he had seen it already obtained. So spirited and so prophetick a soothsayer would in ancient times have received the highest veneration. His predictions were accomplished and the army returned in triumph, with the loss only of one man, August 26, 1637.

In the next year after this expedition, the Ancient and Honourable Artillery company took its rise. The first notice of its origin appears in Gov. Winthrop's journal, February, 1638 : ' Divers gentlemen and others being joined in a military company, desired to be made a corporation, but the council, considering from the example of the Pretorian band among the Romans, and the Templars in Europe, how dangerous it might be to erect a standing authority of military men, which might easily in time overtop the civil power, thought fit to stop it betimes, yet they were allowed to be a company, but subordinate to all authority.'

From this note we should infer, that the associates at first asked to be created into an independent company, which was deemed inadvisable. There appears to have been no objection to the association for the purpose of improvement in military tactics, and accordingly we find the company recognized as such in the Colony records of the 17th March 1638 : ' The *Military Company* of Boston, may present two or three to the council to choose a captain out of them.' Also ' Capt. Keayne and the *Military Company* have power to exercise

---

* In the same year Boston was assessed 59*l*. 4*s*. of a tax of 400*l*.] These data give us some idea of the proportion which Boston bore to the whole colony.

where they please, and to make use of so many of the common
arms as they need, and a warrant from any of the council is
sufficient for the delivery of them unto Captain Keayne or
such as he shall appoint.' The following is a copy of their
charter.*

ORDERS

for the Military Company made by the Governour and Council, and confirmed by the General
Court.

'Whereas divers gentlemen and others, out of their care of
the public weal and safety, by the advancement of the military art, and exercise of arms, have desired license of the Court
to join themselves in one company, and to have the liberty to
exercise themselves, as their occasions will best permit ; and
that such liberties and privileges might be granted them, as
the Court should think meet, for their better encouragement
and furtherance, in so useful an employment ; which request
of theirs being referred by the Court unto us of the *Standing
Council*, we have thought fit, upon serious consideration, and
conference with divers of the principal of them, to set down
and order herein as followeth :

IMPRIMIS.

We do order, that *Robert Keayne, Nathaniel Duncan, Robert
Sedgwick, William Spencer*, Gentlemen, and such others as are
already joined with them, and such as they shall from time
to time take into their company, shall be called the *Military
Company of the Massachusetts*.

SECONDLY.

They, or the greater number of them, shall have liberty to
choose their Captain, Lieutenant, and all other officers. Their
Captain and Lieutenant to be always such as the Court or
Council shall allow of ; and no other officer be put upon them,
but of their own choice.

THIRDLY.

The first Monday in every month is appointed for their
meeting and exercise ; and to the end that they may not be
hindered from coming together, we do hereby order, that no
other training in the particular towns, nor other ordinary
town meetings, shall be appointed on that day ; and if that
day prove unseasonable for the exercise of their arms, then
the sixth of the same week is appointed for supply. This not

---

* 'As extracted from the original records of the colony' and published in Whitman's Historical Sketch of the Company—to which the reader is referred for a fund of interesting information. *Shaw* has given a copy which contains the following article between the 3d. and
4th. 'None of the said Military Company (except such as shall be officers of any other trained band in any particular town) shall be bound to give attendance upon their ordinary trainings.'

to extend to Salem, or the towns beyond, nor to Hingham, Weymouth, Dedham, nor Concord.

FOURTHLY.

They have liberty and power to make orders amongst themselves, for the better managing their military affairs; which orders are to be of force, when they shall be allowed by the Court or Council; and they may appoint an officer to levy any fines or forfeitures, which they shall impose upon any of their own company, for the breach of any such order, so as the same exceed not twenty shillings for any one offence.

FIFTHLY.

The said *Military Company* are to have one thousand acres of land, (in some such place as may not be prejudicial to any plantation,) to be granted by the Court to some of the said company, and such as shall succeed in the same; to be improved by them within a time convenient, for providing necessaries for their military exercises, and defraying of other charges, which may arise by occasion thereof.

SIXTHLY.

The said company shall have liberty, at the time before appointed, to assemble themselves for their military exercises, in any town within this jurisdiction, at their own pleasure; *provided always*, that this order or grant, or any thing therein contained, shall not extend to free the said company, or any of them, their persons or estates, from the Civil Government and Jurisdiction here established.

JOHN WINTHROP, *Gov.*
THOMAS DUDLEY, *Dep. Gov.*

The company was first organized on the first Monday in June, 1638—when Capt. Robert Keayne was elected commander, Daniel Hough, lieutenant, and Joseph Welde, ensign. Of the two last we have no information: Capt. Keayne was by profession a merchant tailor, and had belonged to the Honourable Artillery Company in London. Many important offices and trusts were committed to his charge, both in town and state affairs. He was a man of large property, was frequently a representative, and in every plan for improvement, or enterprize, his name appears as a patron.

Nathaniel Duncan, the second person named in the charter, was a merchant and lived in Dorchester. Robert Sedgwick, the third charter member and next on the roll, belonged to Charlestown: he was, says Johnson, stout and active in all feats of war, nurst up in the London's Artillery Garden, besides having the help of a very good head-piece. He was the leader of the first train band formed in Charlestown, and afterwards was promoted to the highest military rank in the colony. William Spencer, the fourth and last named in the charter, was also a merchant and resided at Cambridge. Thus it appears the charter was granted to four persons, residing each in a different town, with their associates, and this may serve to correct a mistaken idea, that the company in its origin and progress has been confined to Boston.

It will be observed that the name of this company, which is the 'oldest military establishment in the United States,' was by their charter the *Military Company of the Massachusetts.* The names of the Artillery Company, and the Great Artillery, and the First Artillery, which were early applied to it, originated from the introduction of field pieces into their exercise. The General Court recognized the institution by the name of the Artillery Company as early as sixteen hundred and fifty-seven. The oldest printed sermon, delivered on their anniversary, June 3, 1672, was preached " on the day of the Artillery Election." Cotton Mather, in his sermon 1691, in his address to the company calls them the Artillery Company.

Sept. 2, 1700. The title ANCIENT AND HONOURABLE is first used in the 'original records.' All the sermons printed down to 1708, bear the name of the Artillery Company on the title page, but in the sermon for that year they are styled the Honourable Artillery Company. This is uniformly the style in the title pages until 1738. The address in the sermon for 1720, uses the appellation Ancient and Honourable, and in that for 1737, the words Ancient and Honourable Artillery Company are once introduced. Dr. Colman's century sermon, in 1738, has in the title page the words " preached before the Honourable and Ancient Artillery Company." From that period to the present all the sermons are said to have been preached before the Ancient and Honourable Artillery Company.

The records of the company do not mention either the words Honourable or Ancient until long after these appellations had been applied to them by the publick. The present name appears but once, (in 1762,) previous to the year 1789, when the company was revived after the revolution : the Legislature in their militia laws have since confirmed it to them. It is therefore probable they retained the name of Artillery, after they had relinquished the use of field pieces, by common consent. The addition of Honourable was made by the people, in regard to the many distinguished men, who had belonged to and commanded it, and for the great benefit and service the institution had rendered to the community. This name for the same reason they continue to merit ; and the term Ancient has been added by general usage since the expiration of their first century, with that sort of veneration which untarnished reputation always ensures to gray hairs.*

In May 1639, the whole military of the Bay were mustered at Boston in two regiments, to the number of a thousand soldiers, able men, well armed and exercised. They were headed the one by the Governour (Winthrop) who was General of all, and the other by the Deputy who was colonel. The captains and others showed themselves very skilful and ready in various sorts of skirmishes and other military actions, wherein they spent the whole day.' We notice also another general training in Boston, Sept. 15, 1641, which lasted two days. About 1200 men were exercised in most sorts of land service; yet it was observed that there was no man drunk, though there was plenty of wine and strong beer in the town—not an oath sworn, no quarrel, nor any hurt done. A more lofty but less perspicuous account of one of these military displays, is given in a narrative of the first thirty years by Old Planters. It is said to have taken place at Fox Hill, a spot of rising ground, which formerly existed at the bottom of the Common. The pomp and circumstance of the exhibition were so striking that some people entertained fears, lest offence might be taken in the parent country, as if the colonists were (even then) looking up to a state of independence.

While the soldiery at home were thus improving themselves and amusing their neighbours, our seamen were accidentally raising the fame of Boston abroad.† The Viceroys of New Spain and Peru having advice from the court of Spain, that the attempt for finding a Northwest passage, which had been tried before by Capts. Hudson and James, was again attempted in 1639 by some industrious navigators from Boston, despatched Admiral de Fonte to discover and seize them. He sailed from Lima on the 3d of April 1640. On the 17th of July about lat. 61. N. he came to an Indian town, and the natives told his interpreter, that a little way from them lay a great ship, where there never had been one before. He sailed to the place and found only one man advanced in years, and a youth: the man exhibited the greatest skill in the mechanical parts of the mathematics of any that he had ever met. They informed him that their ship was of New-England, from a town called Boston. The owner and the whole ship's company came on board, and the navigator of the ship told the admiral that his owner was a fine gentleman, and a

---

* See *Whitman's* Sketch, p. 8—12. 104. Mass. H. C. 2. ii. 160. 185. i. xxix. W. W. P. ch. xxvi.

† Memoirs of the Curious, April and June 1708, as quoted in an account of the N. W. passages, 1748.

Major General in the largest colony in New-England, called the Massachusetts. On this he received him like a gentleman, and told him his commission was to make prize of any people seeking a Northwest or West passage into the South Sea, but he would look on them as merchants trading with the natives for beavers and otters and other furs and skins; and so for a small present of provisions which he had no need of, he gave him a diamond ring that cost him 1200 pieces of eight, which the modest gentleman received with difficulty; and having given the brave navigator Capt. Shapely for his fine chart and journals a thousand pieces of eight, and the owner of the ship, Seimor Gibbons, a quarter cask of good Peruan wine, and the ten seamen each 20 pieces of eight, they set sail on a farther expedition. The behaviour of Admiral de Fonte evinced great politeness. He might have taken Shapely's charts forcibly, but chose to give a considerable price for them, on pretence that they were curious, when the true reason was that they might not be used as guides to others.

This story is solemnly related by the Admiral with every particular, and has been copied into foreign works with the remark that the ardour of enterprize at that period seemed to have passed from the English to their colonists at Boston.* It probably originated in the following simple fact,† out of which the Magnalia makes a story as doleful as the foregoing is improbable. About this time came home a small pinnace of 30 tons which had been gone eight months and was given up for lost. She went to Bermuda, but by continual tempests was kept from hence and forced to bear up for the W. Indies, and being in great distress arrived at Hispaniola, and not daring to go into any inhabited place there, the men went ashore in obscure places and lived on turtles and eggs. At last they were forced into a harbour, where lay a French man-of-war with his prize, and had surely made prize of them also, but that the captain, one Petfree, had lived at Piscataqua, and knew the merchant of our bark, one Mr. Gibbons: whereupon he used them courteously, and for such commodities as she carried, furnished her with tallow and hides, and sent home with her his prize, which he sold for a small price to be paid in New England.

Mr. Gibbons brought home an Alligator, which he gave to the Governour. This may be recollected as the first thing of the kind exhibited here; since which almost every living thing has found its way to Boston.

---

* See Hist. Gen. de. Voyages, 1757, tom. 15. p. 161.

† Winthrop, June 1637. Magnalia 2. 297.

12

CHAPTER XVI.

The house of God
They first re-edify, and for a while
In mean estate live moderate. . . . . . .   *Par. Lost.*

THE temper of these early times is manifest in the continued care of the court to guard against extravagance in dress. Mr. Cotton's lectures against veils appear to have been soon forgotten. Some of the magistrates imagined that the women indulged themselves in too much expense. They accordingly conferred with the ministers on the subject, and charged them to address themselves to the consciences of their hearers. The ministers promised a compliance, but it was found that so many of their own and the elders' wives participated in the fault, that there could be little hope of reformation through this means.

The appetite as well as the fondness for dress was put under restraint. Colony records, Nov. 1637: No person shall sell any cakes or bunns either in the market or victualling houses, or elsewhere, upon pain of ten shillings fine, *provided*, that this order shall not extend to such cakes as shall be made for any burial, or marriage, or such like special occasion.

A lesson on morals may be taken from a circumstance which happened in the year 1639. At the General Court holden in November, great complaint was made of the oppression suffered by the people in the purchase of foreign commodities. Capt. Keayne, who kept a shop in Boston was notoriously above others observed, and charged with such particulars as these; for taking in some cases above six pence in the shilling profit, in some above eight pence, and in others two for one. He was convicted and fined. After the court had censured him, he was called to account by the church. He acknowledged his fault with tears and bewailed his covetous and corrupt heart, and a partial defence was set up by him or his friends, on the ground that if a man lost in one commodity, he might make it up in another, and that if through ignorance a man had given more for an article than it was worth in Europe, he might sell it for more than it was worth in New-England.

Some of the members were earnest to have Capt. Keayne excommunicated, but Mr. Cotton did not consider his offence to be of that nature which is condemned in the scriptures, and he was excused with a simple admonition, on the presumption that his errour was rather in his judgment than in his heart: for he was otherwise a liberal man, very hospitable and generous in his contributions towards the church expenses. What would have been the effect on the mercantile character of Boston, if the rigour exercised in this case had continued to be exercised to this day, we leave the reader to surmise.

Towards the close of the year 1639, the congregation meditated the rebuilding of their house of worship. The old one which was erected in 1632, not only having become decayed, but being also too small to accommodate the people, there was no question about the necessity of a new house, but a wide and warm difference of opinion respecting where it should stand. Some of the brethren were for placing it on what was then called *the green*, which was Gov. Winthrop's first lot, and he had yielded it to the church. There is reason to suppose this was the lot which the Old South church now owns, at the corner of Milk and Washington streets. Others, particularly the tradesmen, were inclined to build it still nearer the market than where the old one stood, lest in time it should divert the chief trade from thence. The church referred it to the judgment and determination of a committee of five, who agreed that it ought to be placed near the market, but still for peace sake they proposed it should be decided by lot. When the church met, the matter was debated with some earnestness, and at last Mr. Cotton thought proper to express his opinion. He made it clear that it would be injurious to remove to the green, as many persons had purchased and settled round the market in the expectation of being accommodated in their proximity to the place of worship, whereas it would be no damage to the most to have it by the market-place. It was finally determined with a good degree of harmony to erect the new church on the plat which is now covered by the block of buildings in Cornhill-square.*

---

* We find no records of the dimensions of this house: that it had *a gallery* is certain, and that it was furnished with *a bell* is probable from these records on the town books:

1648. March 27. Sgt. Johnson and Walter Merry are requested to take ye oversight of the boyes in ye galleryes and in case of unruly disorders to acquaint the magistrates therewith.

1649. June 26. 'Richard Taylor is appointed to ring the bell at nine of the clock at night, and at half past four in the morning, at four pounds per annum.' This may be considered *the origin of our nine o'clock bell.*

Hingham meeting-house, which is said to have been built on the same model, has a belfry in the centre of the roof.

The contractors for the work calculated that it would cost
£600. They took the old house for half that sum, and the
balance was to be supplied by voluntary contributions of the
people. The building however cost about £1000, yet the expense was defrayed without any murmurs or assessment, by
weekly collections. ' In some other churches,' says the Governour, ' which did it by way of rates there was much difficulty and compulsion by law to raise a far less sum.' It is
pleasing to see in this incident how early the people of Boston adopted the practice of supporting religion without re-
course to law. Mr. Cotton had before this time advanced
the doctrine, that when magistrates are obliged to provide for
the maintenance of ministers, the churches are in a declining
condition ; and proved in a sermon that the preachers of the
gospel should be supported not by lands, revenues and tithes,
which are the occasion of pride, contention and sloth, but by
the voluntary contributions of their hearers. Their manner
of taking these contributions was different from ours at the
present day. Instead of the deacons passing the box to every
one, and subjecting all to the tax of a groat or the mortifica-
tion of a nod, ' the Governour and all the rest' went down and
put their mites into the box at the deacons' seat.

The religious society was now in a prosperous state. That
disaffection which all, save five or six of the members, had formerly manifested towards the pastor and Mr. Winthrop had
happily subsided, and all was tranquillity and love. A while
since, these gentlemen were treated with slight as men under
a covenant of works and as the greatest enemies of the truth.
But under these suspicions and cool treatment, they had behaved with great meekness, never complaining of unkind usage.
Though often and strongly solicited to withdraw themselves
from the communion, they had withstood the solicitation until
now the odium which was upon them had gradually worn
away, and they found themselves in possession of the wonted
confidence and affection of their friends. The Governour in
particular had a proof of the returning love of the brethren
when suffering a heavy loss through the delinquency of one
Luxford, his bailiff, to whom he trusted the management of
his farm, and who incurred a debt of £2300 without his knowledge. The whole country indeed sympathized with him ;
the Court gave his wife 3000 acres of land and some of the
towns sent in liberally. The whole however did not amount
to £500 whereof near half came from Boston.

Many of the poor to whom lots were assigned in Mt. Wolaston, finding it inconvenient to improve their lands there while
they resided in Boston, petitioned the town for leave to form
a church at the mount, which was eventually allowed on cer-

tain conditions. So on Monday the 16th of September, 1639, they gathered a church in the usual manner, and chose Mr. William Thomson, a pious and learned minister, who was ordained their pastor on the 24th of the same month. Mr. Henry Flint was chosen teacher. The church was the twentieth formed in the colony. This was a principal step towards the final separation, and the erection of a town in that place.

As early as Dec. 10, 1636, measures had been adopted towards accomplishing the separation. ' The Governour (Vane) Dep. Gov. (Winthrop) Messrs. Oliver, Keayne, John Newgate, Colburn, Coggeshall and Brenton, are chosen to consider of the Mt. Wolaston business; how they may be a town and church there with the consent of this town's inhabitants.' On Jan. 17th 1640, the consent of Boston was voted in the following terms. ' It was agreed with our neighbours and brethren of the Mount, namely, William Cheeseborough, Alexander Winchester, Richard Wright, James Penniman, Stephen Kinsley and Martin Saunders, in the name of the rest there, for whom they undertake, that they should give to this town of Boston towards the maintenance [of the ministers] thereof 4s. an acre for every two acres of the seven acres formerly granted to divers y^n of Boston, upon expectation they should have continued with us : and 3s. an acre for every acre that hath been or shall be granted to any others who are not inhabitants of Boston. And that in consideration hereof and after that the said portions of money shall be paid to this town's treasury of Boston, all the said land shall be free from any town rates or charges to Boston, and also from all country charges when the Mount shall be rated by the court and not assessed with the town of Boston ; and upon these terms if the court shall think fit to grant them to be a town of themselves they shall have free liberty to accept thereof.*

Feb. 13, 1640, at a General Court the petition of the inhabitants of Mt. Wolaston was voted and granted them to be a town according to the agreement with Boston : provided if they fulfil not the covenant, it shall be in the power of Boston to recover their due by action against the said inhabitants, or any of them, and the town is to be called *Braintree.*

In February 1792, the people of the first parish in Braintree petitioned to be made a distinct town, and were incorporated by the name of Quincy. This name was adopted in honour of one of the earliest and most considerable proprietors at the Mount. December 14, 1635, a committee of five persons were appointed to go to Mt. W. and bound out lots for Mr. Edmund Quincy and Mr. Coddington, ' what may be

---

* See town records June 26, 1649. Also Appendix No. III. *Winthrop*, Sept. 1636.

sufficient for them :' in 1636, March 14, the bounds are recorded.   Mr. Coddington appears to have given his to Braintree for the support of schools ; the lot assigned to Mr. Quincy
remains in the possession of one of his descendants, the present mayor of the city.

Mr. Quincy was descended from that Sieur de Quincy who
was one of the English barons that made that noble stand, in
the year 1215, which obliged King John to grant the Magna
Charta.   He with his wife joined the church in Boston, Nov.
1633 : within a short time five servants belonging to his family also became members.   He was a representative in 1634,
and died here, aged about thirty-three.   His son Edmund
who was born in 1628, settled in Braintree and was a gentleman of distinction among the fathers of that town : he died
Jan. 7, 1698, leaving a son Edmund, who was born and resided at Braintree, and was a bright ornament and eminent benefactor of that town and of his country.*

Hubbard pronounces the ten years which were now (1640)
closing, the golden age of New-England, when vice was crush-
ed as well by the civil as sacred sword, especially oppression
and extortion in prices and wages.   A remarkable instance
was given in one F. P. who for asking an excessive price for
a pair of stocks which he was hired to frame, had the honour
to sit an hour in them first himself.†   Women were not exempt from publick notice.   One for reproaching the magistrates was condemned to be whipped, and bore her punishment with a masculine spirit, glorying in her suffering.
She was a woman of abilities far before Mrs. Hutchinson,
but she was poor and had little acquaintance.   The free expression of her thoughts brought her again into difficulties for
speaking against the elders, and she was obliged to stand half
an hour with her tongue in a cleft stick.   Church discipline
reached to still nicer points : one brother ' having purloined
out of buckskin leather brought unto him, so much thereof as
would make three men's gloves, to the scandal of sundry
without as well as of his brethren, and also having been by
some of the brethren dealt with for it, did often deny and forswear the same, and was therefore cast out of the church.'

* Hancock's century sermon, 1739, rep. 1811, and sermon on death of Hon. Edmund Quincy, 1738.   Eliot's Biog. Dict.

† See Hubbard, 242, 276.   Emerson's Hist. Sketch, 60—67.   Winthrop's Jo. Dec. 1638.
Sept. and Nov. 1639.   Feb. 1640.   Shaw, 289.   Mass. H. C. 1. x. 2.

CHAPTER XVII.

Let discipline employ her wholesome arts ;
Let magistrates alert perform their parts,
Let active laws apply the needful curb,
To guard the peace that riot would disturb.—*Cowper*.

FROM the time of a permanent establishment of a house of deputies or representatives in 1634, to the court of election in 1639, Boston had the privilege of sending three members. At that court, May 22, in consequence of the increase of the number of deputies with the increase of the number of towns, it was determined for the convenience both of the country and the court, to reduce all towns to two deputies. The expenses were at that time paid out of the public treasury. This alteration excited some suspicions. Many were jealous that it was a plan of the assistants and magistrates to keep the number of deputies on a nearer equality with their own; and the people in some towns were highly displeased with their representatives for consenting to the measure. A motion was made in the next session to return to the former rule ; but after long debate, the order was confirmed, and the reasons for it, and answers to the objections against it, were recorded, and sent to such towns as were dissatisfied. From that period until 1680, Boston sent only two deputies.

An incident occurred in Boston, hardly worthy of notice, which gave rise to a change also in regard to the Assistants. A thoughtless pig strayed from its owner, one good Mrs. Sherman; and, her husband not being at home to look after the creature, it wandered through the town, breaking into every body's corn as its hunger dictated. About the same time a stray pig was brought to Capt. Keayne, who had it cried a number of days, and many people came to see it, but no one would claim the property. He kept it in his yard for nearly a year with a pig of his own. At the proper season the captain had the latter killed. This was no sooner done than forward came Mrs. Sherman, and claimed the dead pig for hers, because she found that the living one had other marks : she went so far as to accuse the captain of wilfully killing her pig. The matter made so much noise that the church investigated it and were satisfied of his innocence.

The woman however was instigated to bring the cause before an inferior court at Boston: there again Capt. Keayne was cleared, and the jury gave him £3 for his costs, and in an action brought by him against her and her instigator for defamation, he recovered £20 damages from each.

This result so vexed Story, a London merchant, who was the woman's adviser, that he searched town and country to find matter against Capt. Keayne about this stray pig. At last he prevailed with one of the captain's witnesses to go into Salem court and confess that he had forsworn himself. Upon this he petitioned the General Court, in June 1642, to have the cause heard again, which the court granted and spent the best part of seven days in examining witnesses and debating the case. Yet when the question was put to vote, no decision could be obtained; for no sentence of law could pass without the consent of the majority, both of the deputies and of the magistrates, and here were thirty deputies and nine magistrates, of whom two of the magistrates and fifteen of the deputies were for the plaintiff, and seven of the magistrates and eight of the deputies for the defendant, and seven deputies standing neutral. There had been great expectation in the country that the case would terminate unfavourably to Capt. Keayne. It happening otherwise, many took occasion to speak disrespectfully of the court, especially of the magistrates, and to attribute the hindrance of the course of justice to their exercise of a negative voice upon the doings of the deputies. Some were of a mind that this power of a negative should be taken from the assistants. Nothing was effected at this time, but occasions of altercation becoming more frequent, and the deputies being dissatisfied that their votes should lose their effect, by the non-concurrence of the magistrates who were so much fewer in number, a formal attempt was made in 1644, to diminish or destroy the power of the latter. Mr. Winthrop and the assistants maintained their right with so much firmness, that the effort was unavailing; and it was therefore moved by the deputies, that the two houses might sit apart, and from that time votes were sent in a parliamentary way from one house to the other, and the consent of both was necessary to an act of court. Provision was made for some cases in which, if the two houses differed, it was agreed that the major vote of the whole should be decisive. This was the origin of our present Senate.

Mrs. Sherman's pig might have been forgotten in the greater interest excited by the difficulties it produced. But she possessed perseverance superior to that of Amy Dardin, in more modern times, and at length the captain yielded to the advice of friends, and relinquished the living pig to the woman, for the sake of the publick peace.*

The Boston church enjoying harmony within itself could not forget its members, who had left their places in the Antinomian controversy. In March 1640, they sent a deputation of three gentlemen to Rhode Island, with letters to Mr. Coddington and the rest, to inquire into their opinions on certain points of doctrine formerly maintained by them, and also to demand that they should give an account of themselves to this church, for their unwarrantable practice of communing with excommunicated persons. When the messengers arrived, they found that these people had formed a church among themselves, and had the independence to refuse to hear the messengers as such, or to receive the Boston letters. When the result of the mission was submitted to the church, the elders and most of the church were disposed to pass a vote of exclusion against them, ' but all not being agreed, it was deferred.' Mr. Emerson observes, the mission was worse than useless : it served to foment a party spirit at home, and to exasperate the minds of those for whose benefit the measure was intended.

In the year 1640, Mr. Dudley was chosen governour, and Mr. Bellingham, deputy-governour, Mr. Winthrop, the former governour, being elected an assistant. The election in 1641, notwithstanding the number of votes was great, was determined in favour of Mr. Bellingham for governour (Mr. Winthrop being his competitor) by a majority of six votes only. Mr. Endicott was chosen deputy-governour. It was disputed whether they fairly had the majority, because the votes of some persons were refused, who it was thought had a right to vote. Mr. Winthrop was silent, though he believed himself injured.

The revolutions which were now taking place in England, excited the attention of the colonial government, and it was determined to send three agents thither, to congratulate the parliament on their successes, and to be ready to improve any opportunity which might offer for the advantage of the colony. The men selected for this purpose were Rev. Messrs. Weld and Peters, and Mr. William Hibbins. The two former never returned to America. Mr. Hibbins was a principal merchant in the colony, and was the first town treasurer of Boston whose name appears on record.†

---

* *Hutch.* Hist. ch. 1. *Winthrop*, June 1642. March 1644. Town records, Sept. 17, 1688.

M r. Winthrop's account would lead us to infer that Capt. Keayne repaid the 3*l.* costs, which was all that he received of the woman ; the pig was worth forty shillings.

† Town records, April 27, 1640. Mass. H. C. 1. x. 30.

13

In the years 1642 and 1643, Mr. Winthrop was chosen governour and Mr. Endicott, deputy. In the latter year, the colony of Massachusetts was divided into four counties, Essex, Middlesex, Suffolk and Norfolk.

Essex contained	*Middlesex.*	*Suffolk.*	*Norfolk.*
Salem	Charlestown	Boston	Salisbury
Lynn	Cambridge	Roxbury	Haverhill
Enon (Wenham)	Watertown	Dorchester	Hampton
Ipswich	Sudbury	Dedham	Exeter
Rowley	Concord	Braintree	Dover
Newbury	Woburn	Weymouth	Strawberry-Bank
Gloucester	Medford	Hingham	(Portsmouth)
Chochickawick	Lynn Village	Nantasket (Hull)	

The four last towns are now in New-Hampshire.

At the election in 1644, Messrs. Winthrop and Endicott exchanged places ; the latter being chosen for governour, and the former for deputy. This success of Mr. Endicott was peculiarly gratifying to ' those of Essex.' Salem had become a very flourishing place, and it was a favourite object with Mr. Endicott to have that town considered the capital of the state. The Essex deputies had introduced a measure at the court previous, by which the deputies of the several counties were directed to meet in the recess and prepare such business as it might be necessary to transact. Under this order they came prepared, and introduced two bills, the object of which was to aggrandize their own section of the country by drawing 1. the seat of government thither : 2. the courts : and 3. a good part of the country stock. They also proposed, 4thly, that four of their neighbourhood should be joined in commission with the magistrates. ' They had made so strong a party among the deputies of the smaller towns, (being most of them mean men, and such as had small understanding in affairs of state) that they easily carried all their points among the deputies. But when the two bills came up to the magistrates, they discerning the plot and finding them hurtful to the commonwealth, refused to pass them. A committee from each house was appointed to consider the reasons of both sides, and then the opinion of the upper house prevailed :' ' Boston being such a convenient mart for business, and other circumstances concurring to increase its population, obtained the preference,' and thereafter ' all hopes were renounced that Salem would become the capital of New-England.*

We shall find the authorities here acquiescing under every change of government which occurred during the civil wars

---

* *Winthrop*, June 5, 1641. Mass. Hist. Coll. 1. vi. 232—234. *Eliot.* Biog. Dict. 195.

in England. The parliament prevailing this year, the General Court passed an order which contains the following article; ' what person soever shall by word, writing or action, endeavour to disturb our peace directly or indirectly, by drawing a party under pretence that he is for the King of England, and such as join with him against the parliament, shall be accounted as an offender of a high nature against *this commonwealth*, and to be proceeded against either capitally or otherwise according to the quality and degree of his offence.' A provision was annexed that this order should not be extended against any that came hither merely for purposes of trade. Very soon after the passing of this order, a London ship of 24 guns, Capt. Stagg, arrived at Boston with a cargo of wine from Teneriffe. A Bristol ship of 100 tons, laden with fish, lay in the harbour at the same time. Captain Stagg said nothing of having any commission, but as soon as he had landed the principal part of his wine, he suddenly weighed anchor and sailed round to Charlestown, placed his ship between that town and the Bristol ship, and moored himself abreast of her. He then ordered the master of the Bristol ship aboard, showed him a commission, turned up a half-hour glass, and demanded that he should surrender by the time the glass was out. The Bristol captain returned to his own vessel and stated the case to his men ; two or three of them were for fighting, and would rather have blown up the ship than have yielded, but the greater part thought best to secure their property and wages, which Capt. S. promised them, as well as their lives, and the ship was therefore surrendered.

In this half hour's time a great many people were gathered upon the Windmill hill (Copp's hill) to see the issue, and as was very natural, some who had an interest in the prize ship (especially a Bristol merchant, a very bold malignant, in the phrase of the times) began to collect a mob and raise a tumult. But some of the inhabitants, apprehensive of serious consequences, seized the said merchant and some others that were strangers and brought them before the deputy, Mr. Winthrop, who put them under guard in a room at a publick house. Others who belonged to town he committed to prison, and sent the constable to require the people to disperse. Capt. Stagg was immediately called to account, and produced his commission from the parliament, which was found to give him sufficient authority to make prize of all Bristol vessels in any port or creek.

Great excitement was produced by this occurrence. Some of the ministers partook of the common feeling, and in their sermons inveighed against the captain, and exhorted the magistrates and all concerned to maintain the people's liberties, which they said were violated by this act. Many were of

opinion that Capt. Stagg should be compelled to restore the
ship ; but the majority of the magistrates were of a different
opinion, on the ground that it would seem like an opposition
to parliament.   For this and other reasons of state, the captain was suffered to enjoy his prize.   The merchants who
were interested in the property on board the Bristol vessel
petitioned to try their right by an action at law, which was
granted : but when the governour and six other magistrates
(for the governour did not send for such as dwelt far off) and
the jury were assembled, the merchants were persuaded not
to insist on the case being submitted to the jury, but to refer
the decision of the whole matter to the court of admiralty,
before which the case must necessarily come.   Thus an affair,
which in its outset threatened to produce no small trouble, ended peaceably.

There was a speck of liberty discernible in the part which
the Boston people took in this affair.   An occasion of a different kind occurred in 1646, in which they manifested their love
of freedom more conspicuously.   There had been an assembly of the ministers and elders in 1643, for the purpose of
discountenancing an attempt at Newbury to establish some
things in the presbyterian way.   It probably was a voluntary
meeting, and Mr. Cotton of Boston acted as one of the moderators.   In 1646, a synod was called by the General Court,
to discuss, dispute and clear up such questions of church government and discipline as they shall think needful and meet,
and to continue so doing till the major part of them should be
agreed upon *one form of got rnment* and discipline, which they
judge agreeable to the holy scriptures, to be presented to the
court for their approbation.   It was of course intended that
what this synod should decree, and the court approve, should
become the law of the land and binding on the churches.
Some of the deputies saw this and opposed the proposition.
It was demonstrated that no new powers were assumed ; but
out of regard to the scruples of some members, it was agreed
that the synod should be convoked by a vote recommending
it to the several churches to send delegates, and not by a positive order.

But, says Mr. Hubbard, whatever gentle words the order
was sweetened withal, some of the churches could not swal-
low it : the principal men who raised objections were some
lately arrived from England, where a vast liberty was allowed
by the parliament, which had also sent orders to the West India colonies, that all men should enjoy their liberty of conscience, and had by their letters also intimated the same to
those of New-England.   Some few of the church in Boston
adhered to these principles, which made them stickle much
against the calling of this synod.

This few formed about three-sevenths of the acting members of the church; they were influenced in a great degree
by the opinion of Mr. Cotton, and their opposition to the measure was so determined, that they presented three formal objections to it; that the interference of the court was unnecessary, that the order originated with the ministers, and that
the decisions of the synod would be binding on the churches,
without their own consent. A motion was however made
that the church should send its proportion of delegates, and
after two Sabbath days' debate, it was carried in the affirmative by a vote of forty against thirty. Here arose a great
difficulty: some members were in favour of proceeding to select and send their delegates: but the church had heretofore
done all business by unanimous votes, and it would have
grieved many to see so important an act as this, carried into
operation on a bare majority. To relieve the difficulty, some
one proposed that the whole church should attend and see for
themselves: but this would appear singular and perhaps be
thought disrespectful. Some external impulse was necessary
to bring the matter to a conclusion. Mr. Norton, then of Ipswich, was at hand, and he was procured to supply the pulpit
as Boston, upon a lecture day, where was a great audience,
and he handled his subject so aptly, and with so much strength
of reason and argument, that on the next Sabbath the Boston
church agreed to send their elders and three of the brethren
as messengers to the synod.

This assembly met at Cambridge and had several adjourn-
ments until October 1648, when its sesssion terminated. Its
labours principally consisted in compiling what is called the
Cambridge platform, which together with the Westminster confession they recommended to the court, and which for a long
time continued to be standard authorities in the congregational
churches in New-England.*

---

* *Hubbard*, 532. *Backus*, i. 185. Magualia, ii. 181—*Emerson*, 31. Mass. H. C. t. x. 3—2. i.
195.

CHAPTER XVIII.

" Great prince and father of our State, receive
The well-earn'd honours that thy Rome would give."

In the beginning of the year 1649, Boston suffered a mournful loss in the death of Governour Winthrop. From the first
moment of placing his foot on the peninsula he had been its
firmest friend. His resolute perseverance in opposition to Dudley's plan of establishing the capital at Cambridge, laid the
foundation of Boston's greatness, and the endeavours of Endicott and his party to obtain the same honour for Salem, were
rendered unavailing through the wisdom and prudence of Winthrop. He was one of the earliest Selectmen and frequently
served on that board. In almost every event of any moment
we find him bearing part, and except for one short period he
was an oracle and favourite with the people. Or, as Cotton
expresses it, he was their friend in all things by his counsel, a
a help for their bodies by physick, and in their estates by
law.

Governour Winthrop was born at the family mansion house
of his ancestors, at Groton in Suffolk, June 12, 1587. Having been educated to the profession of law, he was made a
Justice of the peace at the age of eighteen, and soon became
conspicuous for his many virtues. In his profession he was
exemplary as an upright and impartial magistrate, and in his
private character he manifested the traits of a devout and
practical christian. He had the wisdom to discern and the
fortitude to perform what was right in executing the duties of
his office; and as a gentleman was remarkable for liberality
and hospitality. These qualities rendered him dear to men
of sobriety and religion, and fitted him to engage in the great
and difficult work of founding a colony.

Previous to his embarking for New-England, he converted
a fine estate of six or seven hundred pounds sterling per annum into money, which he expended principally in the service of the plantation. His time, his study, his exertions, his
influence and his interests, were all employed in the publick
service. He maintained the dignity of a governour with the
obliging condescension of a gentleman : his wisdom, patience
and magnanimity were conspicuous in the most severe trials,

and his christian-like behaviour added splendour to all his rare qualifications.

He was a pattern to the people of that frugality, decency, and temperance, which were necessary in their circumstances, and even denied himself many of the elegances and superfluities of life, which he had enjoyed elsewhere. This he did both that he might set others a proper example, and be the better enabled to exercise that liberality in which he delighted. His charity indeed was unbounded. He would often send his servants on some errand, at meal times, to the houses of his neighbours to see how they were provided with food, and if there was a deficiency would supply them from his own table. He mingled with his sterner virtues a happy portion of well-timed wit. In one of the very hard and long winters which he endured in this climate, a man came to the governour with a private complaint that a needy person in the neighbourhood stole wood sometimes from his pile. ' *Does he,*' said Mr. Winthrop, ' *call him to me and I will take a course with him, that shall cure him of stealing.*' The man appeared, trembling under the terrours of the law. ' *Friend,*' said the governour, ' *it is a very cold season, and I doubt you are but poorly provided with wood : you are welcome to supply yourself at my pile till the winter is over.*'

But though condescending and gentle on every occasion of personal ill treatment, yet where the honour of government or religion and the interests of the people were concerned, he was equally firm and intrepid, standing foremost in opposition to those whom he judged to be really publick enemies. He defended the course he had pursued in Mrs. Hutchinson's case, on the ground which he maintained on all occasions : ' I have acted according to my conscience and my oath, and by advice of the elders of the church, and am fully satisfied that it would not have been consistent with the publick peace to have done otherwise.'

His political opinions were not so favourable to the democratical forms of government as were those of some of the wise and good men with whom he was associated. On this subject he has left us these remarkable words; ' the best part of a community is always the least, and of that best part the wiser is still less.' His ideas of the right of a publick officer to exercise his own judgment are thus conveyed : ' When you choose us magistrates, the covenant between us and you is, that we shall govern you and judge your causes according to the laws of God and our best skill; and as for our skill, you must run the hazard of it : if there be an errour, not in the will, but in the skill, it becomes you to bear it.'

Mr. Winthrop, before he left England, was of a more catholick spirit than some of his brethren. After he came to America he yielded somewhat to the reigning spirit of intolerance, but as he advanced in life he resumed his former moderation, and in the time of his last sickness, when Dudley pressed him to sign an order for the banishment of a person who was deemed heterodox, he refused, saying, that he had done too much of that work already.

He met with much affliction in his family, having buried three wives and six children. These and other troubles joined with the opposition and ill treatment he frequently received so preyed upon his nature, already worn by the toils and hardships of planting a colony in a wilderness, that he perceived a decay of his faculties and often spoke of his dissolution as approaching, with a calm resignation to the will of heaven. A fever occasioned by a cold, after one month's confinement, put an end to his life on the 26th of March 1649, æt. 62.

Gov. Winthrop's house stood on the spot occupied by the South Row, about opposite to School street. It was of wood, two stories high, and was demolished by the British in 1775. His remains were deposited in the family tomb, on the north side of the Chapel burial ground. His portrait is preserved in the Land Office at the State House. He is judged to have been about six feet high, not corpulent, long favoured, with a dark blue eye, high forehead, long beard, and dark hair, which he wore in the form of a natural wig.

CHAPTER XIX.

"See wide dominions ravished from the deep,
And changed creation takes its face from man."

WE consider the death of Gov. Winthrop to have completed an epoch in the history of Boston. The town had then been settled about nineteen years; its population had become so numerous that they were meditating the formation of a new church: the necessities of the place and the conveniences it afforded for trade, had given occasion for extensive improvements in the construction of wharves, and other expedients to enlarge the facilities for domestick and foreign commerce: a foundation was laid for the publick instruction of youth, and a regular system of police established. We propose to give in this chapter a view of the progress of these improvements.

The features which in sixteen hundred and thirty were most prominent on the face of Boston have now disappeared. The hill at the north, rising to the height of about 50 feet above the sea, presented then on its northwest brow an abrupt declivity, long after known as Copp's hill steeps. Its summit, almost level, extended between Prince and Charter streets towards Christ's church. Thence south a gentle slope led to the water, which washed the south side of Prince street below, and the north side above Thacher street as far as Salem street. Eastward from the church, a gradual descent led to the north battery, which was considered the bottom of the hill. South-easterly the slope was still more gradual, and terminated at the foot of the north square, leaving a knoll on the right, where at present stands the meeting-house of the Second church.

This hill was the spot selected for the site of the first windmill used in the colony, when it was brought down from Watertown, in August 1632, because it would not grind there but with a westerly wind. Hence it obtained the name of Windmill hill. Most probably it was at some period called Snow hill; but about the time of the revolution in 1775, it bore the name of Copp, which it retained so long as any portion of it was left standing.

William Copp was the earliest proprietor of that portion of the hill which latterly bore his name. This appears from the following record in the first *book of possessions.*

"The possession of William Copp within the limits of Boston.

"One house and lott of halfe an acre in the Mill field bounded with Thomas Buttolph southeast: John Button northeast: the marsh on the southwest: and the river on the northwest."

Copp's hill was at one time in possession of the Ancient and Honourable Artillery Company. In 1775 the common was occupied by the British troops, and that company was refused admittance there to perform their exercise and evolutions. Major Wm. Bell, who was then commander, therefore marched the company to Copp's hill. Some years after, a question arose in town meeting, ' to whom this hill belonged:' some one said, ' to the Ancient and Honourable.' Col. Joseph Jackson, their treasurer and past commander, was sent for, and declared that he considered it their property, a mortgage upon it to them having long since run out, and that Capt. Bell, with the company, had taken possession of it in 1775. Capt. Bell was then interrogated by Col. Thomas Dawes, the moderator. Why did you march your company to Copp's hill? Answer. I was prohibited from entering the common,

14

conceiving this hill to be the property of the company, I marched them there, as a place no one had a right to exclude them from. Question by moderator. Supposing a party of British troops should have been in possession of it, and should have forbidden you entrance, what would you have done ? Answer.   I would have charged bayonets, and forced my way, as surely as I would force my way into my dwelling house, if taken possession of by a gang of thieves.   The late Col. William Tudor, who was then present, said, ' Mr. Moderator, The hill clearly belongs to that company, and I wish they would execute a quit claim of it to me for a fair price.'   The mortgage was afterwards discharged.

The British left a small fort standing on this hill, (near the southwest corner of the burial ground,) which remained a favourite resort for the recreation of school-boys, until the improvements commenced in 1807, that have terminated in the levelling of the hill, and the erection of buildings on its summit and base.*

Lynn-street and Ann-street, as far south as Richmond-street, occupy what was the foot of Windmill hill on the seaboard.   The land between Richmond-street on the north, and Portland and Elm-streets on the south, was a narrow neck, on either side of which was a spacious cove.   Southerly from Richmond-street, Ann-street probably follows the shore, till we reach the Mill creek, where a natural inlet commenced, which extended to and covered what is now Hatter's square.

As near as can be ascertained the name of ' the cove' was applied to all the water which flowed between the head of Hancock's wharf and the bottom of State-street.   All the records of possessions north of the former speak of the sea or the bay (as Josselyn called it) for the bounds on the north and east.   Then comes Thomas Joy who has the cove southwest; Mr. Thomas Clarke next has it south, which probably was at the foot of North-square, (for some time called Clark's square.)   Southerly from him various owners have the cove southeast, east and north till we come to Edward Tyng, who has the bay on the east, and the cove on the north.

The western extremity of this, which we will call the market-cove, has of late years been known as the Town dock ; it was formerly called Bendall's dock, from Edward Bendall, who owned a lot near the head of it.   His deed gives him the cove north and east, which brought him not far from the corner of Dock-square opposite the Sheep-market : a creek is mentioned near his new house, April 1639.   The water flowed near to the foot of Brattle-street. The whole of Dock-square

---

* Whitman's hist. sketch, p. 66.   Winthrop's Journal.

and Market-square, and the west side of Union-street as far as Creek lane, and all east of that to the Mill creek were daily covered by the tide.

Between the inlet, which now forms the Mill creek, and the principal arm of the cove, there was a narrow point of low marsh projecting, in the form of a triangle. This was anciently granted to Mr. Bellingham. In 1644 he sold one half to Christopher Lawson, and the other half in 1646 to Joshua Scottow, who in 1650 appears also to have purchased of James Everill another portion of the same marsh, which was the identical spot on which lately stood the triangular warehouse.

THE TRIANGULAR WAREHOUSE.

VIEW FROM S. E. CORNER OF FANEUIL-HALL.

The origin of that singular building is involved in a happy obscurity, which has given rise to much curious speculation. It stood at the head of the Town dock, as it was in July last, on the north side of the same. It occupied precisely the space marked by the small triangle, which is to be seen in square $H e$ on our plan for 1824, and opposite to the swing bridge, which is shewn on the plan for 1722. It measured on the side facing the dock forty-eight feet: on Roe-buck passage fifty-one, and on the back side fifty-five feet. It was built of brick, on a stone foundation, and had a slated roof. There were two principal stories in the building with a good cellar underneath. The lower story appeared to have been arched, with very many doors and windows. On each cor-

ner, and in the centre of the roof there was a tower, such as is
represented in the plate, topped with a ball. The centre ball
was of wood ; the others were of stone, all fixed on iron spires
set in lead. Conjecture has made this edifice to have been a
fort built for the protection of the town, or a custom-house
for the accommodation of government ; there is, however,
good reason to believe that it was not erected for any publick
purpose, but that it was built about the year 1700, by London
merchants, for a commercial warehouse. It had been a place
of considerable business and for some time the publick scales
for weighing large draughts were kept there. Of late years
it had been occupied for minor purposes, until August last,
when it was taken down to make room for the great improvements commenced in the vicinity of the market. It was constructed with great strength, the bricks were of a larger size
than those now used, and the foundation stood upon a sandy
marsh ; beneath which there is found a solid blue clay, at
about thirteen feet below the level of Ann-street.

State-street was a primitive highway. The owners on both
sides, about 1640, can be traced. Edward Tyng before mentioned, owned the North-east corner, which, as we suppose,
was the South-west corner of Merchants'-row. William Hudson, senior, held a house and yard at the lower end on the
south side, which appears to have been the only lot between
the corner of that street and the commencement of Mr. Winthrop's marsh, which afterwards came to be known by the
name of Oliver's dock. This lot was probably situated near
the corner of Kilby-street now occupied by the New-England
bank. From between that corner and the bottom of Milk-
street, a cove run up westward as far as Spring-lane, where
there was a remarkable spring. Mr. Winthrop's garden lay
on the south side of that lane, and was said to be bounded
north with the springate. Mr. Hibbins lay east of him, having also the springate north. Then came John Spoore, who
had ' the creek' north, and the marsh east of him. These
three lots bring us down to the block between Congress and
Kilby (late Adams) street. Passing the intervening piece of
marsh, (or water course,) we then have three lots which have
the marsh still on the north, and at the water side have John
Compton's house and garden ' bounded with the cove on the
east and the fort-hill on the south.' The lots on the north
side of Spring-lane and Water-street are all said to be bounded south, either by the springate or the marsh.

We have taken the pains to trace out the above points on
the original records, to show how accurately tradition and the
memory of our aged citizens agree with the facts thus ascertained. They substantiate the account in Shaw's description,
which we here insert.

' *Oliver's Dock*, not many years since, came up to Kilby-
street.   A fish-shop owned by Mr. Solomon Hewes, used to
stand over the water, and parallel to the street.   On the side
of the dock stood the famous stamp office, occupied by Lieut.
Governor Oliver.   This small building was tumbled into the
water by the patriotic mob in 1765, and with it was over-
thrown the scheme of taxation which led to the revolution.
The building, now (1817) occupied as a grocer's shop, by J.
Welsh, stands on the same spot.

' The greater part of Quaker-lane (Congress street,) is *made*
land.   An aged gentleman, who lived near the spot, says that
when the foundation of Joy's buildings was preparing, the
remains of the hull of an old vessel, or large boat, with frag-
ments of canvass, and tarred rope, were dug up : which shews
the place had been once used for a graving yard, or some
similar purpose.   A relative of our informant, remembered
when lighters and boats came up the creek (then so called,)
as far as the *wheat sheaf*, now the estate of Mr. Kendall, the
baker.   On the spot now covered by the corner of Joy's
buildings, stood a shop, improved by one Kent, a tanner.   His
tan-yard was in the rear, and in front was a wharf, for the
accommodation of his small vessels.   This was one branch
of the creek.

' Another branch may be traced thus :—A Mr. Marshall
remembered, when a boy, smelts were caught at the head of
the creek, near the meeting-house in Federal-street, where is
now the drain and common sewer.   A man descended in this
some years ago, and groped his way under ground, till he
came out at Oliver's dock.—Here were a number of cooper's
shops ; the workmen used to soak their hoops in the water,
now covered by an oyster shop, and buildings occupied by
painters and others.   From a view of the ground, there is
reason to believe that the greater part of Congress-street, the
whole of Kilby-street, and Liberty-square, are built on flats
once covered by salt water.   In noticing the great storm and
tide, in 1723, the writer says, " we could sail in boats from
the southern battery to the rise of ground in King-street."

' Another aged inhabitant states, that he has seen a canoe
sail, at different times, over the spot which now makes the
corner of Congress and Water-streets ; and thinks he has
seen the water three feet deep in Federal-street.   He remembers having heard Dr. Chauncy say, that he had taken smelts
in the place, now improved as a garden, belonging to the estate of the late Judge Paine, in Milk-street, [at the west corner of Federal-street.]

' Passing on southerly from the bottom of Milk-street to
Battery-march, you walk over a spot, which was formerly occupied by Mr. Hallowell as a ship-yard.—Where the Custom-

house, and the adjoining stores now stand, vessels of great
burthen have been built ; and a large and beautiful ship, completely rigged, owned by Capt. Fellows was launched there,
within the recollection of many now living.

' In very high tides the water has flowed up to the corner
of State-street, formerly called the Admiral Vernon tavern,
now occupied by Mr. Sumner as a crockery store.   At the
bottom of this street not many years since, logs were dug up
in a sound state, which, from the knots and remains of the
boughs, must have been felled near the spot.'

The grocery shop mentioned in this account stood at the
corner of Kilby-street, which makes the north-east corner of
Liberty-square, being very near the centre of *H h.* Joy's
buildings are on the west side of Congress-street, corner of
Water-street.   The southern branch of the creek covered a
part of the lower end of Pearl-street, and extended across
the Atkinson estate, which lay between Pearl and Atkinson-
streets, as appears on an ancient plan deposited in the Athenæum, and is also evident from the course of the larger drain.
The head of the creek reached towards Summer-street, and
in very high tides, has nearly united with the water from
South-street at the late Mr. Ebenezer Parsons' garden, now
Winthrop-place.   In digging for the foundation of the very
elegant stone stores recently erected by Waterston, Pray, &
Co. at the corner of Kilby and Water-streets, it was necessary to pass through marsh and dock mud, and the tide water
daily filled the trenches, until the discovery that it was all let
in by one aqueduct log.   The Admiral Vernon tavern noticed
by Shaw, was at the corner of Merchants'-Row.

From the south-east margin of this, which we will call the
middle-cove, the eastern hill commenced its ascent, and extending gradually to the south and west rose to the height of
30 feet above the sea.   Its eastern side was also a ragged cliff,
that seemed placed by nature in front of the entrance to the
harbour for the purposes of defence, to which it was very
soon applied, and from which it obtained its present name of
Fort-hill.   It was before called Corn-hill.   Southerly and
westerly it slopes towards Purchase and Atkinson, and down
High-street to the foot of Summer-street.

The estates east of High-street had the bay on the east,
and when we arrive to the lots now in South-street and Essex,
they are said to have the cove on the south, which we call
the *southern cove.*   Windmill point at the bottom of Sea-street
makes one limit of this cove, and South Boston the other, with
Dorchester and Roxbury south, and the neck on the west.

' The neck now so called within the limits of Boston is one
mile and thirty-nine yards in length.   A part of it has been

greatly widened and improved by building, and the whole extent has been raised by art above its original level : otherwise the neck has undergone but little alteration. It is hardly necessary to state that the neck has been overflowed in
many parts, within the recollection of people now living.'

On the west side of the neck we have the receiving basin of
the mill-dam, and as we advance north from that we enter
Charles River, which washes the western shore of the peninsula, and empties itself into the bay between Copp's hill and
Charlestown. There its breadth is about 600 yards : towards
the south part of the town it widens into a bay of considerable extent, but the channel becomes narrow and innavigable
by large vessels at low tide. Formerly also there was a
spacious cove on the Boston side, still nearer the mouth of
the river. This afterwards became the mill pond by the
erection of the causeway from Prince-street *G c* to Leverett
street *D d*. The waters of ' the *mill cove*' came up to the
south-west side of Prince-street below Thacher-street, where
they took a turn northerly and up towards the bottom of
Snow-hill-street. The northerly end of Thacher-street lay
open till within a very few years. The south side of Prince-
street above this spot was marsh, and so was the west side of
Back-street. A causeway was also erected on this side, for
the convenience of passengers to the mill ; it lay east of the
present site of the First Baptist meeting-house, and opened a
few rods east of Thacher-street.

Until 1807, when the mill pond began to be filled up, about
one half the Baptist meeting-house mentioned stood over the
water, and the margin of the pond ran in a south by west line
to the south mills, which stood at the entrance on Mill-pond-
street, near the furniture warehouse of Mr. Beals. Verging
thence a little more westerly, it passed across Union, Friends'
and Portland-street towards the bottom of Hawkins', whence
it took a westerly course across Pitt's and Gooch-street to the
entrance from Leverett-street, which at one time bore the
name of Mill-alley. Not far from this spot we find the record
of a ' small creek,' as the west bounds of an estate, Alexander Beck's, which had ' the cove north, and John Leverit
south,' from whom Leverett-street has probably derived its
name.

The descent to the water here was very steep. The south-
west side of Leverett-street, opposite this opening, stands on
rising ground from which we may commence our ascent to
one portion of the chief of the three hills. A street was
early laid out in the vicinity, if not in the very course of
Temple-street, and those among us not very old can well remember Beacon hill steps, which stood at the head of it, to

conduct us to a spot that we shall ever recollect with pleasure and regret.

The top of this beautiful hill was 138 feet and a half above the level of the sea. It afforded ' an extensive and most enchanting prospect of the country round,' and of the islands in the harbour. The spirit of speculation has in an evil hour laid it low, and posterity must satisfy themselves with a dull description instead of enjoying the reality.

Beacon hill with its two eminences embraced about a hundred acres of ground, extending through the centre of the peninsula, from the river to the coves. The view given in page 46, exhibits as exact a representation of its original appearance seen from Charlestown, as we have been able to obtain. Probably it was better wooded. Of late years, while it laid open as a pasture ground for cattle, the barberry and the wild rose grew upon it. The eminence almost contiguous to Beacon hill on the east, was rather higher than that on its western side. It reached towards Tremont-street (lately so called) and thence with a very slow descent in three directions led to the Springate, the Market cove, and the Mill pond, through Sudbury-street. The grounds occupied by the gardens of Messrs. Phillips, Green, and Lloyd, we conjecture to have been ' the three little rising hills,' from which arose the name of *Trea-Mount*, as the street was first officially designated in 1708.*

The westernmost eminence or left shoulder of this hill, as Johnson might call it, making no unapt comparison of the three to the head and shoulders of a man, was farther from the beacon, and occupied what is now called Mount Vernon. The highest points were probably between Sumner and Pinckney-streets, giving an easy descent towards Cambridge-street on the north, and a more rapid one to Beacon-street south. On the top, directly opposite the Charles-street meeting-house, there was, and continues to be, a boiling spring, which is now open in three places, at a height not less than eighty feet above the water. The west side of this hill appears to have been rough and precipitous, though several streets are now constructed over it, which afford a more gentle, if not entirely safe approach to the river.

' A certain writer, in mentioning this river, quaintly says, the subject is *dry* though *watery ;* and is not considerable, otherwise than in settling the south line of the Massachusetts colony. It is, however, worthy of particular description, in an account of Boston.†

---

* Miscellanies in library of Historical Society.
† See *Shaw*, p. 60, 70, 73, 81, 101, 116. *Winthrop*, May, 1632. *Hale's* Survey, p. 20.

'The source of the principal branch of this river, is a pond, bordering on Hopkinton. It passes through Holliston and Bellingham, and branches of it divide Medway from Medfield, Wrentham and Franklin, Dover from Sherburne, and passing in a north-easterly course through the S. E. corner of Natick, it there turns to the eastward, and separating Needham and Dover, pursues its way into Dedham; where at about nine miles from Boston, a stream called Mother Brook runs out of this river into the Neponset, and forms a sort of canal between the two. From this place the course of the Charles is northerly between Needham and Newton to the bounds of Weston, whence bending eastward it separates Weston and Waltham from Newton. From the south-east corner of Waltham, it has Watertown and Cambridge on the north, Newton, Watertown (at the village), Brighton and Brookline on the south, till it reaches the harbour of Boston. The junction of the Charles and Neponset by the medium of Mother Brook, forms a beautiful island of the towns that lie within them, to wit, Brookline, Brighton, Newton, part of Dedham, Dorchester, Roxbury and Boston. These rivers are interrupted by several elegant falls, and afford a number of seats for mills and manufactories.

Besides the hills and water spots mentioned there was one of each, of which nothing now remains to be seen; Fox hill which is delineated on our old plan at the bottom of the common, and the town's watering place, which was afterwards called ' the pond,' on the north side of Bedford-street, near the opening into Chauncy-place. It is most likely that ' Mr. Coddington's swamp' was situated in that vicinity, farther down the street. There was also a considerable extent of marsh on the north side of Cambridge street below Blossom street. The plans of the town so late as 1796 exhibit no land west of a line from the foot of Centre, (No. 69 in *B f*,) to Brighton street, in *B d.*

An enumeration of the islands in the harbour will now complete our design of bringing into one view the original appearance of Boston. The following table was made in 1793 by that distinguished antiquary Mr. Thomas Pemberton, with great care. 'The distances are from actual survey according to Des Barre's excellent chart. Although not all the islands in the table belong to Boston, the propriety of inserting it entire will be manifest. The bay or harbour extends from Nantasket to Boston, and spreads from Chelsea to Hingham, containing about 75 square miles. It is bespangled with upwards of 100 islands or rocks, and receives the waters from Mystick, Charles, Neponset and Manatticut Rivers, with several other smaller streams.'

15

Islands and Rocks.	Distance from Long Wharf, Boston.	Situation.	In what place.
Apple Island - - - -	2 3-4 miles.	Between Snake and Green islands - - - -	Boston.
Apthorp's, a part of Calf Island - - - - - -	9 ,,		
Bird Island. Soil washed away, but dry at low water - - - - - -	1 1-12 ,,	Between Noddle's and Governour's island -	Boston.
Great Brewster. Contains about 25 acres. A high cliff, towards the sea; it is lessening every year.	7 3-4 ,,	Between Lovell's and Light-House island -	Hull.
Middle Brewster. Rocks, with a small portion of soil - - - - - -	8 1-8 ,,	Between the Great and Outer Brewster - -	Hull.
Outer Brewster - - - -	8 1-4 ,,	East from the Middle Brewster - - - -	Hull.
Bumkin Island - - - -	9 1-4 ,,	Between Nantasket and Little Hog island - -	Hingham.
Button Island - - - -	11 1-4 ,,	Between Sailor's island and Hingham - - -	
Calf Island. A rock, covered in some parts with soil.	7 3-4 ,,	Between the Great Brewster and Green island -	Hull.
Castle Island, (Fort Independence) - - - - -	2 1-3 ,,	Between Thomson's island and Boston - - - -	Boston.
Chandler's Island, called Langley's, in Des Barre's Chart - - - - - -	10 3-4 ,,	Between Bumkin island and Hingham - - -	Hingham.
Deer Island. Wasting towards the sea, and gaining on the inside, and at the East point - - -	4 1-4 ,,	Between Shirley point and Lovell's island -	Boston.
Egg Rock. A bare rock.	8 3-4 ,,	East from Light-House	
Gallop's Island - - - -	6 ,,	Between Lovell's and Rainsford's islands -	
George's Island - - -	6 1-2 ,,	Between Lovell's and Pettick's islands - -	Hull.
Governour's Island, containing about 70 acres -	1 7-8 ,,	Between Deer and Bird islands - - - - -	Boston.
Grape Island - - - -	8 7-8 ,,	Between Bumkin island and Weymouth - -	
Graves. Bare rocks - -	9 1-4 ,,	E. by N. from Green island - - - - - -	
Green Island. Rock, covered with soil in most parts - - - - - -	7 7-8 ,,	Between Calf island and the Graves rocks - -	Hull.
Half Moon Island - - -	6 1-8 ,,	Between Nut island and Squantum - - - -	
A small island - - - -	4 3-4 ,,	Near Half Moon island -	Dorchester.
Hangman's Island - -	5 7-8 ,,	Between Pettick's and Moon islands - - -	

Islands and Rocks.	Distance from Long Wharf, Boston.	Situation.	In what place.
Harding's Rocks. Visible at low water - - - -	10 3-4 miles.	S. E. 1-2 S. from the Light-House - - -	
Hog island - - - - -	2 1-2 ,,	Between Noddle's island and Chelsea - - - -	Boston.
Little Hog island - - -	3 7-8 ,,	Between Nantasket and Bumkin island - - -	Hull.
Light-House island. Rock, with 3-4ths of an acre of soil. A bar, dry at low water, connects it with the Great Brewster -	8 1-2 ,,	S. 69 deg. E. Between Point Alderton and the Middle Brewster - - - - - -	Hull.
Long island - - - - -	4 3-4 ,,	Between Nick's Mate and Spectacle island - -	Boston.
Lovell's island - - - -	6 1-4 ,,	Between Long island and the Great Brewster -	Boston.
Moon island - - - - -	4 3-4 ,,	Between Thomson's and Hangman's islands -	Dorchester.
Nick's Mate. Nearly washed away by the sea -	5 3-4 ,,	Between Long island and Gallop's island - - -	Boston.
Noddle's, or Williams's island - - - - - -	3-4 ,,	Between Boston and Hog island - - - - - -	Boston.
Nut island. Joins the main at half tide - -	7 1-4 ,,	Between Pettick's island and Germantown - -	
Pettick's island - - -	6 7-8 ,,	Between George's island and Braintree Great Head - - - - - -	Hull.
Rackoon island - - - -	8 1-4 ,,	Between Sheep island and Germantown - - -	Quincy.
Ragged island - - - -	10 3-4 ,,	Near Chandler's island -	Hingham.
Rainsford island - - -	5 7-8 ,,	Between Gallop's and Hangman's islands -	Hull.
Rainsford rocks - - -	6 ,,	S. S. W. from Rainsford island - - - - - -	
Sailor's island. Called Sarah's island in Des Barre's chart - - -	11 ,,	Between Bumkin island and Hingham - - -	Hingham.
Sheep island - - - - -	3 3-8 ,,	Between Bumkin and Pettick's islands - - -	
Slate island - - - - -	9 3-8 ,,	Between Bumkin island and Weymouth river	
Snake island - - - -	3 1-4 ,,	Between Apple island and Shirley point - - -	Boston.
Spectacle island - - -	3 5-8 ,,	Between Castle and Long islands - - - - -	Boston.
Sunken island - - - -	6 1-12 ,,	Between Long island and Pettick's island - -	
Thomson's island - - -	3 1-2 ,,	Between Moon island and Dorchester - - - -	Dorchester.
A small island Marsh in Mystick river - - -	2 1-4 ,,	Near Malden bridge - -	Charlestown.
Shirley point - - - -	4 1-2 ,,		Chelsea.
Alderton point - - - -	9 1-2 ,,		Hull.

CHAPTER XX.

——It would be no unprofitable thing for you
to pass over the several streets and call to mind *who lived here so many years ago.*

Increase Mather.

SHAW introduces the above quotation from a lecture preached in 1698, entitled the Bostonian Ebenezer, and adds ' who does not regret that the learned preacher has not given us the result of these profitable inquiries? Retrospection lingers with melancholy delight on the spot to which talents and learning and piety once gave importance.' Presuming that our readers partake in some degree of this feeling, we have been the more minute in our researches regarding the early period of our history. We have incidentally noticed the places where Cotton and Winthrop and Vane resided. The book of possessions to which we have referred, enables us to point out those of other eminent characters, about the period of 1645.

Gov. Winthrop's neighbour on the opposite corner of the springate was Elder Thomas Oliver, who from several notices in the town records and in the Governour's journal, appears to have been an experienced and skilful surgeon. He came to Boston quite early, and was a right godly man, and his wife also a very godly woman that could bear the severest of afflictions with much patience and honour.* Elder Thomas Leverett, who prior to his removal hither had been an ancient and sincere professor in Mr. Cotton's congregation in England, had his house and garden on the east side of the old meeting-house, with the street on the north, and the marsh of Mr. Winthrop on the south. That part of Congress street north of Water street was long called Leverett's lane or street, in remembrance of him. He was father to John Leverett, who became a very distinguished man in our annals. This last resided at the south-east corner of Court street.

His next neighbour on the south was Richard Parker or Brackett, whose name we find on the colony records as prison keeper so early as 1638. He had ' *the market stead* ' on the east, the prison yard west, and the meeting house on the south. The other corner of Cornhill square, which used to be called Church square, was owned by Valentine Hill, a

---

* Magnalia, ii. 306. *Winthrop.* Jan. 9, 1683. Sept. 17, 1644. Town Records, Sept. 1644. Jan. 1647.

man of eminence in town affairs. From these data we ascertain the fact, that the county prison was originally located about the spot where the jail lately stood, and that the spot now occupied by the Old State-house was the ancient market-place.

Mr. Coggan, who set up the first shop in Boston, lived on the north side of the market, at the corner of State street. He probably purchased of Mr. Wilson the minister, who owned north and east of him. On this lot Mr. Wilson had a house, two gardens, a barn and a yard : out of this he sold a lot of 45 feet in front, between him and Mr. Coggan, to John Davies, which makes it quite likely that his dwelling house was very near the new Branch bank, and that Wilson's lane takes its name from him. We may be permitted to add the hope that the name will always be retained. It can do posterity no harm to be reminded that there were good men, though it may be irksome to imitate them.

Capt. Keayne lived on the other corner of State street, opposite the market-stead : Major (so they called Major General) Edward Gibbons' dwelling house, with other housing and a garden, were situated on the bend opposite the lower end of Market street, so as to give him the street on the west and the north. William Pierce owned an estate, extending from State street north to the cove, in the direction of Flagg alley, which a long time bore his name. Samuel Cole, who in the name of Richard, figures so demurely by the side of his wife in the *Peep at the Pilgrims*, lived on the west side of Merchants' row, mid-way from State street to Faneuil Hall, and there kept his tavern ; which it will be remembered was the first in the town, and which Lord Leigh declared was so well regulated, that he could be as private there as he could have been at the Governour's own house.*

Capt. William Tyng, sometime treasurer for the country, had a house, one close, a garden, one great yard and one little yard *before the hall windows*, bounded with Mr. Richard Bellingham and the street that goes to the dock southwards. This sets him on the tongue of land between Brattle and Washington streets, now known as Market Row, and gives Mr. B. an estate about the end of Market street. The latter probably resided there, but he had also a garden plot next but one to Mr. Cotton's on Common (late Tremont) street.

Mr. Henry Dunster, first president of Harvard college, owned the north east corner of Court street. Daniel Maud, one of the earliest schoolmasters, lived next south of Mr. Cotton, now the noble mansion of Lt. Gov. Phillips. The corner of Beacon street opposite the chapel was Mr. Coggan's estate, and had then the burying place adjoining it on the east. On

---

* *Winthrop*, June, 1637.

the other side of this burial ground, fronting south on School
street, was the house and garden of Thomas Scottow, joiner,
who, in Feb. 1644, was appointed to superintend the graves,
gates and fences.   He and Mr. Richard Hutchinson divided
the north side of School street.   Zaccheus Bosworth lived at
the corner on the west end, and those southward of him had
the common on their west.   The south-east corner of School
street was the estate of Mr. Atherton Hough, (sometimes spelt
Hoffe:) he was often a representative of the town in the general courts. His neighbour on School street was Arthur Perry,
worthy of note as town drummer on all important occasions.
His services entitled him to a salary of £5 in 1638, and provision was made in 1643, for the instruction of such as were
candidates to become his successors.   A barber by the name
of Francis Lisle* kept opposite to where the Old South stands,
and three doors above him was William Aspinwall, who was
a notary publick and recorder, after his return from banishment.   His estate extended from the main or high street, to
the common, and we find the name of Bomsted near him.
   At the south-east corner of Winter street was the widow
Jane Parker, and on the opposite corner, Robert Blott.
Boylston market place belonged to an Oliver, and the opposite
corner to Robert Wing.   Deacon Colburn westward of whom
there were six lots, Belcher, Talmage, Snow, Walker, Brisco,
Flacke, lived on the high street at the northerly corner of
Elliot street, and deacon Jacob Elliot, from whom the street
derived its name, was his neighbour on the south corner. We
find no private property south of this : and the next allotment
on the east side of the high street was Garret Bourne's, at the
head of Essex street, but so far down as to give him the cove
on the south.   His next neighbour was Edward Rainsford,
whose name is still retained for the lane that was afterwards
opened in the vicinity of his estate.   Griffith Bowen was on
the north corner of Essex street, and Mr Thomas Fowle's
possession was one house and garden five estates north of him.
Robert Woodward lived at the south and Thomas Wheeler at
the north corner of Bedford street, the latter having the lane S.
the high street W. *the watering place* E. and Wm. Blaintaine
N. who also had the watering place east.   The widow Elizabeth Purton lived at the south-west corner of Summer street,
and Nath. Woodward, sen. who had a numerous family, opposite to her.   Robert Reinolds owned the corner of Milk
street opposite the Old South, and two estates below him was
Nath. Bishop, from whom came the name of Bishop's alley,
once appropriated to Hawley street.

---

* It is not certain whether he was the *barber chirurgeon,* who lost his life in a snow storm,
while on his way to Roxbury to draw a tooth.   W. W. P. b. 2. ch. 15.

Jeremy Houchin, who was a tanner by trade, was located at the corner of Hanover and Court streets (Concert hall) and had his tan-pits and tan-yards there. Down that side of Court street were the families of Makepeace, Thwing, Joshua Scottow, (of whom we have a memoir in the fourth volume of the Hist. Coll. 2d. Series.) Beck, Brown and Biggs. Thomas Marshall, who was a shoemaker besides being ferryman, owned a lot which falls near the block between Union street and Marshall lane. He had the street S. W. and N. W. and the marsh south-east: the extent of his lot was about half an acre. At the north end the whole sea board was *lotted out*, beginning at the mill creek and following the shore to the north end of Snow-hill-street: we shall have occasion to name the families hereafter. Sudbury street was occupied on both sides, and lots extending from the cove on the north to the lane (Green st.) on the south were improved with dwelling houses and gardens as far as 'Mill alley.' The rest of the north and west parts of the town was owned in large lots, said to be in the mill field and new field. Among others we notice Thomas Buttolph who had about five acres in each of those fields, an acre and a half between Essex and Bedford streets, besides his house and garden midway between Market and Court streets. The name of Buttolph street may probably be traced to him. Capt. Christopher Stanley was also a large owner of estates in various parts, and was Buttolph's neighbour on the north. Ensign Thomas Savage at one time owned in the same neighbourhood, and a little above them Capt. Thomas Hawkins, which last had also an estate in the vicinity of the street that bears his name. Near Fort hill we find among others the names of Richard Gridley and Edward Belcher. Part of Purchase street formerly was called by the name of the latter, and we have now in that quarter a Gridley lane.

These researches have informed us of the number and extent of most of the high ways, which existed at the period of twenty years after the settlement of the town. The first orders on record upon this subject were passed in October, 1636: we have given some extracts on page 83, and shall be the more copious here, to save the labour of future inquirers.

There was a high way, sometimes called the high street, laid out from the head of the dock to Mr. Colburn's field, a little south of Elliot street, and beyond that was the 'foot way unto Samuel Wilbour's field next Roxbury.' On the east side of this high way Essex street was laid out, but had no particular name: so was it with Bedford street, which was afterwards called Pond-street, with reference to the watering place to which it led. Summer street and High street had the name of Mill street or lane, because they led to the widow

Tuttle's mill. Milk-street was called the Fort street, it being the thorough fare from the high street to the works at Fort hill. State street is called the Water street in Mr. Wilson's deed. Court street as far as Market street had the name of Centry hill street. From the chapel burial ground north and from Market street west to the bottom of Sudbury street, the way was known as Sudbury street, doubtless in reference to the part of England from which many of the Boston people emigrated. In March 1640 it was ordered that the street from Mr. Hough's to the Centry hill should be kept open forever: this was School street and part of Beacon street. Winter, Boylston and Elliot streets were at that time lanes. The first has at some period borne the name of Blott's lane, from Robert Blott, the first proprietor of one of the eastern corners.

Hanover street north from the mill-creek, and also Marshall's lane, we think are described in the following provision: 1636, October. 'The streete waye from the gates next James Everill's, toward the Mylne, is to runne straight along in an even line to John Pemberton's house, and to rainge betweene Thomas Marshall's house and Serjeant Savage's, and to bee within the street betweene payle and payle on each side, two poles broad.*

'A layne to goe from cove to cove, between Thomas Paynter and Thomas Marshall's, one pole and a half between payle and payle.'

We can trace nothing of Hanover street farther north: in a deed from Thomas Clarke of Dorchester, merchant, to Christopher Stanley we find something like the original of Fleet and Tileston st. though it surprises us to see one of them 'thirty six foote broad unto the lowermost highway and from thence to low water marke thirty foote,' whereas the other 'going towards *the mill hill,*' was only twelve foote. This lowermost highway was Ann Street 'upon the sea bank,' and before Walter Merry's at the North battery it was 16 ft. broad. It followed the shore, as we have supposed, to the mill creek inlet, and was completed in the following order.

'The land at the head of the cove, round about by John Glover's, Geo. Burden's, Hugh Gunnison's, Capt. W. Tyng's, Wm. Franklin's, Robert Nash's and eight foot to eastward of it, is high way—as also from the eastward side of the 8 feet, and round about by the corner of Edw. Bendall's brick house, and so by S. Cole's house, as also to E. Tyng's wharf

---

* 1635. Dec. 4. *Ordered,* a fence to be made between the two necks.

shall go a high way of twenty foot.'* Here E. Tyng had a house, yard, warehouse and brew-house.

There was also a passage way of seven foot, up from the creek near Bendall's to the lower part of Mr. Keayne's garden at his mud-wall house, in 1639, which probably answers to Wilson's lane or Exchange street. And there was a lane by the old meeting house : Henry Webb, a merchant who lived at the corner had the market place north, and on the east the old meeting house and the lane, which terminated at the Springate or high way by the spring.

CHAPTER XXI.

" Full were our cities with the sons of art,
And trade and joy in every busy street
Mingling were heard."

'STRAITS and difficulties,' says Hutchinson, 'at the beginning of the colony had produced industry and good husbandry, and then they soon raised provisions enough for their own support, and an overplus for exportation. We hear but little of trade for the first seven years, except a small traffick with the natives, by barter of toys, and the few utensils, tools and clothing they at first thought necessary, in exchange for furs and skins. What the planters brought with them consisted principally of materials for their buildings, necessary tools for their husbandry, stock for their farms, and clothing for themselves and families; and those who had more estate than was sufficient for these purposes, were country gentlemen, unacquainted with commerce, and never employed themselves in it. People in general turned their minds to provide comfortable lodgings, and to bring under improvement so much land as would afford them necessary support, and this was enough to employ them. After a few years, by hard labour, and hard fare, the land produced more than was consumed by the inhabitants ; the overplus was sent abroad to the West-Indies, the Wine-Islands, and other places. Returns were made in the produce of the respective countries, and in bullion, the most of which, together with the furs produced from the natives, went to England,

---

* Town Records, Feb. 1649. The precise location of Glover, &c. is less certain than that of almost any other persons, whose names occur to us. We conclude they were situated along Union street and Dock square, and accordingly have ventured to express ourselves thus in defining the extent of the dock.

to pay for the manufactures continually necessary from
thence. As hands could be spared from husbandry and labour in providing their houses, they were taken off, and some
employed in sawing boards, splitting staves, shingles and
hoops, others in the fishery, and as many as were capable of
it, in building small vessels for the fishery, and for coasting
and foreign trade. Thus gradually and insensibly they seem
to have fallen into that trade most natural to the country, and
adapted to their peculiar circumstances, without any premeditated scheme, or projection for that purpose. Their primary views in their removal, were the enjoyment of civil and
religious liberty. Merchants and others, for the sake of gain,
when they saw a prospect of it, afterwards came over, and incorporated with them, and caused a great increase of commerce, and led the legislators to measures for the further improvement of it. For encouraging the fishery, an act was
made in 1639 to free all estates, employed in catching, making
or transporting fish, from all duties and public taxes, and all
persons were restrained by a penalty from using any cod or
bass fish, for manuring the ground ; and all fishermen during
the season for business, and all ship-builders, were by the
same act excused from trainings.

  ' In the year 1642 the House of Commons passed a memora-
rable resolve in favour of the Massachusetts colony, containing this ordinance : " that all merchandizing goods, that by
any person or persons whatsoever, merchant or other, shall
be exported out of this kingdom of England into New-England
to be spent, used or employed there, or being of the growth
of those colonies, shall be from thence imported hither or
shall be laden or put on board any ship or vessel for necessaries in passing to and fro, and all and every the owner or
owners thereof *shall be freed and discharged of and from paying
and yielding any custom, subsidy, taxation or other duty, either
inward or outward*." It had, however, this proviso, " until
the House of Commons shall take further order therein to
the contrary." '

  Johnson's account of the extent of our commerce and its
beneficial effects is too lively to be omitted. ' Those,' says he,
' who were formerly forced to fetch most of the bread they eat
and beer they drank a thousand leagues by sea, are through the
blessing of the Lord so encreased, that they have not only
fed their elder sisters, Virginia, Barbadoes and many of the
Summer islands, that were preferred before [them] for fruitful-
ness, but also the grand mother of us all, even the fertile isle
of Great Britain. Beside, Portugal hath had many a mouth-
ful of bread and fish from us, in exchange of their Madeira
liquor, and also Spain ; nor could it be imagined that this wilderness should turn a mart for merchants in so short a space.

' Many a fair ship had her framing and finishing here, besides lesser vessels, barques and ketches. Many a master, beside common seamen, had their first learning in this colony. Boston, Charlestown, Salem and Ipswich, our maritan towns, began to increase roundly ; especially Boston, the which of a poor country village, in twice seven years is become like unto *a small city* and is in election to become a mayor town suddenly, chiefly increased by trade by sea.

' All other trades have here fallen into their ranks and places, to their great advantage ; especially Coopers and Shoemakers, who had either of them a Corporation granted, enriching themselves by their trades very much, Coopers having their plenty of stuff at a cheap rate and by reason of trade with foreign parts abundance of work. As for Tanners and Shoemakers, it being naturalized into these occupations, to have a higher reach in managing their manufactures, then other men in N. E. having not changed their nature in this, between them both they have kept men to their stander hitherto, almost doubling the price of their commodities, according to the rate they were sold for in England, and yet the plenty of Leather is beyond what they had there, counting the number of the people, but the transportation of Boots and Shoes into foreign parts hath vented all however : as for Tailors, they have not come behind the former, their advantage being in the nurture of new-fashions, all one with England ; Carpenters, Joiners, Glaziers, Painters, follow their trades only ; Gun-smiths, Lock-smiths, Blacksmiths, Nailors, Cutlers, have left the husbandmen to follow the plough and cart, and they their trades ; Weavers, Brewers, Costermongers, Feltmakers, Braziers, Pewterers and Tinkers, Ropemakers, Masons, Lime, Brick, and Tilemakers, Cardmakers, to work and not to play, Turners, Pumpmakers, and Wheelers, Glovers, Feltmongers, and Furriers, are orderly turned to their trades, besides divers sorts of Shopkeepers, and some who have a mystery beyond others, as have the Vintners.'

It would be wrong to pass unnoticed the exertions of Hugh Peters towards exciting a commercial spirit. ' He went from place to place, labouring both publickly and privately to raise up men to a publick frame of spirit,' and induce them to engage in the fishing business and foreign commerce.* It was to his influence that Salem owed her first glory, and his counsel advanced her to that rank in commerce which enabled her to dispute preeminence with Boston when local advantages gave superiority to the latter.

The first page of the record September 1, 1634, speaks of ' a common landing place between the creeks' and contains an

---

* *Winthrop,* Nov. 1635. May 1686. Mass. H. C. 1. vi. 259.

order for keeping the same clear of all annoyances.* The numerous shipping which visited Boston from Holland, France,
Spain and Portugal, according to Johnson, early required the
erection of wharves for their accommodation.   It appears by
the records of Jan. 1639, that some important undertaking of
this kind had been commenced prior to that time, in which the
town felt considerable interest : for on the 21st of that month
'there is granted to the overseers of the wharfes and crane an
hundred acres of land at Mt. Wolaston next to the allottment
already granted, towards the repairing and maintaining of the
said wharfs and crane.'   Other wharves are mentioned in
1641 ; particularly, Nov. 29th, Valentine Hill and associates
are authorized and agree to build certain wharves, and keep
them in repair, on condition that for every hundred pounds
thus laid out within five years, they are to have the improvement nine years thereafter, and to receive tonnage and wharf-
age.   There are no traces by which we can ascertain where
the two first of these wharves were situated, or whether the
last was not a continuation of the same.   This cost per account £818. 13s. 4d. and the company was granted four score
years to possess and improve.

   There is no doubt that this improvement embraced some of
the wharves between the Town dock and Long wharf.   At
the expiration of the term specified in the contract the wharf
and buildings thereon were to revert to the town and all be
left in good repair.   It is apparent from this circumstance
that the town claimed the right of ownership in the marsh or
dock : the same thing is inferrible from the fact that individuals desiring to wharf before their lots were obliged to ask liberty of the town, and in granting that, the town reserved the
right to inhabitants of coming to and going from such wharves
free of charge, on their own accounts ; but no man was allowed to sail for hire from another man's wharf.   Numerous
grants of this nature were made almost every year from this
time till 1673, when the great work of constructing what has
since been called the *Old Wharf* was accomplished.

   The origin of the mill creek is to be traced in the following
record.   July 31, 1643.   There is granted unto Henry Simons, G. Burden, John Button, John Hill and their partners
all that cove (already bounded) on the N. W. side of the
causey leading toward Charleston, with all the salt marish
bordering thereupon, round about, not formerly granted to
any other, reserving liberty from time to time to make use of
any part thereof for repairing the said causey, to have and
enjoy the said cove and marsh to them and their heirs and
assigns for ever.

* *Shaw*, 72.

2. The said grant is for this intent and upon this condition; that the said grantees shall within the space of three years erect and make upon or near the premises one or more corn mills and maintain the same forever.

3. Provides for a flood gate.

4. Appropriates 300 acres of land at Braintree for the use and encouragement of the said mills.

5. That if they shall carry their mill stream through the marsh on the northeast end of Goodman Low's* house, they have 60 feet in breadth throughout the said marsh granted unto them.

6. They shall have liberty *to dig one or more trenches in the highways* or waste grounds, so as they make and maintain sufficient passable and safe ways over the same for horse and cart.

7. The town will not allow any other common mill to be erected, except the necessary occasion of the town require it.

8. The selectmen shall procure what free help they can, by persuasion, upon any pressing occasion of use of many hands, about making the banks or trenches etc. for the better furtherance of the work to be speedily effected.

The grantees proceeded to carry into execution their part of this project. We sometimes find the trench which was thus formed called the ditch: but it soon acquired in deeds the name of Mill creek which it still retains. The causey mentioned was not what has in late years been known as such, but the one alluded to, page 111, and in the following record.

1640, March 30. C. Stanley shall have all the marsh on the east side of the way toward Charlestown ferry for £1. 10. reserving eight feet in breadth all along the side of the ditch by the said high way: and *the swamp* compassed by his upland for 6s. 8d. being about half an acre.† The same is also mentioned in 1655. Oct 29. Respecting the great causeway we are not able as yet to say any thing more than we find in Shaw, ' that the Indians had a foot path over the highest part of the marsh or flats, which was raised and widened by a Mr. Crabtree to retain the water of the pond.' There was such a man and he was by trade a joiner.

In process of time mills for various purposes were erected at three places on the margin of the pond thus formed. One at the west end of the creek, which was called the South mills; others at the north-east end of the causeway called

---

* Goodman Low's marsh was at the extremity of the triangle.

† The same paragraph provides that there shall be a high way reserved through the mill-field, *two rods* in breadth, from the W. corner of M. Chaffith's garden unto the little house by the said swamp, and from thence to the wind mill *as directly as the land will bear.*

the North mills and the Chocolate mills, and another at the
south-west end of the causeway.   This however did not take
place seasonably to prevent the erection of a mill at Fox-hill in
1649, at which time there was also one at Fort hill and another in the new field.   There was a watermill previously at
Mt. Wolaston, in 1639 : the " first in the colony " was erected
at Dorchester, on Neponset river in the year 1633.   The
creek very soon became a sort of boundary (which has continued to this day) between the north and south parts of the
town, and we find it so recognised in the appointment of two
superintendants of streets in 1651, of whom one was ' for the
Northend and one for the Southend, *the mill creek to be the
division.*'
     The Northend people seem to have undertaken at their
own expence the construction of the north battery.   The affair with Captain Stagg had made the Bostonians a little jealous of the armed vessels which visited their port, and they
had been at great cost to put the castle and Fort hill in a
state of defence.   Another difficulty of a similar nature occurred in 1644 with one Capt. Richardson, who undertook to
make seizure of a Dartmouth ship that lay in the harbour, but
which the authorities here had determined to seize themselves, by way of reprisal for a Boston ship that had been
taken in Wales by the king's party.   Officers were put on
board the vessel, and Capt. R. was warned to desist; this he
either could not or would not do ; his men boarded the vessel
and the captain of her was made prisoner.   The Governour
hereupon ordered Capt. R. to come on shore to account for
his conduct.   His men were so unruly that he feared to leave
them, and he declined obeying the command.   Upon this a
warning piece was fired at him from the battery, which cut a
rope in the head of his ship: one of his men was about to return the fire but was providentially prevented.   A stranger
who was in the battery fired another gun, without orders,
which however did no damage, except a slight injury to the
prize ship in question.   Forty men were then sent aboard
and took possession of her, and Capt. Richardson came ashore
and acknowledged his errour and his sorrow for what he had
done.   ' So we ordered him to pay a barrel of powder, and
to satisfy the officers and soldiers we had employed and
other expenses, and dismissed him.'   The reason of their being so easy with him was that ' there was no hurt done, nor
had he made one shot; for if he had, we were resolved to
have taken or sunk him, which we might easily have done,
lying close under our battery so as we could have played

---

* Mass. H. C. 1. ix. 164.   Town Records, Jan. 1651.   † *Winthrop*, Sept. 1644.

upon him, with whole culverin or demi-culverin, six hours together.'

It is not improbable that such occurrences as these led the north-end people to think it prudent to have a suitable work of defence, for the protection of their part of the town from insolent aggressions. Accordingly, preparations were made for fortifying somewhere about Walter Merry's point. It was the point now known by the name of Battery or North Battery wharf. The position was well selected, commanding the entrance of the harbour, and the river also, as high up as vessels of large size would have been likely to venture. The work was completed in the course of the year 1646, when we have the following record concerning it :

' Proposicions presented to the townsmen, on the behalfe of the inhabitants of the north end of the towne of Boston, the ratification whereof is desired, and the registeringe of them in the towne records,

' 1. That we of this end of the towne, whose harts the Lord hath made willing to set about erecting and maintenance of a fortification att Walter Merry's point, may for the future bee freed from all rates and assessments to what other fortifications bee in the towne, until such time as the other part of the towne, not joyning with us herein, shall have disbursed, and layd out in equall proporcion of their estates with ours, as by trew account may appeare.

' 2. That the land gained at the towne's charge, and stacked out to the towne's service by those deputed for that end, to the raysinge of a work upon, may not by any to their private occations, be imployed or made use of ; as that the ground nor flatts, before the sayd worke may not be disposed of by the towne unto any particular man's imployment, to the prejudice of the said worke.'

It is easy to imagine what must have been the spirit of the times, when so great a work was undertaken in such a way : it evinced a growing readiness in the people to maintain their rights with their lives, their fortunes and their sacred honour. Johnson's account of the castle affords us a pleasant view of this subject. 'To say right,' (says he, b. ii. ch. xxvi.) ' some particular persons may be penurious in laying out their estates upon ammunition, but the general of Officers and souldiers are very generous that way : the reverend Doctor Wilson gave bountifully for the furthering this Wilderness-work, the which was expended upon great Artillery, his gift being a thousand pound ; beside many persons that came over, the Lord was pleased to indow with a large portion of the things of this life, who were not backward liberally to dispose of it, to procure means of defence. And to that end there was a castle built on an Island, upon the passage into the Mattachu-

Bay, wholly built at first by the country in general, but by reason the country affords no Lime, but what is burnt of Oyster-shels, it fell to decay in a few years after, which made many of the Towns that lay out of the defence thereof to desert it, although their safety (under God) was much involved in the constant repair and well-mannaging thereof; hereupon the next six Towns take upon them to rebuild it at their proper cost and charges, the rest of the country upon the finishing thereof gave them a small matter toward it; upon this there was a Captain ordained, and put in possession thereof by the country, having a yearly Stipend allowed him for himself and his souldiers, which he is to keep in a constant readiness upon the Island, being about eight acres of ground.

' The Castle is built on the North-East of the Island, upon a rising hill, very advantageous to make many shot at such ships as shall offer to enter the Harbor without their good leave and liking; the Commander of it is one Captain Davenport, a man approved for his faithfulness, courage and skill, the Master Canoneer is an active Ingineer; also this Castle hath cost about four thousand pounds, yet are not this poor pilgrim people weary of maintaining it in good repair; it is of very good use to awe any insolent persons, that putting confidence in their ship and sails, shall offer any injury to the people, or contemn their Government, and they have certain signals of alarums, which suddenly spread through the whole country.'

CHAPTER XXII.

―――― It being as unnatural for a right N. E. man
to live without an able Ministery, as for a Smith to worke his iron without a Fire.
W. W. P.

It has been so often repeated that it is now generally believed the north part of the town was at that period the most populous. We are convinced that the idea is erroneous. We have reason to suppose that almost every householder in Boston was a member of the first church, and it appears there had been admitted only 306 men, down to the latter end of 1652. Of these we know some had died and others removed. The book of possessions records the estates of about 250, the number of their houses, barns, gardens, and sometimes the measurement of their lands. It seems to embrace the period from 1640 to 1650, and we conclude, gives us the names of almost, if not quite, all the freemen of Boston. They were settled through the whole length of the main street on both sides, from Elliot-street to the market, excepting only the small green near the Old South. The cross streets on either side were all occupied : Elm-street, the upper part of Hanover-street, Sudbury-street, and Green-street on the north side, were all appropriated for house lots. It is evident too, that the most wealthy and influential characters lived in what is now the centre of the town. We discover only about thirty names of residents north of the creek. Among them were Copp, *Goodwin*, Shoare, *Sweet*, Seaberry, Bourne, *Clark*, *Joy*, Rawlins, Cullimer, *Merry*. Passmer, *F. Hudson*, Chaffie (a shipwright,) Gallop, Meekins, Millam, John Hill, *Bennett*, *Phillips*, *Gibson*, *Jones:* some others were owners of field lots : C. Stanley owned fifteen acres.*

It is probable, however, that an increase of business began to be perceived at the north end about this time, and that removals began to be made into it, which resulted in its becoming ' for many years the most populous and elegant part of the town.' For we find that when another meeting house was judged necessary, to accommodate the population, it was deemed expedient to place it in that quarter. This was done in 1649, when the house was erected at the head of the North Square. A church was gathered there on the fifth day of June the next year, and consisted at first of seven members. Their names were Michael Powell, James Ashwood, Christopher Gibson, John Phillips, George Davis, Michael Wills, John Farnam. A sermon was preached on the occasion, by Samuel Mather, a graduate of Harvard College. He was earnestly solicited to remain as pastor of the new church, but declined the invitation.†

---

* The 306, mentioned in this paragraph, joined after Mr. Cotton's arrival : 130 had joined before that : the removals carried away very many to Charlestown, Rhode Island, Exeter, the Somers Islands, besides those who were settled at Braintree, Romney Marsh and Muddy river, and others who had returned to England.

† *Rev. Mr. Ware's* Historical Discourses.

Covenant of the Old North Church.

We whose names are hereunto subscribed, being called of God to enter into church fellowship, knowing and considering our own great unworthiness and unfitness for so near approaches to so holy a God, and how apt we are to start aside from him and from the rules of his gospel and government over us, we therefore desire to lament as in his sight the inconstancy of our own spirits with him and our former neglects of him, and pollutions of his house and holy things by our personal corruptions and unworthy walkings : and do beseech him for his name's sake to prevent us with mercy, and accept us under the wings of his own everlasting covenant.

And in dependance upon his free grace therein, in his name and strength we freely this day, in the presence of the everliving God, do avouch the Lord to be our God, and ourselves to be his people, and so yield up ourselves to him by an holy covenant of faith and love and

17

This event brings us near to the time when Johnson sketched his description of Boston, which was ready for publication in 1651. We present the twentieth chapter of his first
book, without variation, that our readers may have one specimen of the manner in which the work was executed.

JOHNSON'S DESCRIPTION.

' After some little space of time the Church of Christ at
Charles Towne, having their Sabbath assemblies oftenest on
the South side of the River, agreed to leave the people on
that side to themselves, and to provide another Pastor for
Charles Towne, which accordingly they did. So that the
fourth Church of Christ issued out of Charles Towne, and
was seated at Boston, being the Center Towne and Metropolis of this Wildernesse worke (but you must not imagine it to
be a Metropolitan Church) invironed it is with Brinish flouds,
saving one small Istmos, which gives free accesse to the Neighbour Townes ; by Land on the South side, on the North-west,
and North East,* two constant Faires are kept for daily
traffique thereunto, the forme of this Towne is like a heart,
naturally scituated for Fortifications, having two Hills on the
frontice part thereof next the Sea, the one well fortified on
the superfices thereof, with store of great Artillery well mounted, the other hath a very strong battery built of whole Timber, and filled with Earth, at the descent of the Hill in the
extreme poynt thereof betwixt these two strong armes lies
a large Cove or Bay, on which the chiefest part of this Town
is built, over-topped with a third Hill, all three like over-top-
ping Towers keepe a constant watch to fore-see the approach
of forrein dangers, being furnished with a Beacon and lowd
babbling Guns, to give notice by their redoubled eccho to all
their Sister-townes, the chief Edifice of this City-like Towne
it crowded on the Sea-bankes, and wharfed out with great industry and cost, the buildings beautifull and large, some fairely

---

loyalty, to cleave to him and to one another in him, to cleave to God in Christ as our sovereign good, and to the Lord Jesus Christ as the only mediator and surety of the covenant,
as our only high priest and atonement to satisfy for us and to save us, and as our only
prophet to guide and teach us, and as our only king and lawgiver to reign over us : as
also to attend upon him and the service of his holy will, by walking together as a congregation and church of Christ in all the ways of his worship and of mutual love and special
watchfulness one over another, according to his will which is revealed to us by his word ;
subjecting ourselves in the Lord to all his holy administrations in his church, beseeching
him to own us for his people, and to delight to dwell in the midst of us, that his kingdom
and grace may be advanced by us.

Which sacred covenant that we may observe and all the branches of it inviolate forever
we desire to deny ourselves, and to depend alone upon the promise of his spirit and grace,
and upon the merits and mercies of the Lord Jesus Christ for assistance and for acceptance,
for healing and forgiving mercy for his own sake.

* [There is access by ferries, from Charlestown and Winnesimet?]

set forth with Brick, Tile, Stone Slate, and orderly placed with comly streets, whose continuall inlargement presages some sumptuous City. The wonder of this modern Age, that a few yeares should bring forth such great matters by so meane a handfull, and they so far from being inriched by the spoiles of other Nations, that the states of many of them have been spoiled by the Lordly Prelacy, whose Lands must assuredly make Restitutions. But now behold the admirable Acts of Christ, at this his peoples landing, the hideous Thickets in this place were such, that the Wolfes and Beares nurst up their young from the eyes of all beholders, in those very places where the streets are full of Girles and Boys sporting up and downe, with a continued concourse of people. Good store of Shipping is here yearly built, and some very faire ones : both Tar and Mastes the Countrey affords from its own soile ; also store of Victuall both for their own and Forreiners-ships, who resort hither for that end : this Town is the very Mart of the Land, French, Portugalls and Dutch, come hither for traffique.'

Respecting the second church, which he makes the thirtieth in the colony, he says (Book iii. ch. 7.) ' the north-east part of the town being separated from the other with a narrow stream cut through a neck of land by industry, whereby that part is become an island, it was thought meet that the people inhabiting the same should gather into a church body, and build a meeting-house for their assembly, the which they have already done, but not as yet called any one to office.'

Several of the distinguished ministers of that period, who were officers in other churches, but likely to remove from their places, were invited unsuccessfully to take charge of this congregation. For a few years, therefore, one of the brethren, Michael Powell, conducted the worship, and to such satisfaction that he would have been ordained teacher, had it not been for the interference of the General Court, who ' would not suffer one that was illiterate, as to academical education, to be called to the teaching office in such a place as Boston.' There was a law in existence that no minister should be called into office, in any church in this jurisdiction, without the approbation and allowance of some of the magistrates. Mr. Powell was a man of sense and good character ; the objection to him was not that he was a layman, but that he was wanting in learning, and they would not suffer him to be a publick teacher, lest occasion should be given to introduce such more generally, if allowed in a particular instance. The court recommended Mr. Reyner from Plymouth.

After four years passed in this condition, Mr. John Mayo, who on account of some difficulties and discouragements had left his people at Nosset, (Eastham?) was called to the pastoral

office here, and ordained the 9th of November, 1655. At the
same time, Mr. Powell was ordained as ruling elder of the
church. Mr. M. administered the seals, and Mr. P. continued to preach publickly in a constant way.

We are told that 'the gathering of this church was evidently
very much to the disadvantage of Mr. Cotton, in many of his
interests; but he was a JOHN, who reckoned his joy fulfilled
if in his own decrease he could see the interests of his Master
advance; and therefore, with exemplary self-denial, he encouraged its foundation :' he had not the happiness, however,
to live to see it established under any other instructions than
those of Mr. Powell.

CHAPTER XXIII.

> —— "his reverend lockes
> In comelye curles did wave,
> And on his aged temples grewe
> The blossomes of the grave."

THE death of Mr. Cotton took place towards the close of the
year 1652. In the course of the fall, he had been urgently
desired to visit the college at Cambridge and preach a sermon
to the students. He was exposed to the wet, in his passage
across the ferry for that purpose, and took cold, which was
followed with an inflammation of the lungs, attended with
asthmatick affections and other symptoms of alarming character. He preached occasionally afterwards, and his last sermon was on the Lord's day Nov. 21, from John i. 14. *We
beheld his glory, the glory as of the only begotten of the Father.*
His impressions of his near approach to the grave were so
strong, that at the preceding Thursday lecture he had hastened to close his exposition of the second of Timothy, and dwelt
with increased emphasis on the last words, GRACE BE WITH YOU
ALL : thus, as it were, he bade his people farewell, and his
appearance on this sabbath was both to him and to them, like
a visit from the unseen world. He spent the succeeding day
in private devotion, and on quitting his study at night, said to
his wife, I shall go into that room no more!—The event proved the correctness of his forebodings: from that time he went
no more out.

While he thus lay sick, the magistrates, and the ministers
of the country, and christians of all ranks, resorted to him
as to a publick father, full of sad apprehensions for the loss

they were about to sustain. A short time before his death he desired to be left alone, that he might fix his thoughts, without interruption, on his great and last change. So, lying speechless a few hours, he expired about noon, on Thursday the 23d of December, having just completed his sixty-seventh year.*

Strange and alarming signs appeared in the heavens, while his body lay, according to the custom of the times, till the Tuesday following, ' when it was most honourably interred, with a most numerous concourse of people, and the most grievous and solemn funeral, that was ever known, perhaps, upon the American strand ; and the lectures in his church, the whole winter, were but so many funeral sermons upon the death and worth of this extraordinary person.'

Mr. Cotton's memory did not receive so much attention from his cotemporaries without his well deserving it : for in the language of the ' *Old Men's Tears*' he was in his life, light and learning, the brightest and most shining star in their firmament. He was born at Derby, December 4, 1585. His father, Mr. Roland Cotton, was a lawyer, a man of piety and respectability, and his mother a pious woman. Without a great property to encourage them, they resolved on giving their son a learned as well as religious education. He was accordingly qualified for the university, and at the age of thirteen was admitted into Trinity college, Cambridge. His proficiency in his studies excited admiration, and procured him an invitation to Emmanuel college, where he was soon elected to a fellowship, and afterwards became head-lecturer, dean, and catechist. He acquired so exact a knowledge of the Hebrew as to be able to converse in it, was perfectly familiar with the Greek, and wrote the Latin language with Ciceronian elegance.

In his twenty-eighth year he removed from Cambridge and settled at Boston in Lincolnshire. There his labours and his usefulness were immense, and he was exceedingly beloved by the best, and reverenced by the worst of his hearers. Through all the times of trouble, which visited the non-conformists, he was maintained in his place by the unanimity of his people. But after the government of the church fell into the hands of Bishop Laud, divisions arose among the parishioners of Mr. Cotton. An information was lodged against him, (by a dissolute fellow, who thought in that way to revenge himself on some of Mr. C's friends, for a restraint they had put upon him,) and being cited to appear before the high-commission court, he thought it more prudent to flee his country, than to expose himself to perpetual imprisonment. He was

---

* Magnalia, *Emerson.* The town Register of deaths says 15th Dec. 1652,

hesitating whether to choose Holland, Barbadoes or New-England for the place of his retreat, when his mind was determined by letters received from Gov. Winthrop, inviting him in the name of the church to come to Boston. He arrived here in 1633, which was the forty-eighth year of his age, and immediately commenced the career of usefulness, which ended only with his life. Nineteen years and odd months he spent in this place, doing good publickly and privately to all sorts of men.

Mr. Cotton's personal appearance was strikingly impressive. His complexion was clear and fair, and his countenance florid : in size he was rather short and inclining to corpulent, but in the whole of an agreeable mediocrity. In his youth, his hair was brown, but as he advanced in life it became as white as the driven snow. The colour of his eye his ' prosopographer' omitted ; but we know its glance flashed the keenest rebuke on every appearance of evil, and smiled the heartiest approbation on every worthy action. He had a clear, neat and audible voice, which easily filled the largest halls. His delivery was not noisy and thundering, yet it had in it a very awful majesty, set off with a natural and becoming motion of his right hand. His style of preaching was plain, designed to be understood by the meanest capacity, while his more discerning hearers could perceive from it that he was a man of more than ordinary abilities and research.

He generally devoted twelve hours in a day to his studies, and composed his written sermons with great care, though he sometimes preached without any preparation. It was his practice to expound, both from the old and new testaments, in course, and to draw from each subject a series of ' doctrines and uses.' In this manner he went through the whole bible once, and had proceeded some ways a second time, when he was cut off by the hand of death.

The political and religious opinions of so influential a personage were matters of importance to the infant plantation. The scope of both may be gleaned from his writings, and they are substantially apparent in many of our customs and laws at the present day. The Magnalia tells us that upon Mr. Cotton's arrival, the points of church order were revived with more of exactness, and received by the churches already formed, and the same were adopted by such as rose afterwards.

' It was an uncommonly interesting epoch to the Boston church. A fraternity was to be formed of discordant materials. Many of those who composed the church had been educated Episcopalians, and were therefore disinclined to vary from established forms. Others had come to New-England rather as adventurers than as christians, and could hardly be subjected to any ecclesiastical or political rules. But the sagacity and ever-watchful discipline of Mr. Cotton was astonishingly efficacious towards conforming all descriptions of characters to habits of obedience and order.'

He prepared a book which was published in 1644 with the title of *The keys of the kingdom of heaven,* in which the principles of Congregational church government are explained and defended. This work was long a standard reference and guide to the New England congregationalists.

On doctrinal points Mr. C. was a calvinist. He used to say to his private friends, that he knew of no difficult place in the bible which he had not studied somewhat to satisfaction, and that he always loved to sweeten his mouth with a piece of Calvin before he went to sleep.

His political writings show him to have been friendly to an elective government, administered on the principles of the Mosaic laws. In a communication to Lord Say and Seal, in 1636, he expresses himself thus : ' Democracy I do not conceive that ever God did ordain as a fit government, either for church or commonwealth. As for monarchy and aristocracy, they are both of them clearly approved and directed in Scripture, yet so as referreth the sovereignty to himself, and setteth up theocracy in both.' But he says in another place, ' the authority of the father is no where communicated with his honours to all his posterity : if God should not delight to furnish some of them with gifts for magistracy, we should expose them rather to reproach and prejudice, and the commonwealth with them, if we should call them forth to publick authority.'

One instance of Mr. Cotton's conduct in a political affair is worthy to be repeated. ' It was moved in caucus by a man of some influence, that two of their deputies of long standing, who had fallen into low circumstances should be dropped from office. Mr. C. hearing of the project, took occasion on the next lecture day, pointedly, though prudently, to condemn it. He taught that if old and faithful officers had grown poor in the publick service, they should be maintained at the publick expense. The reproof was clearly understood, and pungently felt : for the motion was never renewed.'

Mr. C.'s private virtues and domestick life were equally exemplary. His control over his own passions was almost perfect, and his family government was strict, while his corrections were cool and deliberate. He was liberal of his own property, and, when the necessities of any required his exertions, would apply to the hearts of others for their assistance. On one occasion he thus collected £200 from the members of his own church, for the relief of a persecuted minister and his people. He lost his first wife a few years before his removal to this country. His second, whose name was Sarah,

accompanied him to Boston. They had three sons and three
daughters. The oldest daughter and the youngest son died
during their father's lifetime, both of them near together, of
the small-pox, which was then (1649) for the first time raging
in Boston. Of the other four, the elder daughter (and her
only child) died within a few years : the youngest became
the wife of Increase Mather : Seaborn, the elder son, was settled in Hampton, and John, the younger, in Plymouth, both
ministers of the gospel.

Mr. Cotton left a will, in which he provided, that on certain contingencies the one half of his estate should revert to
Harvard College and the other half to the support of the
free school in Boston. Those contingencies never happened.
He gave the church a piece of silver plate to be used in communion service, which may have been the first they had, for
at one time they made use of wooden chalices.

Others of the first settlers were about this time paying the
debt of nature. Capt. Stanley is mentioned in April, 1649,
as having left a lot of land in his will to the school's use.
The widow Mary Hudson bequeathed ten pounds to the same
purpose. William Paddy left something to the town in 1658,
and Mr. Henry Webb in 1660 demised £100 to be appropriated either for the use of the school, or the building some neat
house for the relief of the poor, or supplying them with needful articles, as the selectmen might deem best. Capt. Keayne
died on the 23d of March, 1656 : he also remembered Boston
in his will. This unparalleled document occupies 157 folio
pages of the Probate records, and besides providing handsomely for his relatives and his idol, the Great Artillery, for
Harvard college, and his revered pastor and teacher, and the
poor of the church, he bequeaths to the town about £500 worth
towards the erection of a market place and town house, and
granary for the benefit of the poor, a conduit for security
against fire, and the foundation of a library, and £50 for the
free school ; appropriating a portion withal for his own decent
and civil burial, which he desired might be performed in a
military way. His whole estate which he enjoined should be
appraised at its fair value, not at half price as the custom of
some *was*, amounted to £2843 19*s*. 3*d*. The estate of Wm.
Tyng who died about the same time was valued at £2774 14*s*.
4*d*. each about 15000 dollars. The amount of Mr. Cotton's
inventory was £1038 4*s*. We add a fac simile of his writing.

CHAPTER XXIV.

"I'll tear her to pieces!
And dissecting her heart, find the witchery there."

ACCORDING to usage formally established, by a vote in 1646, appointing eight o'clock A. M. 'of the second second day of the first month, in every year,' as the time to meet for the choice of town officers, the inhabitants assembled in general meeting on Monday the fourteenth of March, 1653, when the town government was organized as follows:

Deputies to General Court.

Capts. John Leverett,
Thos. Clarke.

Selectmen.

Ensigns Edw. Hutchinson,
Jere. Houchin,
Messrs. Wm. Brenton,
Sam. Cole,
Cornet Peter Oliver,
James Oliver,
Thos. Marshall.

Commissioner to carry in votes for Magistrates.

Mr. Nath. Duncan.

Constables for town.

Mr. Joseph Rock,
Henry Bridgham,
Barth. Chevers,
Wm. Wenborn.

For Romney Marsh.

John Doolittle.

For Muddy River.

Peter Aspenwal.

Clerks of the Market.

Thomas Buttalls,
Corporal Henry Pounding.

Sealers of Leather.

Wm. Courser,
Robert Reade.

Surveyors of high ways.

Matthew Barnes,
Richard Bennet,
Thos. Wiburne,
James Pemert [?] at
Rom. M.

Packers of flesh and fish.

Serjeant John Barrell,
Wm. Dinsdale.
and
Isaac Collimor
{ is chosen to look to carriages and wheels of the Great Artillery and to be paid by the Selectmen.

These offices had been established from time to time as the exigencies of affairs demanded: usually there was some vote of the court sanctioning or recommending them, and conferring or limiting their powers.

In June, 1650, a petition had been presented from Boston, that they might become a corporation, which was granted, *provided* the articles and terms, privileges and immunities asked, may be such as rationally should appear, (respecting the mean

18

condition of the country) fit for the court to grant, and that they shall be ready for examination at the next session of the court. The records of that session show nothing that was done upon the subject. Suits at law, however, grew more frequent, and many crimes were committed especially in the town of Boston, by reason of the great concourse of people and the increase of trade.*   On this account,

'At a sessions of the general court in October, 1651, an act or order was passed, empowering the town of Boston to choose seven commissioners, to be presented to the court of assistants ; and, being authorized by them and sworn before them, or before the governour, they or any five of them, or any three together with one magistrate, might hear and determine all civil actions not exceeding ten pounds in value, and all criminal actions where the penalty or fine should not exceed forty shillings, the parties being such as were inhabitants of Boston neck or Noddle's island, or such as did not belong to the jurisdiction ; and the county court was not to take cognizance of any such actions. This law was made for one year for trial.'

The commissoners were authorised to appoint their own clerk, and ordered to keep a book of records for the entry of all causes, evidences and testimonies, sentences and judgments *as the law provided in like cases.*

At the second election under this order in October, 1652, Messrs. John Leverett, Nathaniel Duncan, Anthony Stoddard, William and Edward Tyng, T. Savage and T. Clark were chosen for the year ensuing. The first five had served the year before. These gentlemen, together with those in the foregoing list of town officers, probably comprised the most active and influential part of the citizens in the year 1653.

The duties of the Selectmen were very solemnly detailed in a power which was drawn up by a committee appointed for the purpose, in this form :

' 24, 1 mo. 1651.—Directions for the selectmen of Boston commended unto them from the town.

Having chosen you for orderinge of towne affaires, this year ensuing, though we doubt not to confide in your wisdom, fidelity, and care, in seeking and promoting the good and welfaire of the towne, yet according to court we commend unto you the instructions following.

First, in generall we require your special care that the good and wholesome orders already made, which you have the records of, be observed and duly executed, and what other acts and orders, shall be established for future benefit

---

* Colony records.

of the towne, that you allsoe cause them to be published and
put in execution, and further according to power given, and
several lawes of the country to be found in the book of printed lawes, under these titles, Townships, Ecclesiastick, Freemen, High-ways, small Causes, Indians, Corn-fields, Masters
and Servants, Pipe Staves, Swyne, Weights, Measures, and
any other order in force which concerne your place to regulate yourselves and carry on your worke, and where you finde
defect of power to bring your desires to a good issue for well
ordering the town, you may draw some good orders in forme
to be approved by the towne, and so to be presented to the
Generall Court, and our Deputyes for consideration.

Secondly, there are some particulars necessary to be considered of and ordered by you—as first about accepting and
entertaining new inhabitants into the towne and herein,

First, it is required that you make some effectuall orders,
with such penalty as you have powers to impose, that none
transplant themselves from other parts of the country to inhabit here without giving you notice thereof.

Secondly, to inquire of such as so present themselves for inhabitants, what calling or employment they will undertake,
and if they will live under other men's roofs as inmates, then
to deal with them, according to the order of such persons,
comprehended under the title of Towneshipes.

Thirdly, if such persons were poor and impotent, such as
had reliefe in the district whence they came, then to deal with
them according to the ordering of settling poore people under
that title of poor.'

These instructions were continued in force by an annual
vote of the people for many years.

Before the year 1637 the townsmen served without compensation, (as the fashion now is) and defrayed incidental expenses. In that year it was agreed that their charges at their
meetings be borne by the town in general. And in 1641 we
find a charge of two pounds eighteen shillings for a selectmen's dinner. The number of the Selectmen (who used to be
chosen twice a year,) varied in different years, from eleven to
seven, till 1647, after which seven continued for a long time to
be the number.

The year 1653 is rendered memorable by the first great fire.*
Neither the part of the town nor of the year in which it occurred, is precisely ascertained by us. We infer that it was near
Cornhill, from some expressions in Capt. Keayne's will, where
he recommends having a conduit, as ' a good help in danger of

---

* ' A most terrible fire happened iu Charlestown, in 1650, in the depth of winter, which
by a violent wind was blown from one house to another to the consuming of the fairest
houses in the town.' W. W. P. iii. 9.

'fire, the want of which we have found by sad and costly experience, not only in other parts of the town, where possibly
they have better supply of water, but in the heart of the town
about the market place—and many fair buildings there be
round about it.' We also date it before the 14th of March,
for on that day we find a body of regulations adopted for the
better preservation of the town from fire. Before this a man
was liable to 10s. fine, if he suffered his chimney to become
so foul as to take fire and blaze out at the top. Now every
house was to be provided with a ladder to reach to the ridge
thereof, and a pole about 12 feet long with a good large
swabb at the end of it, to reach to the roof of the house. Six
good and long ladders were to be furnished by the selectmen
and kept at the meeting houses, and four strong iron crooks
with chains and ropes fitted to them, and this crook fastened
on a good strong pole. No person was to recover damage for
his house, if pulled down to stop the progress of fire; but no
house should be so pulled down without the consent of the
major part of the magistrates, or commissioners and selectmen
present. No fire was to be allowed on board any vessel or
near any warehouse after nine o'clock. Bell men are appointed to go about during the night. Fire buckets are mentioned soon after, and the selectmen are authorized to agree
with Joseph Jenks for an engine to carry water in case of fire.
Chimney sweepers were also appointed 'with liberty to cry
about the streets, that they may be known:' Robert Wyatt
and William Lane had the honour to receive the first appointments. In these ordinances we trace the rudiments of our
present system for the management of fires.

The most remarkable occurrence in the colony in the year
1655 was the trial and condemnation of Mrs. Ann Hibbins of
Boston for witchcraft. Her husband, who died July 23, 1654,
was an agent for the colony in England, several years one of
the assistants, and a merchant of note in the town; but losses
in the latter part of his life had reduced his estate, and increased the natural crabbedness of his wife's temper, which
made her turbulent and quarrelsome, and brought her under
church censures, and at length rendered her so odious to her
neighbours as to cause some of them to acuse her of witchcraft. The jury brought her in guilty, but the magistrates
refused to accept the verdict; so the cause came to the general court, where the popular clamour prevailed against her,
and the miserable old lady was condemned and executed in
June 1656. Search was made upon her body for tetts, and
in her chests and boxes for puppets or images, but there is no
record of any thing of that sort being found. Mr. Beach, a
minister in Jamaica, in a letter to Dr. Increase Mather, says,
' You may remember what I have sometimes told you your

famous Mr. Norton once said at his own table, before Mr. Wilson the pastor, elder Penn and myself and wife, and others, who had the honour to be his guests:—That one of your magistrates' wives, as I remember, was hanged for a witch only for having more wit than her neighbours. It was his very expression ; she having, as he explained it, unhappily guessed that two of her persecutors, whom she saw talking in the street, were talking of her, which proving true, cost her her life, notwithstanding all he could do to the contrary, as he himself told us.'

This was the third instance of execution for witchcraft in New England. The first occurred in Connecticut : the second was the case of Margaret Jones of Charlestown, who was executed at Boston in June 1648. She was charged with possessing a malignant touch, which immediately infected with some violent ail, whoever came in contact with her. Had she lived in our day, she would only have been sent to Rainsford's island.

It is not strange that her husband should have been a suspicious character. After witnessing her tragical end, he very naturally desired to leave the scene of distress, and sought passage in a vessel bound to Barbadoes, which was for some cause denied him. The vessel lay in the river between Boston and Charlestown, and ' on a sudden she was seen to roll from side to side as if she would turn over.' She was of 300 tons, in light ballast, and had eighty horses on board. Poor Mr. Jones was accused as the probable cause of this accident, and warrant issued for his apprehension. The constable, as he crossed the ferry, had the prudence to present the warrant in view of the ship ; and the same instant she began to stop her motion and to swim upright, and as soon as Jones was safe lodged in prison, she never moved in that kind any more : so says ' history.'

We have the authority of Hutchinson to say, that about this time the scrupulosity of the good people of the colony was at its height. Soon after Mr. Winthrop's death, Mr. Endicott the most rigid of any of the magistrates, being governour, he joined with the other assistants in an association against the wearing of long hair, as a thing uncivil and unmanly, fit only for Russians and barbarous Indians. They had a law too against long boots, on account of the waste of leather, and a law against dancing on ordinary occasions. Some good men finding that laws were rather ineffectual used the severer lash of ridicule. The *Simple Cobler of Aggawam* thus lectures our extravagant grandsires and grandames :

' Methinks it should break the hearts of English men to see so many goodly English women imprisoned in French cages, peering out of their hood-holes for some men of mercy to

help them with a little wit, and nobody relieves them. We
have about five or six of them in our colony : if I see any of
them accidentally, I cannot cleanse my phansie of them for a
month after.

' It is a more common than convenient saying that nine
taylors make a man : it were well if nineteen could make a
woman to her mind : if taylors were men indeed, well furnished but with meer moral principles, they would disdain to
be led about like apes, by such mymick marmosets. It is a
most unworthy thing, for men that have bones in them, to
spend their lives in making fiddle-cases for futulous womens
phansies ; which are the very pettitoes of infirmity, the giblets
of perquisquilian toyes. I am so charitable to think, that
most of that mystery would work the cheerfuller while they
live, if they might be well discharged of the tyring slavery
of mis-tyring women : it is no little labour to be continually
putting up English women into out-landish caskes ; who if
they be not shifted anew, once in a few months, growe too
sowre for their husbands.

> He that makes coats for the moon
> Had need take measure every noon;

and he that makes for women as often, to keep them from
lunacy.

' It is known more than enough, that I am neither nigard, nor
cinick, to the due bravery of the true gentry : if any man
mislikes a bullymong drossock more than I, let him take her
for his labour : I honour the woman that can honour herself
with her attire : a good text always deserves a fair margent ;
I am not much offended, if I see a trimme far trimmer than
she that wears it : in a word, whatever christianity or civility will allow, I can afford with London measure : but when I
hear a nugiperous gentledame inquire what dress the queen is
in this week : what the nudiustertian fashion of the court ;
with egge to be in it in all haste, whatever it be ; I look at
her as the very gizzard of a trifle, the product of a quarter of
a cypher, the epitome of nothing, fitter to be kickt, if she were
of a kickable substance, than either honoured or humoured.'

He is very serious on the subject of dressing the head.
' Knew I how to bring it in, I would speak a word to long hair
whereof I will say no more but this : if those who are termed
rattle-heads and Impuritans would take up a resolution to begin in moderation of hair, to the just reproach of those that
are called Puritans and round-heads, I would honour their man-
liness as much as the others' godliness, so long as I knew
what man or honour meant. If neither can find a barber's
shop, let them turn in to Psalms, Jeremiah and Corinthians,
where they may obtain certain directions. If it be thought

no wisdom in men to distinguish themselves in the field by scis-
sors, let them remember, he is ill kept that is kept by
his own sin : a short promise is a far safer guard than a
long lock. Though it be not the mark of the beast, it may be
the mark of a beast prepared to slaughter : I am sure, men
used not to wear such manes : I am also sure, soldiers used to
wear other marklets or notadoes in time of battle.'

There must have been something more agreeable than a
universal gloom in the society, where a man could be found,
and he a minister and solitary widower, whose thoughts could
run in such a train. We have been too long taught to believe
that in the first generation, every thing bore marks of a poverty, which though voluntary was real : that austerity of manners did well enough agree with the horrours of a wilderness,
and that content extended only to the supply of the first wants,
and to a cabin, which the waste of fuel rendered inhabitable.
Those who heard the late Dr. Bentley's Antiquarian discourse will recollect how happily he combated that opinion,
by introducing his hearers into the mansions of some of the
early settlers, and displaying the articles found in the inventories
of their estates. His researches were made in Essex : our
own Probate records exhibit similar facts. We find in the principal houses a great hall ornamented with pictures and a great
lantern, and a velvet cushion in the window seat, which looks
into the garden. On either side is a great parlour, a little parlour, or study. These are furnished with great looking glass-
es, turkey carpets, window curtains and valance, pictures and
a map, a brass clock, red leather-back chairs and a great
pair of brass andirons. The chambers are well supplied with
feather beds, warming pans, and every other article that
would now be thought necessary for comfort or display.
The pantry is well filled with substantial fare and dainties,
prunes, marmalade and madeira wine. Silver tankards, wine
cups, and other articles of plate, are not uncommon : the
kitchen is completely stocked with pewter, copper, and iron
utensils. Very many families employed servants, and in one
we see a Scotch boy valued among the property and invoiced
at £14. The wardrobe of Mrs. Hudson exhibited as many
articles of finery as usually deck a modern toilet.

These legal records furnish the best of testimony concerning the extent of individual wealth, and the manners of the
times. Such things existed in other places as much perhaps
as in Boston, but a knowledge of them is not on that account
less necessary to those, who would be familiar with the distinguishing traits of our ancestors.

The business of the most importance in the town at this
period was the erection of the first Town House. A proposal
had been made in 1649, 'that those that shall undertake to

build a house for the courts to be kept in, shall have the income of any rents that might arise, forever.' In Capt. Keayne's will the subject was renewed and urged with much earnestness : he calculated the expenses and bequeathed a sum which he thought would nearly defray the whole. In 1657 a model was presented ; in 1659 the town house is mentioned, and at the meeting that year, which we suppose to have been held in that house, a rule of proceeding was adopted that ' there shall be a moderator chosen annually to regulate publick meetings and for this present year Wm. Davis [apothecary] is chosen.' Thomas Joy appears to have been the carpenter that built the town house, and a final settlement was made with him in January 1661, when he received £680 ' whereby all contracts with him were performed.' This was double the amount of Capt. Keayne's calculation. Whether any individuals bore part of the expense, does not appear : but in 1664 the town hired some part of the premises for a watch-house.

CHAPTER XXV.

" A lowering storm, from envy brewing,
Shall at a distance menace ruin ;
While slander, malice and detraction
A host of fiends shall bring in action."

THE Massachusetts colony originated in the commencement of the reign of King Charles I. The true intent of their patent or charter was, that the government of the colony should be under a corporation in England. The great change which the company made, by transferring the government into New England, produced a clamour against them, and a quo warranto was issued and prosecuted, and judgment obtained against the patentees in 1638. But the troubles which were increasing in the kingdom, and other circumstances, prevented the execution, and no further demand was made during the life of the king. After various vain expedients to retain his authority, Charles was brought to a trial, condemned and beheaded on the 30th of January 1649. The parliament of Scotland took no part in this transaction, and formally protested against it. On his death they proclaimed his son Charles II. their sovereign. Against him Oliver Cromwell maintained the field, and destroyed the royal army at Worcester in September 1651. England was now a sort of republick, and continued so till April 1653, when Cromwell assumed the power and became lord protector of the three kingdoms. He maintained his place till 1658, when he fell into disease and died, leaving the protectorate to his son Richard, who being utterly unfit for that hazardous situation resigned his office in April 1659. General Monk, taking advantage of the crisis, determined to make an effort to restore the exiled monarch, which was successful, and Charles II. was proclaimed in London, May 29, 1660.

The news of this fact arrived in July, but the government did not think proper to proclaim the king here at that time. In November, official information was received from Mr. Leverett, the colony's agent, that petitions and complaints were preferred against the colony to the king and to the parliament. Thereupon the governour and assistants met and prepared a very loyal address, which was very graciously received and answered in February, 1661. There was, notwithstanding, no small degree of fear, lest the revolution in England should produce as great a change in the form of their government, both in church and state. A sort of prudential committee was appointed, to consider what measures the state of things required to be taken, which produced a declaration of rights and duties, which was adopted by the court.* The king was proclaimed and acknowledged in August, but this submission did not cause all their difficulties to subside. Further complaints were made, and an order was received from the king, that some persons should be sent over to make answer. Mr. Bradstreet, one of the assistants, and Mr. John Norton, teacher of the first church, were sent, and were well received. They made but a short stay, and returned with a letter from the king. It offered to confirm and renew the charter and other privileges, which all thought very favourable ; but then it required among other things, that all, who desired it, should have liberty to use the book of common prayer, and perform their devotions according to the service established in England ; and that all freeholders of competent estates, though of different persuasions concerning church government, should be electors, and be eligible to all offices for which their wisdom, virtue and integrity qualified them. The old law of 1631 had been enforced by authority in 1660, making church members the only freemen ; and these requirements entered the sanctum sanctorum of our fathers' prejudices, and were admitted with reluctance. The agents met with a very unkind reception on their return. Mr. Norton died soon after (April 5, 1663) of an apoplectick fit : his friends attributed his death to the treatment

* See Hutch. vol. 1. app. No. 13.

19

he experienced : the Quakers pronounced it a judgment of God upon him, for the part he had taken in their persecution.*

The years 1664 and 1665 afforded the people greater occasion for fears, than they had met with, at any time before. Their compliance with the requisitions of the king's letter were so slow, that his Majesty determined to send over several gentlemen of distinction, with a commission to hear and determine all matters of complaint, and to settle the peace and security of the country, according to their discretion. With such powers, four commissioners arrived in July, 1664. They were Col. Richard Nichols, Geo. Cartwright, esq. Sir Robt. Carr, and Sam'l. Maverick, esq : the latter an implacable enemy to the colony, ever after an unsuccessful petition was preferred by him and others for certain privileges in 1646. They had various charges to advance and many demands to make of the government here : numerous interviews took place, and differences in opinions about mutual rights were unavoidable. Nothing definitive was effected by their labour ; the commissioners had to deal with men, who were their equals in knowledge, and their superiors in every other qualification. Some light is thrown upon the characters of both by the following story.

' The commissioners with other gentlemen meeting sometimes at a publick house in Boston, called the Ship tavern (it was at the corner of Clark and Ann streets, then kept by John Vyal, vintner,) one of the constables, named Arthur Mason, expected to find them there upon a Saturday evening, which would have been a breach of law ; but before he came, they had adjourned to Mr. Kellond's, a merchant, who lived opposite to the tavern. Another constable, who had been at the tavern before, had been beaten by them. Mason, who had more courage and zeal, went into the company with his staff and told them he was glad to see them there, for if he had found them on the other side the street he would have carried them all away ; and added that he wondered they should be so uncivil as to beat a constable and abuse authority. Sir Robert Carr said, it was he that beat him, and that he would do it again. Mason replied, that he thought his Majesty's commissioners would not have beaten his Majesty's officers, and that it was well for them that he was not the constable who found them there, for he would have carried them before authority. Sir Robert asked, *if he dare meddle with the king's commissioners ? Yes*, says Mason, *and if the king himself had been there, I would have carried him away.* Upon which, Maverick cried out, *Treason ! Mason, thou shalt be*

_____

* Mr. Norton left 10 pounds by will to the poor of Boston.

hanged within a twelvemonth! Sir Robert Carr spake to Sir Thomas Temple and some others of the company, to take notice of what passed; and the next day Maverick sent a note to Mr. Bellingham, the governour, charging Mason with high treason for the words spoken, and requiring the governour to secure him. The governour appointed a time for Maverick to come to his house, and to oblige himself to prosecute the constable at the next court of assistants; but Maverick, instead of appearing, thought proper only to send another note, promising to appear against the constable, and charge him home, and therefore required his person should be secured. The governour thought it advisable to cause Mason to recognize, as principal, in five hundred pounds, with two sufficient sureties in two hundred and fifty each, for his appearance; but the day before the court, Maverick sent another note to the governour, desiring to withdraw his charge, being " satisfied that although the words were rash and inconsiderate, yet there was no premeditated design in Mason to offer any injury to the king or his government." The governour returned for answer, " the affair was of too high a nature for him to interpose in, Mason being bound over to answer." Upon his appearance a bill was laid before the grand jury, wherein he was charged with maliciously and treasonably uttering the treasonable words mentioned. According to liberty taken by grand juries at that day, they only found " that the words charged were spoken;" and Mason being brought upon trial, and the words fully proved, the court of assistants suspended judgment, and referred the cause to the next general court, where it was resolved, that although the words were rash, insolent, and highly offensive, yet, as his accusers and witnesses all cleared him from any overt act, or evil intended against the king, the court did not see cause to adjudge him a capital offender, but sentenced him to be admonished in solemn manner by the governour.'

Sir Robert Carr was in his turn summoned by Mr. Leverett to appear at his house, with his man James Deane, and answer to a complaint exhibited against them for ' royatous and abusive carriage to one of his Majesty's officers, Richard Bennet, one of the constables of the town, that the honour and authority of H. M. or his officers, may be preserved, with the greatest respect to yourself the case will admit of.' We find no record of the result.

The commissioners drew up a report, in which they speak of Boston as ' the chief town in the colony, seated upon a peninsula, in the bottom of a bay, which is a good harbour and full of fish. It was fortified this year, 1665, with two block houses —Their houses are generally wooden, their streets crooked with little decency and no uniformity; and there, neither

months, days, seasons of the year, churches nor inns are
known by their English names.—One of the king's loyal subjects was derided for being so civil as to accompany a commissioner from the town where he lived to Boston, and others
in Boston derided those of Rhode Island, for having yielded
so much to the commissioners.

' At our first coming over, many untruths were raised and
sent into the colonies—Major Hawthorne made a seditious
speech at the head of his company, and the late governour*
another at their meeting house in Boston ; but neither of them
were so much as questioned for it by any of the magistrates.'

The town had for several years given instructions to their
deputies in the general court. The first on record are those
for the year 1665, and are not without interest, as exhibiting
the first publick act of Boston in support of ' just privileges.'

May 4. 1665. Instructions for the deputies, it is agreed to
present these ensuing :

First, that there may be an amicable compliance with his
Majesty's hon. commissioners according as duty to God and
allegiance to H. M. obligeth, without any receding from our
just privileges according to the patent.

2dly. Inasmuch as the number of freemen in this town of
B. (consisting of row distinct churches,) is very large, that
either the number of deputies their representatives may be
enlarged, according to proportion of freemen, or that there may
be [?] show deputies.

3dly. That whereas there be divers offices, as sealers of
leather, &c. who after election by law o$^{gt.}$ to be sworn to
the execution thereof, who yet refuse the same, that there may
be some penalty inflicted upon the refuser of the same, that so
the work may not be frustrated.

4thly. That whereas the standard for weights in towns
exceeds not four pounds, that it may be enlarged to 56lb.
weight, whereby fraud may be prevented in greater drafts.

5thly. That whereas for the future there may be more use
of bricks than formerly, for prevention of damage ; that the
law relating to tiles may be enlarged to bricks, as to clay they
are made of, and that there may be a size appointed for their
dimension, and that their moulds may be shod, &c.'

The representations of the commissioners produced another
letter from the king, dated April 10, 1666, and requiring that
five persons, of whom Gov. Bellingham and Major Harthorne

---

* Gov. Endicot died March 23, 1665. He had made Boston his place of residence for
some time. His will is dated here May 2, 1659, and speaks of the house he lived in, which
was on the lot now occupied by Gardiner Greene, esq. He left four pounds to the poor of
Boston.

were to be two, should be sent over to answer for the conduct of the colony. The court excused themselves with much sagacity from a compliance with this demand. An increase of troubles at home directed the king and council's attention from the colonies, and the people here had a respite on these matters till 1675.

CHAPTER XXVI.

We see the ground whereon these woes do lie,
But the true ground of all these piteous woes
We cannot without circumstance descry.

Romeo and Juliet.

SOME few of the first settlers in New England were persons inclined to the sentiments of the Baptists, and the rulers of the colony had used every effort to check the spread of their opinions. Some they fined : some they whipped : some they imprisoned : some they banished : and some were subjected year after year to ecclesiastical discipline, and delivered up to Satan for not hearing the church.

But now, the king's commissioners, having declared that they would have liberty given to all sorts and sects of men, the baptists in and near Boston took advantage of their presence and formed a society, which was the origin of the First Baptist church.* The first record on their books gives the following account of this transaction :

'The 28th of the 3d Month, in 1665, in Charlestown, Massachusetts, the Church of Christ, commonly (though falsely) called Anabaptists, were gathered together and entered into fellowship and communion with each other; engaging to walk together in all the appointments of their Lord and Master, the Lord Jesus Christ, as far as he should be pleased to make known his mind and will unto them by his word and spirit ; and then, were baptized Thomas Gould, Thomas Osborne, Edward Drinker, John George—and joined with Richard Goodall, William Turner, Robert Lambert, Mary Goodall, Mary Newell, who had walked in that order in Old-England —and to whom God hath joined since, Isaac Hull, John Farnum, Jacob Barney, John Russell, jun. John Johnson, George Farlow, Benjamin Sweetser, Mrs. Sweetser, all before Ellis Callender who was received Nov. 9, 1669.'

---

* This was the first church of the denomination in Massachusetts proper : there had been one in Rehoboth, which was then in Plymouth colony, since 1663.

This act of the baptists was in defiance of a standing law of the colony, as the formation of the first church had been contrary to a law of the kingdom. Shortly after the departure of the commissioners, Aug. 20, a warrant was issued to the constable of Charlestown to labour to discover where these people were assembled, and to require them to attend the established worship ; upon refusal to do this, they were brought before the court of assistants in September, when they presented a confession of faith, setting forth their distinguishing sentiments.[*] The court were not satisfied, but declared Mr. Gould and his company to be no orderly church assembly, and sentenced them to be disfranchised, and on conviction of any further meetings, to be committed to prison. In April of the next year they were again indicted for non-attendance on publick worship, and plead their own constant meetings in defence. This was considered an aggravation, and Gould, Osborne and George were fined £4 each, and ordered to give bonds for their appearance at the next court. This they refused, and were therefore committed to prison. They remained in confinement, for a long time, making occasionally appeals for release, but in vain. In March, 1668, Gould appealed for himself, but the court of assistants again affirmed the judgment against him, and he was recommitted. But the same court appointed him and his associates a day to hold a publick dispute in defence of their principles, ' for their orderly conviction by the labours of some of the reverend elders.' When the day arrived, April 14th, the baptists appeared with some of their friends from Newport, and the six selected divines were attended by the governour and other magistrates and ministers. A memorandum of the proceedings is preserved in the Historical Library, but as it remains undeciphered, we can only say that 'the conference seems from the quick alternation of the dialogue, as the speakers' names indicate, to have been more animated than might have been expected, but the eloquence and argument of each is lost in an impartial oblivion.' The result was more palpable. In the following May, Gould, Turner and Farnum were ordered to remove from the jurisdiction before the 20th of July ; and if seen after that time, they were to be thrown into prison, and there to remain without bail or mainprise. Mr. Gould was thereupon set at liberty, that he might prepare to go into banishment : in the mean while, the court ordered that no meeting should be held or ordinances administered. The baptists were determined to suffer imprisonment rather than go into exile. One of them, Turner, lay in prison Nov. 1670, and warrants were then in two marshals' hands against Mr. Gould,

---

* Rev Mr. Winchell's Jubilee sermon.

but he was not then taken ' because he lived on Noddle's Island, and they waited to take him at town.' Many influential men in the town ' laboured abundantly as if it had been for their best friends in the world to obtain their release,' and from the documents left on record, we should suppose the opposition to this church was more from the country than from the people of Boston.* The church at this time held their meeting at Noddle's Island every sabbath : Mr. Gould officiated as their pastor, and John Russell, senior, who had joined them from Woburn, held the office of elder. This Mr. Russell and another of their members by the name of Foster, were confined in prison for nearly six months in 1672, and in the spring of 1673, two others were fined for withdrawing from the publick meetings.

Gov. Bellingham, who had been opposed to the baptists, had died Dec. 7, 1672, and was succeeded at the May election by Maj. Gen. John Leverett, who had always objected to the measures pursued against them : and one of their number writes in Jan. 1674, ' the church of the baptized do peaceably enjoy their liberty !' Their pastor died in October, 1675. Encouraged by the lenity of Gov. Leverett's administration, they resolved, in Jan. 1678, to erect a place of worship in Boston. They proceeded with so much caution in building their house, that it was not known for what purpose it was erected until it was completed. After it was finished, the church purchased the house, with the land it was built upon, of Philip Squire and Ellis Callender for £60 ; and they met in it for worship on the 15th of February, 1679. It was situated on part of the lot now owned and occupied by the church, nearer to the street than the present meeting-house stands. The society did not enjoy it long unmolested ; in May, their leaders were convented before the court and admonished, and an order was then passed that no meetings should be held in any house, erected without the consent of the town in which it might be, on penalty of forfeiture or demolition. They therefore refrained from meeting, (in the mean time ordaining Mr. Russell as their pastor) until another letter came, July 24, 1679, from the king, forbidding that any of his subjects, not being papists, should be subjected to fines or forfeitures or other incapacities for serving God in the way they might desire. Then they ventured to meet again ; and again they were summoned to

---

* A petition (which see in *Backus* i. 380) was offered to the court in behalf of the prisoners. Henry Shrimpton, who died after the 17th of July, 1666, when he made his will, left 10 pounds ' to the society of christians that doth now meet at Noddle's Island, of which is Gould and Osborn and the rest, *as a token of my love.*' Mr. S. left property worth 10,000*l.* of which he gave some to each of the other churches, and 50*l.* to the town, on condition that he might be buried in the tomb with his former wife, otherwise nothing.

desist, and the court ordered the marshal to nail up the house, which he did on March 8, 1680, and posted on the door a paper in these words:

' All persons are to take notice, that by order of the Court, the doors of this house are shut up, and that they are inhibited to hold any meeting therein, or to open the doors thereof, without license from authority, till the Court take further order, as they will answer the contrary at their peril.'

' The church met in the yard, next Lord's day, and in the week ensuing erected a temporary covering ; but coming the second Lord's day, they found the doors of the house open, and they continued meeting in it till the General Court met in May following, when, having been admonished in open Court, by the Governour, and charged not to meet in their house, they were dismissed ; and the Court agreed to suspend any further proceedings against them.

Thus were the baptists ' left to worship God as they chose, although the law forbade it; but neither the church nor the rulers afterwards regarded this prohibition.'

While the baptists were thus earnestly contending for the application of baptism to believers only, a question arose among the pedobaptists themselves, of most peculiar ' exercise and concernment respecting the ecclesiastical state of their posterity.' To some unpleasant disagreements on this subject is to be traced the origin of the Old South Church.

In 1657 the first church had voted, that it was the duty of a church to exercise church power regularly over the children of their members, who had been baptized in infancy, and to take care that their life and knowledge might be answerable to the engagement made by their relatives. This duty they put into practice. This opinion was sanctioned by a council, and another proposition was adopted, which gave to such persons the right to bring their children for baptism, on condition of their owning the covenant before the church, though they might not have sufficient confidence of their own regeneration, to justify themselves in partaking of the sacrament. This was the commencement of the half-way covenant.

Some persons feared that a consequence of adopting this rule would be, that before the churches should be aware, ' a worldly part of mankind might carry all things into such a course of proceeding, as would be very disagreeable unto the kingdom of heaven.' Among those who were of this opinion was the Rev. John Davenport, of New Haven. It happened very singularly that the first church, which had acted on the principles recommended by the synod, and whose pastor, Mr. Wilson, had decidedly approved them, should, when called to fill the vacancy occasioned by his death, choose Mr. Davenport. Yet so the major part did, in opposition to a

large minority.   Mr. Davenport accepted their invitation,
and he and the Rev. James Allen, from England, were ordained, the former as pastor, and the latter as teacher of the
church, on the 9th of December, 1668.   This step created so
great a division, that the minority withdrew, and formed a
new society, by the advice of ' councils fetched from other
churches in the neighbourhood.'

The names of the thirty ' brethren which came off and laid
the foundation of the third [pedobaptist] church, partly on
May 12, and partly on May 16, 1669, were Capt. Wm. Da-
vis, Messrs. Hez. Usher, John Hull, Edw. Raynsford, Peter
Bracket, Jacob Eliot, Peter Oliver, Tho. Brattle, Edw. Raw-
son, J. Scottow, Benja. Gibbs ; Major T. Savage, Messrs. Jo.
Rocke, Theodore Atkinson, John Wing, Richard Truesdale,
Theophilus Frarye [and] R. Walker, John Aldin, Benja.
Thurston, Wm. Salter, John Morse, Josiah Belcher, Seth Per-
ry, Jas. Pemberton, Wm. Dawes, Jo. Davis, Mr. Thomas
Thacher [and] Joseph Belknap.'

The heading of their covenant* says the church was gathered in Charlestown, on the 12th of May, 1669.   In July a

---

* *Covenant of the Old South Church.*

We whose names are underwritten, being called of God to join together into a church, in
heart sense of our unworthiness thereof, disability thereunto, and aptness to forsake the
Lord, cast off his government, and neglect our duty one to another, do in the name of J. C.
our L. trusting only in his grace and help, solemnly bind ourselves together as in the presence of God, constantly to walk together as a chh. of Christ, according to all those holy
rules of God's word given to a chh. body rightly establ. so far as we already know them,
or they shall be hereafter farther made known unto us.   And particularly, we do first of all
acc. to the tenor of the everl. cov. give up ourselves and our offsp. unto God our chief yea
only good : unto our L. J. C. as the only mediator, our only spotl. head and Lord, receiving
and relying on him not only as our h. p. for satisf. and interc. but also as our prophet to t.
and King to reign over us, and unto the H. S. to be a temple to him, that by his dwelling
and working in us we may have and be establ. in fellowship with God in C. and one with
another.   And for the furth. of this blessed fp. we do likewise promise to end. to establ. am.
ourselves and convey down to post. all the holy truths and ordin. of the g. committed to the
chhs. in faith and observance, opposing to the utm. of our chh. power whatever is diverse
therefrom or cont. thereto.   Also we do give up ours. unto one an. in the L. and by the will
of G. hereby prom'g to cleave one to an. as fellow m. of the same b. in brotherly l. and holy
watchf. unto mutual ed. in C. J. and to be subj. in and for the L. to all the adm. and censures of the congr. so far as the same shall be ord. acc. to the rules of God's most holy wd.
& finally we do hby. cov. and prom. thro. the help of the same grace to hold, promote &
maint. sisterly fp. and comm. with all the chh. of saints in all those holy ways of order app.
betw. ym. by our L. J. C. to our utmost. esp. wt. those among wh. the L. hath set us ; that
the L. may be one and his n. one in all these chh. thro'out all gen. to his et. gl. in C. J.
And now the good Lord be merciful unto us, pardg. acc. to the greatness of his gr. as all
our past sins so esp. our chh. sins in negligence & unfreq. of former enjoym. & accept us a.
sweet savour in J. C. this our offg. up oursv. unto him in this work—filling this his house
with his own glory—making us faithf. to himself, & one unto an. acc. to himself, for his holy
name sake.   Amen.

20

council was called by Gov. Bellingham, ' fearing,' as he says
in the order, ' a sudden tumult ; some persons attempting to
set up an edifice for publick worship, which is apprehended
by authority to be detrimental to the publick peace.'   But
the council thought best not to interpose any farther than to
caution those, who were about to erect the house, to conform
to the laws on that subject.   They accordingly applied to
the selectmen, who passed a vote 26, 5, 1669, ' that there is
need of another meeting-house to be erected in this town ;'
though they judged it did not belong to them to determine the
placing of it.   The house was erected on the spot where the
Old South now stands, and the abovenamed Mr. Thacher
was installed as pastor of the church, Feb. 16, 1670.*

Mr. T. was from Salisbury in England, where his father,
Mr. Peter Thacher, was minister. He arrived in this country in 1635, at the age of fifteen, and received his education
under Mr. Charles Chauncy, who was afterwards president
of the college.   In 1644 he was settled at Weymouth, where
he remained more than twenty years, till after the death of
his first wife, when upon marrying a second, who belonged to
Boston, he removed hither, and engaged himself in the practice of physick, to which he had devoted considerable attention : this he did not entirely relinquish, after he became
pastor of the Old South.   He was the author of the first medical tract which appeared in this state, which was a discourse
on the subject of the small-pox and measles, published 1677.

CHAPTER XXVII.

Sermons in stones, and good in every thing.
Shakspeare.

We shall devote this chapter to a variety of miscellaneous
facts, which were interesting at the time of their occurrence.

The following useful regulation is found in the town records,
March 14, 1664.   For the more orderly and deliberate carrying on of the affairs of the town, it is ordered, that henceforth there shall be no alteration made in the way of elections, or other matters of moment and publick concernment,
that hath not been duly considered of, and proposed at a pub-

---

* Mrs. Norton had conveyed the land to several of the above gentlemen in their associate
capacity, by a deed, April 1, 1669.

lick town meeting, orderly called, before the meeting when the final determination shall be put to vote.

ELEVEN O'CLOCK BELL.

The origin of our eleven o'clock bell is found under date of 25. 5. 1664. ' For the more convenient and expeditious despatch of merchants' [and maritime] affairs, or any other relating to strangers or our inhabitants, it is ordered that the bell shall be rung at eleven of the clock every working day, to give notice thereof to all persons concerned ; and that the ringer shall be allowed 12d. a year by every person that commonly resorts thereunto, and that they may assemble in the room under the Town-house, for the space of one hour, for the ends above expressed.'

NORTH AND SOUTH BATTERIES.

Some of the letters from the king in 1665 had recommended to the court to fortify against the Dutch and other enemies ; how faithfully they obeyed, appears in the subjoined report, which is found in the colony records for 1666, p. 222.

' We the subscribers being appointed a committee by the Hon. Court, to view the batteries lately erected by Maj. Gen. John Leverett, with the advice of the committee of the militia in Boston, accordingly attended to that service, and under the conduct of the said Maj. General we entered a well contrived fort called Boston Sconce, the artillery whereof is of good force and well mounted, the gunner attending the same. The form thereof is suitable to the place, so as to scour the harbour to the full length of their shot every way ; it is spacious within, that the traverse of one gun will not hinder the other's course; and for defence the foundation is of stone, and well banked with earth, for dulling the shot, and hindering execution. Finally, we apprehend it to be *the completest work* of the kind, which hitherto hath been ordered in this country. We also took survey of another work, on the north side of Boston, called Merry's point, raised with stones ; the foundation is defended from the violence of the sea with spyles and planks ; the wall of a considerable thickness, yet less so than by reason of the sharp edges next the cannon, and wideness of the ports within, which (being faced with strong timber as intended) will be much better. To conclude, we judge the defence to be considerable, and the offence to be available (by God's blessing) for the thing intended, for which the actors and contrivers, whereof Maj. Gen. L. hath been the chief, both in contriving, acting and disbursing, deserve the thanks of this court and all due encouragement. Boston Sconce hath nine guns mounted and four more intended with-

out, and seven at Merry's point.' Then follows a vote of
thanks to Gen. L. and £100 grant for his services.

DEATH AND CHARACTER OF REV. MR. WILSON.

The death of Mr. Wilson, the first pastor of the First
Church, occurred in 1667, on the 7th. of August, in the 79th
year of his age. He left an amiable character, and is represented as one of the most humble, pious, and benevolent men.
Cotton Mather, who tells us he never would sit for his like-
ness, says ' if the picture of this good, and therein great man,
were to be exactly given, great zeal with great love would be
the two principal strokes, that joined with orthodoxy should
make up his portraiture.' He was the son of Dr. Wilson, a
prebend of St. Paul's in the reign of Queen Elizabeth, and
received his education at King's college, Cambridge. His
cotemporaries considered him an excellent poet, though nothing which he has left behind would lead us to form that opinion of him. His principal forte lay in the making of ana-
grams upon the names of his friends, and the happy faculty
he possessed, of flattering them in that way for their virtues,
probably gained him their compliments in return. His heart
was full of compassion for the distressed and of affection for
all : his house was renowned for hospitality, and his purse
was continually emptying itself into the hands of the needy.
This disposition was so remarkable, that it could not escape
unnoticed. One day as he was present at a general muster
of the military corps, a gentleman standing by said to him,
' *Sir, I'll tell you a great thing : here's a mighty body of people,
and there is not seven of them all, but what loves Mr. Wilson.*'
On which he instantly and pleasantly replied, ' *Sir, I'll tell
you as good a thing as that : here's a mighty body of people, and
there is not so much as one of them all but Mr. Wilson loves
him.*' The witty Mr. Ward, (the simple cobler,) passed a
very neat encomium on him, when he gave as an anagram of
his name, I PRAY COME IN, YOU ARE HEARTILY WELCOME. And
the following lines upon his hearse are far from being inex-
pressive, though ' some thought the Muses looked very much
dissatisfied' at them:

Anagram.

JOHN WILSON.

Oh ! change it not. no sweeter name or thing,
Throughout the world, within our ears shall ring.

Magnalia.

Mr. Wilson met with his share of the difficulties of the wilderness. He lost his houses several times by fire ; buried his wife and some of his children and grand children, under trying circumstances ; outlived two of his friends and associates in the ministerial office ; saw errours stalking into the churches, in forms which appeared to him dreadful in the extreme ; and died lamenting, that the zeal and pious devotion of the first generation had died with them, and that their children promised nothing better than to prove degenerate plants. He left a little property, which was valued at £419. 14s. 6d. and distributed it in small portions to many individuals, not forgetting the poor of his own church. The foregoing fac simile represents the signature to his will.*

SIGNS OF THE TIMES.

The relation of an incident in 1668 will show us the character of the age. ' There appeared a meteor in the heavens in the beginning of March, in the form of a spear, of a bright colour, something thicker in the midst than at either end. It was seen several nights together, in the west, about half an hour within night : it stood stooping, one end pointing towards the setting of the sun, and moved downwards by little and little, till it descended beneath the horizon.' This and some other occurrences excited the magistrates to make an effort towards ' a reformation of manners :' for it was observed, that the youth of the age had degenerated very much from the strictness of their fathers. A brief was therefore issued to all the ministers in the colony, urging them to a more strict performance of their duty of visiting and instructing families, with the hope, that ' the effectual and constant prosecution hereof will have a tendency to promote the salvation of souls, to suppress the growth of sin and profaneness, to beget more love and unity among the people, and more reverence and esteem of the ministry, and it will assuredly be to the enlargement of your crown, and recompense in eternal glory.'

It is evident, that the face of society was now becoming changed, and so strongly marked, that the line was plainly to be drawn, between those who maintained a regard for primitive holiness, and those who preferred to follow the inclination of their own hearts. This comports well with the observation of Hutchinson, that the colony about this time (1669) made a greater figure than it ever did at any other time. Their trade was as extensive as they could wish : no

---

* " 1668. May 3. Dorchester chh. records. Role-on-God, the son of Mr. John Cotton, is baptized by virtue of communion of churches : his father being a member of the church at Boston, *but there is no officer there to dispense the ordinance at present.*"

custom-house was established. The acts of parliament of the
12th and 15th of king Charles II. for regulating the plantation trade were in force,* but the governour, whose business it
was to carry them into execution, was annually to be elected
by the people, whose interest it was that they should not be
observed. Some of the magistrates and principal merchants
grew very rich, and a spirit of industry and economy prevailed through the colony.'

DEATH AND CHARACTER OF REV. MR. DAVENPORT.

The first church lost their senior pastor, on the 11th. of
March 1670, Mr. Davenport dying suddenly of apoplexy,
aged 72. 'Although his career in Boston was short and
troublous, it had been long and glorious in New-England.
Few men were better qualified for planting the gospel in a
new world, and seldom has any man made a happier use of
his natural and moral energies. His intrepidity saved king
Charles' judges, Whalley and Goffe, who fled to New-Haven,
in 1661, and who were hidden in his house, whilst he was
preaching in publick, before the officers in pursuit of them, a
sermon from the following words: "Take counsel; execute
judgment; make thy shadow as the night in the midst of the
noon day: hide the outcasts; bewray not him that wander-
eth; let mine outcasts dwell with thee. Moab, be thou a
covert to them from the face of the spoiler." Mr. D. agreed
in sentiment with Mr. Cotton respecting the civil as well as
religious polity of the bible, and endeavoured a system of
order, which should nearly correspond with the Hebrew
institutes and the usages of the primitive christians.'

JOSSELYN'S DESCRIPTION.

Mr. Josselyn, whose former travels are noted in page 82,
visited Boston again in 1663 and was hereabouts till 1671,
when he published the result of his inquiries. We give the
substance of them, omitting somewhat, which he borrowed
from Wood and Johnson.

'Boston the metropolis of this colony, or rather of the whole
country, is in longitude 315 deg. and 42 deg. 30 min. of north
latitude. The buildings are handsome, joining one to the
other, as in London, with many large streets, most of them
paved with pebble; in the high street toward the common
there are fair buildings, some of stone, and at the east end of
the town, one among the rest, built by the shore, by Mr.
Gibbs, a merchant; being a stately edifice, which, it is
thought, will stand him in little less than £3000, before it be
fully finished. The houses are for the most part raised upon

* These acts forbade the introduction of foreign produce, except from England.

the sea banks, and wharfed out with great industry and cost,
many of them standing on piles [?] close together on each
side of the streets as in London, and are furnished with many
fair shops.

' The town is not divided into parishes, yet they have three
fair meeting-houses, or churches, which hardly suffice to receive the inhabitants and strangers that come in from all
parts. There is also a Town-house built upon pillars, where
the merchants may confer : in the chambers above they hold
the monthly courts. Here is the dwelling of the governour
[Bellingham]. On the south there is a small but pleasant
common, where the gallants, a little before sunset, walk with
their marmalet madams as we do in Moor-fields, till the nine-
o'clock bell rings them home to their respective habitations :
when presently the constables walk the rounds to see good
order kept and to take up loose people.'

DEATH AND CHARACTER OF MR. BELLINGHAM.

Gov. Bellingham, who from the time of his first arrival, in
1635, had been an inhabitant of Boston, died Dec. 7, 1672.
He appears to have been a popular man, and was strongly
attached to the liberties of the people. He was by education
a lawyer. As a man he was benevolent, upright, and active
in business : it is always mentioned as a singular part of his
character, that he would never take a bribe. As a christian
he was devout, zealous, and attentive to external forms. In
politicks, he leaned rather to the democratick side, but in the
church was a violent opposer of the new sects, that contended
for religious freedom. He was sometimes subject to melancholy and mental derangement, lived to the age of 80 years,
and was the only surviving patentee named in the charter.
His will left a large property for charitable and pious uses,
but it was made in such a manner, that, after some years'
dispute, the general court thought it necessary to supply the
defects of it, by making a disposition of his estate themselves.*

THE OLD WHARVES.

We gather the history of the origin of the *Old Wharf*,
so called, from the following documents :

' Boston, N. E. Sept. 10, 1673. Whereas the Honourable
Council of this jurisdiction have lately recommended to the
consideration of the selectmen of this town, the necessity of
erecting a wall or wharf, upon the flats before the town,
from the Sconce to Capt. Scarlett's wharf, or using some

---

* ' March 21. 1673, the castle, at the entrance of Boston harbour, being of timber, was
burnt down by accident. A new fortress of stone was erected, said then to be a strong work.'

other means for securing the town from fireships, in case of
the approach of an enemy, which the selectmen represented
to the inhabitants, at a publick meeting, Sept. 5, 1673 ; and
whereas the said inhabitants did on that day, by two publick
votes, *first* deny to have the said work carried on at the publick charge of the town, and *secondly*, did grant and give
power to the selectmen, that they might order and dispose of
the flats before the town, from the Sconce aforesaid to Capt.
S.'s wharf for the better security of the town, as they shall
think best—Now the aforesaid selectmen, having taken into
their serious consideration the necessity of something to be
done to the end aforesaid, and of some way of encouragement
to such as shall undertake so great a work, do propound to
the inhabitants of this town as followeth :

1.   That a wall or wharf of wood or stone be erected from
the said sconce to Capt. Scarlett's wharf, which is in length
about 2200 ft. ; that it be made in breadth 22 ft. at bottom,
and to be raised 6 feet high at the least, with all expedition ;
and afterwards as soon as may be to add thereto in height, as
shall be judged convenient for a breastwork to play guns on,
which is supposed to be 14 or 15 ft. high in all, and so carried up to be 20 ft. broad at the top, to be made substantial
and uniform, and continued and maintained at the cost and
charge of the undertakers according to these propositions.

2.   For encouragement hereunto the said selectmen of this
town of B. in behalf of themselves and their successors in the
office, do, according to the power committed to them, hereby
order and declare, FIRST, that such of the inhabitants of this
town as shall undertake and carry on the said work
as above expressed, shall possess and enjoy, and hereby is
granted to them, their heirs and assigns forever, all those flats
that lie before the town, between the town and the said wall
or wharf so to be built ; 200 feet whereof back towards the
town, and next adjacent to said wall or wharf, shall be free
for them the said undertakers to build wharves and warehouses upon as they shall see cause, proportionably in breadth
to what they build on in the front : the remainder to be for
dock or shelter for ships or vessels :

Except always, and it is hereby reserved to such of the present abutters or borderers on the said flats, as shall come in
undertakers of said w. or wh. and carry an end the
same in convenient time, with the rest of the u. that they shall
have liberty of carrying out their present wharves, before
their own land, in proportion with others about 100 ft. beyond
the Hon. Gov. Leverett's and Mr. Alford's present wharves,
and to improve it, for the best advantage of them, their heirs
and assigns forever, as shall be staked out in a *Circular Line,*
according to a plot or map now taken of the said cove :

Reserving also to such others of the present abutters or borderers on the said flats, who refuse to join in the said wall or whf. aforesaid, liberty of egress and regress of vessels, and lying at their wharves for loading and unlading and graving before them. SECONDLY,

That the said u. and carriers an end of said w. or whf. shall, according to and in proportion to what they build in front, have right, unto all income, advantages and emoluments that may arise or accrue, by dockage or anchorage of any such vessels as shall harbour or be secured within the said cove, as also by fishing within the said cove, or in the mouth thereof, and all other liberties and privileges, which may arise by virtue of this grant of the selectmen, between the said wharf or wall, now to be erected, and the wharves and docks now bordering on said flats, or to be made as above expressed, except what is reserved as above. It is further ordered and declared, that no man shall subscribe or undertake for less than twenty feet of said wall or wharf.'

The foregoing propositions were signed by the selectmen ; forty-one persons very soon undertook the work in parcels from 20 ft. to 120 feet in front, and their agreement ' being read to the council Nov. 11, 1673, it was accepted.'

The circular line, mentioned in this document, is a very important boundary at the present day. A question having arisen concerning it so soon as 1678, it was then, Oct. 28th, determined that the southernmost part of Capt. Scarlett's wharf is meant and understood to be the northerly bounds thereof, and the Sconce to be the southerly bounds, and ' from these two places lines to be run the nearest or shortest cut into the channel before the town, and the channel to be the eastern or easterly bounds, and the western or westerly to be 100 ft. without the Hon. Gov. Leverett's and Mr. Wm. Alford's wharf.' Gov. L.'s wharf was at that time the wharf on the south side of the bottom of State-street, and Mr. Alford's that on the north : the Long wharf has since been built between them. Capt. Scarlett's wharf was that at the bottom of Fleet-street, and the Sconce was situated not far from the head of India wharf.

Stupendous as this undertaking was, for the period when it was projected, it was carried into execution, and the proprietors received an act of incorporation from the council of the colony, May 11, 1681. Happily there never was occasion to employ the works for the ends for which they were designed ; *no enemy having ever passed the castle.* The profits from the concern were found so small, that the wharves were soon suffered to go into decay, and no trace is now to be seen of them. We have been favoured with the use of a plan, taken after Long-wharf was built, which exhibits the cove and all the '

21

wharves between the two extremities of the circular line, the
out wharf crossing the Long at the T. with a ' gap or passage
of 80 ft. wide into the cove' on the north side of the T, and
another narrower gap on the south side of Long wharf.

CHAPTER XXVIII.

Or fighte with mee, or lose thy lande,
No better termes may bee.

Remains of Ancient Poetry.

WHATEVER concerned the welfare of the colony was deeply
felt in Boston, and scenes were about opening in 1674, which
kept alive the publick anxiety from that time, till the colonial government was settled under a new charter.

The Indians within the Massachusetts bounds were not subject to one general sachem, but divided into smaller cantons
or tribes.   These, one after another, had submitted themselves to the jurisdiction of our government.   There was the
appearance of amity and good correspondence on all sides,
and for forty years together, the people had suffered no great
concern from fears of any irruption.   But about the year
1670, suspicions were excited by some strange conduct on the
part of the Indians, and measures of precaution were taken
against them.   Philip, sachem of Mount Hope, was the chief
who was destined to give the greatest annoyance.   He was a
man of high spirit, and could not bear to see the people of
Plymouth colony extending their settlements over the dominions of his ancestors : and although his father had at one time
or other conveyed to them all that they were possessed of,
yet he had sense enough to distinguish a free, voluntary covenant from one made under a sort of duresse, and he could
never rest until he brought on the war, which was to end in
his destruction.

While Philip was making professions of peace and friendship, he was secretly laying a plot, that all the Indians should
rise at once, in all quarters, in the spring of 1676, and drive
the English entirely out of the land : but circumstances concurred to bring on a rupture at an earlier period, that ended
in quite a different result.   In this contest the people of Boston took a very efficient part.   Philip's men made an attack
on some persons at Swansey, on the 24th of June, 1675, and
information being immediately brought to Boston, a company

of foot under Capt. Daniel Henchman, and a troop of horse under Capt. Thomas Prentice were despatched to their relief on the 26th. An eclipse of the moon, which happened that evening, produced fearful discouragements in this little army. Some melancholy fancies imagined that they saw an unusual black spot in her centre, resembling an Indian's scalp, and this brought to recollection other ominous signs. ' But after the moon had waded through the dark shadow of the earth, and borrowed her light again,' the two companies marched on and arrived at Swansey. within a quarter of a mile of Philip's dominions, some time before night on the 28th. A party of the Boston troop, unwilling to lose their time, made an excursion into the enemy's territory, but were compelled to retreat with the loss of one man, Wm. Hammond, killed, and one man, corporal Belcher, wounded.

The whole body of the forces (Mass. and Plymouth) made a sally the next morning, crossed the bridge that led to Mt. Hope, and drove the enemy before them, a mile and a quarter on the other side of it. ' Ensign Savage, that young martial spark,' says Hubbard, ' scarce twenty years of age, had at that time one bullet lodged in his thigh, another shot through the brim of his hat, by ten or twelve of the enemy discharging upon him together, while he boldly held up his colours in the front of his company.' Major Savage arrived soon with supplies and took the command : Capt. Edw. Hutchinson also came up shortly after, with reinforcements and further orders from Boston. A few skirmishes routed the Indians in that quarter ; Philip fled to the western part of the colony, and some of our troops returned. Capt. Henchman started again from Boston, in November, with another company. Near to Mendon they heard of a party of Indians, and it was resolved to give them a camisado, as they called it, in their wigwams. The captain and his lieutenant, Philip Curtis, accordingly led their men out to the fight, but most of them flinched in the moment of need, and Capt. H. and Lieut. C. were left with only five men to finish the combat. The lieutenant and one man were killed, and the object of the excursion was lost.

The following winter was marked with numerous rencontres, in which the Indians were sometimes victorious and sometimes obliged to retreat. They, however, advanced towards Boston, and some of them expressed the hope, that they should yet see that town in ashes. *What me will, me do*, was their motto, and the people believed so much in its appropriateness, that they set a watch at the entrance of the town, and no Indian whatever, friendly or not, was allowed to enter unguarded. Next to Philip in insolence, there was a John Monahco, or One-eyed John, who had threatened hardest and boasted loud of what he should accomplish : but before the year was closed, Philip himself was hunted to his dens, by Capt. Church, and shot by a friendly Indian ; and this John, ' with a few more bragadocios like him was taken, and was seen marching towards the gallows, through Boston streets, which he threatened to burn at his pleasure, with an halter about his neck, with which he was hanged at the town's end, Sept. 26, 1676.' Thus ended king Philip's war.

What the malice of the savages was not permitted to effect, took place through other means. On the 27th of November, the town was alarmed by the discovery of ' a sad fire, accidentally kindled by the carelessness of an apprentice, that sat up too late over night, as was conceived, which begun an hour before day, continuing three or four, in which time it burned down to the ground 46 dwelling-houses, besides other buildings, together with a meeting-house* of considerable bigness. Some mercy was observed, mixt with the judgment, for if a great rain had not continued all the time, (the roofs and walls of their ordinary buildings consisting of such combustible matter) that whole end of the town had at that time been consumed.'

This is Hubbard's account in his ' Indian wars.' Hutchinson says, ' it broke out about five o'clock in the morning, at one Wakefield's house, by the Red Lion.' The wharf, which opens next north of Richmond-street (late Proctor lane), was formerly called the Red Lion wharf, and from the number of buildings destroyed, and the names of persons mentioned in the town records, as interested in the improvements afterwards made in the width and course of the streets, we infer that the fire extended from that lane as far north as Clark-street.† Great pains appear to have been taken that the new streets might be both wider and straighter than before, and the selectmen had as much difficulty to persuade the owners to give up an inch of ground then, as the city authorities now have. Some of the wooden houses now standing in Ann-street were probably built immediately after this fire. The house at the head of the slip below Richmond-street is thought by the occupant to be 150 years old. It is of two stories ; the second projecting about 18 inches over the first. There are houses in several parts of the town, built in the same style.‡ The fashion is said to have been introduced here

---

* The church met at Dea. Phillips' house, Dec. 3, and took measures for the erection of a new house of worship : it was ready in the course of the next year. No pew was to be built with a door into the street : and if the builder of the pew left the house, the pew was to revert to the church.

† Town Records, Jan. and Aug. 1677.

‡ The house on the north side of the New Brick meeting-house is a specimen of this structure, and the one on the south side, at the corner of (late) Proctor-lane, is in the previous fashion of two low stories with a high, peaked roof : until late years it retained the ancient small glass windows with leaden sashes.

from the country, where this structure was found expedient, to furnish protection from the assaults of the natives. This is not improbable ; but another opinion, that it was the fashion of the times and prevailed also in France at the same period, is quite as likely.

We do not find that the engine authorized in 1654 was ever obtained, but after this fire the town appears to have sent abroad for one.

Town Records, 1679. Jan. 27. ' In case of fire in the town, where there is occasion to make use of the engine lately come from England, Thomas Atkins, carpenter, is desired and doth engage to take care of the managing of the said engine, in the work intended, and secure it the best he can from damage, and hath made choice of the several persons following to be his assistants, which are approved of, and are promised to be paid for their pains about the work :—' The persons who formed the first engine company, were Obadiah Gill, John Raynsford, John Barnard, Thomas Elbridge, Arthur Smith, John Mills, Caleb Rawlins, John Wakefield, Samuel Greenwood, Edward Martin, Thomas Barnard, George Robinson.'

The following record shows us the antiquity of their privileges. May 28, 1683. It is agreed that Ralph Carter and seven others, one man out of each company of the train bands, should take the care and charge of the water engine, to keep it in good order, and be ready upon all occasions to attend the use and service thereof, when the said Carter shall require it, or there be any noise or cry of fire breaking out in any part of this town : In consideration whereof, with consent of the several captains, they shall be exempt from training, and are to attend the said service upon the penalty the law prefixeth for not training.

Another ' terrible fire began about midnight, August 8, 1679, at one Gross's house, the sign of the Three Mariners, near the dock. All the warehouses and a great number of dwelling-houses, with the vessels then in the dock, were consumed. It continued till near noon the next day ; the most woful desolation that Boston had ever seen ; eighty odd dwelling houses and seventy odd warehouses, with several vessels and their lading consumed to ashes. The whole loss computed to be £200,000.' Hubbard says (N.E. 649) ' it was set on fire* by

---

* 1679, October 13. p. 242. Colony Records. Whereas the persons hereafter named are under vehement suspicion of attempting to burn the town of Boston, and some of their endeavours prevailed to the burning of one house, and only by God's providence prevented from further damage : This court doth order that Edward Creeke and Deborah his wife, Hepzibah Codman, John Avis, John Easte, Samuel Dogget, Wm. Penny, Richard Heath, Sypron Jarman, and James Dennis, shall depart the jurisdiction and never return, and be kept in prison until ready for their departure.

some malicious wretches, as is justly suspected, and half ruined the whole colony, as well as the town.' This devastation occasioned such a demand for house timber, that the town
petitioned the court to forbid its exportation for a time.
It also increased the watchfulness of the people, and in some
new regulations adopted, we find the singular one that a man
should be stationed on each meeting-house during service on
the sabbath day, to give the alarm in case of any fire being
discovered.

A law was made about this time to prevent the erection of
wooden buildings, and the houses and warehouses near the
town dock, which were rebuilt after the great fire in 1679,
were either constructed with brick, or plastered on the outside
with a strong cement intermixed with gravel and glass, and
slated on the top. They were two stories high, with a garret in the high peaked roof.* One of them is yet standing,
and is represented in the following plate.

ANCIENT BUILDING

AT THE CORNER OF ANN-STREET AND MARKET-SQUARE.

VIEW FROM THE N. E. CORNER OF ELM-STREET.

---

* Mass. Hist. Coll. 1. iv. 189.

This, says a description furnished by a friend, is perhaps the only wooden building now standing in the city to show what was considered elegance of architecture here, a century and a half ago. The peaks of the roof remain precisely as they were first erected, the frame and external appearance never having been altered. The timber used in the building was principally oak, and, where it has been kept dry, is perfectly sound and intensely hard. The outside is covered with plastering, or what is commonly called rough-cast. But instead of pebbles, which are generally used at the present day to make a hard surface on the mortar, broken glass was used. This glass appears like that of common junk bottles, broken into pieces of about half an inch diameter, the sharp corners of which penetrate the cement in such a manner, that this great lapse of years has had no perceptible effect upon them. The figures **1 6 8 0** were impressed into the rough-cast to show the year of its erection, and are now perfectly legible. This surface was also variegated with ornamental squares, diamonds and flowers-de-luce. The building is only two stories high, and is about 32 feet long and 17 wide ; yet tradition informs us that it was once the residence of two respectable families, and the front part was at the same time occupied for two shops or stores. The water of the dock flowed on the south and southwest sides of it, as represented on the plan for 1722. The principal apothecary' shop in the town was once kept there, and one part of it continues to be improved for the same business.

CHAPTER XXIX.

He's gone, and who knows how he may report
Thy words, by adding fuel to the flame ?
Expect another message more imperious,
More lordly thund'ring than thou well wilt bear.

Samson Agonistes.

'In the height of the distress of the Indian war, and while the authority of the colony was contending with the natives for the possession of the soil, complaints were making in England, which struck at the powers of government ; and an inquiry was set on foot, which was continued from time to time, until it finally issued in a quo warranto and judgment thereupon against the charter.'

The compliance of the colony with the requisitions of the king had been slow and occasional, as necessity impelled, and whatever alterations they might make in their polity from rea-

son and conviction, of their own motion, they were not easily
led to adopt the same when required by a sovereign, to whom
they held themselves subject only according to their charter.
There were different opinions in regard to the course, which
the colony ought to pursue, and from this period we may date
the origin of two parties, the patriots and prerogative men,
the whigs and tories, between whom controversy scarcely in-
termitted, and was never ended, until the separation of the
two countries.*

A jealousy concerning their political rights infused itself
into the people, and henceforward we discover in the acts of
the Bostonians an increased sensibility to every shadow of
encroachment upon their liberties, whatever may be its source.

Thus in April, 1676, in conformity to custom, the town chose
by ballot Mr. John Hayward, to be nominated to the county
court for the office of clerk of the writs. For reasons not assigned on the town records, that court saw fit to disregard the
nomination, and the town resented the affront at a publick
meeting, on the 25th of August following.

' Then was presented a paper to the inhabitants, by Richard Knight, in the name of himself and others of the town, to
represent their dissatisfaction and grievance for a breach of
their liberties and privileges, as they apprehend, by the Hon'd.
County court's putting in another clerk of the writs than what
was nominated by a major vote of the inhabitants, the 24th of
April, 1676.

The question being put, whether the motion therein should
be considered at this time, Resolved in the affirmative.

Secondly, it was voted, that Mr. Thomas Deane and Mr.
John Fairweather join with the selectmen to represent the
dissatisfaction and grievance of the inhabitants to the hon'd.
county court, and humbly desire *that their privileges and liberties, that do belong to the town,* may be continued and enjoyed without any obstruction, and may have satisfaction in their
present complaint.'

This was an evil of trifling moment, when compared with
the troubles that awaited them, in common with their brethren
of all New-England. That same summer, king Charles II.
sent over to the colony, as bearer of despatches ' to the governor and magistrates of the town of Boston,' Edward Randolph, a man who became infamous and hated by the people as
a spy upon their liberties ; whose business it was, they said, to
go up and down seeking to devour them. The court complied
with the principal demands of the king, and sent agents (Wm.
Stoughton and Peter Bulkley) to answer the complaints against
them. Randolph returned upon their heels, and reported that

'the colony refused any obedience to the acts for regulating the trade of the plantations.'

'Several laws were made by the court, while the agents were in England, to remove some of the exceptions which were taken, and the king's arms were ordered to be carved and put up in the court [town] house. But it was a more difficult thing to conform to the acts of trade : they acknowledge in their letter to their agents that they had not done it. They apprehended them to be an invasion of the rights, liberties and property of the subjects of his majesty, *they not being represented in parliament*; however, they had made provision by a law, that the acts should be strictly observed from time to time, although it greatly discouraged trade, and was a great damage to his majesty's plantation.' Here we perceive that the government of Massachusetts avowed the principle, that taxation and representation ought to go together, a hundred years before the united colonies declared that they should.

Randolph kept a continual watch upon the colony, and went divers times to England with complaints, and returned with fresh orders and powers. In 1678 he came over with authority from the commissioners of the customs as an inspector, and to make seizures for breaches of the acts of trade ; but he was generally, if not always, condemned in costs. In his list of 'articles of high misdemeanour exhibited against a faction of the general court,' besides accusing them of aiming at independence, he alleges that in opposition to him, they had 'confirmed the place and powers of the collector of the customs and imposts, laid upon wines and strong waters imported into their colony, set up by a law made in their colony in 1645 ;' which officer, he says, had been chief collector of these duties above a year before his own office was ordered.

Even this collector, though appointed by the court, it seems met with some refractory spirits, who were not disposed to submit to the 'acts of trade.' Town Records, 1678, Aug. 26, 'Mr. Paul Dudley, collector of the customs in this port of Bostone, complaining that Robert Orchard, who had received several goods from England, had neglected to make any entry, and refused to produce an invoice of them, the said Mr. Dudley desired the assistance of the selectmen to rate the said Orchard for the said goods, according to their best discretion, as the law directs. And the said collector with the selectmen do, according to the law, rate the said Orchard to pay to the collector £10 in money, for the custom of the said goods.'— And the constable thereupon attached 19 lbs. of beaver, as security for the same.

Governour Leverett, who had been annually continued in office, from the time of his being first chosen in 1673, died on the 16th of March, 1679. He had been a soldier in early

22

life, and distinguished himself in several actions abroad. Upon his return he was chosen a deputy to the general court
for Boston ; in 1664 he was appointed major-general, and
elected assistant in 1665 : he succeeded Mr. Francis Willoughby in the deputy-governour's office in 1671, and held
that place till he became governour. The weighty affairs of
the war and of the agency during his administration, conducted with prudence and steadiness, caused him to be greatly
respected, and he was so beloved by the colony, that his election was never contested, and he descended with honour to
the grave. His funeral was attended with great solemnity :
a sermon was preached by Mr. [Samuel] Nowel, and military
honours were conferred on the occasion.*

The agents returned in 1679. In 1681, Randolph obtained
a commission from the crown, for collector and surveyor and
searcher of the customs, in New England. He laid his commission before the general court, and desired he might be aided in the execution of his office with their countenance and
authority : but no notice being taken of his application, he set
up his advertisement in the town-house, to acquaint all persons concerned, that an office was erected, and they must
govern themselves accordingly. This, he said, was taken
down by the marshal, by order of the general court, or some
of the members. He, therefore, demanded a final resolution
of the court, whether they would admit his commission to be
in force or not, that he might know how to order his proceedings. What was their reply to Randolph we have not found ;

---

* Order of march at the funeral of Governor Leverett, who died 16 March 1678, and was
buried the first day of the next year, 25 March, 1679.

Mr. John Joyliffe
Mr. James Whetcombe
Mr. Wm. Tailer
Mr. Rics. Middlecot } to carry each a Banner Roll at the 4 corners of the Herse.

To march next before the Herse as followeth.

{ Mr. Sam. Shrimpton, or in his absence Capt. Clap to carry the helmet.
{ Mr. John Fairweather to carry the Gorget.

{ Mr. E. Hutchinson   Brest
{ Mr. Charles Lidgett   Back

{ Mr. Samp. Sheafe   one tace
{ Mr. John Pincheon   one tace   Mr. Dummer in case

{ Capt. Nich. Page   one Gauntlet
{ Capt. Jona. Curwin   one Gauntlet

{ Lieut. Edw. Willys   the Target
{ Capt. Edw. Tyng   the Sword

{ Mr. Hez. Usher   one Spur
{ Mr. Peter Sargeant   one Spur

Capt. Wm. Gerrish to lead the Horse per the Rain and Return Waite (as Groom) per
the headstall.

Mr. Lynde
Mr. Saffin
Mr. Rock
N. Green } to carry Banners mixt with the Banner Roles above.

but in an answer to the king we find them declaring, that he
' was acknowledged collector, and his commission enrolled.'

Charles II. remained dissatisfied, and required that other
agents should be sent over, without delay, with powers to
submit to such regulations of government as his Majesty should
think fit. Mr. Joseph Dudley, a son of the first deputy-governour, and Mr. John Richards, a wealthy merchant of Boston,
a man of fair character and one of the assistants, were chosen, and despatched with all practicable speed. They arrived
at London on the latter end of August, 1682, and Randolph
was not long after them, ready to disclose every thing they
might wish to conceal. They found ' his majesty greatly provoked;' and in their first letters to the general court represented the case of the colony as desperate, and left it to the
court to determine, whether it was advisable to submit to his
pleasure or to suffer a quo warranto to issue. Upon receipt of
these advices it was made a question, not in the court only,
but amongst all the inhabitants, whether to surrender or not.
On the whole, the agents were instructed to make no concessions of any privileges conferred upon the colony by the
charter. Upon receiving this final resolution of the court,
their business was at an end : it was immediately determined
a Q. W. should go forth, the agents returned to Boston, Oct.
23, 1683, and Randolph arrived the same week with the instrument of death.

' The next day after Randolph arrived, a destructive fire
happened in the richest part of the town. Some of the people in their rage and jealousy supposed it to have been kindled by his procurement. It was on the south side of the
dock's mouth, and consumed a great number of dwelling
houses, warehouses and vessels.'

The Bostoneers, as Randolph called them, were forward to
oppose his Majesty's demand : this is the record :

1684, Jan. 21. At a meeting of the freemen of this town
upon lawful warning, upon reading and publishing his Majesty's declaration dated 26 July, 1683, relating to the quo warranto issued out against the charter and privileges claimed by
the governour and company of the Mass. Bay in N. E. It
being put to the vote, whether the freemen were minded, that
the general court should make a full submission and entire
resignation, of our charter and privileges therein granted,
to his majesty's pleasure, as intimated in the said declaration
now read, the question was resolved in the negative, NEMINE
CONTRADICENTE.

It is impossible to pronounce the two last words without
perceiving that the clerk felt himself animated with the assurance, that he was recording the sentiments of the whole popu-

lation.* Yet the proposition divided the legislature. The
Governour (Bradstreet) and the major part of the assistants
says Minot, voted not to contend in law, but to submit to the
pleasure of the King; but the representatives, after a fortnight's consideration, refused to give this vote their concurrence; and a letter of attorney was sent to a suitable person
to appear and answer in behalf of the Colony.

' It seems that this process was issued from the Court of
King's bench, where the attorney was accordingly authorised
to appear ; but from some reason or other proceedings were
not further prosecuted there, and a scire facias was issued
against the colony from the Court of Chancery, on the 16th
day of April, and was not received until the return day had
expired ; by means of which, judgment was given against the
colony on the 18th of June, 1684, subject to an appearance
and defence on the next term, without their being heard, or
receiving timely notice to appear. Thus fell the good old
charter, valuable for its defects so happily supplied, as well
as its powers. But with it fell not the habits it had engender-
ed, nor the principles which the settlement of the country
had inspired.'

' The loss of the charter was followed within a few months
with the death of King Charles II. (Feb. 6, 1685,) which occasioned such a crowd of business at home, that the plantations were neglected for some time. King James II. was
proclaimed with great ceremony in the high street in Boston
on the 20th of April. As soon as he was settled in his throne
he sent over a commission to Col. Joseph Dudley, to take the
government of New-England upon him, under the title of President, and appointed him a new council, of his majesty's own
nomination, with Wm. Stoughton as deputy president. Mr.
D. received it (by the Rose frigate, the first we have noticed
as arriving in Boston harbour) on the 15th of May, 1686, and
it was made publick on the 25th, when the president and
council met in form.†

' Mr. Dudley considered himself and the council appointed
to preserve the affairs of the colony from confusion, until a
governour should be appointed, and a rule of administration
be more fully settled. Hutchinson says, that ' in general the
former laws and established customs, so far as related to
judicial proceedings, seem to have been their rule, although
the government which framed them was dissolved. The

---

* See Remarkables of Increase Mather, who attended the meeting and made a spirit-stir-
ring speech on the subject.

† *Neal*, N. E. ch. x. *Hutch.* Hist. 1. ch. iii. The old magistrates had continued to exercise authority, as a thing of necessity, until May 12, 1686, the date of the last old charter
record, when Mr. Bradstreet was chosen Governour.

affairs of the towns were likewise managed in the same manner as formerly.'

The power of granting taxes being transferred to the President and council, it was necessary for the town of Boston to make application for liberty to assess and collect their usual rates. The following articles, from the town records, are the more interesting from the consideration that Randolph thought to have destroyed the publick records from 1686 to 1689. The town record next after May 14,1686,reads thus:

'Upon the constables' delaying or neglect to collect the rate for the alms-house or work-house, within mentioned, the President and council were pleased to endorse the warrant following upon each constable's list.

By the President and Council.

The order and agreement of the town of Boston relating to the alms or work house having been considered, the rate in this paper is allowed, and to be paid as formerly ordered by the Committee and Selectmen, reserving liberty to complain as formerly, to such as are oppressed or aggrieved : and where any have subscribed or made promise and refuse payment, the treasurer or his attorney hath power to recover the same by action before any two justices of the peace, if the subscriptions exceed not 40s. or otherwise by the county court.

per Edward Randolph, Sec'y.

By the President and Council, June 2, 1686.

In answer to the motion of the selectmen of Boston showing that their town treasury is so exhausted that they stand in need of a present supply, for the maintenance of the poor, mending the highways, finishing the alms house, and other necessary town occasions, which have been formerly and particularly referred to their care and management, the Pres't and council for the present exigency, and having seen the town's votes allowing the said selectmen's power, accordingly do approve the same, and order them to give notice of the sum necessary and to proceed in due and equal manner to levy the same upon the inhabitants and estates of the town.

Sec.

Copy of a return to the Council, June 7th.

Whereas the President and council, June 2, 1686, in answer to the motion of the Selectmen of Boston for the supply of money to maintain the poor, mending of the highways, and other necessary town's occasions, ordering to give notice of the sum to defray the charge, it is found according to former experience, that rating the town about £600, rate pay, being customary to abate one third part if paid in money, which brings it to £400, and abatements for such as have been rated and found not able to pay, and for such as have died, and such as have gone to sea, removed to other places, before they have been paid, and such as have been abated on complaint of being overrated, commonly brings it to £340 or £350. And the standing charge of this town at this time is about £400 per ann. and about 200 of which is in maintaining three free schools, mending the highways in Boston, Romney Marsh and Muddy river, the rest to several that have standing salary for service in the town, and to poor people, that are not likely to get their livings as long as they do live, besides clothing and burying the poor, and giving to people's necessities transiently, repairing the town-house and school-houses, maintaining bastards and poor people when they are sick and nurses for them, and powder for the town's occasions, paying house rent for it, and blowing up of houses, and finding powder for the town as the law requires.

Subscribed per Edward Willis, treasurer.

CHAPTER XXX.

Thy sons, Edina, social, kind,
With open arms the stranger hail,
Gay as the gilded summer sky,
Thy daughters bright thy walks adorn.
Address to Edinburgh.

FROM this review of the course of publick affairs we turn now to exhibit to our readers a picture of private society and manners in the same period : and we shall do it in the words of the facetious John Dunton, who visited Boston in 1686, and published an account of his life and errours in 1705.

' We weighed out of the Downs, Nov. 2, 1685 ; and made the best of our way for the Beachy.—We were above four months at sea, and at last reduced to that extremity that each of us had no more than the allowance of one bottle of water for four days. When we came within ken of Boston, we were all overjoyed, being just upon the point of starving ; we put off to land in the long boat and came ashore near the Castle, which stands about a mile from Boston. The country appeared at first like a barren waste, but we found humanity enough when we came amongst the inhabitants. We lodged

the first night at the Castle, and next morning we found the
way to Boston lay over the ice, which was but cold comfort,
after we had been stowed up so many months in a cabin.
The air of New England was sharper than at London, which,
with the temptation of fresh provisions, made me eat like
a second Mariot of Gray's Inn. The first person that welcomed me to Boston was Mr. Burroughs, formerly a hearer of
my reverend father-in-law, Dr. Annesly. He heaped more
civilities upon me than I can reckon up, offered to lend me
monies, and made me his bedfellow, till I had provided
lodgings.

As I was rambling through Boston, I met both with lodgings, and a warehouse at Mr. Wilkin's, whose family deserves
as well of me, as any in New England. Being thus fixed, I
delivered the letters of recommendation I had brought with
me from England. I had one from the Reverend Mr. Richard
Stretton, to Mr. Stoughton, the deputy governour: and Mr.
Morton of Newington-Green, sent another to major Dudley,
afterwards president, which, with other letters to the magistrates, had the good effect that I was made freeman of Boston,
though very much obliged for it to the friendship of Mr.
Burroughs. Immediately upon this, captain Hutchinson
gave me an invitation to dine with the governour and the magistrates in the town hall. The entertainment was very rich
and noble, and the governour, deputy-governour, major Dudley, and the other magistrates gave me a very friendly welcome to Boston, and kindly wished me success in my undertaking.

He that trades with the inhabitants of Boston, should be
well furnished with a Grecian faith : he may get promises
enough, but their payments come late. However, under all
the disadvantages of that kind, I was now resolved to run the
risk of it, and in order to promote the sale, I made a visit to
the Reverend Mr. Increase Mather, the metropolitan clergyman of that country, and rector of Harvard College. He is
master of a great stock of learning, and a very eminent divine.
His son, the Reverend Mr. Cotton Mather, was then upon
finishing his Magnalia Christi Americana, which has lately
been published here in England. There is abundance of
freedom and familiarity in the humour of this gentleman ;
his conversation and his writings are living evidences that he
has read much, but there are many that won't allow him the
prudence to make a seasonable use of it. His library is very
large and numerous, but had his books been fewer when he
writ his history, 'twould have pleased us better.

I was next to wait upon the Reverend Mr. Willard, minister of the South-Meeting in Boston ; he is well furnished with
learning and solid notion, has a natural fluency of speech,

and can say what he pleases. Afterwards I went to visit the
Reverend Mr. Allen, he is very humble and very rich, and
can be generous enough, when the humour is upon him.   His
son was an eminent minister here in England, and deceased
at Northampton.   Mr. [Joshua] Moody was assistant to Mr.
Allen, and well known by his practical writings.   Leaving
Mr. Allen's house, I went next to Mr. John and Mr. Thomas
Baily.   These two are popular preachers, and very generous
to strangers;   I heard Mr. John upon these words,—*Looking
unto Jesus*, and I thought he spake like an angel.   They express a more than ordinary kindness to Mr. Wilkins, my landlord, and (being persecuted in Limerick for their nonconformity) came over with him from Ireland.   Reader, I might
be large in their character ; but when I tell you they are true
pictures of Dr. Annesly (whom they count as a second St.
Paul) 'tis as high as I need go.

   The sun being now gone to bed (for though I was up before
him, he got to his lodging first) I bid good night to these two
brothers, who gave me a hearty welcome to Boston, and assured me of all the service that lay in their power.

   Having first paid my visits to the clergy of Boston, and
given a character of them, pray give me leave to ask my
brethren the booksellers how they do, and that shall be all.
For though I know they love to be respected, yet at the same
time I am satisfied, that I'm as welcome to them as sour ale
in summer, for they look upon my gain to be their loss, and do
make good the truth of that old proverb, that interest will not
lie ; but I must begin my addresses to them.

   Mr. [John] Usher, your humble servant.   This trader
makes the best figure in Boston ; he is very rich, adventures
much to sea ; but has got his estate by book-selling ; he proposed to me the buying my whole venture, but would not
agree to my terms, and so we parted with a great deal of
seeming respect.

   Mr. Phillips, my old correspondent !—'Tis reason I should
make you the next visit.   He treated me with a noble dinner,
and (if I may trust my eyes) is blest with a pretty obliging
wife ; I'll say that for Sam (after dealing with him for some
hundred pounds) he is very just, and (as an effect of that)
very thriving.   I shall add to his character, that he is young
and witty, and the most beautiful man in the town of Boston.

   But leaving Phillips, I rambled next to visit Minheer Brunning, he is a Dutch bookseller from Holland, scrupulously
just, plain in his clothes, and if we will believe the printers in
Boston (who are notable criticks in such cases) a most excellent paymaster.   Brunning is versed in the knowledge of all
sorts of books, and may well be styled a complete bookseller.
He never decries a book, because 'tis not of his own printing ;

there are some men that will run down the most elaborate
pieces, only because they had none of their midwifery to
bring them into publick view, and yet shall give the greatest
encomium to the most nauseous trash, when they had the hap
to be concerned in it. But Brunning was none of these ; for
he would promote a good book whoever printed it ; and I
found him a man of that great interest, that I made him my
partner in printing Mr. Mather's sermon, preached at the execution of Morgan, who was the only person executed in that
country for near seven years. From the Dutch, I went to
the Scotch bookseller, one Duncan Cambel, he is very industrious, dresses all-a-mode, and I am told, a young lady of
a great fortune is fallen in love with him.

Having visited all the booksellers, I will next give an account of what acquaintance I had in Boston.   I shall begin
with Mr. Willy, who fled thither on the account of conscience,
(and is brother-in-law to the Reverend Mr. Baily) he is a
man of a large heart, one who, in relieving others' wants, con-
siders not so much his own ability, as their necessity. This
Monmouth's forlorn fugitives experienced often, to whom he
was the common refuge. The next I shall mention is Mr.
White, a merchant, who by trading has clasped islands to the
continent, and tacked one country to another ; his knowledge, both of men and things, is universal.——The next was
Mr. Green, a printer ; I contracted a great friendship with
this man ; to name his trade, will convince the world he was
a man of good sense and understanding; he was so facetious
and obliging in his conversation, that I took a great delight in
his company, and made use of his house to while away my
melancholy hours. Another of my acquaintance was Captain Gery [Gerrish?] a man as eminent for his love to his
country, as Junius Brutus and the famous Scævola among the
Romans.——Another of 'em was George Monk. a person so
remarkable, that had I not been acquainted with him, it would
be a hard matter to make any New England man believe that
I had been in Boston; there was no house in Boston more
noted than George Monk's, or where a man might meet with
better entertainment; he was so much the life and spirit of
the guests that came to his house, that it was almost impossible not to be cheerful in his company. Another was captain
Townsend, a gentleman very courteous and affable in his conversation.

I might here ramble to Mr. Jollyff, justice Lines, Macarty,
and some others; but least I tire you quite, I will next come
to a distinct head, which shall be those of my countrymen
that have rambled into this country as well as myself. such of
them, I mean, as I came acquainted with in the course of my
business: and these were, first, Mr. Mortimer, who came from

23

Ireland ; he was an accomplished merchant, a person of great modesty, and could answer tne most abstruse points in algebra, navigation, dialling, &c.

The next to these was Mr. King: love was the cause of this gentleman's long ramble hither; sure his mistress was made of stone, for King had a voice would have charmed the spheres, he sang, *All Hail to the Myrtle Shades*, with a matchless grace, and might be called an accomplished person.

Another acquaintance was Mr. York, he had his soft minutes as well as other men, and when he unbent the bow, for he was very industrious, he treated the fair sex with so much courtship and address, as if loving had been all his trade.

The next I mention shall be Andrew Thorncomb, bookseller from London ; his company was coveted by the best gentlemen in Boston, nor is he less acceptable to the fair sex ; for he has something in him so extremely charming, as makes them very fond of his company. However, he is a virtuous person, and deserves all the respect they showed him. He visited me often in Boston, and I here declare I've a particular kindness for him.

Another acquaintance was Mr. Heath ; were I to write the character of a pious merchant, I would as soon take Heath for the exemplar, as any man I know. There are two things remarkable in him, one is, that he never warrants any ware for good, but what is so indeed ; and the other, that he makes no advantage of his chapman's ignorance, where the conscience of the seller is all the skill of the buyer; he doth not then so much ask as order what he must pay ; and in such cases he ought to be very scrupulous. Bishop Latimer being told he was cozened in buying a knife, no. replied Latimer, he cozened not me, but his own conscience. This person was my daily visitor, and brought me acquainted with one Gore, of New York, with whom I traded considerably.

Mr. Watson shall be the next; formerly a merchant in London, but not thriving there, he left the exchange for Westminster Hall, and in Boston has become as dexterous at splitting of causes, as if he had been bred to it. He is full of fancy and knows the quirks of the law ; but to do him justice, he proves as honest as the best lawyer of 'em all.

Another acquaintance is Mr. Mason. He was a blunt, honest Christian ; he will speak his mind, take it how you please.

The next I'll mention shall be Mr. Malinson, he is a stiff Independent, (which is rare in a fencer,) and so great a critick, that he would even find a knot in a bullrush. Malinson was one of those unfortunate gentlemen that engaged with Monmouth, and I'm told this day at the Royal Exchange, he now teaches young gentlemen to fence in Boston.

I was so happy as to find *particular friends* in Boston, whose characters I shall next give you, and I'll begin with Dr. Oakes.—He is an eminent physician, and a religious man; at his first coming to a patient he persuades him to put his trust in God, the fountain of health; the want of this hath caused the bad success of most physicians, for they that won't acknowledge God in all their applications, God won't acknowledge them in that success which they might otherwise expect.   He was a great dissenter whilst he lived in London, and even in New England retains the piety of the first planters; I was recommended to him by Mr. Gilson, as also by a relation of his in Ratcliff, and I must own, the doctor gave me a generous welcome to Boston.—From Dr. Oakes I pass to my good friend Dr. Bullivant, formerly my fellow citizen in London ; I must consider him both as a gentleman and a physician.   As a gentleman, he came of a noble family, but his good qualities exceeded his birth ; he is a great master of the English tongue, and the Northampton people find him a universal scholar ;   his knowledge of the laws fitted him for the office of attorney general, which was conferred upon him on the revolution in Boston ; it is true he sought it not. but New England knew his worth, and even forced him to accept of it.

While he held this place of attorney general, he was so far from pushing things to that extremity as some hot spirits would have had him, that he was for accommodating things, and making peace.   His eloquence is admirable, he never speaks but 'tis a sentence, and no man ever clothed his thoughts in better words.

I shall next consider him as a physician, his skill in pharmacy was such as had no equal in Boston, nor perhaps Northampton ; he is as intimate with Galen and Hippocrates, at least with their works, as ever I was with Iris.   He is so conversant with the great variety of nature, that not a drug or simple escapes his knowledge, so that he never practises new experiments upon his patients, except it be in desperate cases, where death must be expelled by death.   This also is praiseworthy in him, that to the poor, he always prescribes cheap, but wholesome medicines, not curing them of a consumption in their bodies, and sending it into their purses, nor yet directing them to the East Indies to look for drugs, when they may have far better out of their gardens.

I proceed in the next place to Mr. Gouge, a linen draper from London, son to the charitable divine of that name.   He is owner of a deal of wit, his brain is a quiver of smart jests. He pretends to live a bachelor, but is no enemy to a pretty woman.   He's high church, yet so great a lover of his father's " christian directions," that he bought two hundred

of me to give away, that so he might, as he used to say, make
the Bostonians godly. And this was a noted quality in him,
that he would always tell the truth ; which is a practice so
uncommon in New England, that I could not but value his
friendship.

But I must not forget Mr. Tryon. Mr. Tryon is a man of
a sweet temper, an excellent husband, and very sincere in
his dealings. The next I shall mention is Mr. Barnes, he was
clerk to the government, a matchless accomptant, a great musician, bookish to a proverb, very generous to strangers, and
at our first interview, declared a particular friendship to me.

To return to my own affairs, the booksellers in Boston perceived I was very diligent to bring custom to my warehouse,
and thereupon began to make terms with me for my whole
venture, but that would not do for me, because there's the
loss of thirty per cent. in the return of their money. The
books I had with me were most of 'em practical, and well
suited to the genius of New England, so that, my warehouse
being opened, they began to move apace. Palmer, my apprentice, was very honest and diligent, took the whole charge
of my business off my hands, and left me to ramble and divert myself as my fancy would suggest.

But I must make a transition to arms. It is their custom
here for all that can bear arms, to go out on a training day ;
but I thought a pike was best for a young soldier, and so I
carried a pike. And between you and I, reader, there was
another reason for it too, and that was, I knew not how to shoot
off a musquet, but 'twas the first time I ever was in arms.
Being come into the field, the captain called us all into our
close order, in order to go to prayer, and then prayed himself. And when our exercise was done, the captain likewise
concluded with prayer. I have read that Gustavus Adolphus,
the warlike king of Sweden, would before the beginning of a
battle kneel down devoutly, at the head of his army, and
pray to God, the giver of victory, to give them success against
their enemies, which commonly was the event ; and that he
was as careful also to return thanks to God for the victory.
But solemn prayer in the field upon a day of training, I never
knew but in New England, where it seems it is a common custom. About three of the clock, both our exercise and prayers being over, we had a very noble dinner, to which all the
clergy were invited.

Summer was now well advanced, however my time did not
lie much upon my hands, for upon my return from Roxbury,
I found several of my friends making ready for a journey to
Natick. Every summer there's an Indian lecture preached
there, which has been kept on foot ever since the Rev. Mr.
Elliot gathered a church there of the converted natives. I

was glad of the opportunity to acquaint myself with the manners, religion, and government of the Indians. When we were setting forward, I was forced, out of civility and gratitude, to take madam Brick behind me on horseback ; it is true, she was the flower of Boston, but in this case proved no more than a beautiful sort of luggage to me. We had about twenty miles to Natick, where the best accommodations we could meet with, were very coarse. We ty'd up our horses in two old barns, that were almost laid in ruines, however we cou'd discern where they had stood formerly. But there was no place where we cou'd bestow ourselves, unless, upon the greenswerd, till the lecture began.

The wigwams, or Indian houses, are no more than so many tents, and their way of building 'em is this ; they first take long poles, and make 'em fast in the ground, and then cover them with mats on the outside, which they tye to the poles. Their fire-place is made in the middle, and they leave a little hole upon the top uncover'd with the mats, which serves for a chimney. Their doors are usually two, and made opposite to each other, which they open or shut according as the wind sits, and these are either made of mats, or of the barks of trees.

While we were making such discoveries as these, we were informed that the sachim, or the Indian king, and his queen, were there. The place, 'tis true, did not look like the royal residence, however we cou'd easily believe the report, and went immediately to visit their king and queen ; and here my courage did not fail, for I stept up and kissed the Indian queen; making her two very low bows, which she returned very civilly. The sachim was very tall and well limbed, but had no beard, and a sort of a horse face. The queen was well shaped, and her features might pass pretty well, she had eyes as black as jet, and teeth as white as ivory ; her hair was very black and long, and she was considerably up in years ; her dress peculiar, she had sleeves of moose-skin, very finely dressed, and drawn with lines of various colours, in Asiatick work, and her buskins were of the same sort ; her mantle was of fine blue cloth, but very short, and tied about her shoulders, and at the middle with a zone, curiously wrought with white and blue beads into pretty figures; her bracelets and necklace were of the same sort of beads, and she had a little tablet upon her breast, very finely decked with jewels and precious stones ; her hair was combed back and tied up with a border which was neatly worked both with gold and silver.

The Natick lecture was done about four in the afternoon, and we had twenty miles to Boston, so that we were obliged to mount immediately, and make the best of our way. Upon my coming to Boston, I heard that the Rev. Mr. Morton, so much celebrated in England for his piety and learning, was just arrived from England, and with him, his kinsman, Dr. Morton, the physician.   Mr. Morton did me the honour to declare he was very glad to see me ; and I am sure I was glad to see him ; not only as he brought me letters from Iris, but for his own personal worth.

In the same ship with Mr. Morton, came over one Mrs. Hicks, with the valuable venture of her beautiful person, which went off at an extraordinary rate ; she marrying ˀa merchant in Salem worth thirty thousand pounds.

By this time there were about two thirds of my venture of books gone off, and I was fearful to sell any more at Boston, till the old scores were discharged ; for besides all the money I had taken, there was about four hundred pounds owing me in Boston, and the towns adjacent, at my return from Natick. It began to run in my head, that Mr. Sewel, one of the magistrates in Salem, had invited me thither, and told me, if I sent part of my venture there, he'd do me all the service that was possible, in the sale of them ; upon these thoughts, I made a journey to Salem.

Having staid some little time, with my worthy friend Mr. Steward, myself and Mrs. Comfort took our leaves, and made the best of our way for Boston ; where we arrived to the great satisfaction of my good landlord and his wife.

I had now no more business in New England, but just to pay a farewell to Mr. Burroughs, (that was so kind to me at my first landing) and to shake hands with Mr. Wilkins (my landlord) his wife, and daughter.

And here I shall first take my leave of Mr. Francis Burroughs, for I wanted till now, an opportunity to thank him for the many civilities he heaped upon me in Boston ; for he not only lent me money (the true touch-stone of friendship) but made me his bed-fellow, got me the freedom of Boston, and was the chief person I advis'd with under any difficulty.

" His person is handsome (I don't know whether he knows it or no) and his mind has as many charms ; he's a man of remarkable chastity, of a great deal of wit, and his repartees are so quaint, apposite and genteel, 'tis a pleasure to observe how handsomely he acquits himself ; in the mean time he's neither scurrilous nor prophane, but a scrupulous, honest, conscientious man, so that he's what we may call a religious merchant, and (I was going to say) he hates vice almost as much by nature as grace."   And this I think is his true character ; but I must remember Captain Leg is ready to sail, and I have other farewells to make, and so worthy friend adieu.

I come next to honest Wilkins, my landlord, for I should think myself very unkind, should I leave Boston, without shaking hands with a person I lived with near eight months. His person is tall, his aspect sweet and smiling, and (though but fifty years old) his hair as white as snow. He was formerly a bookseller in Limerick, and fled hither on the account of conscience. He is a person of good sense, keeps up the practice of religion in his family, and (upon a nice search into all his affairs) I found it had a general influence on all the actions of his life : he was deservedly chosen a member of Mr. Willard's church, and I do think he's a pious man, if there's such a thing in Boston. But dear sir, adieu, for the wind is fair, and I must be gone ; but I leave your company with as much regret as ever I did any earthly blessing.

My next farewell shall be to Mrs. Wilkins my obliging landlady.

" She's a tender wife, a kind mother, and is a woman well poised in all humours ; or, in other words, Mrs. Wilkins is a person of an even temper, which rendered her conversation more agreeable than those that laugh more, but smile less : some there are, who spend more spirits, in straining, for an hour's mirth, than they can recover in a month, which renders them so unequal company ; whilst she is always equal, and the same. 'Tis virtue to know her, wisdom to converse with her, and joy to behold her ; or (to do her justice in fewer words) she is the counterpart of her pious husband, who without her, is but half himself." I might inlarge, but I fear if I write on, I shall lose my passage, and so (kind landlady) adieu.

Having taken leave of the father and mother, my last visit must be to the daughter, and sheer gratitude obliges to this farewell ; for you Mrs. Comfort may well take it amiss, if I should forget your favours to me in your father's house, your pleasant company to Ipswich, your assistance when I was ill, and the noble looking-glass you sent my dear, and all this with a world of innocence.

When the ship was ready to sail, I was attended on board by Dr. Bullevant, Mr. Wilkins, Mr. York, Mr. Gouge, Mr. Heath, Mr. Tryon, Mr. Green, and some other of my Boston friends. The captain entertain'd them with wine, beer, cyder, and neats' tongues.

So soon as ever my friends were gone off to shore, our captain ordered all his guns to fire, which were accompanied with huzzas and shouts, and shaking of hats, till we had lost all sight of our friends.

Kind Boston adieu, part we must, though 'tis pity ;
But I'm made for mankind, and all the world is my city.
Look how on the shore. they whoop and they hollow,
Not for joy I am gone, but for grief they can't follow.

CHAPTER XXXI.

" And now the trying hour came on,
That each must act a gallant part ;
Fate on one grand manœuvre hung,
One mighty stroke, prompt, dangerous, and bold."

Mr. Dudley's presidentship was of short duration. Sir Edmund Andros, who had formerly been governour of New York, arrived Dec. 19, 1686, with a commission from king James II. dated July 3d, constituting himself governour of the whole country, and empowering him with four of his council to make laws, and raise money without a general assembly or any consent of the people. He landed at Boston, the 20th of Dec. and his commission was published the same day.* The beginning of his administration gave great encouragement, but it was too soon evinced that his disposition and aims were tyrannical : many of his council deserted their seats ; a few only who lived in or near Boston attended constantly, and some of those complained that he had always three or four of his creatures, ready to say yes or no to every thing he proposed, after which no opposition was allowed. It was not long before the case of some, who apprehended themselves oppressed, came under consideration, and one of the council told them, ' they must not think the privileges of Englishmen would follow them to the ends of the world.' It was an incautious speech, but it sounded an alarm through the country, and was never forgotten.

The Boston records present the following communication, made Feb. 25, 1687, ' To his Excellency the Governour and Council of H. M. territory and dominion of New England.'

' The humble petition of the selectmen of Boston humbly showeth, that forasmuch as this town, being the principal seat of trade within this his M.'s territory, the growth and flourishing whereof will necessarily influence the prosperity and well-being of the whole, and there having been of late years considerable visible decays in the estates thereof, through the adversity of the Indian war, desolation by fire, and the failing of trade. which have greatly impoverished the town, so that the number of the poor is much increased, and notwithstand-

---

* He was accompanied by 60 red coats, whom he landed at Fool's wharf (now Central street), and marched to Mr. Gibbs' house on Fort-hill. *Holmes.* Mass. H. C. 2. ii. 261.
Aug. 31, 1687. An official return gave 1447 male persons above 16 years of age.

ing some former essays, as yet no effectual remedy is provided for easing the charge of the town, by setting them to work ; there being also several common nuisances, in said town, very offensive and prejudicial to the inhabitants, and occasion of charge to the town ; we therefore pray, that your Ex. and council will please to order and appoint a committee of some of the members of your council, who are best acquainted with the state and condition of the town, unto whom we may represent what we conceive to be necessary for the well ordering and regulating of the affairs of this populous town, respecting the poor, idle, and disorderly persons, with what else we may propose as conducible to the good and welfare of the place, that so what we shall offer therein may be stated and prepared to be laid before your Ex. and Council for consideration and approbation, as in your wisdom you shall judge fit. And your petitioners as in duty bound shall ever pray.'

The people endured insolence and privations of various kind and degree under the new government, yet it is observed, that they were, in general, patient.* Opportunely for them, a revolution was about taking place in England, which was to furnish them with a plausible pretext for the overthrow of their oppressors. James second was a devoted papist, and aimed to restore the catholicks to power : the nation was not prepared to submit to such a change. James had three children, one of which, Mary, was married to William, prince of Orange. William aimed at the throne of England, and, taking advantage of the discontent of the people, he landed with an army, Nov. 15, 1688, and expelled James from the kingdom.

An account of this event reached Boston in April, 1689. Mr.———Winslow, who brought a printed copy of the Prince of Orange's declaration, was imprisoned on the charge of bringing a ' traitorous and treasonable libel into the country.' He offered £2000 bail, but it could not be accepted. A proclamation was issued by Sir Edmund, charging all officers and people to be in readiness to hinder the landing of any forces, which the Prince of Orange might send into these parts of the world. The old magistrates and heads of the people silently wished, and secretly prayed for success to the glorious undertaking, and determined quietly to wait the event. The body of the people were more impatient. The

---

* In 1684, Boston had increased the number of its selectmen from 7 to 9 : in 1688 ' by virtue of an act of the Gov. and Council,' it was reduced to 8. ' Every town was suffered to meet once a year, to choose their officers, but all meetings at other times or for other purposes were strictly forbidden.' And the phraseology of the records is altered specially from ' a meeting of the freemen' to ' a meeting of the *freeholders and other inhabitants.*'

flame, which had been long smothering in their breasts, burst
forth with violence on Thursday, the 18th of April ; when
Andros, and such of the Council as had been most active,
were seized and confined, and the old magistrates were re-
instated. The most circumstantial account of this exploit is
contained in the following letter to the governour of
Plymouth.

' Boston, April 22d, 89.

' Hon'd Sir,

' The consideration of my sending you a blank, wherein
only the declaration was enclosed, seems to deserve a check,
and constrains me to an apology, not having so much as liberty granted me by the messenger to write two or three lines,
whereby you might have understood the present state of
things, which by this time you are doubtless acquainted with ;
but lest it should prove otherwise, I have taken the pains to
give a brief account—I knew not any thing of what was intended, until it was begun ; yet being at the north end of the
town, where I saw boys running along the streets, with clubs
in their hands, encouraging one another to fight, I began to
mistrust what was intended, and, hastening towards the town-
dock, I soon saw men running for their arms ; but before I
got to the Red Lion, I was told, that Capt. George and the
master of the frigate* were seized and secured in Mr. Colman's house at the north end ; and when I came to the town-
dock, I understood, that Bullivant and some others of them
were laid hold of ; and then, immediately, the drums began
to beat, and the people hastened and ran, some with and some
for arms.

' Young Dudley† and Colonel Lidget with some difficulty
attained to the fort. The governour immediately sent Dud-
ley on an errand, to request the four ministers,‡ Mr. Joyliffe,||
and one or two more, to come to him at the fort, pretending
that, by them, he might still the people, not thinking it safe
for him to go to them. They returned for answer, that they
did not think it safe for them to go to him. Now, by this
time, all the persons, whom they concluded not to be for their
side, were seized and secured, except some few who had hid

---

* The Rose.

† Mr. Dudley, his father, was absent, holding court in the Narraganset country. Some
of Providence went out and seized him. He was brought to Roxbury, and a guard placed
round his house, to secure him, as the order expresses it, against violence. He was afterwards committed to prison.

‡ Messrs. Allen and Moodey, of the First Church,—Willard, of the Old South,—and Cotton Mather, of the Old North.

|| A person, who had been many years a leading man in town affairs in Boston, and
recorder or town-clerk at the time.

themselves, who afterwards were found, and dealt by as the rest. The governour, with Palmer, Randolph, Lidget, West, and one or two more, were in the fort. All the companies were soon rallied together at the town-house ; where assembled Capt. Winthrop,* Shrimpton,* Page,† and many other substantial men, to consult matters ; in which time the old governour‡ came among them, at whose appearance there was a great shout by the soldiers. Soon after, the jack was set up at the fort, and a pair of colours at Beacon-hill, which gave notice to some thousand soldiers on Charlestown side that the controversy was now to be ended ; and multitudes would have been there, but that there was no need. The frigate, upon the news, put out all her flags and pendants, and opened all her ports, and with all speed made ready for fight, under the command of the lieutenant, he swearing that he would die before she should be taken ; although the captain sent to him, that if he fired one shot, or did any hurt, they would kill him, whom they had seized already ; but the lieutenant, not regarding, kept those resolutions all that day.

' Now, about four of the clock in the afternoon, orders were given to go and demand the fort ; which hour the soldiers longed for ; and had it not been just at the nick, the governour and all the crew had made their escape on board the frigate, a barge being sent for them ; but the soldiers, being so near, got the barge. The army divided, and part came up on the back side of the fort, part went underneath the hill to the lower battery or sconce, where the red coats were, who immediately upon their approach retired up to the fort to their master, who rebuked them for not firing on our soldiers and, as I am informed, beat some of them. When the soldiers came to the battery or sconce, they presently turned the great guns about, and pointed them against the fort, which did much daunt those within ; and the soldiers were so void of fear, that, I presume, had those within the fort been resolute to have lost their lives in fight, they might have killed an hundred of us at once, being so thick together before the mouths of the cannon of the fort, all loaden with small shot ; but God prevented it. Then they demanded a surrender, which was denied, until Mr. West and another should first go to the council, and after their return, we should have an answer, whether to fight or no. Upon their return, they came forth from the fort, and went disarmed to the town-house,

---

* They were both of them of Sir Edmund's council.

† He married president Dudley's sister.

‡ Other accounts say, that he and the old magistrates were guarded by the militia with great formality.

and from thence, some to the close jail, and the governour, under a guard, to Mr. Usher's house.*

' The next day, they sent the two colonels to demand of him the surrender of the castle, which he resolved not to give ; but they told him, if he would not give it presently, under his hand and seal, he would be exposed to the rage of the people, and so left him ; but he sent and told them that he would, and did so ; and they went down, and it was surrendered to them with cursings ; and they brought the men away,† and made Captain Fairweather commander in it. Now, by the time that the men came back from the castle, all the guns, both in ships and batteries, were brought to bear against the frigate, which were enough to have shattered her in pieces at once, resolving to have her. It is incident to corrupt nature to lay the blame of our evil deeds any where rather than on ourselves ; so Captain George cast all the blame now upon that devil Randolph, (for had it not been for him he had never troubled this good people,) earnestly soliciting that he might not be constrained to surrender the ship, for by so doing both himself and all his men would lose their wages, which otherwise would be recovered in England, giving leave to go on board and strike the topmasts and bring the sails on shore ; and so he did. The country people came armed into the town, in the afternoon, in such rage and heat, that it made us all tremble to think what would follow ; for nothing would satisfy them, but that Gov. Andros must be bound in chains or cords, and put into a more secure place, and that they would see done before they went away ; and, to satisfy them, he was guarded by them to the fort.'——

None of the magistrates appear to have been privy to the rising of the people on this occasion : but the former governour, Mr. Bradstreet, with several of the assistants chosen in 1686, assembled immediately at the town-house, and assumed the direction of affairs, under the title of ' a council for the safety of the people and conservation of the peace,' and associated 22 others with them. Mr. Bradstreet was chosen their president. They recommended to the towns to send deputies (not exceeding two for each town, except Boston four‡) to form an assembly on the 9th of May. This assem-

* Mr. John Nelson, a young gentleman of Boston, at the head of the soldiers, demanded the fort the second time ; and then the governour came down, and surrendered himself and the fort. *Neal.*

† Ensign John Pipon was at that time commander there. The veteran Roger Clap, who had succeeded Capt. Richard Davenport in 1665, resigned his office rather than submit to the requisitions of Andros. *Prince*, Chr. Hist. p. 71.—Col. Rec. 1689.

‡ After many successive petitions for an increase in the number of her representatives, Boston had been allowed to choose three in 1681.

bly declared the officers chosen in 1686 to be the rightful government ; and adjourned to the 22d, when warm disputes occurred on the expediency of reassuming the old charter. This was not done.

‘ On the 26th, a ship arrived from England, with advice of the proclaiming of King William and Queen Mary. This was the most joyful news ever received in New-England. The fears of the people, of any very bad consequences from their late actions, were now over. On the 29th, the proclamation was published in Boston, with greater ceremony than had been known ; the governour and council, civil and military officers, merchants of the town, and principal gentlemen of the town and country, being on horseback ; the regiment of the town, and many companies of horse and foot from the country, appearing in arms ; a grand entertainment was prepared in the town-house, and wine was served out to the soldiers.’

On the 5th of June, the representatives from the several towns, on a new choice, assembled at Boston. The council immediately proposed to them to consent to the enlargement of the ‘ gentlemen seized by the people,’ upon security ; but this was not agreed to : and on the 27th they resolved, that they were not bailable, and sent up articles against them. Sir Edmund and his friends remained in close custody for upwards of twenty weeks ; excepting the knight himself, who was absent a short time, on his way to Rhode Island, having made his escape through the craftiness of a servant, that ‘ enticed the centinel to drink, and then to suffer him to be on guard in his stead :’ but ‘ there, Major Sanford stopped him and sent him back to the castle again.’ At last an order was received from the king, approving the course pursued by the people and old magistrates, and directing, that Andros and the rest of their prisoners should be sent forthwith to England. This order arrived late in the year, and on the first opportunity, (Feb. 1690,) Sir Edmund with Mr. Dudley* and several others embarked for England.

---

* ‘ Of all that were concerned in the late government, Mr. Dudley felt most of the people's resentment. He writes to C. Mather, June 1st, ‘ I am told that this morning is the last opportunity for rolling away the stone from the mouth of this sepulchre, where I am buried alive, in which I yet trouble you for your assistance.’ To governour Bradstreet, Sept. 12th, ‘ After twenty weeks unaccountable imprisonment, and many barbarous usages offered me therein, the last seven weeks whereof are upon account of your letters to me, I have now to complain, that on Monday the whole day I could be allowed no victuals till nine of the clock at night, when the keeper's wife offered to kindle her own fire to warm something for me, and the corporal expressly commanded the fire to be put out.—I may be easily oppressed to death.—God will hear them that complain to him.—I pray your directions for your oppressed kinsman.   J. D.’

CHAPTER XXXII.

"This is a beaten track." "Is this a track
Should not be beaten ? Never beat enough
Till enough learnt the truths it would inspire."

THERE were, in the company of first emigrants, a very few who entertained sentiments in unison with the church of England. We hear very little of them until the year 1646, when Dr. Child, Maverick, Fowle, and others, presented a petition to the court, in which, among other grievances, they complain that ' divers sober, righteous, and godly men—members of the church of England—and their posterity are detained from the seals of the covenant of grace, because, as it is supposed, they will not take these churches' covenants' ; and ' humbly intreat—liberty to the members of the Church of E.—to enjoy all those liberties and ordinances Christ hath purchased —till inconveniences hereby be found, prejudicial to the churches and colony.' This petition met with so unfavourable a reception, that it is probable the episcopalian brethren made no attempts afterwards to establish a society of their order for several years. In 1662, the court declared in an official document, that ' none as yet among them had appeared to desire to use the book of common prayer.' But when the commissioners from K. Charles II. were at Boston, in 1665, they had a chaplain with them, and the agents of the colony in England, and the general court, in their answers to complaints made against them in 1677, had promised that no person should be hindered from the performance of church services. From that time a society seems to have been forming, and in the year 1686 Randolph writes to the Archbishop of Canterbury, that ' there are 400 persons who are daily frequenters of our church, and as many more would come over to us, but some being tradesmen, others of mechanick professions, are threatened by the congregational men to be arrested by their creditors, or turned out of their work, if they offer to come.'

In disregard, however, of all such discouragements, a meeting was held on the 15th of June, of that year, which may be considered the origin of the first episcopal society in Boston. The persons who then associated were ' Mr. Robert Ratcliffe, our minister, Edw. Randolph, Esq. one of His M.'s council, Capt. Lidgett, Mr. Luscomb, Mr. White, Mr. Maccarty, Mr. Ravenscroft, Dr. Clark, Mr. Turfrey, Mr. Richard Banks, and Dr. Benja. Bullivant ; and at a subsequent meeting, July 4, Mr. Proctor, Mr. Steph. Wessendonck, Mr. Thomas Brinley, and Mr. Mallet, are also named. Dr. Bullivant and Mr. Banks were elected the first wardens.

At those meetings it was agreed, that an humble address should be made to the king, to be signed by the gentlemen first named, ' to implore H. M.'s favour to our church, and it is consented that all true sons of the Church of E. may join with us in the same.' In the same method, letters were to be sent ' to the Right Reverend Father in God, the Lord Archbishop of Canterbury, and to the Reverend Father in God, the Lord Bishop of London, to implore those prelates' favour.' It was also agreed, that there be a sacrament the second sabbath in August, and that the prayers of the church be said, every Wednesday and Friday in the year, for the present in the library chamber in the town-house in Boston, and that a sober and fit person be sought after for a clerk. Mr. Thomas Hill was selected and held the first office of that name. Mr. —— Smith was the first sexton. He was a joiner, and was employed to make 12 forms [settees] for the service of the church, and also to clean, place, and remove the pulpit, forms, table, etcetera, and ' do all other things, which shall be convenient and necessary, in their place of publick assembling.'

The first step towards the erection of a church was an address to the [President and] Council, for ' liberty and authority, by a brief, to pass through the whole territory of H. M. in N. E. and therein to collect and receive all such voluntary donations, as all persons whatsoever shall be disposed to give us, for and towards the building of a church, in Boston, to be erected for the service of God and for the use of the church of E. as per law established.' This was in July, 1686.* Gov. Andros arriving in Dec. of that year, and not finding the church so well accommodated as the congregations were, made application for the use of one of the meeting-houses, and having examined *the three,* made choice of the Old South, and sent Randolph to ask for the keys. The proprietors declared, that they could not in conscience suffer the house to be occupied for such a purpose as the governour proposed. Andros however persisted, and on Friday, the 25th of March, 1687, had a service performed there : ' good man Needham, though he had resolved to the contrary, being prevailed upon to ring the bell and open the door at the governour's command.'

---

* ' Aug. 5. Mr. Harris, boddice-maker, is the first buried with Common Prayer : he was formerly Randolph's landlord.' *Sewall's* Diary in *Holmes'* Annals.

It is probable, that the council acceded to the request of the church, and granted them a brief for obtaining subscriptions, for they proceeded to build a house of worship. It is usually said to have been founded in 1688 : the first record, that speaks of it as if finished, is dated July, 1689, and is a list of those ' that contributed' towards the house. They were 106 in number, and the amount of their contributions was £256. 9s. 0d. The cost of the house was £284. 16s. 0d. exclusive of some items for which no charge was made. It was a wooden building, with a steeple, and occupied part of the land on which the Stone Chapel now stands. How the society obtained possession of the lot does not appear. It had been the property of the town ; but whether Johnson, as is the opinion of some, had reserved a portion of it for the site of a church, or whether, according to another opinion, Andros exercised the power, which the annihilation of the charter was supposed to give the king over all landed estate, and of his own will appropriated it to the use of the church, must remain undecided.   At first there were no pews in the house ; in 1694, fifty-three persons subscribed toward the building of pews ; those probably were all attendants on the service of the church. Down to May, 1698, we find the building called His Majesty's chapel ; in November, King's chapel, and in 1713, Queen's chapel, in honour of queen Anne.

Mr. Ratcliffe, the first rector (who had an assistant by the name of Robert Clarke) came over with Mr. Dudley. He is noticed by Dunton, who says, he ' read the common prayer in his surplice and preached in the town-house on Lord's days. He was an eminent preacher, and his sermons were useful and well dressed : I was once or twice to hear him, and it was noised about, that Dr. Annesley's son-in-law was turned apostate : but I could easily forgive 'em, in regard the common prayer and surplice were religious novelties in New-England.'

It may be noted here, that, under the charter government, the clergy had never performed any part of the ceremonies at marriages or funerals, except an occasional prayer, ' lest it might in time introduce the customs of the English church.' Upon Mr. Dudley's being appointed President, in 1686, he published an order of council, authorizing and empowering ministers and justices to " consummate marriages :" and in 1688, we find Mr. Ratcliffe persisting in the performance of the burial service at the grave of one Lilly, in opposition to the will of his executors. After that time our present customs in these respects came slowly into vogue.

CHAPTER XXXIII.

She deals in charms—can read the book of fate,
And tells the future with unerring skill.

Atheneum.

THE execution of Mrs. Hibbins for witchcraft had been disapproved by many people of note, and it is not unlikely that her death saved the lives of many, who might have been made the victims of a delusion, which, in the thirty years succeeding, had brought many to believe that there might exist such a thing as a witch, or person favoured with uncommon communications from the prince of darkness. In 1687 or '88 an instance occurred in Boston, which was more alarming than any that had preceded it. It certainly entitles us to divide the credit, which our sister town of Salem has borne away so long.

' Four of the children of John Goodwin, a grave man and a good liver at the north part of Boston, were generally believed to be bewitched. I have often heard persons, who were of the neighbourhood, speak of the great consternation it occasioned. The children were all remarkable for ingenuity of temper, had been religiously educated, and were thought to be without guile. The eldest was a girl of thirteen or fourteen years. She had charged a laundress with taking away some of the family linen. The mother of the laundress was one of the wild Irish, of bad character, and gave the girl harsh language ; soon after which she fell into fits, which were said to have something diabolical in them. One of her sisters and two brothers followed her example,, and, it is said, were tormented in the same part of their bodies at the same time, although kept in separate apartments, and ignorant of one another's complaints. One or two things were said to be very remarkable ; all their complaints were in the day time, and they slept comfortably all night ; they were struck dead at the sight of the assembly's catechism, Cotton's milk for babes, and some other good books, but could read in Oxford's jests, Popish and Quaker books, and the common prayer, without any difficulty. Is it possible the mind of man should be capable of such strong prejudices, as that a suspicion of fraud should not immediately arise ? But attachments to modes and forms in religion had such force, that some of these circumstances seem rather to have confirmed the credit of the children. Sometimes they would be deaf, then dumb,

25

then blind ; and sometimes all these disorders together would come upon them.   Their tongues would be drawn down their throats, then pulled out upon their chins.   Their jaws, necks, shoulders, elbows, and all their joints would appear to be dislo- cated ; and they would make most piteous outcries of burnings, of being cut with knives, beat, &c. and the marks of wounds were afterwards to be seen.   The ministers of Boston and Charlestown kept a day of fasting and prayer at the troubled house ; after which, the youngest child made no more com- plaints.   The others persevered, and the magistrates then interposed, and the old woman was apprehended ; but upon examination would neither confess nor deny, and appeared to be disordered in her senses.   Upon the report of physicians, that she was *compos mentis,* she was executed, declaring at her death the children should not be relieved.   The eldest, after this, was taken into a minister's family, where at first she be- haved orderly, but after some time suddenly fell into her fits. The account of her affliction is in print ; some things are mentioned as extraordinary, which tumblers are every day taught to perform ; others seem more than natural; but it was a time of great credulity.   The children returned to their or- dinary behaviour, lived to adult age, made profession of reli- gion, and the affliction they had been under they publickly declared to be one motive to it.   One of them I knew many years after.   She had the character of a very sober, virtuous woman, and never made any acknowledgment of fraud in this transaction.   The printed account was published, with a pre- face by Mr. Baxter, who says, ' the evidence is so convincing, that he must be a very obdurate Sadducee, who will not be- lieve.'   Says Hutchinson, from whom this account is taken, ' it obtained credit sufficient, together with other preparatives, to dispose the whole country to be easily imposed upon by the more extensive and more tragical scene, which was pres- ently after acted at Salem and other parts of the county of Essex.'

In 1690, August 3d, a fire near the Mill bridge, across the creek in Hanover street, consumed several houses : and the fire known as THE FIFTH GREAT FIRE happened September 16th, near the [Old] South meeting-house, greatly endangered it, and burnt several houses.   A lad was burnt to death in the house where it began.

1691, June 30th, in the sixth great fire, which happened at the King's Head, by Scarlett's wharf, North-end, several houses were consumed.

CHAPTER XXXIV.

The senate owns its gratitude to Cato,
Who with so great a soul consults its safety,
And guards our lives, while he neglects his own.
Addison.

HOWEVER true the observation may have been, that the people in general were patient under Andros's government, some of the principal men had thought it an object to endeavour to obtain relief from their sufferings, by a representation of their grievances to King James. It was proposed ' that some one should be sent with an address of thanks to the king, for his gracious declaration, wherein he does promise us the free exercise of our religion, and that he will maintain us in the enjoyment of our rights and possessions.' Mr. Increase Mather, (then pastor of the Old North church, in conjunction with his son Cotton,) was selected for this purpose, and on propounding the matter to his church, Dec. 11, 1687, he found them all willing that he should go. He was ready to sail in April, 1688, and did so, notwithstanding the machinations of Randolph, who, on false pretences, was bringing an action against him about the same time. Mr. Mather was obliged to keep himself concealed, to avoid the service of the writ ; and when the vessel was ready to sail, some of his church carried him aboard, in the night, in disguise.

Mr. Mather was the man of all the clergy, on whom the mantle of the departed Cotton seems to have rested. His influence on the character of the town, and particularly on that part of it in which he resided, was equal to that of his revered exemplar. ' Ardent, bold, enterprising, and perhaps ambitious ; conscious of his own power, religiously sensible of his obligations to exercise it usefully ;* born and trained in a young colony struggling with hardships, and forcing its way through peril and fear ; his mind fashioned by a father, who for conscience' sake had quitted all and settled in this hopeless land, and who had all the zeal and firmness which characterized the puritans of that age, a race eminently formed " to do and to dare ;"—thus gifted and educated, he became peculiarly fit, and no wonder it was felt that he was fit, to have an ascendency and exercise a control. He had re-

* Rev. Mr. Ware's Discourses.

ceived the best education of his own country, he had completed it abroad, he had been driven from place to
place, suffering for his religion, and presented with
strong temptations to abandon it, thus acting a hurried
and various part in the most trying times in the mother
country—and after this discipline, so calculated to give firmness and character, he returned to labour in the service of
this infant state. Nothing can be conceived more likely to
prepare a man to act well his part in so peculiar a scene. He
soon became eminent. Talents, learning, and virtue are always commanding. In that age a religious spirit was indispensable to honour and power. Mather had all. He was
conspicuous for rigid piety where all were rigid, and eminent
for talents and knowledge, where many had been eminent before him. It therefore is not strange that he acquired a control to which few are equal, and received and held honours
which would not now be bestowed upon ministers.'

Mr. Mather's exertions and remonstrances with James II.
were unavailing, and he determined to wait the event of the
Prince of Orange's expedition. Soon after the withdrawal of
James, he was introduced to the prince, and obtained some
partial favours, and royal promises of more. Mr. M. improved all his time in unwearied efforts to secure friends for his
country. Besides several of the nobility and principal commoners, he had engaged the whole body of the dissenting
ministers, whose weight at that time was far from inconsidera-
ble. Before any thing was completed, the general court
thought it advisable to send over two of their members to join
with Mr. Mather and Sir Henry Ashurst (whose services he
had retained) in maintaining their charges against their oppressors, as well as in soliciting the restoration of the charter,
with such additional privileges as should be thought proper.
The persons appointed were Doctors Elisha Cooke and
Thomas Oakes, both practitioners of medicine in Boston, just
rising into eminence in the political theatre, in which both
sustained very eminent parts afterwards. The result of all
their petitions and remonstrances, suggestions and objections
was, that a new charter was formed, in which ' the colony of
New Plymouth, the province of Maine and the country of
Nova Scotia, with the lands between the two latter, were
joined to Massachusetts.'

Sir William Phips was appointed the first governour under
the new order of things. He arrived at Boston with the
charter, Saturday the 14th of May, 1692, towards evening.
On Monday he was conducted from his house to the town-
house, by the regiment of Boston, the military companies of
Charlestown, the magistrates, ministers, and principal gentle-

men of Boston and the adjacent towns. The charter was first published, then the governour's commission ; and thereupon the venerable old charter governour Bradstreet resigned the chair ; not without a deep sigh from many of the spectators. After publishing the lieutenant-governour's commission, and administering the oaths, the governour was conducted, with the same parade, to the place appointed for a publick dinner, and from thence to his house again.'

His residence was in Charter-street at the corner of Salem-street, which was then called Green-lane, in the house now occupied by the Asylum for indigent boys. It is a three-story brick house, in an elevated situation, commanding a delightful view of the harbour and of the surrounding country.

The charter named the persons who were to form the council for the first year, and made provision for the organization of an assembly or house of representatives. Writs were issued without delay, and the first court under the new charter met on the 8th of June, 1692. Although a party was formed, which opposed submission to the charter, a majority of the court " thankfully accepted it, and appointed a day of solemn thanksgiving to Almighty God, for granting a safe arrival to *his excellency* the Governour and the Rev.Mr. I. Mather, who have industriously endeavoured the service of this people, and have brought over with them a settlement of government, in which their majesties have graciously given us distinguishing marks of their royal favour and goodness."

The court interpreted their powers with regard to the apportionment of representatives so as to allow Boston four members in the house, which continued to be her number until the revolution in 1775.

CHAPTER XXXV.

"Just a stained stone,
To mark the spot so holy once,
And with gray moss o'ergrown."

THE Society of Friends and the French Protestant Church having both become extinct in Boston, we shall introduce in this place the information we have been able to obtain concerning their history. The denomination of Quakers took its rise in Leicestershire (E.) in 1644. The first that came to Boston were Mary Fisher and Anne Austin, who arrived from Barbadoes in the fore part of the 5th month, 1656. These

women were made prisoners on board the vessel; the books
they brought with them were burnt, and they were taken to
gaol and confined, as were seven others, in about a month
after.   Nicholas Upshall, an aged member of a Boston
church, whose humane and tender feelings induced him to
apply to the gaoler for leave to furnish them with provisions,
and even to purchase that liberty at the price of 5s. a week,
was for thus doing and bearing his testimony, weeping, against
the persecution of these people, fined £20, and banished the
colony, though he was both a freeman and freeholder in the
town.   He was permitted to return in about five years, and
opened his house, and furnished a room in it, for the use of
travelling Friends.

Such was the dread of the influence of this sect, that severe
laws were immediately passed to prevent their entrance into
the jurisdiction, on penalty of fines, stripes, and imprisonment.   This not proving effectual, it was enacted, that any
Quaker found here should have one of his ears cut off for the
first offence, and lose the other for a second, and have his
tongue bored through with a hot iron for the third.   Three
Quakers, Holden, Copeland, and Rouse, lost each his right
ear under this law, by the hand of the hangman, in Boston
prison, Sept. 16, 1658.

All this severity was of no avail ; the persecutors seem to
have been infuriated, and their fury drove the Quakers to
acts of desperation.   They still came into the colony : the
court ordered some to be sold as slaves for the payment of
their fines ! this frightened the particular objects of the order,
and they were suffered to go to their own homes.   The sect
grew under all these disadvantages, and several families went
over to it : the magistrates were more provoked, and the general court passed a law to banish all Quakers, not inhabitants,
upon pain of death.   Four persons suffered death at Boston
by virtue of this law ; viz. Wm. Robinson, Marmaduke Stevenson, Wm. Leddra, and Mary Dyer; the last on the first of
June, 1660.   She had been conspicuous in Mrs. Hutchinson's
controversy, and that probably aggravated her guilt.   Her
son came forward and plead for her pardon, but in vain.   One
of the officers under the gallows at the time of her execution,
Edward Wanton, was so affected at the sight, that he became
a convert to the cause of the Friends.   The Quakers discovered, that this law was an exercise of power not authorized
by the patent, and made such complaints to the king that no
further execution of it ever took place : whipping at a cart's
tail, through all the towns in their way out of the jurisdiction,
was substituted for death.

The first meeting of Friends in Boston, of which we have
account, was at the house of Mr. Wanton, on the 4th of May,

1664, when a warrant was issued to apprehend the preacher, and report the names of his hearers to the governour. The spirit of persecution was kept alive and manifested itself in various ways, after this. On the 9th of August, 1675, there were apprehended, at their ordinary place of meeting, Robt. Edmund, Edw. Shippen, John Soames, Jere. Debee, George Danson, Miles Foster, Humphrey Hodges, Bridget Phillips, Tho. Scott, Wm. Neal, Eph. Stratton, Elizabeth Bowers (senior and junior), Geo. Walker. Twelve of these 14 were whipped ; the other two paid their fine. At the next meeting day, 15 were whipped, viz. the eight first abovenamed, with Wm. Richardson, Thomas Holburn, Rebecca Levy, Josiah Southwick, Wm. Mumford, Eliphalet [?] Stratton, and Anna Wilson. We have mentioned the names, to give the best account we can obtain, of the number of men Friends in and near Boston at the time.*

Under the new charter, the Quakers, Baptists, and Episcopalians were placed on more equal ground with their neighbours, and some laws passed in 1692 exempting them from taxation. In 1694, the Quakers had a lot in Brattle-street, measuring 108 by 25¼ ft. for a meeting-house and burying lot, and built a brick house thereon 24 by 20 ft. which was secured to the society by Messrs. Mumford, Shippen, Soames, Wanton abovenamed, and Walter Clark of Newport and Wm. Chamberlain of Hull, ' to the only, sole, and proper use, for the service and worship of Almighty God, by the society or community of people called Quakers.' In 1708, it was concluded to sell the old meeting-house and build a new one, if leave could be obtained to build of wood ; but in 1709 the committee, Walter Newberry, John Wing, and Thomas Richardson, reported their disappointment in this respect, and it was therefore concluded to build of brick, a house 35 ft. long and 30 ft. wide. This was the building now standing in Congress-street, which is dated on the old plans of the town as if erected in 1710 ; the deed, however, by which the lot was conveyed to the society, June 10, 1717, speaks of ' the brick meeting-house lately erected thereon,' which would leave a doubt whether it was built so early. This is the oldest of

---

* For this and other information we are indebted to a venerable professor of the denomination.

Town Records, 1678. Alex'r. Coleman, shoemaker, ' the Quaker that came into the third meeting-house in a bloody coat,' is presented to the county court as a person unfit to abide here. At another time Tho. Newhouse went into a meeting-house with a couple of great glass bottles, and breaking them against one another, in the face of the congregation, said, *Thus will the Lord break you in pieces.* Similar acts of imprudence are attributed to others : all which seem to be the result of phrensy, induced by the equally senseless cruelty with which they were goaded.

the meeting-houses now standing in the city. It was burnt in
the great fire of 1760, and in the same year it was concluded
by the yearly meeting to repair it, which was done.

The Friends were never numerous in this place. ' In the
eleventh month, 1774,' says our informant, ' I was in Boston
and visited every family, and took account of their names as
follows : Ebenezer Pope, John Pope, Samuel Pope, James
Raymer, John Phillips, Ephraim Silsbee, Nathanael Low,
Ezra Collins, Ezra Curten, Daniel Silsbee, Josiah Gorham :
these eleven were all the members belonging to Boston meeting of Friends. I was at a monthly meeting there, which was
small ; it was held alternately at Boston and Lynn or Salem ;
they were then in a declining state.' Their numbers diminished after that, and the meetings were discontinued by a
regular vote in   . The house has been deserted,
the burying-ground undisturbed for several years, and we
know not now of a single professed Friend in Boston.

The French church became embodied about the same time,
but did not flourish so long as the Quakers. After having
endured severe persecutions, the Protestants in France were
relieved from their distresses by the edict of Nantes, issued
by Henry IV. in 1598. Lewis XIV. confirmed it in 1652,
but soon after suffered its provisions to be violated.* The
protestants were deprived of all offices, hundreds of their
churches desolated, and at last, in 1685, the edict was formally revoked, and multitudes were compelled by this act to
flee from the country. Some sought shelter in England and
Ireland: others directed their way to America, and some of
these settled in Boston. Those who arrived here probably
came in the summer of 1686, for contributions were taken on
their behalf at Salem, in September of that year ; and we also
find in Cotton Mather's MS. notes of sermons, under date of
Sept. 12. and Oct. 7. minutes of discourses by a Mr.
Laurie, from the tenour of which it is is apparent that he was
of the number. Pierre Baudouin (the ancestor of the Bowdoin family) fled first to Ireland, and thence came to Maine in
1687, and soon after to Boston. The first notice we discover
of the church in this place is in the Magnalia, (i. 86) where
the author enumerates among the churches in Boston, ' a
French congregation of Protestant refugees, under the pastoral care of Monsieur Daille.' †

---

* ' John Touton, a French doctor and inhabitant of Rochelle in France, made application to
the court in behalf of himself and other protestants expelled from their habitations on account of their religion, that they might have liberty to inhabit here, which was readily granted to them.' *Hutch.* vol. i. Col. rec. 1662. p. 413.

† The records of this church are supposed to be in existence, but we have not been able to
discover them. A bible presented by Queen Anne is also mentioned in Mass. H. C. 1. iii. 264.

M. Daille continued to be pastor of this church till his death, which took place on the morning of Friday, May 20, 1715. He was about 66 years of age ; ' a person of great piety, charity, affable and courteous behaviour, and of an exemplary life and conversation : much lamented, especially by his flock.' Monsieur D. had buried two wives, Esther-Latonice, who died Dec. 14, 1696, and Seike, who died, Aug. 31, 1713 ; and he left a widow, whose name was Martha. His will required, that his body should be ' decently interred' according to the discretion of his executor, Mr. James Bowdoin, ' with this restriction, that there be no wine at my funeral, and none of my wife's relations have any mourning clothes furnished them, except gloves.' All the ministers of the town, together with Mr. Walter, are presented with gloves and scarfs : his books are given to form a library for the church ; £100 for the benefit of the minister, and £10 to be put to interest, until the church should erect a meeting-house, when it was to be appropriated towards the expenses of the same. He remembers his brother ' Paul Daille Vaugelade in Amsfort in Holland,' and signs himself *Daille*, omitting his baptismal name of Peter.

From the above notice of a meeting-house, it appears that the French church, which once stood in School-street, on the lot next east of the Universal meeting-house, was not erected till after 1715. The lot had come into their possession, Jan. 4, 1705, by a conveyance from ——— Mears to ' John Tartarien, Francis Breedon, Jean Depuis, elders of the said French church, in behalf of themselves and the rest of the congregation—being to erect and build a church upon for the use of the F. congregation in Boston, to meet therein for the worship and service of Almighty God, according to the way and manner of the reformed churches of France.' On the 7th of Feb. 1705, ' John Portree, F. Breeden, and John Dupee,' petitioned the selectmen for licence to erect a wooden building for a meeting-house of 35 by 30 ft. on that piece of land. It was judged ' not convenient to grant the same, since they have the offer of the free liberty to meet in the new school-house, as they had for some years past done in the old, and that being sufficient for a far greater number of persons than doth belong to their congregation.' The brick building was probably erected in 1716 : it is mentioned by C. Mather in Jan. 1717.

M. Daille's successor was the Rev. Andrew Le Mercier, whose name is found on the town records in 1719. He published a church history of Geneva, in 1732, from which it appears that he was educated in that country. This church did not increase in number sufficiently to enable them to

26

support the expenses of a separate house of worship and on
that account the society was discontinued.   On the 7th of
March, 1748, the proprietorship of the house in School-street
was transferred to several gentlemen as trustees of a new congregational church.   The transfer was made by Stephen
Boutineau, only surviving elder, Zach. Johonnot, Jean Ar-
nault, John Brown, Andrew Johonnot, James Packonett, Wm.
Bowdoin, Andrew Sigourney, members, and Mr. Le Mercier,
the minister.   Mr. Le M. after that resided at Dorchester, but
removed again to Boston, and died here, March, 31, 1764,
' after a long indisposition of body, in the 72d year of his
age.'   One of his daughters and Mr. Z. Johonnot were joint
executors of his will.

CHAPTER XXXVI.

Buck. You are too senseless obstinate, my lord,
Too ceremonious and traditional.
Shakspeare.

THE seventh religious society formed in Boston was the
fourth Congregational, or Brattle-street church.   ' A number
of good men,' says Dr. Thacher's century sermon, ' distinguished for their liberality of thinking, as well as for their
regard to the gospel and its ordinances, laid the foundation
of this church.'   The earliest date, at which we find them
associated, is Jan. 10, 1698, on which day Thomas Brattle,
Esq. conveyed to them a piece of land called *Brattle's close*,
which makes part of the lot now in possession of the church.
The grantees were Thos. Clark, Thos. Cooper, Benja. Walker, Benja. Davis, Wm. Keen, Richard Draper, Wm. Harris,
Zech. Tuthill, John Colman, Jos. Allen, John Kilby, John
Mico, Thos. Bannister, Timo. Clark, Stephen Minot, Abr.
Blush, Thos. Palmer, James Meers, Elkanah Pembroke,
Addington Davenport.

' As to the doctrines of religion, these good men did not differ
professedly from their brethren of other churches, while they
thought that in some respects the religious practices of the
day might be improved.   Under these circumstances it was
necessary for them to choose a minister, who agreed with
them in sentiment,' and accordingly, in the spring of 1699,
they sent a letter of invitation to Mr. Benjamin Colman, a
native of Boston and graduate of Harvard College, who was
then pursuing his studies in England.   ' From an apprehension that he might meet with difficulty in procuring ordination

here, they requested him to ask it of the ministers in London, who readily granted his desire, and the solemnity was attended on the 4th day of August, after a publick lecture, at the meeting-house of the Rev. Mr. Christopher Taylor.'

On the first of the following November, Mr. Colman arrived at Boston ; and on the 17th of that month a publication appeared, with the title of ' A manifesto or declaration, set forth by the undertakers of the new church, now erected in B. in N. E.' in which, ' for preventing all misapprehensions and jealousies,' they say, ' we think it convenient to publish our aims and designs herein, together with those principles and rules we intend, by God's grace, to adhere unto.' ' On Tuesday, Dec. 12th, at a private meeting at Mr. Mico's house, after solemn calling upon God,' the eleven grantees first abovenamed, with Mr. Brattle and Messrs. John and Oliver Noyes, united to form the church, and ' declared their consent and agreement to walk together in all the ordinances of our Lord Jesus Christ.' The 24th instant, being Lord's-day, was agreed upon for their first meeting in their ' pleasant new-built church.' Mr. Colman preached on the occasion from 2 Chron. vi. 18. The ' Manifesto' and other ' miscarriages,' which this society had ' fallen into,' gave so great offence, that some of the clergymen of the town refused to unite with them in the observance of a day of prayer ; but by some means, an accommodation took place prior to Jan. 31, 1700, when both the Mathers and Mr. Willard joined with them on a similar occasion.

The doctrines which this church espoused could not have been exceptionable, for they declare, ' we approve and subscribe the confession of faith put forth by the assembly of divines at Westminster ;' but they introduced some changes as to ' modes of order and discipline,' which probably were the cause of alarm and dissatisfaction. They adopted the custom of reading some part of the holy scriptures, and ' concluded to have the Lord's prayer used once in each season of publick worship.' The admission to full communion was deemed, by the first settlers of this country, as matter of great importance. The general opinion was, that none should partake of this privilege but such as were truly born of God. ' In order that the church might judge of this fact, a relation of his christian experiences, either written or oral, was required of every candidate for this privilege. This usage had degenerated into a matter of mere form, and such a similarity prevailed in these instruments, as gave too much occasion for ridicule. In this church, therefore, the practice was disused ; at least it was not required, while every one was left at liberty to do it.'

' In ancient days the choice of minister (as well as the choice of civil officers) was confined to those who were in full communion with the church. In this respect also they differed from the general practice. " We cannot, say they, confine the right of choosing a minister to the communicants alone, but we think that every baptized adult person, who contributes to the maintenance, should have a vote in electing."—But there were many men, some from a reverence to ancient institutions, and a convicton of their propriety, some from dread of innovation, and others from a fear that this new and popular society would diminish their own societies and lessen the influence they held, who exclaimed loudly against this new establishment, which they called, by way of derision, the *Manifesto church.* Respectable and opulent as were the men who formed it, they found it difficult for a time to stem the torrent of publick opinion which ran strongly against them, and overcome the jealousy which their neighbours felt of being eclipsed by them.*

Following the order of time, we mention here that the By-laws of the town, which had been accumulating for seventy years, were put into order and renewed by a vote in 1701, and first published in a printed form in 1702.

The Seventh Great Fire happened in the year 1702, on the 11th of March, near the dock. Three ware-houses were blown up to stop its progress. The destruction of property was so extensive, as to be mentioned in official papers ' as a great loss to the town.'

In 1704 the first newspaper published in the English colonies in North America, appeared in Boston. It was printed on half a sheet of pot paper, with a small-pica type, folio, and was entitled,

𝔑. 𝔈.   𝔑𝔲𝔪𝔟. 1.

The Boston News-Letter.

𝔓𝔲𝔟𝔩𝔦𝔰𝔥𝔢𝔡 𝔟𝔶 𝔄𝔲𝔱𝔥𝔬𝔯𝔦𝔱𝔶.

From 𝔐𝔬𝔫𝔡𝔞𝔶, April 17, to 𝔐𝔬𝔫𝔡𝔞𝔶, April 24, 1704.

The proprietor's name was John Campbell, a Scotchman, who was established here as a bookseller. The imprint is, " Boston ; printed by *B. Green.* Sold by *Nicholas Boone,*

---

* This church voted to dispense with the custom of singing the psalms in publick worship line by line, Dec. 20, 1699. Between 1717 and 1724 they had a *singing society*, which was the first in the town, that introduced singing by note.—Chh. Rec.—Mass. H. C. 2. iv. 304. Also Appendix, No. IV.

at his Shop near the Old Meeting-House." Green was Campbell's printer, and Boone was for some weeks his publisher.*

The first number contained the following prospectus :—
' This News Letter is to be continued Weekly ; and all Persons who have any Houses, Lands, Tenements, Farmes, Ships, Vessels, Goods, Wares, or Merchandizes &c. to be sold or Lett ; or Servants Runaway : or Goods Stoll or Lost may have the same Inserted at a Reasonable Rate ; from Twelve Pence to Five Shillings, and not to exceed ; Who may agree with *Nicholas Boone* for the same at his shop next door to MajorDavis's,Apothecary in *Boston* near the old Meetinghouse.

' All Persons in Town and Country may have said News-Letter Weekly upon reasonable tearms agreeing with John Campbell Post Master for the same.'

So early as Dec. 8, 1686, the inhabitants at Muddy river had obtained an order from the president and council, that said hamlet should henceforth be free from town rates to the town of Boston, and have the privilege of meeting ' annually to choose three men to manage their affairs.' The conditions were, that they should support their own expenses, erect a school-house, and maintain a reading and writing master. After the overthrow of Andros, the town of Boston disannulled this order, by a vote, in March, 1690, ' that M. R. inhabitants are not discharged from B. to be a hamlet by themselves, but stand related to B. as they did before the year sixteen hundred and eighty-six.' As the inhabitants there increased in numbers and in wealth, they were emboldened again to seek a complete separation. Accordingly, in March, 1701, they requested the consent of Boston, ' to be a district or hamlet separate from the town.' Instead of granting their request, the inhabitants of Boston rigorously exercised over them all the authority they possessed. Finding their application to Boston ineffectual, they resolved to apply to still higher powers. They therefore in June, 1704, petitioned the governour, council, and assembly. On this, the inhabitants of Boston had several meetings, warmly remonstrated against the petition, and represented the request as highly ingrateful in this people, after having experienced so many favours. Their petition was at this time rejected. They however persisted in their request, and in the summer of 1705, presented a petition to be incorporated, signed by 32 freeholders, which was finally granted, and the signature of the governour to the act incorporating them as a distinct town, by the name of

* At the time this paper was first published, and for many years afterward, there were licensers of the press. " Published by authority," I presume means nothing more than this —what appeared in this publication was not disapproved by the licensers.—*Thomas'* Hist. of Printing in America. ii. 191.

BROOKLINE, was passed November 13, 1705. It is supposed that this name was adopted from the circumstance, that Smelt brook is a boundary between that town and Cambridge, and that another brook, which falls into Muddy river, is a boundary between it and Roxbury.*

OLD FRANKLIN HOUSE,

IN MILK-STREET.

VIEW FROM THE SOUTH SIDE OF THE OLD SOUTH MEETING-HOUSE.

The year 1706 is memorable in the annals of Boston for giving birth to Benjamin Franklin. His parents were named Josiah and Abiah : his father ' was a native of England, where he was bred to the trade of a silk dyer ;' but after settling in Boston, he devoted his attention to the business of a soap and tallow chandler.

Franklin was born on the sixth of January, and is recorded as baptized on the same day, in the Old South church books.

---

* See the order of the P. and C. in Town Records, 1686. We are also referred (Mass. H. C. 2. ii. 142,) ' for this and all other information relating to the incorporation of Brookline, to a bundle of documents on file in the secretary's office of this commonwealth, under the date of 1705.'

From this circumstance some have inferred that he was born in the house, which lately stood where the Furniture warehouse now stands, in Milk-street, nearly opposite the south door of that meeting-house, and where it is known that his father lived at some period. But we have the testimony of his own declaration to a lady, now living, that the scene of his nativity was at the sign of the Blue Ball, corner of Union and Hanover-streets, where his father exercised his trade. The other house, however, having been more remarakble in its appearance, and a drawing of it having been taken shortly before it was burnt (Dec. 29, 1810,) we have given it a place here.

We have no record of any attempt to change the form of town government from that established in 1651 (see p. 138) until the year 1708. The seven Commissioners were annually chosen during the old charter government, and the selection was made from the most honourable among the inhabitants : the last choice was in August, 1691. On the 8th of Dec. 1708, the selectmen made the following proposals to the town, respecting a charter of incorporation.

' That the orders and by-laws of this town already made, for directing, ordering and managing the prudential affairs thereof, have not answered the ends for which they were made, and the principal cause thereof is a general defect or neglect in the execution, without which the best laws will signify little, and one great reason why they are no better executed, is the want of a proper head, or *town-officer*, or officers empowered for that purpose, the law having put the execution of town orders into the hands of the Justices only, who are not town, but county officers ; and it cannot be expected that they should take the trouble and care, or make it so much their business, as a town officer or officers particularly appointed or chosen thereunto must needs do, and indeed, for any body or society of men as a town is, to be vested with power to make rules and by-laws for their own good regulation, and not have power to appoint and choose the head officer or officers, who shall have power to execute their own orders and by-laws, seems incongruous. And good order is not to be expected while it remains so ; for while a town grows more populous, it will stand in need of a more strict regulation. The selectmen do, therefore, propose that this town do now choose a committee of a considerable number of the freeholders and other inhabitants of the town to draw up a scheme or draught of a *Charter of Incorporation*, [or any other projection] for the encouragement and better government of this town, in the best methods as they shall think suitable, and of the best and most suitable means for procuring and obtaining thereof. and to present the same to the town at their annual meeting.' Accordingly thirty-one of the most respectable citizens, including the selectmen, were chosen, seventeen of whom were to be a quorum.

March 14th, 1709, the committee presented a draught to the town, which was read in the audience of the meeting. On the question whether the town will refer the consideration of the said scheme to some publick meeting to be warned for the same purpose ?—voted in the negative.   On the question —whether the town do accept of the scheme or charter now read. yea or nay ?—voted in the negative.

Hutchinson tells us, that most of the principal inhabitants were in favour of the measure.   But the people entertained the opinion of a champion, who, when the subject was discussed in town-meeting, concluded his speech with the prophetick warning, " *It is a whelp now*, IT WILL BE A LION BY AND BY : *knock it in the head :* Mr. Moderator, put the question."   His hearers were ready, and the plan was rejected by a great majority, with a vote of thanks to the gentlemen, on whom they had imposed the labour of preparing it.

CHAPTER XXXVII.

. . . . . . " higher still
The blazing tide rose awfully." . . . .

MR. HENRY DEERING had proposed to the town ' to build a house to contain several offices, and a wharf below the Townhouse-street,' in December, 1707, but it does not appear that he met with any encouragement.   The subject was renewed in 1709, by Dr. Oliver Noyes and others, and the town referred the consideration of it to the selectmen, who made the following report on the 10th of March, 1710.

' Whereas the selectmen for the year past were by a vote of the inhabitants of this town, at their publick meeting on the 19th day of Dec. last past, appointed a committee to consider the proposals of Capt. Oliver Noyes and some other gentlemen, about their building out a wharf from the lower end of King-street down to low-water mark, and to make report to the next town-meeting of what they shall think proper for the town to do concerning the same, the said committee have now presented their report thereof, and is as followeth, viz.

' We are of opinion that the proposal made by Dr. Oliver Noyes and other gentlemen, now signed by them and given in to the town at this meeting, will be a means to have the out-wharves brought into good repair, the doing of which,

with the planting of guns as proposed, may be a great safety
to this town, in case of the attack of an enemy, and will be of
publick and general good to the town, *Provided* the undertakers be under penalty to perform what they have there proposed and what is intended, viz. that the street shall forever
be open, its full breadth, from the end of King-street to the
Circular line, and be no ways incumbered by them.

' The aforementioned proposals made by Dr. Oliver Noyes
and other gentlemen, signed by them and given in to the town
at this meeting, and being read are as followeth, viz.

' We the subscribers, some of the inhabitants of the town
of Boston, do hereby promise and engage, that we and our
associates will at our own cost and charge erect and build a
wharf with a sufficient common sewer, at the approbation of
the selectmen, at the end of King-street to the Circular Line,
as delineated by the plan, and that from thence we will erect,
build, and maintain a wharf, the width of King-street, between
Mr. [East] Apthorp's and Mr. [Andrew] Faneuil's, and continue the same in a direct line to the [out] wharves, commonly called the new wharves, and unto low-water mark, leaving
always a way of 30 feet wide, on one of the sides thereof, as
a highway for the use of the inhabitants of the said town and
others, and to extend from one end of the same unto the
other, forever ; and leaving a gap of 16 ft. wide, covered
over, for lighters and boats to pass and repass, about the middle of said wharf, or where the selectmen shall direct, as also
a passage way on the new wharves,on each side,for carts,etc.
leaving the end of said wharf free for the town, when they
shall see reason to plant guns for the defence of said town.

' In consideration whereof, the freeh. and other inhabitants
of the town of B. shall, do, give, grant, bargain, enfeoffe, and
confirm unto us, the said subscribers, our heirs, assignees, and
associates forever, the said wharf or flats, to be maintained
as aforesaid, unto low-water mark, with all the liberties, privileges, commodities, and appurtenances whatsoever, thereunto
belonging, to our only, proper, and absolute use and behoof
forever : and that the town of B. shall always defend us in
the possession and peaceable improvement of the granted
premises from any claim of the town, etc. And that no wharf
beyond the said Circular Line be permitted to join or come
nearer to us than sixty ft. forever ; and we do engage and
promise to finish said wharf within the space of four years
next after the date of the grant, if the right of the outwharves
for 120 ft. where this line will fall can be procured by us.
In witness whereof, we have hereunto set our hands, the 20th
day of Feb. anno reginæ viii. A. D. 1709—10.

Oliver Noyes,   James Barnes,   John Gerrish,
Daniel Oliver,   John George,   Anthony Stoddard.'
27

Whereupon the town voted ' a grant to Capt. O. N. and company, according to their said proposals and the committee's report, so as not to prejudice former grants.' The selectmen were empowered to execute proper instruments in writing for confirming the grant, which they did on the 13th of May. The work was accomplished within the time limited.

In the same year, 1710, it was voted, that a line of defence be forthwith made across the neck between Boston and Roxbury. This constituted the *Fortifications*, which were constructed of stone and brick work for a foundation, with a parapet of sod work. A convenient number of great guns were ordered to be placed there, and a gate extended across the road.

Something like the rudiments of a Post-Office is discoverable in the colony records, May, 1677, when upon petition of several merchants of Boston, the court appointed Mr. John Hayward, scrivener, ' to take in and convey letters according to their direction.' And the office of post-master appears to have been regulated by the colonial government until 1710, when an act of parliament established the office of P. M. general. who had liberty to keep one chief letter office in New York, and others at other convenient places in America. Campbell, the publisher of the News-Letter, who had been in the office for several years, was appointed at Boston. In 1711, a southern and eastern mail, to Plymouth and Maine, ran once a week, and a western mail to Conn. and N. Y. once a fortnight.

The prosperity of Boston, which seemed now to be growing rapidly, received a check this year by a fire, that broke out on the evening of Tuesday, October 2d, about 7 o'clock. It originated in a building belonging to Capt. Ephraim Savage, in Williams's Court, from the carelessness of a poor woman, one Mary Morse, who suffered the fire ' to catch the oakum, which she was employed in picking of.' All the houses on both sides of Cornhill, from School-street to the Dock-square, were laid in ruins The wind being southerly, the meeting-house of the First Church was early found to be in danger, and some sailors went up into the steeple or cupola to save the bell. Whilst they were engaged in this service, the house was on fire below, and the stairs were consumed. They were seen at work just before the roof fell in, and all perished in the flames. All the upper part of King, or what is now called State-street, together with the Town-house, was lost, and some desolation made in Pudding-lane (Devonshire-street), and between Water-street and Spring-lane, before the violence of the flames could be conquered. There were then but two engines in the town, and the method taken to stop the progress of the fire, by blowing up the houses, had a contrary effect, and served to scatter it. The number of houses destroyed was computed near a hundred, and, by the best account, about a hundred and ten families were turned out of doors. It being also a place of much trade, and filled with well-furnished shops of goods, not a little of the wealth of the town was now consumed. The rubbish from the ruins was used to fill up the Long-wharf.

The houses which were built after this fire ' were of brick, three stories high, with a garret, a flat roof, and balustrade.' Some of them remain on each side of Cornhill ; one, now numbered 38 Washington-street, bears the date of **1712** on the front, with a coat of arms and the letters **S. L.**

The First Church commenced building on the same spot where their old house had stood, on the 14th of April, 1712. They erected a large brick edifice of three stories in height, which was ready for use, and the first service performed in it May 3, 1713.*

The general court at their next session after the fire, passed a law creating the Board of Firewards, whose number was originally ten. We recognize their symbol of authority in the badge of ' a staff of five feet in length, coloured red, and headed with a bright brass spire of six inches long.' The same court also proposed a plan for rebuilding the Townhouse, which was concurred in by the town, Nov. 16, 1711. The Province was to bear one half of the expense, the county of Suffolk and town of Boston each one quarter. The house was so far finished, that a town-meeting was held in it, March 8, 1714.

CHAPTER XXXVIII.

To know, and knowing worship God aright,
Is yet more kingly : this attracts the soul,
Governs the inner man, the nobler part.

Paradise Regained.

In the winter of 1712, seventeen substantial mechanicks associated for the purpose of establishing another church at the north part of the town, which, when formed, they named the New North Church. Their first meeting was at the house of

---

* This being the first Congregational meeting-house built of brick, obtained in time the name of the *Old Brick.* It stood till the year 1808; the last service being performed in it on the 17th, and the first in the house in Chauncy-place on the 21st, of July, in that year.

Matthew Butler, who seems to have been the father of the association, and whose descendants have formed a part of the society to the present time. The projectors were joined by others, and obtained liberty of the proper authority to erect a wooden building.* They procured a lot of land of Col. Thomas Hutchinson, at the corner of Hanover and Clark-streets, set up a house of small dimensions, and finished it, " as is observed in an ancient manuscript, without the assistance of the more wealthy part of the community, excepting what they derived from their prayers and good wishes."

The house was dedicated on the 5th of May, 1714. The two Dr. Mathers officiated in the ceremonies of giving the right hand of fellowship to the new church, and the prayers were as usual on such occasions. On the evening of the same day, the church met at the house of Mr. Butler and signed their covenant. On the 2d of August they came to the choice of a pastor. At the first trial, the suffrages were divided between Mr. John Barnard and Mr. John Webb. The majority was for Mr. Webb : on a second trial, he had a unanimous vote. The election was immediately communicated to the congregation, who were convened in another place, and they " universally" concurred in the choice. An invitation was presented on the 4th and accepted on the 27th of the same month, and the ordination of Mr. Webb took place on the 20th of October following. Dr. I. Mather acted as moderator, Dr. C. M. made the first prayer, and the pastor elect preached. The covenant was read and acknowledged : the church confirmed their choice, and Mr. Webb his acceptance ; the moderator then gave the charge, and his son the right hand of fellowship, and the exercises were closed with singing and a blessing.

The seventeen first associates were, Solomon and Elias Townsend, Erasmus Stevens, Moses Pierce, Caleb Lyman, Alex'r. Sears, Eben. Clough, John Goldthwait, Sam. Gardner, Wm. Parkman, John Bassett, Joshua Cheever, Matthew Butler,—John Pecker, Isaac Pierce, John Goff, and James Barnard. The first thirteen, together with Mr. Webb, Benja. Gerrish, Nath. Kenney and Lately Gee, were the original signers of the church covenant.†

At the session of the general court, July, 1715, a law was passed ' that there be a *Light-house* erected at the charge of the province on the southernmost part of the Great Brewster, called Beacon Island, to be kept lighted from sunset to sunrising.'

---

* The governour might grant a licence on certificate of approbation from the justices of peace and selectmen of Boston, by the law of 1699.

† See Appendix, No. IV.—Historical Notices of the New North.

The formation of the New South Church and Society was the next event of moment. The first meeting on the subject was ' at the Bull [tavern, in Summer-street] in Boston, on Thursday, the 14th of July, 1715,' when it was voted, ' that the money received of Mr. Nath. Glover, except the charges arising thereon, viz. the balance, be given towards the erecting a meeting-house at the south-end of Boston, where the major part of the proprietors [in Mr. G.'s donation ?] shall be concerned.' Forty-four subscribers were soon found to engage in ' so good a work,' and ' a petition was drawn and presented to the town, on Tuesday, the 20th of Sept. 1715, and was as follows :

' To the inhabitants of the town of Boston, the petition of sundry inhabitants at the southerly end of Boston, showeth, That whereas we the subscribers have entered into a design, if we obtain leave, to erect a meeting-house for the publick worship of God at the south end of Boston, therefore desire a grant from this town of that piece or parcel of land, called Church Green, in Summer-street, for the erecting a meeting-house of 65 ft. long and 45 ft. broad, it being a suitable place for that service, and by the situation and name thereof intended, no doubt, by our forefathers for that purpose, and pray that the present selectmen of the town may be empowered to make a conveyance to the undertakers underwritten. Subscribed by Thomas Peck, Nicholas Boon, Samuel Adams, Eneas Salter. jun. Sam'l Greenleaf, Henry Hill, Jona. Simpson, Eleaz. Dorby, David Craige, Wm. Engs, Eneas Salter, Thomas Salter, John Barton, Daniel Legre.'

The town granted the petition, ' Provided the said meeting-house be erected and improved to that use within the space of three years next ensuing.' This was done, and the dedication took place on the 8th of Jan. 1717. Rev. Benj. Wadsworth of the Old South and Cotton Mather both preached. Copies of their sermons were desired and published. Jan. 11, a committee was appointed to supply the pulpit, with authority to allow 20s. for each sermon. Sept. 24, 1718, Mr. Samuel Checkley, of Boston, was unanimously chosen out of several candidates, and invited to become pastor of this church. He accepted, and was ordained, April 15, 1719. The covenant was signed on the same day, by H. Hill, T. Peck, John Clough, T. Salter, S. Adams, Sam'l. Bridgham, Benja. White, and Thos. Downe.*

---

* *Covenant of the New South Church.*

We, whose names are hereunto subscribed, apprehending ourselves called of God to joyne together in church communion, and acknowledging our unworthiness of such a priviledge. and our inability to keep covenant with God, or to perform any spiritual duty, unless Christ shall enable us thereunto ; doe (humbly depending on free grace for assistance and accep-

The Sixth Congregational church originated in a difficulty respecting the settlement of a colleague with the Rev. Mr. Webb, of the New North. Preparatory to that step, the church had adopted the following regulations, on the 13th of May, 1719. " *First*, the church shall go before and lead in the choice, according to the professed principles and practice of the churches in N. E.—2d. Since the edification of the brethren of the congregation is to be considered on such an occasion, we are willing they should join with us in the call of a minister : that is to say, after the church have expressed their satisfaction with any particular person, we are willing that a major vote of the church and congregation, assembled together, as is usual in country towns, shall determine wheth- er the person, first chosen as aforesaid by the church, be finally settled in the pastoral office over us. And we all of us promise to make ourselves easy, and sit down contented by such determination, and purpose by the grace of God to do so, unless some weighty and conscientious reason oblige us to the contrary : but upon this condition, that our brethren of the congregation are willing to act upon the same princi- ples and to submit to the same rules." And those persons were to be allowed the privilege of voting, who had been con- stant hearers and contributors towards the support of publick worship, and should sign a declaration of their assent to the above rule.

The 9th of September following was set apart as a day of prayer, and as soon as the exercises of the day were ended, the members of the church proceeded to cast their votes ; but lest there should be a breach upon the solemnities of the day, they were sealed up, without examination. On the morn-

---

tance) in the name of Christ Jesus our Lord, and in the presence of God himself, the blessed angels, and all his servants here present, freely covenant, and solemnly bind ourselves, to serve the God, whose name alone is Jehovah, Father, Son, and holy Ghost, the only living and true God ; cleaving to him, as our chief good, and to our Lord Jesus Christ, as our only Saviour, Prophet, Priest, and King of our souls, in a way of Gospel obedience ; avouch- ing the Lord to be our God, and the God of our children, whom we give unto him, counting it, as a high favour, that the Lord will accept of us, and our children with us, to be his people. We do also give ourselves, one unto another, in the Lord ; covenanting to walk together, as a Church of Christ, in all the ways of his worship—according to the rules given us in his holy word ; promising, in brotherly love, faithfully to watch over one another's souls, and to submit ourselves to the discipline and power of Christ, in his Church, and duly to attend the Seals and Censures, or whatever ordinances, Christ has commanded to be ob- served by his people, so far, as the Lord, by his word, and Spirit, has or shall reveal unto us, to be our duty ; beseeching the Lord, to own us for his people, and to delight to dwell in the midst of us ; and that we may keep our Covenant with God, we desire to deny our- selves, and to depend entirely on the free mercy of God, and the merits of Jesus Christ, and wherein we shall fail, to wait on him for pardon, through his name ; beseeching the Lord, to own us as a Church of Christ, and to delight to abide in the midst of us,

ing of the 10th, the church met, when the votes were counted, and the Rev. Peter Thacher had 34 out of 44. On the
16th day of the same month, the congregation met, by desire,
to express their concurrence. if it might be, with the vote of
the church. When the question was proposed to the convention, a protest against the proceedings was produced, signed
by 6 members of the church and 39 of the congregation, in
which they charged the church ' with the base design of en-
snaring them,' by the vote passed professedly in favour of the
congregation. They refused to leave this memorial of their
grievances, and probably retired, as the records state that the
other brethren brought in their votes, which were 46, and all
for Mr. Thacher.

The 27th of Jan. 1720 was appointed for the installation.
The five Congregational churches in Boston, the first in Salem, and those at Cambridge, Dorchester, Romney-Marsh,
and Milton, were invited to attend. A few days before the
time appointed for the installation, ' the aggrieved brethren,'
by the advice of Boston ministers, proposed that their differences should be referred to a council. The church declined
acceding to the proposal, on account of the time and manner
in which it was brought forward.

The appointed day arrived, and not one of the Boston ministers appeared to sit in the council : of those invited from the
neighbouring towns, only Mr. Cheever from Romney Marsh,
and Mr. Peter Thacher of Milton came ; one with the consent of his church, accompanied by delegates, the other,
alone, in opposition to the vote of his church. They met at
the house of Mr. Webb, which was at the corner of North
Bennet and Salem-streets. The aggrieved brethren were assembled at the house of Thomas Lee. Esq. which is the house
in N. Bennet-street, next to the Universal meeting-house, and
was to be passed, if the council should use the common streets
to get to the New North. A deputation from the aggrieved
brethren waited upon the council, with a remonstrance against
their proceeding to business, which they wished to prevent,
peaceably, if they could : if that could not be done, they had
resolved to prevent the council from going to the meeting-
house, by force.

After some consideration and debate, the council resolved,
that there was nothing offered or objected, which was of sufficient weight to prevent their proceeding to business. As
going through the publick streets was likely to produce confusion and uproar, Mr. Webb, after notifying the church that
the council were ready, led them out of a back gate into
Love-lane (now Tileston street), and through an alley (Robinson) which opens immediately opposite to the meeting-house,
and thus got quiet possession of the pulpit. The house was

nearly filled with a promiscuous multitude, among whom were some of the aggrieved. These began to raise a clamour, and sent for their friends at Mr. Lee's, who ran to the house in a tumultuous manner, forced their way into the galleries, and in a menacing style forbade the proceedings. Some were very unruly and indecent, almost beyond credibility. Silence was repeatedly ordered without effect.

The council at length determined to go on, in the best manner they could. Mr. Cheever put the question to such members of the church as were present, who were about 40, ' Whether they confirmed their call of the Rev. Mr. Thacher ?' which being passed in the affirmative, Mr. T. then publickly declared his acceptance of the invitation. Mr. C. thereupon proclaimed ' the Rev. Peter Thacher to be the pastor of the New North church, regularly introduced to the charge.'

The disturbance being still continued, the disaffected party were called upon to say what they wished for. One of them answered, ' that the matters in dispute might be heard and considered by a council.' The Rev. Messrs. W. and T. with the members of the church, severally assented to the proposal. Mr. Thacher, of Milton, then made a prayer ; the newly inducted pastor preached a sermon, prayed afterwards, and the assembly was dismissed with a blessing.

On the next day, Mr. Webb sent to every one of the disaffected brethren of the church, in number nine or ten, to meet at his house, in order to adjust the business of convening a council. Four only appeared, and they refused to have any thing to do about it. The plan of forming another church began to be contemplated.

The discontented members had made preparations for the erection of a new meeting-house, as appears from the following record :—' Sundry of the north end of the town, being moved by the Providence of God for to build a house for the publick worship of God, met sundry times for the promoting of said work, and (Nov. 14, 1719) at a meeting of Alex'r Sears, Solo. Townsend, John Waldo, Owen Harris, James Tileston, Nath. Jarvis, Thomas Lee, Jona. Mountfort, Wm. Arnold, Thaddeus Macarty, James Pecker, Eben'r Bridge, Benj. Edwards, Peter Papillon, Thos. Dogget, Daniel Ballard, Rob't Oring, Edw. Pell, Sam'l Burnell, Fras. Parnell, Jas. Barnes, Jas. Halsy, Ephr'm Moore, they voted that some of them should treat with Mr. Thomas Roby, of Cambridge, for a certain tract or piece of land, it being the land that the meeting-house now standeth on.' December 20th, a building committee was appointed, and the number of proprietors increased to forty before the work was completed. Mr. Edward Pell drew the plan of the house,* which was dedicated on the 10th of May, 1721. A church† was gathered among the worshippers, on Wednesday, the 23d of May, 1722 ; and on the same day Mr. William Waldron was ordained the first pastor.

---

* The same house is now occupied by the Second and Sixth, united as the Second Congregational Church. It was proposed by some to denominate it the Revenge Church, but instead thereof it obtained the name of North Brick, and afterwards of *New Brick.* The figure of a cock was, however, placed as a vane upon the steeple, in derision of Mr. Thacher whose christian name was Peter.

† A. Sears, S. Townsend, J. Waldo, Moses Pierce, J. Tilestone, Josiah Baker, from the New North, together with Wm. Lee, Nath. Loring, Daniel Pecker, and Henry Wheeler and Wm. Waldron, were the original signers of the Covenant of the New Brick church.

Covenant of the New Brick Church.

We, whose names are hereunto sub. apprehending ourselves called of God into a chh. state of the gospel, do first of all confess ourselves to be unworthy to be so highly favoured of the Lord, and admire that free and rich grace of his, wh. triumphs in weakn. and unworthin. and then with an humble reliance upon the aids of grace, promised to them that are conscious of their own inability to do any good thing and humbly wait on the L. for the addition of this thing :—We now thankfully lay hold on his cov. and would choose the things that please him.—We declare our serious belief of the christian religion, as contained in the S. S. and heartily resolve to conform our lives to the rules of that holy r. as long as we live in this world.—We give up ourselves to the L. Jehovah, who is the Father, Son, and Holy Spirit, and avouch this day to be our G. our Leader, and receive him as our portion.—We give up ourselves to the blessed Jesus, who is the L. Jehovah and adhere to him, as the L. of his people in the cov. of God, and rely on him as our prophet, priest, and king, to bring us to et. blessedness.—We ackn. ourselves under inevitable obligations to glorify G. in all the duties of a godly, sober life, and esp. in the duties of a chh. state in obedience to Christ, and the enjoym. of him in all the ord. of the gospel : and we therefore depend on his gracious assistance for the faithful discharge of the duties thus incumbent on us.—We desire and intend, and (depending upon promised grace) we engage to walk together as a chh. of the L. J. C. in the f. and order of the gospel, so far as we shall have the same revealed to us, conscientiously attending the worship of G. the sacraments of the N. T. the discipline of his kdm. and all his holy institutions, in communion with one another, lovingly watching over one another, and watchfully avoiding all sinful stumbling blocks and contentions, as becomes a p. professing godlin. called of the L. into such a holy cov. relation with G. and one another.—We do also at the same time present and offer our seed to the L. purposing with divine help to do our part in methods of a religious edu. training ym. up in the way of the L. that so they may be his.—We do all this, flying to the blood of the ev. cov. for the pdn. of our sins and past failings, praying that the glorious L. who is the sh. of his sheep, would prepare and strengthen us for every good work, working in us that which will be well pl. in his sight, to whom be glory forever. Amen.

See *Rev. Mr. Ware's* Discourses.

28

CHAPTER XXXIX.

Of newspapers a constant feast,
And something there to every taste.

Carrier's Address.

' THE second newspaper which made its appearance in British America was the Boston Gazette, which was first published for Wm. Brooker, who succeeded Campbell as postmaster. No. 1 was issued from the press on Monday, Dec. 21, 1719, on a half sheet of printing foolscap, on a small-pica type, folio ; and it was continued on a half sheet of that size of paper for several years, excepting occasionally a whole sheet, and then one page was often left blank. It had a cut of a ship on the left, and one of a postman on the right of the title, and was "published by authority." Its imprint was, " Boston : printed by J. Franklin, and may be had at the Post Office, where advertisements are taken in." There were three Boston Gazettes in succession before the revolution. This was the first of them.'

The people of Boston had suffered severely at five different periods* from the small pox, prior to 1721. Nineteen years had intervened since its last appearance, when it was introduced a sixth time, by the Sal Tortugas fleet, in April of that year. More than half of the inhabitants were probably liable to it. It continued its ravages till the spring of 1,22, when the following account was taken.

Number of inhabitants above the Mill-creek			-	-	-	6018	
"	"	at	North end	-	-	-	4549=10,567
Of these, had the small pox S. of Mill-creek			-	-	-	3217	
"	"	at	North end	-	-	-	2596= 5,813
		Died—S.				490	
		"	N.			281=	771

It was at this time that the practice of inoculation was introduced. Dr. Zabdiel Boylston ' is known to be the first physician in the British dominions that dared to do it.' He commenced with his own family, inoculating his son Thomas and two of his servants on the 26th of June : and he met with success, which at that time seemed wonderful. The clergy of the town supported and encouraged him, but the physicians joined the populace and opposed the practice with

---

* In 1649, '66, '78--79, '89--90, 1702.

all possible vehemence. By Dr.Boylston's account it appears that of 5759, who had had the disease in the natural way, 844 died ; whereas of 247 cases attended by himself, and 39 by Drs. Roby of Cambridge and Thompson of Charlestown, only six terminated fatally.

A third newspaper appeared on Monday, August 17, 1721. It was the *New England Courant*, printed and published by James Franklin, on a half sheet of crown size printing paper, on a small-pica type. Imprint, ' Boston : Printed by James Franklin, in Queen-street, where advertisements are taken in.' We suppose it to have been at the Franklin Head, Court-street. The Courant contained very little news and very few advertisements. More than half the paper was, with few exceptions, filled weekly with essays, in which men in office, the clergy, and the prevailing religious opinions of the day were attacked. A society of gentlemen furnished these essays : by moderate people this society was called a set of Freethinkers ; by others it was denominated the Hell Fire Club. Their essays were at times opposed in the Gazette and News-Letter, and these papers were in turn warmly attacked in the Courant, but rather by satire than argument. The Courant soon had warm advocates and zealous opposers. It roused the attention of the government and of some of the clergy. Dr. I. Mather openly denounced the paper in an address to the publick, Jan. 29, 1722. James Franklin was shortly after imprisoned and forbidden to print, and the paper was for some time issued in the name of his brother Benjamin, who was an apprentice with him, and was the unknown author of some interesting pieces, that were inserted in the Courant.

The Second Episcopal society is that which worships in Christ-Church, Salem-street. Its records begin thus : ' Laus Deo. Boston, N.E. the 2d September, 1722. At the request of several gentlemen, who had purchased a piece of ground at the north end of Boston, to build a church on, the Rev. Samuel Myles ordered his clerk to give notice to his congregation, that all those who were willing to contribute towards erecting another church, at the north end of Boston, were desired to meet at King's Chapel, the Wednesday following. Agreeably to which notification, several persons assembled and chose Mr. John Barnes, treasurer, Thomas Greaves, Esq. Messrs. Geo. Craddock, Anthony Blount, John Gibbins, Thos. Selby, and Geo. Monk, a committee to receive subscriptions and build a church on said ground at the north end of Boston.' The preamble to their subscription ran thus : ' Whereas the Church of England, at the south part of Boston, is not large enough to contain all the people that would come to it ; and several well disposed persons having already bought a

piece of ground at the north part of said town to build a
church on : We, the subscribers, being willing to forward so
good a work. do accordingly affix to our names what each of
us will cheerfully contribute.'

The list of subscribers and benefactors contains the names
of 214 persons, whose subscriptions amounted to £727. 18s. st.

On the 15th day of April, 1723, the corner stone of Christ
Church was laid by the Rev. Samuel Myles, minister of
King's chapel, accompanied by the gentlemen of his congregation.   The ceremony was concluded with these words,
" May the gates of hell never prevail against it."   The building was completed during the succeeding summer and autumn,
and first opened for publick worship on the 29th day of Dec.
in the same year, by the Rev. Timothy Cutler, D. D. the
first rector of this church.   The appropriate passage of scripture from which the preacher addressed a numerous audience on this interesting occasion was, " For mine house shall
be called an house of prayer for all people " Isaiah lvi. 7.

At the opening of the church, the usual audience is stated
to have been about 400 persons : the number of purchasers
of pews was fifty-three.*

The great tide, (which we alluded to, p. 109,) occurred on
the 24th of Feb. 1723, and is thus described by Cotton
Mather : ' It rose two feet higher than ever had been known
unto the country, and the city of Boston particularly suffered
from it incredible mischiefs and losses.   It rose two or three
feet above the famous Long Wharf, and flowed over the other
wharves and streets, to so surprising an height, that we could
sail in boats from the Southern battery to the rise of ground
in King-street, and from thence to the rise of ground ascending toward the North meeting-house.   It filled all the cellars,
and filled the floors of the lower rooms in the houses and
warehouses in town.'

The New-England Courant ceased to be published in the
beginning of the year 1727, and on Monday, the 20th of
March in that year, the fourth newspaper, being the *New-
England Weekly Journal*, appeared.   It was issued on a half

---

* See Rev. Mr. Eaton's Historical Discourse.

Purchasers of Pews in North or Christ Church, 1723. Wm. Abraham, Jos. Amy, Anthony
Blount, —— Bissell, —— Ballard, —— Bedgood, Thos. Bennet, Walter Brown, Geo. Barrow,
—— Boulderson, Dan'l Crackford, Wm. Clarke, Isaac Dickenson, Timo. Daniel, Dr. Thomas
Graves, Mary Gibbs, Increase Gatchell, —— Hooton, John Howard, Rob't Harris, Wm.Hislop,
Rob't Harrison, —— Hender, North Ingham, —— Jenkins, Wm. Jones, James King, ——
Lawlor, —— Moall, Gillam Phillips, Wm. Patten, Wm. Priggs, John Petell, Wm. and Thos.
Price, Geo. Pemberton, Henry Pigeon, Step. Perks, John Rachell, Nich. Roach, Wm. Ride-
out, Geo. Skinner, Edw. Stanbridge, John Sowerby, Arthur Savage, Adam Tuck, Rob't
Temple, Thos Tippen, Mary Tomlins, Henry Venner, Maj. Vassall, Rob't Ward, Abr.Winter.

sheet of foolscap size, folio. Imprint, ' Boston ; Printed by
S. Kneeland, at the printing-house in Queen-street, where ap-
vertisements are taken in.' Several literary gentlemen furnished this paper with short essays on miscellaneous subjects,
more of a moral than of a political nature, and which, although well written did not occasion an excitement in the publick mind like that produced by the writers for the Courant.

CHAPTER XL.

.... fair Religion's beauteous temples rise,
The altars of the heart's best sacrifice ;
Various their names, yet still alike their plan.

N. H. Wright.

THE Church in Federal-street (which was the thirteenth religious society in Boston) was originally constituted by a number of Presbyterian families from the North of Ireland, the
descendants of emigrants from Scotland to Ireland in the
reign of James I. They arrived in Boston in the year 1727,
accompanied by the Rev. John Moorhead, by whose pious
zeal and assiduity the society was established. They purchased a convenient lot at the corner of Bury-street and Long-
lane (now called Berry and Federal-streets), and altered a
barn, which stood on the ground, into a house of worship.
This was in 1729, and the congregation having increased, they afterwards added two wings to the building. This rude and lowly
edifice was their place of worship until 1744, when a new and
convenient church was erected. At that time the society was
in a flourishing condition. There were twelve elders, correspondent to the number of districts or sections, into which the
congregation was divided. Mr. Moorhead (whose settlement
took place March 30, 1730) was most cordially attached to
his flock, and they cherished for him a reciprocal affection.
With the zealous enforcement of doctrines which he sincerely
espoused, he was unwearied in his endeavours to promote and
maintain virtuous practice among his people. He was favoured with a strong constitution and his labours were uninterrupted, until a few days before his decease, December 2,
1773, in the seventieth year of his age. We are not informed particularly of the history of the church in the interval
between the death of Mr. Moorhead and the instalment of the
Rev. David Annan as their pastor in 1783. Mr. A. was dismissed at his own request by the Presbytery in 1786 ; and

soon after that event, the society in Federal-street relinquished the Presbyterian regimen and embraced the Congregational order.

'Dr. Douglass, in his Summary, speaking of Mr. Moorhead's congregation, has the following note. " They erected
a Presbyterian meeting-house in Boston, Mr. John Morehead
their presbyter, as appears by an inscription, in two columns, and not elegant.

THE FIRST COLUMN.

This chh. of presbyterian strangers was congregated an. dom. 1729.
Anno. dom. 1744, *by a small but generous*
Illa manebit. Labilis e contra si sit erana
Suprema. Desiderio J. M. hujus ecclesiæ.

THE SECOND COLUMN.

This building was begun anno. dom. 1742, *and finished*
Number. Hujus fundamen saxum est. Domus
Peribit. Gloria Christi lex nostra
Christique pastor, and first preached in May 6th.

Latin and English interlarded is new, excepting in bur-
lesque ; likewise the disposition of these lines is singular, and
to be rightly understood must be read by joining the several
lines of each column."

' This inscription was probably in collateral columns. It
is perplexing to read it in the form in which it is placed by
Dr. Douglass, and it may be acceptable to have it presented
in a more intelligible arrangement. In doing this we take the
liberty to include the Latin portion in a parenthesis, and to
correct a probable typographical error in the third line of
the inscription, substituting the word *arena* for *erana*.

' This Church of Presbyterian strangers was congregated
Anno Dom. 1729. This building was begun Anno Dom.1742,
and finished Anno Dom. 1744, by a small but generous number. (Hujus fundamen saxum est. Domus illa manebit.
Labilis è contra si sit arena peribit. Gloria Christi lex nostra suprema. Desiderio J. M. hujus ecclesiæ, Christique
pastor) and first preached in May 6th.'*

---

* ' We should infer from Dr. D. i. 368, that this inscription was placed in the church.
There was none such in the house within the recollection of any of the society.'—*See* Memoir
appended to the Rev. Dr. Channing's sermon at ord. of Rev. Mr. Gannett.

The record of baptisms for the two first years of this church gives us the following family
names Campbell, Knox, Miller, Sloan, Little, McCurdy, Hogg, Moor, Watts, Crosier, Ruth-
erford, Morton, Smith, Tom, Kirkland, Wilson, Young, Hodge, Shirlow, Hutchinson, Patterson, Patrick, Walker, Lee, Maxwell, Chesnut, MaClure, Harper, Tatt, MaQuistion, Speer,
Whipple, MaClean, Stewart, Sinclair, Mitchell, Gwinn, Nicols, Dixon, MacDugall, Pharr,
Ross, Mickleravie, Awel, Black, Quigg, Bryant.

The Hollis-street Church claims the next rank in point of age. ' Upon a motion made by his Ex. Jonathan Belcher, Esq. unto William Pain, Esq. that if he with a convenient number would associate themselves together and build a house for the publick worship of God, on a piece of land belonging to His Excellency, in Hollis-street, at the south part of Boston, that he, viz. His Ex. would make them a present of said land for that use ; upon which motion, divers persons met at the house of Mr. Hopestill Foster, on the 21st of January, 1730–1 [?] and after mature consideration and debate, the following persons subscribed,' viz. Wm. Pain, Esq. Sam'l Wells, Esq. John Clough, Caleb Eddy, John Bennett, Silence Allen, Thos. Walker, John Walker, Israel How, John Blake, Henry Gibbon, Jos. Payson, James Day, Hopestill Foster, Eben'r Clough, Thos. Trott, Thos. Milven, Thos. Clough, Sutton Byles, Alden Bass, Benja. Russell, Jos. Hambleton, Nath. Fairfield, John Goldsmith, Isaac Loring, Wm. Cunningham.

On the 2d of March, the governour conveyed the land, and they proceeded to erect a house 40 feet by 30, with a steeple. It was finished and dedicated June 18, 1732. On the 14th of November, ' the church was gathered, with fasting and prayer, assisted by the ministers of the town. The person who more immediately formed them was the Rev. Dr. Joseph Sewall,' of the Old South, who drew the church covenant.*

---

* *The Hollis-street Church Covenant.*

We, whose names are hereunto subscribed, apprehending ourselves called in the providence of God, though unworthy, to unite in chh. fellowship, and seek the settlement of all the gospel institutions among us, do now enter into covenant with G. and one another, as follows : 1. We declare our belief of the S. S. as the word of G. and perfect rule of faith and obedience, resolving, by his grace, to conform to them ; and we adhere to the faith and order of the gospel as exhib. by these chbs. in their conf. of faith and platform of chh. discipline, for the substance of them. 2. We give up ourselves in an everlasting covenant to the L. Jehovah, who is the Father, the Son, and the Holy Spirit, as to our creator, redeemer, and sanctifier, to love, obey, and serve him forever. 3. We own and submit to the L. J. C. as the head of his body the chh. receiving and relying upon him as the great high priest, prophet, and king of our salvation. 4. We give ourselves each to other by the will of G. engaging by his help to carry it towards one another as fellow members in chh. society, to watch over one another in brotherly l. and to walk together in a due subjection to, and attendance upon the orders and ordinances appointed by C. and enjoined his chhs. in the gospel. 5. We thankfully acknowledge, that our posterity are included in the gospel covenant, and accordingly promise to bring them up in the nurture and adm. of the L. and to own them in their covenant relation, according to the rule of God's word. 6. We promise to do our endeavour to procure the settlement and continuance of all the offices and officers appointed by C. the great shepherd for the edification of his chh. and to do our duty faithfully for their maintenance and encouragement, and to carry it towards them as the gospel requires. 7. We promise to preserve communion with the chhs. of C. walking together in the faith and order of the gospel, by giving and rec. mut. counsel and assistance in all cases wherein it shall be needful. And now we repair to the blood of the great sacrifice for the

The names of the first members were John Clough, Jos. Payson, Henry Gibbon, Jas. Day, Jona. Neal, Hopestill Foster,
Eben'r Clough, Nath. Fairfield, John Cravath, Alden Bass,
John Blake, Thomas Trott, Isaac Loring.   November 20th,
they ' voted to call the Rev. Mr.Mather Byles to take the pastoral care and charge of them,' and ' after this the congregation were also called together and allowed the privilege of a
written vote.'   They unanimously concurred, and Mr. Byles,
having ' advised with the united ministers of the city,' accepted the call, and was ordained on Wednesday, the 20th of
December, preaching his own ordination sermon, from 2 Tim.
ii. 17.

' By reason that the Chapel was full, and no pews to be
bought by new comers,' the first step towards the formation
of Trinity Church appears to have been taken on the 25th of
April, 1728, when the piece of land on which the building
stands, at the corner of Summer-street and Bishop-alley (now
Hawley-street) was conveyed by Wm. Speakman to Leonard
Vassall, John Barnes, John Gibbens, apothecary, on condition
that they shall and will with all convenient speed immediately after the said conveyance endeavour to procure a
building to be erected on the said land, for the worship of
God :—which building or church they, any or either of them,
shall take care to be contrived and disposed, both within and
without, as they or any or either of them, in the absence of
the other, shall find and judge most conducing to the decent
and regular performance of divine service, according to the
rubrick of the common prayer book, used by the church of
England, as by law established.'   A subscription was commenced April 6, 1730, and continued Oct. 17, 1733, and the
subscribers were to be ' repaid, in proportion as money arises
from the sale of the pews, or any benefactors.'   The corner-
stone was laid, April 15, 1734, and bears the following inscription : *Trinity Church.   This corner stone was laid by the Rev.
Mr. Commissary Price, the 15th April,* 1734.'

On the 15th of August, 1735, ' the Rev. Mr. Thomas Har-
ward read prayers according to the rubrick of the church of
England, and the Rev. Roger Price, his lordship's [the
Bishop of London's] commissary preached the first sermon in
Trinity church, from Heb. x. 23—which sermon was preach-
ed before a large number of people, His Excellency Jonathan
Belcher, Esq. being present.'   Services were somewhat sta-

pardon of all our sins, depending entirely upon our L. J. C. for acceptance with G. and for
his good spirit to enable us to keep his holy covenant. And we humbly ask the prayers of God's people, that we and our offspring may obtain all the blessings of this
covenant, for the sake of Jesus Christ, to whom with God the Father, and God the Holy
Ghost, be glory in the churches forever. Amen.

tedly performed in this church, by the [episcopal] ministers of the town, until Mr. Addington Davenport, who was assistant to Mr. Price at the chapel, (and a very popular man among the dissenters,) was invited to become their minister. The first overtures were made to him, Dec. 5, 1737, and he expressed his assent on condition ' the Bishop of London should grant him leave.' A correspondence was instituted to effect this object, which was accomplished ; and on ' May 8, 1740, Mr. Davenport came into the church, with the committee, and accepted the invitation : thereupon by the proprietors was presented and inducted into the church, invested in all the benefits and perquisites of the same, and accordingly put into possession in the manner of a donative church.'*

There had been several ineffectual efforts towards the establishment of a regular market in Boston, previous to the period to which our history has advanced. At length a vote was obtained March 11, 1734, ' to choose a committee to think of and assign three suitable places for erecting markets, and the cost and charge thereof :' 517 being the number in favour of the proposal, and 399 against it. April 24th, in town-meeting, ' It is voted and ordered, that Three places be, and hereby are at present assigned for the aforesaid Market. And that they may be made fit and commodious for the reception of such as from time to time may bring their Commodities there for Sale, that the Sum of *seven hundred pounds* be allowed and paid out of the Town-Treasury, to Thomas Fitch, Edward Hutchinson, Thomas Palmer, Jacob Wendell, Esqrs. Messieurs Nathanael Cunningham, James Watson, Francis Willoughby, and John Steel, to enable them to Effect the Buildings, and other necessarys at the Three several places assigned for that use. And that a piece of Land,—fronting on the main street leading to Roxbury, known by the Name of Orange-Street, over against the House and Land of Thomas Downe, there measuring seventy feet, is pitch'd upon for one of the Places. That the Town's Ground, or open space on the Town Dock or Wharf commonly call'd Dock-Square, be another Place. And that the Open Space before and about the Old North Meeting-house, is fixed upon and determined for the third Place, where the Market is to be kept and carried on.'

---

* The first officers of Trinity church were, Wm. Speakman, Joseph Dowse, *Wardens,*—Lawrence Lutwich Charles Apthorp, Wm. Coffin, James Griffin, John Marrett, Henry Laughton, Peter Kenwood, John Arbuthnot, Benjamin Faneuil, Rufus Green, Philip Dumaresq, Thomas Aston, John Hamack, *Vestry-men,*—John Crosby, *clerk,*—John Hooker, *sexton,* chosen April 24, 1739. ' The holy sacrament of the Lord's supper was first administered June 17th, 1739, by Mr. Davenport ; the Rev. Samuel Seabury, of New-London, assisted.'

29

Clerks of the market were appointed to attend at each of those places, and with other rules for regulating the markets, it was

' *Ordered,* that every Day in the Week, except the Lord's Day, or other Days set apart by this Government for Religious Service, be a Market Day, and that a Bell be daily rung at the Opening of the Market, which shall be at the Rising of the Sun, through the whole Year, from which Hour till the Hour of One, *Post Meridiem,* shall forever hereafter be deemed and held Market Hours.'

The Court of general sessions of the peace approved the scheme adopted by the town, and publick notice was given by Samuel Gerrish, town clerk, ' that the said markets will be opened on Tuesday the fourth day of June next.' The News-Letter of June 6th, gives the following account and remarks. 'On Tuesday morning last, being the 4th of June, at Sunrising, the Bell rang the first time for opening the publick Markets the first time in this Town, at the three several places assigned, and now conveniently prepared therefor, agreeable to an Order or By-Law of the Town, legally approved, ratified, and confirmed by the Court of General Sessions of the Peace for the County of Suffolk : which Order has been published in this and the other publick News Papers. The Concourse of People (Sellers, Buyers, and Spectators) at the Market Places was very considerable ; abundance of Provisions were brought thither for Sale. Those that exceeded in Goodness and Cheapness, went off quick, but those that were poor or dear, more slowly. It's tho't the said Markets carried on conformable to the Restrictions, Limitations, and Regulations of the said Order, will by Experience be found very beneficial, as to this great Town in general, and to our Country Friends in particular, in many Respects, but more especially in having certain fixed Places of Resort both for selling and buying the Necessaries of Life from Day to Day : And the cheaper and better the Commodities brought for Sale are, certainly the more vendable they will be ; which no doubt will induce our Country Neighbours to endeavour to bring as good to the Markets as they can :—*Their* Interest, as well as the *Town's,* has been jointly consulted and aimed at herein.'

Many people were dissatisfied with this experiment, and in the course of three years the clerks were discontinued, the South end market converted into shops, the North taken down to be used in constructing a work-house, and the one at the Town-dock was demolished by a mob.

We proceed to notice the formation of the Ninth Congregational society or the church in Lynde-street, called the West church, which was ' gathered,' to use the technical language of our fathers, 'on the third of January, 1736. The covenant was subscribed by seventeen persons, after solemn prayer and preaching, in presence of Thomas Prince, pastor of the Old South, and Thomas Foxcroft, pastor of the First church. On the same day Mr. Wm. Hooper, who was employed as a private tutor in a family near town, was unanimously chosen their pastor. Mr. H. was a native of Scotland, a man of more than ordinary powers of mind, of a noble aspect, an eloquent, popular preacher : it was on his account chiefly, as there is reason to think, that this church was formed. He was ordained on the 18th of May, 1737. The persons who formed the church were Hugh Hall, Wm. Stoddard, from the Old South ; James Gooch, jr. John Darroll, John Daniells, from the First church ; Jos. Ricks, John Pierce, Samuel Sprague, Jos. Badger, from Brattle-street ; Wm. Williams, from first church in Cambridge ; Eph. Copeland, Abijah Adams, John Scot, from the New North ; Wm. More, from the Old North ; and Jas. Watson, Robert Watt, John Moffatt, not before church members. All the Congregational churches in town, together with Mr. Le Mercier's, were invited to assist in the ordination. All the parts in the solemnities were assigned by the church, except the right hand of fellowship, which the council claimed a right to assign.*

* See Rev. Dr. Lowell's Historical Disc. Dec. 31, 1820.

Covenant of the West Church.

1. We declare our belief of the S. S. as the word of God, and perfect rule of faith and obedience, resolving by his grace to conform to them. And we adhere to the faith and order of the Gospels, as exhibited by these churches in their confession of faith and platform of church discipline for the substance of them. 2. We give up ourselves in an everlasting covenant to the Lord Jehovah who is the Father, the Son and the Holy Spirit, as to our Creator, Redeemer and Sanctifier, to love, obey and serve him forever. 3. We own and submit to the L. J. C. as the head of his body the church, receiving and relying upon him as the great High Priest, Prophet and King of our Salvation. 4. We give ourselves each to other by the will of God, engaging by his help to carry it towards one another as fellow members in chh. society, to watch over one another in brotherly love, and to walk together in a due subjection to and attendance upon the orders and ordinances appointed by Christ, and enjoyned his churches in the Gospel. 5. We thankfully acknowledge that our posterity are included in the gospel covenant, and accordingly promise to bring them up in the nurture and admonition of the Lord, and to own them in their covenant relation according to the rules of God's word. 6. We promise to do our endeavour to procure the settlement and continuance of all the officers appointed by Christ the great Shepherd for the edification of his church, and to do our duty faithfully for their maintenance and encouragement, and to carry it towards them as the Gospel requires. 7. We promise to preserve communion with the churches of Christ walking together in the faith and order of the Gospel, by giving and receiving mutual counsel and assistance in all cases where it shall be needful.——And now we repair to the Blood of the great Sacrifice for the pardon of all our sins, depending entirely upon our L. J. C. for acceptance with God, and for his good Spirit, to enable us to keep his holy covenant. And we humbly ask the prayers of God's people, that we and our offspring may obtain all the blessings of this covenant, for the sake of J. C. to whom with God the Father, and God the Holy Ghost, be glory in the churches forever. Amen.

In 1738 the district of Romney Marsh was separated from Boston, and incorporated into a town by the name of CHELSEA. There was great opposition to this step on the part of the old town, and the principal objection was raised on the ground that it would lessen the ability of the town to bear the burden of taxes, some of the wealthy inhabitants residing or owning property at the Marsh, which would thus be placed beyond the reach of the assessors. An attempt had been made two years before, by the country towns in the county of Suffolk, to rid themselves of the expense of a connection with Boston, by having the town erected into a county by itself, but the opposition from Boston was at that time successful.

The religious world had now experienced a state of quiet for more than fifty years. Primitive zeal in practice and strictness in principle had given place to feelings, which savoured more of indifference and unconcern. Individuals were sometimes emboldened to lift their voices to warn or to reprove, but it was only to be heard and be disregarded. The arrival of the celebrated George Whitefield roused the whole continent from this sort of lethargy. Wherever he appeared, crowds thronged to hear his exhortations. Multitudes attended him in his journeys from place to place, and his progress was regularly reported in the papers of the day. We find his entrance and stay in Boston thus related :—

'On Thursday evening (Sept. 18, 1740) the Rev. Mr. Whitefield arrived here by land from Rhode Island, being met on the road and conducted to town by several gentlemen. The next day in the forenoon he attended prayers in the King's Chapel, and in the afternoon he preached to a vast congregation in the Rev. Dr. Colman's meeting-house ; Saturday, in the forenoon, at the [Old] South church, to a crowded audience ; and in the afternoon to about 5000 people on the Common. Lord's-day, A. M. he went to hear Dr. Colman, and in the afternoon, having preached to a great number of people at the Old Brick church, the house not being large enough to hold those that crowded to hear him, he went and preached in the field to at least 8000 persons. On Monday he preached in the morning at Mr. Webb's, and was to have served in the afternoon at Mr. Checkley's, but for an accident which happened just before the time when the service was to begin. Some person broke a piece of board, in one of the galleries, to make a seat of it. The noise alarmed some that heard it, and they imprudently cried out that the galleries were giving way. The house being prodigiously crowded, the whole congregation was put into the utmost confusion and disorder ; so that, being in the greatest concern how to save their lives, some jumped off the gallery into the seats below, others out of the windows ; and those below pressing to get out of the porch doors in haste, several were thrown down one over another, and trod upon by those who were crowding out. Many were exceedingly bruised, and others had their bones broken : five persons died within two days. Mr. Whitefield's presence of mind did not forsake him ; he led the anxious throng immediately to the Common, and preached to them from the words, Go ye out into the highways and hedges and compel them to come in.' Mr. Whitefield continued this incessant labour here for a week, then travelled eastward a few days, returned and spent the second week of October in and about Boston. He preached his farewell sermon, of a sabbath evening, on the Common, ' where it is supposed upwards of 23,000 people attended.' It is almost needless to observe that opinions were various concerning the benefit achieved by this visit. Whether evening lectures had been in practice before, we know not, but we find it advertised, as if it were something new, that one is now (Oct. 21.) established, to be held weekly, at Dr. Colman's church.

Considering that the Tenth Congregational, the Second Baptist, and the Eleventh Congregational churches, took their rise from circumstances, which ' possibly had some connexion with the religious excitements of this period,' we shall bring an account of those churches into this chapter. The Tenth Congregational was that which is known as Samuel Mather's. This gentleman was a son of the venerated Cotton Mather, and, after his father's death, was chosen, Jan. 28, 1732, to supply his place as colleague with the Rev. Joshua Gee, at the Old North. ' He was recommended to them not only by their respect for the ancient family, but by his own character for diligence, zeal, and learning, of which he certainly possessed an uncommon share. His union with the people of the Old North continued but nine years, when, on account of some dissatisfaction with his preaching, which was thought by some not to be sufficiently explicit upon certain points of doctrine, together with some other grounds of uneasiness, a division took place in the church.' Mr. Mather first asked a dismission in Feb. 1741, which the church declined to grant, and the matter was submitted to a council, in compliance with whose advice they voted, Oct. 23, to dismiss him from his pastoral relation and allow him a year's salary. On the 21st of Dec. following, a number of the ' brethren gave the church to understand, that they conscientiously thought themselves called to promote the building of a new meeting-house,' and were accordingly dismissed. Their number was thirty. On the 29th of the 5th month, 1742, sixty-three women were dismissed to unite with them, and it is probable that their meeting-house was ready to be occupied about that time. It was

located at the corner of North Bennet and Hanover streets.
Mr. M. received a diploma of doctor of divinity from Harvard College in 1773. He continued in the pastoral office
until his death, which took place June 27, 1785, at the advanced age of seventy-nine years. ' He left positive orders that
his interment should be private and without any ceremony—
also signified his desire that he might not have any funeral
encomiums from any quarter.' Most of the persons who were
at that time worshipping with him, returned by his advice to
the church from which they came out, and the house was
soon after purchased and enlarged for the accommodation of
a society of another denomination. It was a wooden building.
　' What is called the Second Baptist church in Boston commenced in the following manner. A number of brethren,
who had for some time enjoyed communion in the First Baptist church in this town, became dissatisfied with the doctrinal
sentiments of their then pastor, Rev. Jeremiah Condy. They
charged him with having departed from the sentiments on
which the church originally covenanted.' After stating their
views to him in writing, under date of Sept. 29, 1742, and not
obtaining any satisfactory answer, they withdrew from his
ministry, and on the 27th of July, 1743, three of their number (James Bownd, John Procter, and Ephraim Bosworth,)
covenanted together as a church, ' purposing, by the Lord's
grace enabling, to hold fast those great though now much ex-
ploded doctrines, of election, justification by faith alone, particular redemption, final perseverance, and original sin
or the total depravity and absolute enmity of all mankind, by
their fall in Adam, to God and the gospel of his Son, until
irresistible grace do change the hearts of those who are the
elect of God.' On the same day, John Dabney and Thomas
Boucher, then Ephraim Bownd, and then Thomas Lewis,
acknowledging the aforenamed persons ' to be the First Baptist church in Boston,' were admitted to be fellow members.
The meeting was then adjourned to the evening, when they
made choice of Mr. Eph. Bownd to take the pastoral charge
of them. His ordination took place on Wednesday, Sept.
7th, at Warwick, R. I.
　This society held their Lord's-day meetings for publick
worship, at the dwelling-house of Mr. James Bownd, in
Sheaf-street, near Copp's hill, from Oct. 3, 1742, until June
3, 1745, when they removed to Mr. Procter's school-house,
and there met until Lord's-day, March 15, 1746, when the
first sermon was preached in their new meeting-house, which
stood on the spot now occupied by the church. It was a
wooden building of 45 by 33 ft. finished in a plain, but decent
style. Near the head of the broad aisle was prepared a font

or cistern, in which their candidates were immersed : it continued in use for more than forty years.*

A narrative of the founding and settling of the new-gathered [Eleventh] Congregational church in Boston, was published by the Rev. Andrew Croswell, their pastor. It states, that on the 17th of February, 1748, a number of persons, almost all of whom were members of other churches, thinking it for the glory of God to be a distinct, but not a separate church, (as was expressed in several letters sent for dismissions,) did, after solemn fasting and prayer, embody into a church state. The articles and covenant with which they were embodied are given at large in Mr. Croswell's narrative. The covenant is almost word for word like that of the New Brick church. In their articles they require ' it as agreeable to Scripture, that those who are admitted members of our church should give an account of a work of the law and of the gospel upon their souls,' first to the minister and afterward to the church. They require the same from any candidate for the ministry, ' to prevent, (say they,) as much as

---

* After an introduction, appealing to the S. S. primarily, and to the London Baptist printed Confession, subordinately, as the rule and standard of their faith and practice and church discipline, we find the

Covenant of the Second Baptist Church.

We whose names are hereafter written, vizt. some that it hath pleased God through the riches of his grace to call out of darkn. into his marv. light, and to reveal his son in us, whereby we know that the L. is our God, and having shown unto us our duty and priv. as believers, (vizt. not only to separate from the world both as to doctrine and practice and worship, but also to congregate and embody ourselves into chh. state,) and being thro' grace well satisfied concerning our mutual nearness to the Lord, and standing together in the person of Christ, and being brought in some blessed measure into oneness of sp. being baptized by one s. into one body, and being agreed in the great and sublime truths of the gospel, we do therefore in the name and fear of the L. give up ourselves unto the L. and unto one another by the will of G. to walk together as a chh. of C. in the fp. of the gospel, and in the observance and practice of the laws and ordinances, wh. C. hath appointed his N. T. churches to be in the pract. of, so far as he hath or shall enlighten us into the kn. of our duty and priv. and as the L. shall please to help us. We will freq. assemble ourselves together, as a chh. of C. to attend upon our L. in the service of his house, esp. every first day of the week; and as we shall be enabled by his grace and conducted by his sp. we will stand up together for the truth and cause of C. against all opp. raised against it by the world and carnal professors; and by the same help we will watch over one another in the L. And as we shall be under the conduct of Jehovah the Spirit, we will keep the doors of God's house open always to believers in C. who are sound in faith about the salv. of God's elect as it is by the Father's grace thro' the Son's redemption; and as our G. will help us, we will keep them always shut ag. unbelievers and profligate persons. And now as a test. of our cordial belief of those former doctrines of f. contained in the printed declaration afsd. and of our holy resolution in the strength of grace to stand and walk together in the fp. of the gospel, we call not only heaven and earth to witness but we also subscribe the same with our hands.

See *Rev. Dr. Baldwin's* Dedication Sermon, 1811, and New Year's Disc. 1824.

in us lies, any unconverted minister being ever concerned
with this church.' They maintain, that, in case of incorrigi-
ble fault in a minister, ' this church hath full power to take
from him that power over them which they gave to him,
though, as we profess ourselves to be Congregationalists, we
think that, in such and other difficult cases, it would become
us as Christians to seek the advice and assistance of other
churches of Christ :' and they acknowledge the Westminster
Confession ' to be an excellent system, though no human com-
posures are perfect and of divine authority.'

Mr. Croswell was invited by this church to become their
pastor. The church in Groton (Conn.) over which he had
been settled, having voted him ' liberty to act as he thought
duty, he gave an answer in the affirmative in publick, declaring to all present, that the design of himself and his friends
was only to be a distinct church, and that they professed no
separation from Calvinistical ministers.'

About the latter end of August, the church sent letters to a
variety of churches to come and assist in the instalment,
which was to be, Oct. 5, 1748. The [Old] South church in
Boston utterly refused to be concerned in the affair, judging
it had ' an unhappy tendency to crumble the other Congregational churches in town into small societies.' The council
considered the objections, but thought them of insufficient
weight to prevent their proceeding ' to the instalment, which
was carried on in a very reverent and godly manner.'

The narrative goes on to say, ' God knew the place where
we assembled was too strait and the difficulties that would
attend our building an house, and therefore he himself found
an house for us.' It was the meeting-house of the French
Protestant church,* which, as we have before related, was
about this time dissolved. They disposed of their right in
the house in School-street to Thomas Fillebrown, James Davenport, Wm. Hickling, N. H. Proctor, and Thos. Handaside
Peck, as trustees of Mr. Croswell's church. We have sought
in vain for the records of this society, and are therefore unable to say how long it maintained a visible standing among
the churches of Boston. Mr. Croswell became blind in the
latter part of his life, but. notwithstanding that infirmity, continued his professional labours ; and could always be depended upon, in cases of emergency, to favour his brethren with
an extempore sermon ; he died ' April 12, 1785, in the 77th
year of his age.' The meeting-house soon after passed into
the hands of another people.

---

* It has not been usual to include this in our enumeration of the Congregational churches : though it appears to have been considered a sister-church in cases of ordination.

CHAPTER XLI.

Oh ! is there not some patriot, in whose power
That best, that godlike luxury is placed,
Of blessing thousands, thousands yet unborn,
Through late posterity ? . . . .   *Thomson.*

AFTER the destruction of the old market-houses, the opinion of the inhabitants continued to be as various as before, some very earnestly desiring, and others as violently opposing the re-establishment of them. In the year 1740, Peter Faneuil, Esq. made an offer to build, at his own expense, a complete structure or edifice on the town's land in Dock-square, to be improved for a Market, for the sole use, benefit, and advantage of the town, provided that the town would pass a vote authorizing it, and lay the same under such proper regulations as should be thought necessary, and constantly support it for the said use. On the 14th of July, a town meeting was held, when a petition of Thomas Palmer and others to the number of 340 was read, praying that the town would accede to the proposal. A vote of thanks to Mr. F. was immediately passed without opposition : but when the question came, whether the town would authorize a market to be built, it was carried by a very small majority : 367 yeas to 360 nays. The work was accordingly commenced on the 8th of the following September, and it was finished Sept. 10, 1742, on which day ' Mr. Sam'l Ruggles, who was employed in building the market-house, waited on the selectmen by order of P. Faneuil, Esq. and delivered them the key of said house.' 'On the 13th, a meeting of the town was held in the Hall, and a motion was made, by the Hon. John Jeffries, Esq. that the thanks of the town be given to Peter Faneuil, Esq. for his noble and generous benefaction of the Market-house to the town, which, as an instance of gratitude in the town to its amiable benefactor, we have thought proper to transcribe.
    ' In Town Meeting, Boston, Sept. 13th, 1742.
    ' Whereas information was given to this town, at their meeting, in July, 1740, That Peter Faneuil, Esq. had been generously pleased to offer, at his own proper cost and charges, to erect and build a noble and complete structure, or edifice, to be improved for a Market, for the sole use, benefit, and advantage of the town; provided the town of Boston would pass a vote for that purpose, and lay the same under such proper regulations as shall be thought necessary, and constantly
30

support it for the said use. And whereas at the said meeting it was determined to accept of the offer or proposal aforesaid; and also voted that the selectmen should be desired to wait upon Peter Faneuil, Esq. and to present the thanks of this town to him, and also to acquaint him, that the town have, by their vote, come to a resolution to accept of his generous offer of erecting a Market House on Dock Square, according to his proposal. And whereas Peter Faneuil, Esq. has, in pursuance thereof, at a very great expense, erected a noble structure, far exceeding his first proposal, inasmuch as it contains not only a large and sufficient accommodation for a Market place, but has also superadded, a spacious and most beautiful Town Hall, over it, and several other convenient rooms, which may prove very beneficial to the town, for offices, or otherwise. And the said building being now finished, has delivered possession thereof to the selectmen, for the use of the town; it is therefore ' voted, That the town do, with the utmost gratitude, receive and accept this most generous and noble benefaction, for the use and intentions it is designed for, and do appoint the Hon. Thomas Cushing, Esq. the moderator of this meeting, the Hon. Adam Winthrop, Edward Hutchinson, Ezekiel Lewis, and Samuel Waldo, Esqrs. Thomas Hutchinson, Esq. the Selectmen and the Representatives of the town of Boston, the Hon. Jacob Wendell, Esq. James Bowdoin, Esq. Andrew Oliver, Esq. Capt. Nathaniel Cunningham, Peter Chardon, Esq. and Mr. Charles Apthorp, to wait upon Peter Faneuil, Esq. and in the name of the town, to render him their most hearty thanks for so bountiful a gift, with their prayers, that this, and other expressions of his bounty and charity may be abundantly recompensed with the divine blessing.'

A number of laws were passed for the regulation of the Market. A Clerk was to be annually appointed, and Mr. Faneuil had liberty to nominate one to serve until the annual meeting, in March.

Another vote unanimously obtained, That in testimony of the town's gratitude to Peter Faneuil, Esq. and to perpetuate his memory, that the Hall over the Market place, be named Faneuil Hall, and at all times hereafter, be called and known by that name. And as a further testimony of respect, it was voted, that Mr. Faneuil's picture be drawn at full length, at the expense of the town, and placed in the Hall; and the Selectmen were charged with the commission, which was accordingly executed.

The building was of brick, two stories in height, and measured 100 ft. by 40. It was esteemed one of the best pieces of workmanship and an ornament to the town. The hall would contain 1000 persons, there were convenient apartments for the offices of the town, besides a room for a naval office, and a notary publick.

Mr. Faneuil did not long survive to enjoy these honours or the gratitude of his townsmen. The town lost its friend by a sudden and premature death, March 3, 1743 ; and at the next meeting of the inhabitants in the hall, March 14th, a funeral oration was delivered by Mr. John Lovell, master of the South grammar school. As the first specimen of eloquence uttered in the future *Cradle of Liberty*, this oration is a precious relick : to preserve it is, moreover, a tribute due to the memory of Faneuil, and we therefore subjoin it to this account.*

FUNERAL ORATION ON PETER FANEUIL, ESQ.

' I stand in this place, my fellow townsmen, and my worthy patrons, at the call of those to whom you have committed the direction of your publick affairs, to condole with you for the loss of your late generous benefactor, the Founder of this house. Certain I am, there are numbers in this great assembly, who should upon this occasion have done more justice to his memory, and have better discharg'd the office that is enjoined me. But the commands of those (for such I must always esteem their desires) who have devolved this charge upon me, and the veneration I have for the virtues of the deceas'd, oblige me to bear what little part I can, in a grateful acknowledgment of the just reward due to the memory of a man, whose name, I am sure, will never be forgotten among us.

' How soon, alas ! is our joy for having found such a benefactor, chang'd into mourning for the loss of him ! But a few months are pass'd, since we were framing votes, and consulting the best measures to express our gratitude for his unexampled favours ; and the first annual meeting within these walls that were rais'd by his bounty, finds us assembled in the deepest sorrow for his decease.

' Instances of mortality are never more affecting than in those whose lives have been publick blessings. Surely then, every breast must feel a more than common distress, for the loss of one, whose largeness of heart equalled, great as it was, his power to do good. Honest industry must mourn, for which the exercise of his bounty found an almost constant employment : And they that know how to pity the calamities of human nature themselves, will mourn for him that always reliev'd them.

---

* March 14, 1744, the town voted to purchase the Faneuil arms, elegantly carved and gilt, by Moses Deshon, to be fixed in the hall. The family of Faneuil was among the French Huguenots that fled from France in 1685. The house occupied by Lieut. Gov. Phillips was built by Andrew F. and the summer-house attached to it bears a grasshopper vane, similar to that on Faneuil Hall. After A's death Peter lived and died there.

' So soon as he arriv'd to the possession of his large and
plentiful estate, instead of fruitlessly hoarding up his treas-
ures, though no man manag'd his affairs with greater prudence
and industry ; instead of wasting them in luxury, though
plenty always crown'd his board ; instead of neglecting the
wants of his fellow creatures, an unhappy circumstance too
often attending the possession of riches, he made it manifest
that he understood the true improvement of wealth, and was
determin'd to pursue it. It was to him the highest enjoyment
of riches, to relieve the wants of the needy, from which he
was himself exempted, to see mankind rejoicing in the fruits
of his bounty, and to feel that divine satisfaction, which results from communicating happiness to others. His acts of
charity were so secret and unbounded, that none but they
who were the objects of it, can compute the sums which he
annually distributed among them. His alms flow'd like a
fruitful river, that diffuses its streams through a whole country.
He fed the hungry, and he cloth'd the naked, he comforted the
fatherless, and the widows in their affliction, and his bounties
visited the prisoner. So that Almighty God in giving riches
to this man, seems to have scattered blessings all abroad
among the people.
' But these private charities were not the only effects of his
publick spirit, which, not contented with distributing his bene-
factions to private families, extended them to the whole community. Let this stately edifice which bears his name witness for him, what sums he expended in publick munificence.
This building, erected by him at an immense charge, for the
convenience and ornament of the town, is incomparably the
greatest benefaction ever yet known to our western shore.
Yet this effect of his bounty, however great, is but the first
fruits of his generosity, a pledge of what his heart, always
devising liberal things, would have done for us, had his life been
spar'd. It is an unspeakable loss to the town, that he was
taken away in the midst of his days, and in so sudden a manner, as to prevent his making provision for what his generous
heart might design. For I am well assur'd, from those who
were acquainted with his purposes, that he had many more
blessings in store for us, had heaven prolong'd his days.
' But he is gone ! The town's benefactor, the comforter of
the distress'd, and the poor man's friend.
' He is gone ! And all his plans of future bounties with
him, they are buried in the grave together. He shall be raised to life again : And his intended charities, though they are
lost to us, will not be lost to him. Designs of goodness and
mercy, prevented as these were, will meet with the reward
of actions.
' He is gone !—And must such men die ! Must the protect-
ors and fathers of the distress'd be taken away, while their

oppressors are continued, and increase in power!—Great God! How unsearchable are thy ways!—We confess our sins, but just and righteous art thou!

' To express your gratitude to your generous benefactor, you have passed the most honourable resolves, and to preserve his memory, you have call'd this house by his name. But in vain, alas! would you perpetuate his memory by such frail materials. These walls, the present monuments of his fame, shall moulder into dust: These foundations, however deeply laid, shall be forgotten. But his deeds, his charities, shall survive the ruin of Nature. And to have reliev'd the miseries of the distress'd, to have still'd the cries of orphans, and to have dry'd the widow's tears, are acts that shall embalm his memory for many generations on earth, and shall follow him beyond the limits of mortality, into those blissful regions where endless charity dwells.

' What now remains, but my ardent wishes (in which I know you will all concur with me) that this Hall may be ever sacred to the interests of Truth, of Justice, of Loyalty, of Honour, of Liberty. May no private views nor party broils ever enter within these walls; but may the same publick spirit that glow'd in the breast of the generous Founder, influence all your debates, that society may reap the benefit of them.

' May Liberty always spread its joyful wings over this place: Liberty that opens men's hearts to beneficence, and gives the relish to those who enjoy the effects of it. And may Loyalty to a king, under whom we enjoy this liberty, ever remain our character. A character always justly due to this land, and of which our enemies have in vain attempted to rob us.

' May those who are the inheritors of the large estate of our deceased benefactor, inherit likewise the largeness of his soul. May the widow, the orphan, and the helpless, find in them a protector, a father and a support. In a word, to sum up all, may Faneuil live in them.

' May charity, that most excellent of graces, that beam from the breast of the Father of Mercies, which so soon as ever it enters our bosoms it begins our happiness; charity, the joy of men, of angels, of Almighty God; which completes the felicity of earth and heaven; may it warm the hearts of those who are like to our departed friend in their fortunes, to resemble him too in his bounties: May there be rais'd up some new benefactors in the room of him we have lost, who shall, if possible, rival Faneuil's spirit. And may there always remain in this town, the same grateful sentiments, the same virtuous dispositions, to remember their benefactors with honour.'

CHAPTER XLII.

"He rights such wrong where it is given,
If it were in the court of heaven."

In the year 1747 there happened a serious tumult in Boston. A fleet of men of war were lying in the harbour of Nantasket, under the command of Commodore Knowles. Some of the sailors having deserted, the commodore thought it reasonable that Boston should supply him with as many men as he had lost, and sent his boats up to town early in the morning of Nov. 17th, ' and surprised not only as many seamen as could be found on board any of the ships, outward bound as well as others, but swept the wharves also, taking some ship-carpenters' apprentices and labouring land-men. However tolerable such a surprise might have been in London, it could not be borne here. The people had not been used to it, and men of all orders resented it ; but the lower class were beyond measure enraged, and soon assembled with sticks, clubs, pitchmops, &c. They first seized an innocent lieutenant, who happened to be ashore upon other business. They had then formed no scheme, and the speaker of the House [afterwards Gov. Hutchinson] passing by, and assuring them that he knew that the lieutenant had no hand in the press, they suffered him to be led off to a place of safety. The mob increasing, and having received intelligence that several of the commanders were at the Gov. [Shirley's] house, it was agreed to go and demand satisfaction. The house was soon surrounded, and the court or yard before the house, filled ; but many persons of discretion inserted themselves, and prevailed so far as to prevent the mob from entering. Several of the officers had planted themselves at the head of the stair-way with loaded carbines, and seemed determined to preserve their liberty or lose their lives. A deputy sheriff attempting to exercise his authority, was seized by the mob and carried away in triumph and set in the stocks, which afforded them diversion, and tended to abate their rage, and disposed them to separate and go to dinner.'

' As soon as it was dusk, several thousand people assembled in King-street, below the town-house, where the general court was sitting. Stones and brickbats were thrown through the glass into the council chamber. The governour, however, with several gentlemen of the council and house, ventured into the balcony, and after silence was obtained,

the governour in a well-judged speech expressed his great disapprobation of the impress, and promised his utmost endeavours to obtain the discharge of every one of the inhabitants,
and at the same time gently reproved the irregular proceedings both of the forenoon and evening. Other gentlemen also
attempted to persuade the people to disperse, and wait to see
what steps the general court would take. All was to no purpose. The seizure and restraint of the commanders and other officers who were in town, was insisted upon as the only
effectual method to procure the release of the inhabitants
aboard the ships.

' It was thought advisable for the governour to withdraw to
his house, many of the officers of the militia and other gentlemen attended him. A report was raised, that a barge from
one of the ships was come to a wharf in the town. The mob
flew to seize it, but by mistake took a boat belonging to a
Scotch ship, and dragged it, with as much seeming ease
through the streets as if it had been in the water, to the governour's house, and prepared to burn it before the house ; but
from a consideration of the danger of setting the town on fire,
were diverted, and the boat was burned in a place of less
hazard. The next day the governour ordered that the military officers of Boston should cause their companies to be mustered, and to appear in arms, and that a military watch should
be kept the succeeding night; but the drummers were interrupted, and the militia refused to appear. The governour did not
think it for his honour to remain in town another night, and
privately withdrew to the castle. A number of gentlemen
who had some intimation of his design, sent a message to him
by Colonel Hutchinson, assuring him they would stand by
him in maintaining the authority of government and restor-
ing peace and order, but he did not think this sufficient.

' The governour wrote to Mr. Knowles, representing the
confusions occasioned by this extravagant act of his officers ;
but he refused all terms of accommodation until the commanders and other officers on shore were suffered to go on board
their ships, and he threatened to bring up his ships and
bombard the town, and some of them coming to sail, caused
different conjectures of his real intention. Captain Erskine,
of the Canterbury, had been seized at the house of Colonel
Brinley in Roxbury, and given his parole not to go abroad,
and divers inferior officers had been secured.

The 17th, 18th, and part of the 19th, the council and house
of representatives, sitting in the town, went on with their ordinary business, not willing to interpose lest they should encourage
other commanders of the navy to future acts of the like nature ;
but towards noon of the 19th, some of the principal members
of the house began to think more seriously of the dangerous

consequences of leaving the governour without support, when
there was not the least ground of exception to his conduct.
Some high spirits in the town began to question whether his
retiring should be deemed a desertion or abdication. It was
moved to appoint a committee of the two houses to consider
what was proper to be done. This would take time, and was
excepted to, and the speaker was desired to draw up such
resolves as it was thought necessary the house should immediately agree to, and they were passed by a considerable
majority, and made publick.

'In the house of representatives, Nov. 19th, 1747.

'Resolved—that there has been and still continues, a tumultuous, riotous assembling of armed seamen, servants, negroes,
and others in the town of Boston, tending to the destruction
of all government and order.

'Resolved—that it is incumbent on the civil and military
officers in the Province to exert themselves to the utmost, to
discourage and suppress all such tumultuous, riotous proceedings, whensoever they may happen.

'Resolved—that this house will stand by and support with
their lives and estates His Ex. the governour and the executive part of the government in all endeavours for this purpose.

'Resolved—that this house will exert themselves by all ways
and means possible in redressing such grievances as his majesty's subjects are and have been under, which may have been
the cause of the aforesaid tumultuous, disorderly assembling
together.   T. Hutchinson, Speaker.'

'The council passed a vote, ordering that Capt. Erskine,
and all other officers belonging to his majesty's ships, should
be forthwith set at liberty and protected by the government,
which was concurred by the house. As soon as these votes
were known, the tumultuous spirit began to subside. The inhabitants of the town of Boston assembled in town meeting in
the afternoon, having been notified, to consider, in general,
what was proper for them to do upon this occasion, and notwithstanding it was urged by many that all measures to suppress the present spirit in the people would tend to encourage
the like oppressive acts for the future, yet the contrary party
prevailed, and the town, although they expressed their sense
of the great insult and injury by the impress, condemned the
tumultuous, riotous acts of such as had insulted the governour
and the other branches of the legislature, and committed
many other heinous offences.

'The governour, not expecting so favourable a turn, had
written to the secretary to prepare orders for the colonels of
the regiments of Cambridge, Roxbury, and Milton, and the
regiment of horse, to have their officers and men ready to
march at an hour's warning, to such place of rendezvous as

he should direct ; but the next day there was an uncommon appearance of the militia of the town of Boston, many persons taking their muskets who never carried one upon any other occasion, and the governour was conducted to his house with as great parade as when he first assumed the government. The commodore* dismissed most, if not all, of the inhabitants who had been impressed, and the squadron sailed, to the joy of the rest of the town.'

On the morning of Wednesday, Dec. 9, of the same year, the Town-house was discovered to be on fire, and the whole interior of it was consumed. The legislature was in session, and made particular inquiry into the occasion of the disaster : they ascertained to the satisfaction of the House, that the fire proceeded from the wood-work under the hearth. The se-lectmen immediately offered the use of Faneuil-Hall, but the court preferred to occupy a room in a publick house ' of the late Luke Vardy.'† The court adjourned on the 12th, and met again in February. When the subject of a new court-house was introduced, a motion prevailed in the House that the same should be built in Cambridge : this vote was re-considered, and another obtained, which proposed to locate it in Roxbury. This was non-concurred, as the former vote had been, by the Council. At length a resolve passed, that the old building should be repaired, and one half the charge be borne by the province, one quarter by the county of Suf-folk, and the other quarter by the town of Boston.

' It was repaired in the year following in its present form, and is in length one hundred and twelve feet, in breadth thirty-six feet, and three stories high. On the centre of the roof is a tower, consisting of three stories, finished according to the Tuscan, Dorick, and Ionick orders. From the upper story is an extensive prospect of the harbour, into the bay, and of the country adjacent.——The lower floor of the building served for a covered walk for any of the inhabitants. On this floor were kept the offices of the clerks of the supreme judicial court and court of common pleas. The chambers over it were occupied by the general court, the senate in one, and the representative body in the opposite chamber. The third story was appropriated for the use of the committees of the general court. On the lower floor were ten pillars of the Dorick order, which supported the chambers occupied by the legislature.'

---

* Mr. Knowles was afterwards an admiral in the British navy, and in 1770, being invited by the empress of Russia, went into her service.

† The Royal Exchange tavern.

CHAPTER XLIII.

" In red and wreathing columns flashed
The flame, as loud the ruin crashed,
And here and there the crackling dome
Was fired before the exploding bomb."

WE pass by the events of a long and anxious war with the French and Indian natives, which, though materially affecting the trade and prosperity of Boston, in common with other parts of the American provinces, were of less immediate interest than the events which we proceed to detail from the registers of the times.

On Wednesday, the 14th of Nov. 1759, a fire happened in some wooden buildings, a little to the southward of Oliver's bridge, and extended to the lower end of Water-street and Milk-st. to Mr. Hallowell's ship-yard. It raged with great violence for two hours. Ten or twelve dwelling-houses, most of them large, besides a number of shops and other buildings, were destroyed, and between 20 and 30 families burnt out. H. Ex. the governour [Pownall] was present during the whole fire, whose direction and influence was very serviceable, and whose paternal care and tenderness for the distressed was quite apparent.

' Between XI. and XII. o'clock at noon on Monday the 17th of March, 1760, a fire broke out at the West part of the town, New Boston so called, by some accident, whereby a joiner's shop was consumed and a large dwelling-house adjoining thereto was a great part of it destroyed and many things therein burnt, and several other houses much damaged in the neighbourhood. The wind blowing very high at N.E. it was a considerable time before it was extinguished. The roof of the West meeting-house caught fire in several places, but by the dexterity of the people and a constant supply of water a stop was at length put to it.' And

On the day following, in the forenoon, ' a store at the upper end of Griffin's [Liverpool] whf. caught fire. The chamber was used as a laboratory by a detachment of the British artillery then here. The circumstance of artillery stores being in the building, gave general alarm, and for a time the citizens were afraid to approach near it. The fire communicated to some powder, and the building blew up. In the explosion some men were hurt : two grenadoes and some small arms went off but did no damage. The extreme parts of the town were affected by the shock of the explosion. A carpenter's shop was also burnt. It stood between the laboratory and some warehouses on the end of the wharf, where the principal artillery stores were deposited ; but the wind being moderate, and a full tide, the flames were prevented from spreading farther.'

The day following, different parts of the town, at different times, were alarmed with the cry of fire : it did not, however, then get to a considerable head any where, so as to become dangerous. By these fires was ushered in, that far greater and more fatal one, which happened on the 20th of March. ' It began about two o'clock yesterday morning,' says a paper of Friday, ' and broke out in the dwelling-house of Mrs.Mary Jackson and Son, at the Brazen Head in Cornhill. At its first appearance there was little wind ; but this calm was soon followed by a smart gale from the N. W. Then was beheld a perfect torrent of blaze, bearing down all before it : in a seeming instant all was flame. Three or four large buildings* in the front of the street were burnt, and a stop was put to it there, at the house improved by Mrs. West on the South, and Mr. Peter Cotta on the North. But the fire raged most violently towards the East, the wind being strong, and carried all before it from the back sides of those houses. All the stores fronting Pudding-lane, together with every dwelling-house, from thence, (excepting those which front the S. side of King-st. and a store of Mr. Spooner's† on Water-st.) to Quaker-lane, and from thence, only leaving a large old wooden house belonging to the late Cornelius Waldo, Esq. it burnt every house, shop, store, out-house, and shed, to Oliver's Dock. And an eddy of wind carrying the fire contrary to its course, it took the buildings fronting the lower part of King-st. and destroyed the houses from the corner opposite the Bunch of Grapes tavern, to the warehouse of Box & Austin, leaving only the warehouse of the Hon. John Erving, and the dwelling-house of Mr. Hastings standing. The other brick warehouses towards the Long-whf. were considerably damaged.

On the S. E. part, the fire extended from Mr. Torrey's, the baker, in Water-st. and damaging some of Mr. Dalton's new shops, proceeded to Mr. Hall's working-house, and from

---

* Mrs. Jackson & Son, Widow McNeal, Jona. Mason, Mrs. Quick [now the sign of the Good Samaritan, formerly Three Kings] northernmost burnt.

† The remains of this old house stood until the summer of 1824, when a new brick building was erected on the spot.

thence to Milk-st. and consumed every house, from the next to Mr. Calfe's dwelling-house [Julien's Restorator], to the bottom of the street.

MR. CALEF'S DWELLING-HOUSE, IN 1760.

JULIEN'S RESTORATOR,

AT THE CORNER OF MILK AND CONGRESS-STREETS, DEMOLISHED IN JULY 1824.

And in the opposite direction from Mr. Dowse's, included, it carried all before it, every house, to Fort-hill, except the Hon. Sec. Oliver's and two or three tenements opposite ; as also every house, warehouse, shop, and store, from Oliver's Dock along Mr. Hallowell's ship-yard, Mr. H.'s dwelling-house, the Sconce of the S. Battery, all the buildings, shops, and stores, on Col. Wendell's whf. to the house of Mr. Hunt, ship-builder. So that, from Pudding-lane to the water's edge, there is not a building to be seen, excepting those on the side of King-st. and the others mentioned above. Besides which, one large ship and 8 or 9 vessels were burnt. The fire did not extend to any part of the North side of King-st. There was a quantity of powder in the Sconce, which blew up, throwing the stones and timber to a great distance, and caused a very great explosion. The rage of the fire was not over till near noon ; but notwithstanding its long continuance, the explosion, and the falling of walls and chimnies, Divine Providence appeared merciful, in that not one person's life was lost, and only a few wounded.'

Means were taken by the authorities of the town immediately to ascertain the amount of losses, and a spirit of sympathy
was every where excited in behalf of the sufferers. Every
individual furnished a schedule of every article he missed,
and his own valuation of it, to a committee appointed for the
purpose : where they considered it just, they adopted such
valuation : where it was thought too high, they curtailed it.
The whole sum,thus ascertained, amounted to £71,112. 7s. 3d.
lawful money : of which £44,121. 6s. 8d. was in real estate.
The Quaker meeting-house, 133 dwelling-houses, 36 barns, 63
stores, 66 shops, in all 299 buildings, were destroyed. Sarah
Ayers and 438 other sufferers petitioned parliament for relief :
our accounts do not say that any was obtained : from other
sources the donations in full, up to the 22d of March, 1763,
were £22,107. 1s. 6d. The town embraced the opportunity
offered for improvements in the streets, and a law was passed,
in the June session succeeding the fire, to regulate the building
of houses on the spots laid waste.

Gov. Pownall sailed from Boston, June 3, 1760. This left
the administration in the hands of Lt. Gov. Thomas Hutchinson, until the arrival of His Ex. Francis Bernard, Esq. on the
2d of August following. He was received with great parade.
The Sheriff of Suffolk (Greenleaf) and a party of the Governour's troop of guards met him at Wrentham, and accompanied him to Dedham, where the Lt. Gov. and some of the
council, attended by Brig. Gen. Royall with the rest of the
troop of guards, waited to receive him. A procession of gentlemen in coaches and chariots escorted them into town and
proceeded to the Province House,* where the company of
of Cadets under Col. Jarvis was drawn up. Thence H. E.
walked in procession to the Court-house [Old State-house],
and the regiment of militia in this town commanded by Col.
Phillips being paraded in the main street, the officers paid the

* The Province House is a large brick building, which stands in the rear of Province-
house row, opposite the head of Milk-st. It is three stories in height, stood back at a convenient distance from the street, having a small garden plat in front of it, and a fence of
iron railing, at the gate of which were two large trees, which agreeably shaded the passage
to the house. The entrance was by an ascent of stone steps. Upon the cupola on the roof
a pedestal supports a figure of bronze, an aboriginal native holding in his hand a bow and
arrow, well executed by Dea. Drowne, formerly an ingenious artist in the town. The front
of the house was ornamented with the king's arms, elegantly carved and gilt : this is preserved in the museum of the Historical Society. The estate has been given by the State to
the Massachusetts General Hospital and Asylum for the Insane ; the trustees have leased it
for 100 years, and the lessees erected a large brick pile in front of it, to be used for shops,
which entirely prevents its being seen from the street. When the Province first obtained
possession of it, we have not ascertained. Its builder and the year of its erection are probably indicated by the letters and date 16 P. S. 79 which appear on the
rail that surmounts the iron balustrade over the portico.

standing salute as H. E. passed by. At the Court-house the
governour's commission was read, and H. E. received the
congratulations of the Court, which was succeeded by three
vollies from the troop of guards, the regiment of militia and
the cadets, and three huzzas from the populace, as also a discharge from the guns at Castle William, the batteries in this
town and Charlestown, and from the Province ship King
George and the other ships in the harbour. After which H.E.
with the Lieut. Gov. and Council, a number of officers civil
and military, and of the clergy and other gentlemen, were
entertained with an elegant dinner, provided at Faneuil-hall.

The death of king George II. took place on the 25th of October, and on the 27th, his grandson George William, prince
of Wales, was proclaimed in London. Authentick advices of
these facts were received at Boston in precisely two months
after their occurrence, and ceremonies very similar to those
just related took place on the proclamation of king George
the Third, from the balcony of the Court-house : 63 guns
being fired at the Castle, a dinner at the Hall, and illumina-
tions in the evening. On the first of the new year, two days
after, there was a general mourning on account of George II.
All the bells in the town began tolling in the morning and continued most part of the day, and minute guns to the number
of 77, the years of His Majesty's age, were discharged at the
Castle. These were the last exhibitions here of a similar
nature on the like occasions, and furnish some notion of the
manner in which such events had been celebrated ever since
the new charter.

In the month of January, 1761, the weather at Boston was
extremely cold, so that the harbour was for two or three days
almost filled with ice. On Tuesday evening, the 13th, ' at
about half an hour after nine o'clock, a violent fire broke out
in one of the shops opposite the north side of Faneuil-Hall
market on Dock-sq. which entirely consumed all the row of
wooden buildings, from the store occupied by the Hon. Thos.
Hubbard, Esq. to the swing bridge. These buildings belonged to the town, and were leased to a number of tradesmen,
some of whom had their whole stock therein, most of which
was either consumed or lost. There were several small
schooners in the dock, but they received little damage, nor
did the fire proceed to the N. side of the dock ; on the contrary, it communicated itself to that stately edifice, Faneuil-
Hall market, the whole of which was entirely consumed, excepting the brick walls, which are left standing. The fire
then proceeded to a number of shops improved by some
tradesmen, on the South side of the market, and consumed
them also. The severity of the weather was such that many
persons could scarce stand it, and the water which issued

NORTH EAST VIEW OF FANUEIL HALL.

A. Bowen Sc.

from the engines congealed into particles of ice before it fell. No dwelling-house was consumed. The records and papers, with such other things as could be conveniently removed, were mostly saved. March 23d, the town voted to repair the building, and the Gen. Court granted the town a lottery for the purpose of defraying the expense.*

CHAPTER XLIV.

I look with rapture at the opening dawn,
And view the glories of the rising morn,
When Justice holds her sceptre o'er the land,
To rescue Freedom from a tyrant hand.

Mrs. Warren.

AT the close of Chapter xxxiv. we quoted the observation that ' a party was formed which opposed submission to the charter.' Their ground of opposition was the extension, which the charter gave to the royal power and influence in and over the colony. It would be an instructive history, that should exhibit to us in minute detail the course pursued by that party, from the commencement of Gov. Phipps' administration to that of Gov. Bernard. We might discover in it the progressive operation of the principles, and the regular and constant increase of the spirit, which in event produced the American Revolution. But such a detail would be too foreign from the subject of this work. The beginning of the reign of George III. was destined to be marked by the more decisive steps of the party alluded to, and we therefore proceed to note the events that occurred in Boston, which we suppose to have been the commencement of the overt acts, which resulted in open rebellion and eventual independence.

' Suffice it to say, that immediately upon the conquest of Canada, in 1759, Great-Britain seemed to be seized with a jealousy against the colonies, and then concerted the plan of changing their forms of government, of restraining their trade within narrower bounds, and raising a revenue within them

---

* The first meeting at Faneuil-Hall, after it was repaired, was on March 14th, 1763. Some slight alterations were made in some parts of the work, but the size of the building remained the same. The enlargement, by which it was extended in width to 80 feet, and a third story added, was proposed by the selectmen in May, 1805, and completed in the course of the next twelve months. The white line in our view of the Hall exhibits the line of demarcation between the original building and the addition.

by authority of parliament. The first demonstration of the
new course, intended to be pursued, was the arrival of an order sent from the Board of Trade to the custom-house officers
in America, to apply to the supreme courts of justice for *Writs
of Assistance*, to enable them to carry into a more rigorous
execution certain acts of parliament called the Acts of trade.
In Massachusetts, Charles Paxton, Esq. who was at the head
of the customs in Boston, directed his deputy at Salem, Mr.
Cockle, in Nov. 1760, to petition the court then sitting in that
town for the grant of such writs. The court expressed great
doubt of the legality of the writ, and of the authority of the
court to grant it : but as the application was on the part of the
crown, it could not be dismissed without a hearing, which
was fixed for the next term of the court, to be held in Feb.
1761, at Boston, when the question was ordered to be argu-
ed. The proposed form of this writ was such as to give the
officer holding it, upon bare suspicion, power to enter any
houses, ships, cellars, stores, chests, or magazines, to search
for goods that had been imported contrary to the acts of
trade.

Beside their natural zeal to merit the approbation of the
ministry, the custom-house officers had the still stronger in-
ducement of the prospect of accumulating wealth, to exercise
rigour in the performance of their official duties. Hence a
rooted aversion subsisted between them and the people concerned in the foreign trade of the province. And while the
question of the issue of Writs of Assistance was pending, a
memorial was framed, apparently with a view to counteract
their project for gain, and presented to the General Court,
Dec. 19, 1760, charging them with appropriating to their own
use, a portion of the goods forfeited, which of right accrued
to the province. The memorialists were 58 in number, and
included the most eminent merchants of Boston ; viz.

John Avery	Sam. Dexter	Thos. Boylston	John Barrett
Jona. Williams	John Greene	John Rowe	Edw. Davis
Tim. Fitch	John Tudor	Tim. Newell	Fitch Pool
John Dennie	Sol. Davis	Jos. Domett	Thos. Greene
John Waldo	John Amory	John Spooner	Henderson Inches
Thos. Greene, jr.	John Gooch	Wm. Greenleaf	Dan'l Malcom
Wm. Molineaux	Jona. Mason	John Welch, jr.	Thos. Tyler
John Boylston	Peter Boyer	John Scollay	Jona. Amory
John Browne	Sam. Grant	John Baker	James Thompson
Benj. Hallowell	Sam. Hughes	Wm. Thompson	Sam. Welles, jr.
Melatiah Bourne	Benj. Austin	Chr. Clarke	Sam. Wentworth
Thos. Gray	Geo. Erving	John Erving, jr.	Arnold Welles
Sam. Austin	Jos. Green	John Powell	Jona. Sayward
Josh. Winslow	Sam. Phil. Savage	Nath. Holmes	James Boutineau
Ezek. Goldthwait	James Perkins		

These may perhaps be considered the first men, who set themselves in open array against the officers of the crown. Their memorial was referred to a joint committee of the House and Council, which reported that the province was illegally and unjustly kept out of £475, 9s. 11d. and that the Treasurer should be empowered to demand and sue for the money. Gov. Bernard opposed his negative to this proposition, but at last assented to it in a message, Jan. 31, 1761, " hoping that they would not require of him such another proof of his great desire of preserving a good understanding with them."*

When the time appointed for the discussion of the question of Writs of Assistance drew near, the mercantile part of the community was in a state of great anxiety as to the result. The officers of the customs called upon James Otis, jun. esq. as advocate-general in the court of admiralty, to argue their cause. But he would not prostitute his office to the furtherance of an oppressive act ; and being unwilling to retain a station, in which he might be expected to argue in favour of such odious measures, he resigned ; and the merchants of Boston and Salem immediately engaged him and Oxenbridge Thacher, jun. esq. to appear in support of a counter petition, which they had presented to the court.

Mr. Otis was a native of the town of Barnstable ; received his education at Harvard College ; graduated in 1743 ; pursued the study of law in Boston under the direction of Jeremiah Gridley, Esq. one of the principal lawyers and civilians of the day ; commenced practice in Plymouth ; and about the year 1750 removed to Boston, and very soon rose to the first rank in his profession. His business as a lawyer became very extensive, and his reputation was firmly established for learning, eloquence, and the most high-minded integrity. He was now in the vigour of manhood, just thirty-six years of age. An opponent describes him as ' a plump, round-faced, smooth skin, short neck, eagle-eyed politician ;' and another writer dresses him in a wig and a black gown.

Mr. Thacher was at this time one of the heads of the bar in Boston. His family had always been distinguished in the province, and his own character and manners were such as to secure affection and esteem : his patriotism was the most pure and ardent, joined to a quick perception of the views of those in power. He was a Bostonian by birth, and now about 41 years of age.

---

* *Minot*, ii. 86. Printed Journal of Gen. Court, pp. 231. 339. Also Sup. Court Rec. Aug. term, 1761, p. 235, where, in an appeal from the Inferior Court, judgment is reversed and Paxton recovers against Harrison Gray, Treasurer, costs taxed 4l. 6s. 9d.

The trial took place in the Council Chamber of the Old Town-house. This room was situated at the east end of that building : it was an imposing and elegant apartment, ornamented with two splendid full-length portraits of Charles II. and James II. The judges in those days, in conformity to European practice, attached a part of their official dignity to a peculiar costume, which in later times they have here discarded. Their dress was composed of voluminous wigs, broad bands, and robes of scarlet cloth. They were five in number, including Lieut. Gov. Hutchinson who presided as chief justice.* The room was filled with all the officers of government, and the principal citizens, to hear the arguments in a cause that inspired the deepest solicitude.

In consequence of Mr. Otis's resignation, the task of supporting the petition for the Writs devolved on Mr. Gridley, who was then attorney-general. He opened the case with much learning, ingenuity, and dignity, urging every point and authority, that could be found upon the most diligent search ; but made all his reasoning depend on this consideration— " *if* the parliament of Great Britain is the sovereign legislature of the British empire." He was succeeded by Mr. Thacher on the opposite side, whose reasoning was pertinent and able, delivered in a tone of great mildness and moderation, which convinced his hearers that he was advocating the cause of truth and justice. As soon as he had concluded, Otis burst forth as with ' a flame of fire : with a promptitude of classical allusion, a depth of research, a rapid summary of historical events and dates, a profusion of legal authorities, a prophetick glance of his eyes into futurity, and a rapid torrent of impetuous eloquence, he hurried away all before him. 'Then and there,' says President John Adams, ' was the first scene of the first act of opposition to the arbitrary claims of Great Britain. Then, and there, the child Independence was born. Every man of an immense crowded audience appeared to me to go away, as I did, ready to take arms against Writs of Assistance.' The court adjourned for consideration, and, at the close of that term, the question was continued to the next.†

' An epoch in publick affairs may be dated from this trial. Political parties became more distinctly formed, and their several adherents were more marked and decided. " *Taxation without representation is tyranny*" (a phrase that fell from Otis in the debate,) became a common maxim in the mouth of

---

* The associate judges were Benja. Lynde, John Cushing, Chambers Russell, Peter Oliver.

† Thus far we follow *Tudor's* Life of Otis, p. 53-86, respecting the Writ.

all the friends of liberty. The crown officers and their followers adopted openly the pretensions of the British ministry and parliament, proclaiming a blind submission as the only safe or reasonable alternative. The people of Boston showed plainly to which party they belonged, by the election of Mr. Otis, almost unanimously, as a representative for the town in the next general court. His colleagues were Royal Tyler, John Phillips, and Thomas Cushing, all of them men of great weight in society. Gov. Bernard perceived the spirit that was rising, and some of his friends, whose wisdom has been proved by events, predicted that ' out of this election a faction would arise, which would shake the province to its foundation.' The Governour, in his speech at the opening of the Gen. Court, advised them to lay aside all divisions, and to give no attention to declamations tending to promote a suspicion of the civil rights of the people being in danger. They replied, that they knew nothing of any such parties as he described, and were not in the least degree suspicious ; but firmly expressed their intention to see for themselves, whether the rights of the people were or were not in danger.

A final ' hearing was had before the Sup. Court of Judicature, upon the petition of the officers of the customs for a Writ of Assistance on Wednesday,' the 18th of November. The whole day and evening, (says the Boston Gazette of the 23d) ' was spent in the arguments, and nothing could have induced one to believe they were not conclusive against the petition, but the judgment of the court *immediately* given in favour of it.' The papers soon exhibited the dissatisfaction which this decision occasioned. On the 7th of Dec. a piece appeared signed ' A fair trader,' complaining that the Acts of trade were no where executed with such rigour as in this colony, and concluding thus : .' We want nothing but to be as free as others are, and that others should be restrained as well as we. This is reasonable. WE HAVE A RIGHT TO CLAIM IT.'

The part, which Mr. Otis had taken, designated him as the friend of the people, and they therefore took deep interest in a controversy which took place in the papers between him and Lieut. Gov. Hutchinson, respecting the currency of the province. Otis improved the opportunity to turn their thoughts to the circumstance of His Honour's enjoying so many lucrative offices as were united in his person, viz. that of Lieut. Gov. with the emoluments of captain of the castle, a member of the Council, Judge of Probate, and Chief Justice of the supreme court. O.'s first piece on this subject appeared Dec. 21, 1761, and the last Jan. 11, 1762. ' The question was settled at the next meeting of the legislature, according to the principles which Otis had advanced.' Having thus obtained an ascendancy, the majority attempted

to retrieve the ground which they had lost by the decision on
the Writs of Assistance, and a bill was prepared, the substance of which was, to prevent the issuing of those writs to
any person but a custom-house officer, and that upon special
information on oath ; but the attempt was checked by the
Governour's refusal to give his assent to the bill. An ineffectual effort was also made to exclude the Justices of the
Sup. Court from a seat in the Council or House of Representatives.   These conflicts, though sometimes unavailing,
served to prove the strength of parties, and to keep alive
the growing jealousy between them.*

Mr. Otis and his colleagues were re-elected in May, 1762,
with a decided approbation, in the Gazette, of the course
they had pursued in regard to the points in controversy.
Brigadier-General Timothy Ruggles, from Hardwick, in the
county of Worcester, the leader of the government party in
the House, was chosen speaker, at the May session ; and the
court was prorogued, June 12th, with some expressions of
pleasure from the Governour for their good conduct. In
September they met again, and ' on the 14th' His Excellency
sent a message informing the house, that, to quiet the fears of
those concerned in the fishing vessels, he had increased the
armament of the Massachusetts sloop, and sent her out for
their protection. A little paper accompanied the message,
with a short account of the difference to the province by the
Gov. and Council's enlarging the establishment, which
amounted to about £72.   This message gave rise to a remarkable discussion, and this trifling expenditure may be
considered as one of the preparatory causes of the revolution. It was not the measure itself, nor the expense of it,
that gave the House so much uneasiness, but the manner of
it ; that is, the enlarging the establishment without the
knowledge of the house, and paying for it without their
privity or consent. The message was referred to a committee, of which Mr. Otis was chairman, who reported a remonstrance, addressed to the Gov. in which they declared that
the proceeding was ' in effect taking from the House their
most darling privilege, the right of originating all taxes.—No
necessity can be sufficient to justify a house of representatives
in giving up such a privilege ; *for it would be of little consequence
to the people, whether they were subjects to George or Lewis, the
king of G.B. or the French king, if both were arbitrary, as
both would be, if both could levy taxes without Parliament.'*

' When the passage in Italics was read, Mr. Paine a member

<hr />

* Town Records, March 8, 1762. ' Upon consideration of that clause in the warrant, viz.
that the town will take such methods as shall be judged necessary for the Incorporation of
it, the question was put, whether the town would take any such steps ? Passed in the negative *almost unanimously.'

from Worcester, cried out, *Treason, treason !* but after a most animated speech from Otis, the answer was passed entire by a large majority, and Otis was appointed one of the committee to present it to the Governour.' H. E. ' was so displeased at this passage that he sent a letter to the speaker, returning the message of the House and recommending earnestly, that it might not be entered upon the minutes as it then stood. After some debate the exceptionable clause was struck out, but enough remained to excite a vindication from the Governour, which he sent by the secretary at the same time that he gave the house notice to attend him in the council chamber to be prorogued.

Soon after this separation, Otis published a pamphlet,* giving an account of all these occurrences and justifying the course pursued by the house. This production has been considered the original source, from which all subsequent arguments against taxation were derived.† The principal stress in the argument of Mr. Otis was laid against the constitutionality of the measure, and the position assumed by the Governour was not only shown to be untenable, but the dangerous tendency of constructive power was pointed out with a clearness and force, that effectually roused the publick attention to guard against every step of arbitrary power in future.

In the winter session of 1762-3 another occasion of dispute was afforded by an application from the Attorney-General for remuneration for his official services, which was so managed as to give the popular party a triumph, at the same time that the officer received the compensation that was honourably due to him. And this subject had not lost its interest, before another excitement was produced on still a different ground. The project of sending a bishop to America had been in agitation for ten or fourteen years,‡ and the minds of people were well prepared for an attack upon the established church. Doctor E. Miller, who was a missionary from the society for propagating the gospel, died   at Braintree where he had been officiating to an episcopal church. The manner in which his death was noticed in one of the Boston papers brought on a controversy, in which most of the dissenters found themselves ranged on one side, in opposition to the few adherents to the church, among whom were most of the dependents on the crown. These writings may therefore be considered as having increased the divisions, which were rising in Massachusetts.

---

* " A Vindication of the conduct of the House of Representatives," &c. by James Otis, Esq, a member of said house." It was published Nov. 15, 1762.

† Franklin had urged similar arguments to Gov. Shirley, 1754. F. was here, Oct. 1763.

‡ See News-Letter, Dec. 13, 1750, and Ev. Post, Aug. 22, 1763.

The people of Boston manifested their adherence to the popular side by the re-election of Otis, Tyler, and Cushing, for their representatives, with the addition of Oxenbridge Thacher Jr. instead of Col. Phillips, who had just deceased (April, 26, 1763.) Great efforts had been made to prevent the choice of Mr. Otis ; his motives had been traduced, and his conduct attributed to personal feeling rather than zeal for the publick good. He had however defended himself, in his own name, to the complete discomfiture of his enemies.

Through the remainder of the year there were occasional publications, calculated to keep alive the spirit, which had displayed itself in the Province : there was no torpor to invite encroachments upon civil rights by stealth, but rather an excessive anxiety about the course, which government might resolve to pursue, relative to the regulations of trade. The first evidence on this point was 'an act for the further improvement of H. M. revenue, for the encouragement of officers making seizures, and for the prevention of the clandestine running of goods,' which was published in Boston, Sept. 22d, and followed on the 16th of November, by Gov. Bernard's proclamation for aid and assistance in the execution of it.

In the opening of the year 1764, Boston was visited again with the small pox, which continued its ravages till the end of June.* The melancholy that attended the prevalence of this horrible disorder, was rendered still more sober, by the daily expectation of unwelcome news from England. Notice of resolutions in parliament proposing duties on various foreign articles imported into the colonies, and a duty upon other articles, the produce of the colonies, exported to any other place than Great Britain, was received early in May. Anticipating the worst, the people of Boston, having re-elected the same representatives on the 15th of May, appointed Richard Dana, Esq. Mr. Samuel Adams, John Ruddock, Esq. Nathl. Bethune, Esq. and Jos. Green, Esq. a committee to prepare such instructions, to be given to the representatives, as the exigencies of the times required. On the 24th the committee reported and the town approved and adopted their report.

In this paper the town claim 'the constitutional right of expressing their mind' to their representatives ' upon particular matters' and charge them to maintain ' the invaluable rights and privileges of the province—as well those rights, which are derived to us by the royal charter, as those which, being

---

* It may be noted here, that the population of the town was ascertained by actual enumeration to be in 1742 - - - - - 16,382 souls, including 1374 blacks.

        1752 - - - - - 15,731 ,,   ,,   1541 ,,

        1765 - - - - - 15,520 ,,

The gazettes of May, 1764, give the names of twenty physicians, (besides Dr. Jackson of Portsmouth,) who inoculated the poor of the town.

prior to and independent on it, we hold essentially as free-born subjects of G. B.' Then they prescribe the course they wish to have pursued in relation to members of the General Court holding offices under the crown or the governour, the excise laws, salaries of judges, war expences; and having mentioned the importance of free trade to the prosperity of the town, and the evils apprehended from the measures of government, they proceed to say,

'There is now no room for further delay, we therefore expect that you will use your earliest endeavours in the General Assembly that such methods may be taken as will effectually prevent these proceedings against us. By a proper representation, we apprehend, it may easily be made to appear, that such severities will prove detrimental to G. B. itself: upon which account we have reason to hope that an application, even for a repeal of the act, should it be already past, will be successful. It is the trade of the colonies that renders them beneficial to the mother country. Our trade, as it now and always has been conducted, centres in G. B. and in return for manufactures affords her more ready cash, beyond any comparison, than can possibly be expected by the most sanguine promoters of these extraordinary methods.

'But what still heightens our apprehensions is, that these unexpected proceedings may be preparatory to new taxations upon us : for if our trade may be taxed, why not our lands? why not the produce of our lands and every thing we possess or make use of ? This we apprehend annihilates *our charter right* to govern and tax ourselves. It strikes at our British privileges, which as we have never forfeited them we hold in common with our fellow subjects, who are natives of Britain. *If taxes are laid upon us in any shape* without our having a legal representation where they are made, are we not reduced from the character of free subjects to the miserable state of tributary slaves?

'We therefore earnestly recommend it to you to use your utmost endeavours to obtain in the Gen. Assembly all necessary instruction and advice to our Agent at this most critical juncture * * * * that he may be able in the most humble and pressing manner to remonstrate for us all those rights and privileges, which justly belong to us either by charter or birth: in acknowledged dependence upon and subordination to G. B. As H. M.'s other N. American colonies are embarked with us in this most important bottom, we further desire you to use your endeavours that their weight may be added to that of this province, that by the united application of all who are aggrieved, all may happily obtain redress.'

The acts were passed, which had been recommended, except that by which it was proposed to lay a stamp duty on

all written or printed papers, in the colonies : this was deferred for one year's consideration, and to obtain the opinion of
the colonists respecting it, The legislature instructed the
Agent in very strong terms, and Mr. Otis published, (July,
23,) a tract entitled ' *The Rights of the British colonies asserted
and proved*,' which was followed on the same side (Sept. 3,)
by ' The Sentiments of a British American' written by Mr.
Thacher.   These two publications gave an importance to the
questions between the ' mother country' and the colonies,
which led to a closer examination of the subjects, on both
sides of the water.

CHAPTER XLV.

" First of your kind ! Society divine !"

WHATEVER other subjects may have engrossed the general
attention, there never has been a period when the people of
Boston lost their interest in those of a religious nature.   The
letters of Robert Sandeman to Mr. Hervey had excited a desire in some people to see the former in this quarter of the
world.   Pressing solicitations were sent to him from different
parts of New England by letter from some of the clergy as
well as of the laity, and he arrived in Boston on the 18th of
October, 1764, in the Ship George and James, Montgomery,
from Glasgow.   On the next sabbath he performed religious
service at Masons' hall.   ' Those who first associated with
him in Boston were, Edward Foster, Alford Butler, and Geo.
Oglevie with their respective wives and families ; and very
soon after, Edw. King, Henry Capen, Adam Chizeau, Ebenezer Allen, Barnabas Allen, Hopestill Capen, Benjamin Davies,
Isaac Winslow, Colburn Barrell, Walter Barrell, Mr. Peck, Hannah Robinson, Susanna Davies, Mary Cotton, Mary West, Ke-
zia West, Mrs. Stayner and some others of both sexes.   Mr.
Joseph Howe and Samuel Harris and wife joined the society at a later period.
  ' They first met in a large room at Mr. Foster's house in
that part of Prince St. called Black Horse lane, but as much
attention was excited, they removed to the Long Room at the
Green Dragon.   They soon built a house at the bottom of a
lane leading to the mill pond, somewhere between the two
Baptist meeting houses.   It was erected for the sole purpose of

a meeting house, by assistance from many friends.' This house was burnt in a fire which happened on Sunday, April, 4, 1773, at 4 o'clock P. M. in a building belonging to Mr. Alexander Edwards, cabinet-maker, and in a short time extended to several other shops and sheds in the neighbourhood. The spot has since been occupied as a bake-house, and is now within the premises of Mr. Joseph Veazie. Engine house, No. 3, stands at the head of the passage way.

The Sandemanian society afterwards convened at Mr. Townsend's in Cross-st. They subsequently built a house in the rear of Middle-street, where they met till within two years, when the attendance became so thin as to occasion the discontinuance of their meetings. A primary school is now kept in the same building.

As to church officers, they always had two elders (teachers) and deacons : no deaconesses are recollected. Daniel Humphreys, esq. (brother to the late Col. Humphreys) was early a deacon here, but soon removed to Danbury, Conn. to officiate as an elder. Mr. H. is still living and resides at Portsmouth, N. H. being Dist. Attorney of the U. S. He is an elder in a small society there, of which Mr. Butler abovenamed is also a living member. Mr. Sandeman died at Danbury, April 2, 1771, æt. 53.

CHAPTER XLVI.

Canterbury. "——— That self bill is urg'd
Which, in the eleventh year of the last king's reign
Was like, and had indeed against us pass'd,
But that ———
Ely. But how, my lord, shall we resist it now ?
Cant. It must be thought on."

It was in vain that all the colonies, in their separate capacities, remonstrated against the passage of the proposed Stamp Act. The king gave his assent to it on the 22d of March, 1765, and an unofficial copy of it was received in Boston on the 26th of May.* It consisted of fifty-five sections, each proposing a stamp duty, from half a penny to twenty shillings, ' on every skin of vellum or parchment or sheet or piece of paper,' on which any thing should be engrossed, written, or printed, which it was possible to imagine could be of any use to any person, to have written, printed,

---

* *Otis's* Botta, Hist. Rev. vol. i. 73, contains a copy.

33

or engrossed.   The Mutiny Act was passed at the same session, which required the colonies to provide for quartering the
king's troops, while on service in the colonies.   The Virginia
legislature were in session when the Stamp Act arrived : it is
well known that they immediately adopted (May 29th) the
resolutions of Patr. Henry, which fact has given to that state
the honour of having been foremost in opposition to the pretensions of parliament.† The Massachusetts legislature convened on the 30th of May, and by resolutions on the 8th of
June, proposed a congress of deputies from all the colonies, to
be held in New York on the first Tuesday of October ensuing.   The Stamp Act was to commence operation on the first
of November.

At this critical moment the cause of liberty lost one of its
worthiest advocates by the death of Oxenbridge Thacher jr.
esq. on the 9th of July.   His place in the house of representatives was supplied by the choice of Samuel Adams.

The gazettes of July abounded with articles, from all quarters, exciting the people to watchfulness, and ' it began to be
said that some provinces resolve not to pay the stamp duties.'
But no business can be legally transacted without the stamps :
the courts cannot proceed, without stamps upon their writs
and processes : no vessel can enter and no clearance can be
had without a stamp : no collegiate diploma can be issued
without a stamp : no marriage can be celebrated without a
stamp upon the clerk's certificate : cards must be stamped ;
newspapers must be stamped ; almanacks must be stamped ;
every thing, in fine, must bear this mark of slavery, or the
execution of the act must be prevented.   What then shall be
done ?

While the considerate part of the community were ponder-
ing this important question, information was received in Boston, that the secretary of the province, Andrew Oliver, esq.
was appointed distributor of stamps for Massachusetts, and
that a cargo of the papers might be daily expected to arrive
in the harbour.   Popular feeling could no longer be suppres-
sed ; and what calm reasoning could not decide, passion, the
love of liberty without restraint, brought to a determination.

Near the head of Essex-street there used to be a grove of
' those majestick elms, of the American species, that form one
of the greatest ornaments in the landscape of this country,'
which obtained the name of Hanover-square, or the neighbourhood of the Elms.   On one of these, which stood in
front of a house opposite the Boylston Market, on the edge of

---

† Aug. 11, 1766. At a celebration in Boston the following toast was given : " *The noble
Virginians, who first asserted their rights with decent firmness.*" B. Gaz.

the street, there was discovered hanging, at break of day, on
the 14th of August, an effigy representing Mr. Oliver, and a
Boot (the emblem of Lord Bute, a promoter of American taxation) with the devil peeping out of it, having the stamp act
in his hand, besides various other satirical emblems.* Some
of the neighbours offered to take it down, but they were given
to know, that would not be permitted. The Lieut. Gov. as
chief justice, directed the sheriff to order the effigy to be taken down, but his officers reported that they could not do it
without imminent danger of their lives.

Business was almost laid aside during the day, and multitudes from the country as well as the town flocked to witness the
sight. As soon as it began to grow dark, the mob, which
had been gathering all the afternoon, came down in procession to the Town-house, bearing the effigy with them; and
knowing that the Governour and Council were in session, they
gave three huzzas by way of defiance, and passed on towards
Kilby-street, where Mr. Oliver had lately erected a building,
which people supposed was designed for a stamp office. That
they instantly demolished, and bearing each man a portion of
the ruins upon his shoulder, they moved in solemn pomp to
Fort-hill, where they made a bonfire in view of Mr. Oliver's
house, and burnt the effigy upon it. Mr. O. had removed his
family, but remained himself with a few friends till the mob
approached, when he was persuaded to withdraw. The mob
got possession of the house, broke the windows and tore down
the garden fences.

' After eleven o'clock, the people seeming to grow quiet, the
Lieut. Gov. and the sheriff ventured to go to Mr. Oliver's
house, and endeavour to persuade them to disperse. As
soon as they began to speak, a ringleader cried out, " The
Governour and the sheriff, to your arms, my boys :" and
presently a volley of stones followed, and the two gentlemen
narrowly escaped, through favour of the night, not without
some bruises. Nothing more being to be done, the mob were

---

* This exhibition was not an original : it was probably an imitation of one in Devonshire,
of which a Boston paper of Aug. 20, 1763, gave the following account :—' About two miles
below Honiton there was suspended on an apple-tree, that grew over the road, a figure as
big as life, dressed in Scotch plaid, with something to resemble a ribbon over one shoulder,
and on a painted board, affixed to the tree, were these lines :

' Behold the man who made the yoke,	Now Britons all, join heart and hand,
Which doth Old England's sons provoke,	His sly-schemed project to withstand,
And now he hangs upon a tree,	That all our sons, as well as we,
An emblem of our liberty.	May have our Cider go scot free.'

' LIBERTY, PROPERTY, AND NO EXCISE.'

left to disperse at their own time, which they did about twelve o'clock.'

In the afternoon of the next day, ' several gentlemen applied to Mr. Oliver, to advise him to make a publick declaration, that he would resign the office, and never act in it ; without which they said his house would be immediately destroyed, and his life in continual danger ; upon which he was obliged to authorize some gentlemen to declare in publick, that he would immediately apply for leave to resign, and would not act in the office (as indeed it was impossible for him to do) until he received further orders.'

An officer addressing the lords of trade, writes thus :— ' After the demolition of Mr. Oliver's house was found so practicable and easy, that the government was obliged to look on, without being able to take any one step to prevent it, and the principal people of the town publickly avowed and justified the act, the mob, both great and small, became highly elated, and all kinds of ill-humours were set on foot.'

' On Monday, August 26, there was some small rumour, that mischief would be done that night ; but it was in general disregarded.   Towards evening some boys began to light a bonfire before the Town-house, which is an usual signal for a mob.   Before it was quite dark, a great company of people gathered together, crying, *Liberty and Property* ; which is their usual notice of their intention to plunder and pull down an house.   They went first to Mr. Paxton's house, who is marshall of the court of Admiralty, and surveyor of the port ; and finding before it the owner of the house (Mr. Paxton being only a tenant) he assured them, that Mr. Paxton had quitted the house with his best effects, and that the house was his ; that he had never injured them, and finally, invited them to go to the tavern and drink a barrel of punch : the offer was accepted, and so that house was saved.   As soon as they had drank the punch, they went to the house of Mr. Story, register-deputy of the Admiralty, [opposite the North corner of the Court-house] broke into it, and broke it all to pieces, and took out all the books and papers, among which were all the records of the court of Admiralty, and carried them to the bonfire, and there burnt them ; they also looked about for him with an intention to kill him.   From thence they went to Mr. Hallowell's, comptroller of the customs, broke into his house, [recently the mansion house of Hon. John Coffin Jones, in Hanover-street, where the new Trinitarian Church is now building] and destroyed and carried off every thing of value, with about 30l. sterling, in cash. This house was lately built by himself, and fitted and furnished with great elegance.

' But the grand mischief of all was to come. The Lieutenant-governour had been apprized, that there was an evil spirit gone forth against him ; but, being conscious that he had not in the least deserved to be made a party, in regard to the Stamp-act or the Custom-house, he rested in full security that the mob would not attack him ; and he was at supper with his family when he received advice that the mob was coming to him. He immediately sent away his children, and determined to stay in the house himself : but, happily, his eldest daughter returned, and declared she would not stir from the house, unless he went with her; by which means she got him away, which was undoubtedly the occasion of saving his life. For, as soon as the mob had got into the house, [it was that now occupied by William Little esq. in Garden-Court street] with a most irresistible fury, they immediately looked about for him, to murder him, and even made diligent enquiry whither he was gone. They went to work with a rage scarce to be exemplified by the most savage people. Every thing moveable was destroyed in a most minute manner, except such things of value as were worth carrying off ; among which were near 1000l. sterling, in specie, besides a great quantity of family plate, &c. But the loss to be most lamented is, that there was in one room, kept for that purpose, a large and valuable collection of manuscripts and original papers, which he had been gathering all his life-time, and to which all persons, who had been in possession of valuable papers of a publick kind, had been contributing, as to a publick Museum. As these related to the history and policy of the country, from the time of its settlement to the present, and was the only collection of its kind, the loss of the publick is great and irretrievable, as it is to himself, the loss of the papers of a family, which had made a figure in this province for a hundred and thirty years. As for the house, which from the structure and inside finishing, seemed to be from a design of Inigo Jones or his successor, it appears that they were a long while resolved to level it to the ground : they worked three hours at the cupola before they could get it down, and they uncovered part of the roof ; but I suppose, that the thickness of the walls, which were of very fine brick-work, adorned with Ionic pilasters worked into the wall, prevented their completing their purpose, though they worked at it till daylight. The next day, the streets were found scattered with money, plate, gold rings, &c. which had been dropped in carrying off. The whole loss in this house is reckoned at £3168. 17s. 9d. lawful.'

The principal citizens, perceiving that such outrages must infallibly injure a cause they considered just, were very strenuous to distinguish this tumultuous conduct from the truly noble opposition which they wished to manifest to the imposition of internal taxes by authority of parliament.

A town meeting was held, as early as possible on the next day, and the town expressed their ' detestation' of the violent proceedings of the past night, and unanimously voted, that the selectmen and magistrates be desired to use their utmost endeavours to suppress such disorders for the future.

In the month of September* a quantity of the stamps arrived, and Gov. Bernard, finding that Mr. Oliver could ' not safely meddle with them,' asked the advice of the Gen. Court, in order that they might be preserved safe and secure, but the Court excused themselves from giving any advice or assistance on the subject, and the stamps were deposited in the Castle for safe keeping.

The first of November had been appointed as a sort of Jubilee, before the riot of the 26th of August happened, and it had for many years been customary to celebrate the fifth of November. The following account of the events of those two days, in 1765, are from the Mass. Gazette, and convey a strong idea of the publick excitement.

' Last Friday being the day the stamp-act *was to* take place, the publick were not much alarmed or displeased at the morning's being ushered in by the tolling of bells in several parts of the town, and the vessels in the harbour displaying their colours half mast high, in token of mourning : and though some previous steps had been taken by authority to prevent any pageantry, fearing lest tumult and disorder might be the consequence, yet the people were soon informed that the Great Tree at the South part of the town (known by the name of the *Tree of Liberty* ever since the memorable 14th of August) was adorned with the effigies of the two famous or rather infamous enemies of American Liberty; G—ge G—nv—e and J--hn H—sk—. The figures continued suspended without any molestation till about 3 o'clock in the afternoon, when they were cut down in the view and amid the acclamations of several thousand people of all ranks, and being placed in a cart, were with great solemnity and order followed by the multitude, formed into regular ranks, to the Court-house, where the Assembly was then sitting ; from thence proceeding to the North end of the town and then returning up Middle Street, they passed back through the town to the gallows on the Neck, where the effigies were again hung up, and after continuing some time were cut down, when the populace, in token of their

---

* Sept. 11. There was a general rejoicing on the change of ministry, of which news was received, and ' On the body of the largest tree was fixed with large deck nails, that it might last (as a poet said, *like oaken bench to perpetuity*,) a copper plate [2 1-2ft. by 3 1-2] with these words stamped thereon in golden letters; *The tree of liberty*, Aug. 14. 1765.'

utmost detestation of the men they were designed to represent, tore them in pieces and flung their limbs with indignation into the air. This being done, three cheers were given,
and every man was desired to repair to his home, which was
so punctually performed, that the evening was more remarkable for peace and quietness than common ; a circumstance
that would at any time redound to the honour of the town,
but was still more agreeable, as the fears of many were great
lest it should prove another 26th of August ; for the horrid
violences of which night we hope the good order of this will
in some measure atone, as it is a proof such conduct was not
agreeable to the sentiments of the town, but was only the
lawless ravages of some foreign villains, who took advantage
of the over-heated temper, of a very few people of this place,
and drew them in to commit such violences and disorders as
they shuddered at with horror in their cooler hours.'

'Tuesday last being the anniversary of the commemora-
tion of the happy deliverance of the English nation from the
Popish Plot, commonly called THE POWDER PLOT, the guns
at Castle William and at the batteries in town were fired at
1 o'clock ; as also on board the men of war in the harbour.

'It has long been the custom in this town on the Fifth of
November for numbers of persons to exhibit on stages some
pageantry, denoting their abhorrence of Popery and the
horrid Plot which was to have been executed on that day
in the year 1685 ; these shews of late years had been continued in the evening, and we have often seen the bad effects attending them at such a time ; the servants and negroes would
disguise themselves, and being armed with clubs would engage each other with great violence, whereby many came off
badly wounded ; in short they carried it to such lengths that
two parties were created in the town, under the appellation of
North-End and *South-End* : but the disorders that had been
committed from time to time induced several gentlemen to try
a reconciliation between the two parties ; accordingly the
chiefs met on the first of this instant, and conducted that affair in a very orderly manner ; in the evening the commander of the South entered into a treaty with the commander of
the North, and after making several overtures they reciprocally engaged on a UNION, and the former distinctions to
subside ; at the same time the chiefs with their assistants engaged upon their honour, no mischiefs should arise by their
means, and that they would prevent any disorders on the 5th
—when the day arrived the morning was all quietness—about
noon the pageantry representing the Pope, Devil, and several
other effigies signifying Tyranny, Oppression, Slavery, &c.
were brought on stages from the North and South, and met in
King-street, where the Union was established in a very cere-

monial manner, and having given three huzzas, they inter-
changed ground, the South marched to the North, and the
North to the South, parading through the streets until they met
again near the Court-house : the whole then proceeded to the
Tree of Liberty, under the shadow of which they refreshed
themselves for a while, and then retreated to the northward,
agreeable to their plan ;—they reached Copps' Hill before 6
o'clock, where they halted, and having enkindled a fire, the
whole pageantry was committed to the flames and consumed :
this being finished, every person was requested to retire to
their respective homes—It must be noticed to the honour of
all those concerned in this business that every thing was conducted in a most regular manner, and such order observed as
could hardly be expected among a concourse of several thousand people—all seemed to be joined agreeable to their principal motto *Lovely Unity*—the leaders, Mr. McIntosh from the
South, and Mr. Swift from the North, appeared in military
habits, with small canes resting on their left arms, having musick in front and flank ; their assistants appeared also distinguished with small reeds, then the respective corps followed,
among whom were a great number of persons in rank : these
with the spectators filled the streets ; not a club was seen
among the whole, nor was any negro allowed to approach near
the stages ;— after the conflagration the populace retired, and
the town remained the whole night in better order than it had
ever been on this occasion.—Many gentlemen seeing the affair so well conducted, contributed to make up a handsome
purse to entertain those that carried it on.—This union, and
one other* more extensive, may be looked upon as the (perhaps
the only) happy effects arising from the S—p A—t.'

To relieve the merchants in some measure from the difficulties to which they were exposed, the custom-house officers
gave to vessels destined for foreign ports a certificate, that no
stamps could be procured in Boston.   Trusting to this security, and perhaps willing to contest the right of parliament
to impose the stamp duty before a court in England, John
Hancock, esq.† despatched the first ship, the Boston Packet,
Capt. Marshall, which arrived safe at London and was admitted without any trouble.   Some other vessels sailed in the
same month of November.

In the early part of December the Sons of Liberty (so
those who espoused the popular side were called, adopting
the appellation given them by Col. Barre on the floor of par-

---

* Referring probably to an agreement not to import goods from England.

† Mr. Hancock was one of the selectmen :   the year preceding he had come into possession of a large estate, left to him by his uncle Thomas H. a great benefactor of the town
and also of Harvard College.

liament) received information, that there was some probability that Mr. Oliver would accept the commission to distribute stamps, notwithstanding his former resignation. He was challenged by an anonymous writer to give a decided answer to the question, whether it were so or not. By the favour of the printer, he was permitted to reply in the same gazette. This was not satisfactory, and he received a note on the 16th, desiring him to appear ' to-morrow, under Liberty-Tree, at 12 o'clock, to make a publick resignation.' Accordingly the selectmen, with the merchants and the principal inhabitants of the town, to the amount of upwards of 2000, assembled at the Tree, at the time appointed. Mr. O. sent a note with ' compliments to the gentlemen assembled,' containing a proposition to have the ceremony performed at the Town-house ; but this not being agreeable, he came up to the Tree and declared as follows :

Whereas a Declaration was yesterday inserted in my name and at my desire, in some of the Boston newspapers, that I would not act as distributor of the Stamps, within this Province, which declaration, I am informed, is not satisfactory :

I do hereby in the most explicit and unreserved manner declare, that I have never taken any measures, in consequence of my deputation for that purpose. to act in the office ; and that I never will, directly or indirectly, by myself or any under me, make use of the said deputation, or take any measures for enforcing the Stamp-Act in America, which is so grievous to the people. *Andrew Oliver.*

Boston, 17 *Dec.* 1765.

Suffolk, ss. *Boston, Dec.* 17*th,* 1765.

The Honourable Andrew Oliver, Esq. subscriber to the above writing, made oath to the same. (Signed) *Ri. Dana, Just. Pacis.*

After which three cheers were given, and then Mr. Secretary made a short speech to the following purport, viz. " That he had an utter detestation of the Stamp-Act, and would do all that lay in his power to serve this town or province; and desired that they would no longer look on him as an enemy, but as another man." After which three cheers were again given him—and Hanover Square was clear in 10 minutes.

It is by no means to be inferred, from the pertinacity with which the people of Boston pursued Mr. Oliver, to compel him to a resignation in their own way, that he was a man of vile or mean character. On the contrary, Dr. Eliot's Biography tells us, ' he was highly respectable for his piety, integrity, and knowledge of the affairs of the province.' But it was his misfortune to differ from the majority ; and we may gather, from the zeal with which the majority could crowd upon such a man, some notion of the height to which popular excitement had reached.

The courts of law continuing closed, a memorial was presented, Dec. 18th, to the Governour in Council, from the town of Boston, urging him to exert his influence, ' that under no pretence whatever, we may be any longer deprived of this invaluable blessing.' The committee to present the memorial

34

were S. Adams, John Rowe, Th. Cushing, J. Ruddock, Saml. Sewall, John Hancock, J. Henshaw, B. Kent, and Arnold Welles. At the same time, Jer. Gridley, James Otis, and John Adams, were 'applied to as counsel to appear in behalf of the town in support of said memorial.' The result of the memorial was not immediately satisfactory ; but the courts were opened shortly after.

Liberty Tree became a sort of idol. On the 14th of February, 1766, ' it was pruned after the best manner, agreeable to a vote passed by the true-born Sons of Liberty,' by a number of carpenters appointed for the purpose, and a gentleman well skilled in these affairs as a director. So that the Tree was now become a great ornament to the street. Thursday the 20th was fixed for burning one of the stamped papers in the principal towns in every colony. In Boston, the ceremony ' was conducted with great decency and good order,' and the effigies of Bute and Grenville, in full court dress, were added to the bonfire. On the 24th a vessel arrived from Jamaica with stamped clearances. The Sons of Liberty immediately sent an order to one of their members ' to go and demand in their names, those marks of Creole slavery.' ' Whereupon the person to whom the above was directed, with a number of others, immediately on the receipt thereof, repaired to the vessel, and being told the captain was gone to enter at the Custom-house, they proceeded thither ; when the above warrant being shown, the said stamped clearance was delivered to them ; they then fixed it on a pole, and carried it to the lower end of the Court-house, where they put the pole in the stocks and exposed the paper to publick view until the time appointed for execution. At one o'clock the warrant was read with an audible voice, the executioner then carried the guilty criminal to the centre of King-street, and with a lighted match set fire to one of the S—p-A—ts, and with that burnt the offspring of that hydra-headed monster ; while the smoke was ascending, the executioner pronounced the following words, viz.—" Behold the smoke ascends to Heaven, to witness between the isle of Britain and an injured people !" Three cheers were then given, and the 'Change was clear in a few minutes, without the least disorder.'

The tone of the writers in the publick journals became more decided. In the B. Gazette, March 17th, we find one exclaiming, ' Since the stamp act imposed upon us is unconstitutional, shall we not then all as one man join in opposing it, and spill the last drop of our blood, if necessity should require, rather than live to see it take place in America !'— This is the first intimation we have discovered, of any thing like the possibility of an appeal to arms : and the author, that his views may not be misunderstood, proceeds. ' any one, af-

LIBERTY TREE, 1774,

CORNER OF ESSEX AND ORANGE STREETS.

ter a thorough search and consideration, would, rather than
lose his liberty, be bored through the centre of life with the
fatal lead.'

Happily the change of ministry was then about producing
a change of measures, which served to avert that crisis till a
more favourable season. Information was received in Boston
on the 16th of May, that the Stamp Act was repealed. It
is impossible to express the joy the inhabitants in general
were in, on receiving this great and glorious news. The bells
were immediately set a ringing, and the cannon fired under
Liberty Tree and many other parts of the town. It is mentioned, as ' worthy of remark, that the vessel which brought
this glorious news is owned by that worthy patriot, John
Hancock esq.'* Monday the 19th was appointed for a day
of general rejoicing on the happy occasion. The ardour of
the people was so great, that, immediately after the clock
struck one in the morning, the bell of Dr. Byles's church (as
being the nearest to Liberty Tree) was set a ringing, which
was soon answered by the bells on Christ Church, at the
other end of the town. Before two, musick was heard in all
the streets, the drums beat and guns fired. As soon as it
grew light enough to see, Dr. Byles's steeple was hung with
banners, Liberty Tree decorated with flags, and colours and
pendants displayed on the tops of houses all round the town.
In the evening the town was universally illuminated and
shone like day : fire works were every where played off,
especially on the Common : the air was filled with rockets,
the ground with bee-hives and serpents. Mr. Hancock gave a
grand and elegant entertainment to the genteel part of the
town, and treated the populace with a pipe of Madeira wine.
Mr. Otis and some other gentlemen, who lived near the common, kept open house. On the common the sons of liberty
had a magnificent pyramid erected, illuminated with 280
lamps. About twelve o'clock, upon a signal given and the beat
of a drum, the populace retired to their respective dwellings,
the lights were put out, and the town was hushed in an unusual
silence. The evening following, all the gentlemen in the town
contributed lanterns to illuminate Liberty Tree, till the
boughs could hold no more, which made a most beautiful and
splendid appearance. These well conducted rejoicings were
ushered in, with a subscription for liberating all the poor persons in gaol for debt, by which the money was raised, and
the debtors were released, to partake of the joy that smiled in
every countenance.

* Otis, Cushing, Adams, and Hancock constituted the Boston delegation in 1766. Mr. H.
was chosen instead of Thomas Gray, who supplied the place of Tyler, chosen into the council in 1764, served also in '65, and this year resigned.

The ministers of religion bore their part in these joyful scenes; the sermons of Mr. Stillman of the Baptist church, Dr. Mayhew of the West, and Dr. Chauncy of the First Church were printed. That of the first was preached on the sabbath after the arrival of the news, Dr. Mayhew's on the Friday succeeding, and Dr. Chauncy's on a day of thanksgiving, set apart for the purpose.

CHAPTER XLVII.

We do say then to Cæsar,
Our ancestor was that Mulmutius, which
Ordain'd our laws, whose use the sword of Cæsar
Hath too much mangled ; whose repair and franchise
Shall, by the power we hold, be our good deed.

Cymbeline.

NOTWITHSTANDING these expressions of universal exultation, the publick mind was not entirely appeased. Gov. Bernard was suspected of having promoted the stamp act and other offensive measures, though he formally disavowed having had any agency in the business. The House of representatives, at the General Election, May 28, 1766, made choice of Mr. Otis of Boston for their speaker. His Excellency saw proper to disapprove the choice, and Mr. Cushing of Boston was elected in his stead. Samuel Adams was at the same time chosen clerk. This act of the Governour may have been the result of sound discretion ; but it served to exasperate the feelings of the House, and they retaliated by leaving out of the list of counsellors, the Lieut. Governour, the Secretary A. Oliver, Judge Peter Oliver, and the Attorney-General Trowbridge, who all had seats at the board in the preceding year. Thus the spirit of division was reciprocally fomented. On the 2d of June, a series of pieces, signed PASKALOS, was commenced in the Boston Gazette, against the Governour, in which his conduct is represented as mean, cowardly, and utterly unworthy of his station, and strong intimations are given that the people would be glad to see some other person in the chair.

The events of the past year were kept in remembrance by a demand from the ministry, that compensation should be made to those who had suffered by the riotous proceedings of the 14th and 26th of August. The demand was brought forward in an offensive form, but was eventually complied with. Another thing, which also kept alive the fears of the patriots was the resolve of parliament, that accompanied the repeal of the stamp act, viz. ' that Parliament had, hath, and of right ought to have full power and authority to make laws of sufficient force and validity to bind the colonies and people of America, subject to the crown of G. B. in all cases whatever.' Against this claim, the writers of the day did not hesitate to declare that ' opposition ought to be made.'

On the 25th of November, ' a large transport ship, having on board a detachment of H. M. Royal train of artillery bound to Quebec, after making many attempts to get up the river in vain, was obliged to put in here.' The Gov. made provision for them, in pursuance of the late act of parliament, the mutiny act. On the 30th of Jan. 1767, the H. of R. begged to be informed, whether this had been done at the expense of this government ; and on learning that it was so, remonstrated in the strongest terms against the proceeding, as an open violation of constitutional and charter rights. On the 28th of May following, twenty-seven recruits were brought in, and the lieutenant, who had charge of them, called for quarters. The Gov. referred the matter to the Council, and they advised him to submit it to the consideration of the House, and the house ' resolved, that such provision be made for these men as has been heretofore usually made for H. M. regular troops, when *occasionally* in this province.'

About the last of July an unexpected change took place in the ministry, and, a short time after, the chancellor of the exchequer (Charles Townsend) moved in the H. of Commons to impose duties on tea, glass, and colours, imported from England into America : he proposed also to suppress the duties on teas, that should be shipped from E. for A. and impose a duty of three pence per pound upon their introduction into the American ports. These two bills were passed without much opposition, and approved by the king. In the preamble, it was declared that the produce of the duties should be applied to defray the expenses of the government in America. It was also enacted that the ministry might, from this fund, grant stipends and salaries to the governours and to the judges in the colonies, and determine the amount of the same. The act was to take effect on the 20th of November, but, as if it was apprehended that the new tax would be too well received by the colonists, and purposely to irritate their minds, by placing before their eyes the picture of the tax-gatherers to be employed in the collection of these duties, another act was passed creating a permanent administration of the customs in America. And to crown the whole, the town of Boston was selected for the seat of this new establishment.

On the 28th of October a town meeting was held, at which Mr. Otis was chosen moderator ; and a written address to the inhabitants, subscribed *Philo Patriæ*, recommending economy and manufactures, being read, the town took into consideration the petition of a number of inhabitants, ' that some effectual measures might be agreed upon to promote industry, economy, and manufactures : thereby to prevent the unnecessary importation of European commodities, which threaten the country with poverty and ruin.' Messrs. *John Rowe, Wm. Greenleaf, Melatiah Bourne, Sam'l Austin, Edw. Payne. Edm. Quincy,* tertius, *John Ruddock, Jona. Williams, Josh. Henshaw, Hend. Inches, Solo. Davis, Joshua Winslow,* and *Thos. Cushing,* were appointed a committee to prepare a subscription paper, for the above object.   Accordingly, they brought forward a form, in which the signers agree ' to encourage the use and consumption of all articles manufactured in any of the British Amer. colonies and more especially in this province, and not to purchase, after the 31st of Dec. next, any of certain enumerated articles, imported from abroad ; and also strictly to adhere to the late regulation respecting funerals, and not to use any gloves, but what are manufactured here, nor procure any new garments upon such an occasion, but what shall be absolutely necessary.'   Copies of these articles were directed to every town in this province, and to all the other principal towns in America, where they were generally approved and adopted.

In November, Wm. Burch and Henry Hulton, esqrs. two of the five commissioners of the customs, arrived in Boston.* On the 11th of Feb. 1768, the House of Representatives addressed a circular to the speakers of other houses on the continent, in which, among other complaints of the acts for raising a revenue, they enumerate the commission of these men, as a grievance which may become dangerous to the liberty of the people.   ' On the 18th of March, being the anniversary of the repeal of the stamp act, and observed as a day of rejoicing, a few disorderly persons, mostly boys, assembled in the evening, paraded some of the streets, and finally repaired to the house of John Williams, esq. the inspector-general. Whether their design was to do him an injury or not, by his address and soft treatment of them, together with the interposition of some of the neighbouring householders, they soon retired and dispersed without doing any mischief at all.'

An occurrence of more importance took place on Friday, the 10th of June.   Towards evening the officers of the customs made a seizure of a sloop, belonging to and lying at the wharf of John Hancock.   The vessel was improved for the

---

* A writer in Sup. to B. Gaz. Dec. 29, 1767, exults that ' the trump of *freedom and independence* sounds again throughout this continent.'

purpose of storing some barrels of oil, for which there was not room in the owner's stores.* One of the officers immediately made a signal to H. M. ship Romney, Capt. Corner, then lying in the stream, upon which her boats were manned and armed and made towards the wharf. Several gentlemen present advised the officers not to move the sloop, as there would be no attempt allowed by the owner to rescue her out of their hands : but notwithstanding this declaration, her fast was cut away, and she carried under the guns of the Romney. This provoked the people who had collected on the shore, and in the dispute, the collector (Harrison), and comptroller, and the collector's son, were roughly used and pelted with stones. The noise brought together a mixed multitude, who followed up to the comptroller's house and broke some of his windows, but withdrew by the advice of some prudent gentlemen that interposed.

By this time they were joined by a party of sailors and vagrants, who were suspicious of an intention to impress them on board the ship. These went in search of one of the man-of-war's boats, and in their way met the inspector (Irvine) : him they attacked, broke his sword, and tore his clothes ; but by some assistance he escaped to a house in King-st. No boat being ashore, between 8 and 9 o'clock they went to one of the docks, and dragged out a large pleasure boat, belonging to the collector : this they drew along the street, with loud huzzaing all the way into the Common, where they set fire to it and burnt it to ashes : they also broke several windows in the houses of the collector and inspector-general (Williams) which were nigh the Common. No other outrage was committed that night.

Several instances of impressment had occurred under aggravated circumstances, and one was even attempted and executed on the Saturday following the above. These things, added to the prospect that the trade and business of the town was in a manner ruined, raised such a spirit of resentment in the people, that the commissioners and their officers, with the collector and comptroller, thought it most prudent to repair on board the Romney, as did also the officers of that ship.

On Monday the people in town were in great agitation, but lest any tumult might arise at night, a notification was issued requesting the Sons of Liberty to meet at Liberty-Hall, on Tuesday, at 10 A. M. The expectation of this meeting kept the town in peace. Early on Tuesday morn the colours were

---

* On the 17th of Aug. the Judge of Admiralty ' decreed the sloop Liberty, seized the 10th of June last, to be forfeited ; but the 200 barrels of oil and six barrels of tar, which were on board her when seized, were cleared.' B. Chron. Aug. 22.–Sept. 19.

flying on Liberty Tree, and, at the hour appointed, vast numbers of the inhabitants appeared ; but the weather being wet and uncomfortable in the street, they adjourned to Faneuil-hall, where it was proposed to have a legal meeting called, which was immediately ordered by the selectmen to take place at 3 o'clock. At three, the inhabitants met, but so great was the concourse, that they were obliged to adjourn to the Old South meeting-house. After very cool and deliberate debates upon the distressed circumstances of the town, a petition to the Governour was unanimously adopted, and a committee of 21 gentlemen appointed to present it. In this petition the town took a bolder stand than any publick assembly here had before taken. Having commenced with a strong declaration of rights and injuries, they say,

' The town is at this crisis in a situation, nearly such as if war was formally declared against it. *To contend with our parent state* is in our idea the most shocking and dreadful extremity : but tamely to relinquish the only security, we and our posterity retain of the enjoyment of our lives and properties, without one struggle, is so humiliating and base, that we cannot support the reflection. We apprehend, Sir, that it is at your option, in your power, and we would hope in your inclination, to prevent this distressed and justly incensed people *from effecting too much, and from the shame and reproach of attempting too little.*'

The Governour received the deputation graciously, but replied to their petition to have the Romney ordered out of the harbour, that he had no authority over H. M.'s ships. Capt. Corner, however, gave publick notice on the 20th, that he would not take any man belonging to or married in the province, nor any employed in the trade along shore, or to the neighbouring colonies. The legislature being in session, the town gave instructions to their representatives, in terms equally strong with those expressed in the above petition : but they had little opportunity to act in conformity to them : for on the first of July, the House was dissolved by the Governour, in consequence of a refusal to rescind and disavow their circular letter of Feb. 11th, in compliance with the orders of the British ministry.

On the first of August, 211 Boston merchants and traders agreed, that, for one year from the last day of the present year, they would not send for or import, either on their own account or on commission, or purchase of any that may import, any kind of merchandise from G. B. except coals, salt, and some articles necessary for the fisheries, nor import any tea, glass, paper, or colours, *until the acts imposing duties on those articles are repealed.* In that month also, another difficulty occurred between some of the town's people and the crew of the Romney, in which the former gained their point and compelled the man-of-war's men to quit the wharf, which they did in great fury. On the 14th, a large company celebrated the anniversary of the first opposition to the stamp act at the Tree of Liberty.

The combination of all these proceedings on the part of the people of Boston, furnished Gen. Thomas Gage, who was commander of the military forces in North America, with a sufficient pretence for sending a portion of regular troops into Boston. His intentions to do so became generally known in July, but nothing certain was determined until September. On the 12th of that month, a town meeting was held on the subject in Faneuil-Hall. The meeting was opened with prayer by the *Rev. Dr. Samuel Cooper*, of Brattle-street church. Mr. Otis was chosen moderator, and Messrs. T. Cushing, Sam'l Adams, Richard Dana, John Rowe, John Hancock, Benja. Kent, and *Dr. Joseph Warren*, were appointed to wait on His Ex. and humbly request him to communicate the reasons on which he supposed troops would be ordered here. A committee was also appointed to request him forthwith to issue precepts for a general assembly. H. E. replied, that his information respecting the troops was only of a private nature, and that the business of calling another Assembly was before the king, and H. E. could do nothing in it without H. M.'s commands.

But it did not please the town of Boston to wait for His Majesty's determination. They met again on the next day, and among other things* resolved to choose ' a suitable number of persons to act for them as a *committee in convention*, with such as may be sent to join them from the several towns in this province, in order that such measures may be consulted and advised as H. M.'s service, and the peace and safety of his subjects in the province may require.' A circular was forthwith addressed to the several towns, and on Thursday the 22d of September, upwards of seventy gentlemen appeared as committees from sixty-six towns,† besides districts. Messrs Otis, S. Adams, Hancock, and Cushing, were the members from Boston. Cushing was chosen chairman. *Their debates and proceedings were open* : and the first step was to prepare a petition to H. E. for the calling of a General Assembly. H. E. begged to be excused ' from receiving a message from that assembly, which is called a Committee of Convention,

---

* One vote was, that ' as there is at this time a prevailing apprehension of approaching war with France,' every inhabitant be requested to provide himself with ' a well fixed firelock, musket, accoutrements, and ammunition,' as the law requires.

† The number afterwards increased to above 100 from 98 towns and districts.

35

for that would be to admit it to be a legal assembly, which I can by no means allow.' On the same day, H. E. sent a message, without a signature, declaring his opinion that this convention was to all intents and purposes ' an assembly of the representatives of the people,' and therefore, says he, ' I do earnestly admonish you, that, instantly and before you do any business, you break up this assembly and separate your-selves.' This message was by vote ordered to be returned to the secretary, and the next day it was sent with the signature of *Fra. Bernard.* On Saturday, the convention sent an an-swer, by way of message, but H. E. refused to receive it. The convention continued their session every day till the 29th, during which time they adopted a letter to be transmit-ted to Dennys De Berdt, the agent of the province, at London, and published ' a result of their conference and consultation,' in which they declared their allegiance to the king, their ab-horrence of riots, and their determination to yield all assist-ance to the civil magistrate towards suppressing them, and also declared their rights, by charter and by nature, and their humble dependence on their gracious sovereign, that their wrongs would be speedily redressed.

It is probable, that the convention effected all that was de-sirable at that moment, and fortunate perhaps that they dis-persed so soon : Otherwise Gov. Bernard might have im-proved the opportunity, as he threatened, to ' assert the pre-rogative of the crown in a more publick manner.' For on the 28th of Sept. six of H. M.'s ships of war, from Halifax, came to anchor in Nantasket. ' On Friday, Sept. 30th, 1768, the ships of war, armed schooners, transports, &c. came up the harbour and anchored round the town ; their cannon loaded and springs on their cables, as for a regular siege. At noon on Saturday, Oct. 1, the 14th and 29th regiments, a de-tachment from the 59th, and train of artillery with two pieces of cannon, landed on the Long-wharf, then formed and marched with insolent parade, drums beating, fifes playing, and colours flying, up King-street : each soldier having re-ceived sixteen round of shot.'*

During various disputes about quarters for the troops, the council maintaining that they were not obliged by law, in-

---

* This quotation is from an engraving of the scene, published by Paul Revere. The view embraces the front of the town from the Old South meeting-house to the North Battery Eight ships of war with tenders are seen lying off the wharves : the Red coats landing on the S. side of Long-whf and a truck placed about midway, under guard, to prevent the peo-ple passing down. It is dedicated thus : ' *To the Earl of Hillsborough, H. M.'s secretary of state for America, this view of the only well-planned expedition, formed for supporting the dignity of Britain and chastising the insolence of America, is humbly inscribed.*'

deed that they were forbidden by law, to quarter them in the town, while the barracks at the Castle were not filled, some of them were lodged in the Town-house, some in Faneuil-hall, and some in stores at Griffin's wharf : and the town was afflicted with all the appearance and inconveniences of a gar-risoned place.

It was about this time that the luxury of Tea became pro-scribed. In Boston 200 families had agreed to abstain en-tirely from the use of it, by the 6th of October : other towns followed the example, and entered into similar agreements ; the students of Harvard College are highly applauded for resolving, ' with a spirit becoming Americans, to use no more of that pernicious herb,' and ' a gentleman in town, finding it very little in demand, shipped off a considerable quantity of the despised article.'

' Amusements that would have been at other times innocent and congenial, were now foregone : especially if they were to be partaken with those, who were held to be the instru-ments of despotism. A striking example was given, the win-ter after the British troops arrived. Some of the crown offi-cers, who thought the publick gloom disloyal, circulated a proposal for a regular series of dancing assemblies, with the insidious design of engaging the higher classes in fashionable festivity, to falsify the assertions of the prevailing distress, and also to undermine the stern reserve, that was maintained towards the army, and thereby allay the indignation against the system, which they were sent to enforce. But, out of the contracted limits of their own circle, they could not obtain the presence of any ladies. Elegant manners, gay uniforms, animating bands of musick, the natural impulse of youth, all were resisted : the women of Boston refused to join in osten-tatious gaiety, while their country was in mourning.' *

CHAPTER XLVIII.

Remember March ! the ides of March remember.
Shakspeare.

' On Monday, the 30th of January, 1769, at about half af-ter 10 o'clock at night, the people adjoining to the gaol were

---

* News-letter, Nov. 10. ' Several transports arrived here this morning from Cork, hav-ing on board part of the 64th and 65th regiments : the remainder are not yet in.'
' We hear, the Honourable the Commissioners of Customs leave Castle William this week. Preparations are making to hold their board in town, [at Concert-Hall,] as heretofore.'

alarmed by the prisoners crying *Fire !* on which the keeper
and a number of persons ran there, and found part of the inside in a blaze. It was some time before the prisoners
could be got out, the inner keys being lost in the confusion,
and the wooden work being so strongly bound with iron, that
it was difficult to cut through the doors and partitions. Capt.
Wilson of the 59th reg. was particularly active in extricating
them. It was expected the fire would be kept under, but the
great quantity of inside timber work, occasioned it to rage
with great violence, and the flames burst through the windows
and reached the roof, which after burning some hours fell in :
the wood work burnt all night, and in the morning nothing
remained but the bare stone walls. During the continuance
of the fire, the town's people behaved with their usual alacrity ; and many of the military were very active in assisting
them ; the commodore was present, a number of officers and
sailors were landed from the ships, and an engine was sent
from the Romney. The commander of the main guard, with
a party offered their service on the first alarm, which was declined ; but they were afterwards sent for and took charge of
some of the prisoners.'   This is the only good deed we have
found attributed to the regular soldiers.

It was generally understood in Boston, that the occurrences
in the town, for some time past, had been represented at home
in an unfavourable light : the selectmen* thought it their duty
to call upon Governour Bernard, in behalf of the town, to
communicate to them such representations of facts as he had
sent to England ; and at the annual meeting in March, the
town addressed the king in a most dutiful and loyal petition,
setting forth their grievances, and in the most affecting strains
begging his royal protection, against their revilers and oppressors.

When the time for the annual choice of representatives
came round, the selectmen waited on Gen. Mackay, who commanded the troops in town, with the request that he would order them out of the town on the day of election. The General declared that it was not in his power, but engaged to confine them within their barracks. The town met on the 5th
of May, and before proceeding to business, entered upon their
records a declaration of their rights, and a protest ' that their
proceeding to an election under such circumstances, is wholly
from necessity, and not to be considered as a precedent at any
time hereafter, or construed as a voluntary receding from the
incontestible rights of British subjects and freeholders on so

* Joshua Henshaw, Jos. Jackson, J. Ruddock, J. Hancock, J. Rowe, Saml. Pemberton,
II. Inches.

interesting an affair.' The next day, Messrs. Otis, Cushing, Adams, and Hancock, were chosen again; H. having 505, A. 503, C. and O. 502, out of 508 votes: a result that speaks strongly of the unanimity of the town.

When the legislature met, they refused to proceed to business in the Town-house, other than the choice of counsellors and officers, unless the fleet and army were removed from the town and harbour. After waiting a fortnight, the Governour adjourned them to Cambridge. There they passed votes of censure upon his conduct. They also passed a petition to the king for his removal, and on the day after (June 28.) he informed them that he was ordered to attend upon the king to lay before him the state of the province. He left Boston, July 31, and Lieut. Gov. Hutchinson officiated in his stead.

The occasions of controversy between the people and the servants of the crown were now almost as frequent as the occasions of intercourse, and every man felt himself interested in every occurrence that interested his neighbour. But the greatest excitement produced by any thing, that more particularly concerned an individual, arose from an attack upon Mr. Otis. His name had been introduced, in an offensive manner, in some paper of the commissioners of the customs, and he therefore advertised them by name, *Henry Hulton*, *Charles Paxton*, *William Burch*, and *John Robinson*, as no more worthy of credit than Sir Francis Bernard, of Nettleham, Baronet. ' The next evening, (Sept. 5th,) about 7 o'lock, Mr. O. went to the British Coffee-house, [it was on the spot where the Massachusetts Bank now stands, in State-st.] where Mr. Robinson was sitting in company with a number of army, navy, and revenue officers. As soon as he came in, an altercation took place, which terminated in Robinson's striking Otis with a cane, which was returned with a weapon of the same kind. Great confusion then ensued. The lights were extinguished, and Otis, without a friend, was surrounded by the adherents of Robinson. A young man, by the name of John Gridley, passing by, very boldly entered the Coffee-house, to take the part of Otis against so many foes ; but he was also assaulted, beaten, and turned out of the house. After some time the combatants were separated ; Robinson retreated by a back passage, and Otis was led home wounded and bleeding. The animosity that existed towards the revenue officers, for their insolent and oppressive conduct, the sympathy and admiration that were cherished for the character, talents, and services of the leading patriot of his day, all conspired to give this transaction the odium of a scheme of assassination. Mr. O. instituted an action against Robinson, and obtained a verdict in his favour for £2,000 sterling damages. This sum he no-bly declined receiving, on a suitable apology from the defendant.*

In January, 1770, the merchants renewed their agreement not to import British goods. They held several meetings in Faneuil-Hall, and appointed committees of inspection, who should examine into the truth of reports, concerning the unfaithfulness of some who had signed the articles. The names of several were reported, and ordered to be published. Lieut. Gov. Hutchinson sent a message to one of these meetings, by the sheriff, (whose name was Stephen Greenleaf,) ' enjoining and requiring them without delay to separate and disperse, and to forbear all such unlawful assemblies for the future.' After a calm consideration of the message, it was unanimously voted to proceed : and a written answer was sent to His Honour, signifying their opinion that the meeting was warranted by law.

Theophilus Lillie, who kept a shop near the New Brick meeting-house, was one of those denounced as *Importers*. On the 22d of February, some persons erected near Lillie's, a large wooden head, fixed on a pole, on which the faces of several importers were carved. One Ebenezer Richardson living in the neighbourhood, (who had acquired the appellation of *Informer*,) endeavoured to persuade some teamsters from the country, to run the post down with their carts ; but they understanding the nature of the pageantry, would have nothing to do with it. Richardson foolishly persisted, and seized the bridle of the horses, but failed of his intent to guide the team against the post. On this. the boys set up a shout, which being resented by Richardson, they pelted him with dirt till they drove him into his own house. The noise gathered a considerable number of people. Hard words passed between Richardson and some of the multitude ; stones were thrown on both sides, till at length Richardson discharged a musket at random from his door, and another from his window. One young man was severely injured, and a boy, Christopher Snider, about eleven years of age, received a mortal wound in his breast. Upon this the bells were set to ringing, and a vast concourse of people drawn together. Richardson, and one Wilmot, a seaman, who had taken his part in the affray, were secured and carried to Faneuil-Hall, where they underwent an examination and were committed for trial.

The boy died in the course of the evening, and was removed to his parents' house in Frog-lane [Boylston-st.] All the friends of liberty were invited to attend the funeral ' of this

---

* *Tudor*, p. 362—In October, 1769, the town published an Appeal to the World, or Vindication of Boston, from the aspersions of Bernard and others.

little hero and *first martyr* to the noble cause.' This innocent
lad was announced as ' the first whose life had been a victim
to the cruelty and rage of oppressors. Young as he was, he
died in his country's cause, by the hand of one, directed by
others, who could not bear to see the enemies of America
made the ridicule of boys.' On Monday, the 26th, his funeral
took place. The little corpse was set down under the Tree
of Liberty, from which the procession began. The coffin bore
inscriptions appropriate to the times ; on the foot ' *Latet an-
guis in herba :*' on each side, ' *Haeret lateri lethalis arundo :*'
and on the head, ' *Innocentia* NUSQUAM *tuta.*' Four or five hundred school boys, in couples, preceded the corpse ; six of the
lad's playfellows supported the pall ; the relatives followed,
and after them a train of 1300 inhabitants on foot, and thirty
chariots and chaises closed the procession.

A more imposing spectacle than this could hardly have
been contrived, or one better adapted to produce a lasting
impression on the hearts of the beholders : but it was only
the prelude to a scene of far greater horrour. The morning
papers of Monday, the fifth of March, which told of this transaction, gave also several accounts of quarrels between the soldiers and different individuals belonging to the town. The
officers were apprehensive of difficulties, and were particularly active in their endeavours to get all their men into their
barracks before night. *Murray's Barracks,* so called, where
the 14th regiment was principally quartered, were in Brattle-
street, in the buildings directly opposite the little alley, which
leads from the bottom of Market-street. The 29th regt. was
quartered in Water-street and in Atkinson-street. As a measure of precaution, there was a sentinel stationed in the alley
before mentioned, (then called Boylston's alley) and this very
circumstance led to the quarrel which terminated in the
Boston Massacre. Three or four young men, who were disposed to go through the alley, about nine o'clock, observed the
sentinel brandishing his sword against the walls and striking
fire for his own amusement. They offered to pass him and
were challenged, but persisted in their attempt, and one of
them received a slight wound on his head. The bustle of
this rencontre drew together all those who were passing by,
and fifteen or twenty persons thronged the alley, and thirty
or forty more, gathered in Dock-square. were attempting to
force their way to the barracks through Brattle-street, (which
was at that time so narrow that a carriage could with difficulty
pass.) Being foiled in this attempt. the party, which was continually increased by accessions, gathered in Dock-square
round a tall man with a red cloak and white wig. to whom
they listened with close attention two or three minutes, and
then gave three cheers and huzzaed for the main guard.

The main guard was regularly stationed near the head of
State-street, directly opposite the door on the south side of
the Town-house. To this place all the soldiers detached for
guard duty were daily brought, and from thence marched to
the particular posts assigned them. On this day the command of the guard had devolved on Capt. Thomas Preston,
and Lt. Basset under him.

As the party dispersed from Dock-square, some ran up
Cornhill, others up Wilson's lane, others up Royal Exchange
lane (now Exchange street.) These last found a single sentinel stationed before the door of the Custom house, which was
the building now occupied by the Union Bank, and then
made one corner of that lane, as the Royal Exchange tavern
did the other. As the sentinel was approached, he retreated
to the steps of the house, and alarmed the inmates by three or
four powerful knocks at the door. Word was sent to Lt. Bassett that the sentinel was attacked by the town's people. He
immediately sent a message to his captain, who instantly repaired to the guard house, where Lt. Basset informed him
that he had just sent a serjeant and six men to assist the
sentry at the Custom house. 'Well,' said the captain, 'I will
follow them and see they do no mischief.' He overtook them
before they reached the Custom house, where they joined
the sentinel and formed a half circle round the steps.

By this time the bells were set to ringing, and people flocked from all quarters, supposing there was fire. The soldiers
were soon surrounded; many of those nearest to them were
armed with clubs and crowded close upon them; those at a
distance began to throw sticks of wood and snow-balls and
pieces of ice at them, while from all sides they were challenged to *Fire, fire if you dare*. At last they thought they heard
the order given, and they did fire in succession from right to
left. Two or three of the guns flashed, but the rest were
fatal. Crispus Attucks, Samuel Gray, and James Caldwell
were killed on the spot, Samuel Maverick and Patrick Carr
received mortal wounds, of which the former died the next
morning, and Carr on the Wednesday of the next week.
Several other persons were more or less injured: the greater
part, persons passing by chance or quiet spectators of the
scene. The people instantly retreated, leaving the three unhappy men on the ground. All this transpired within 20
minutes from the time of Capt. Preston's joining the guard.

' On the people's assembling again,' says Capt. P. ' to take
away the dead bodies, the soldiers, supposing them coming to
attack them, were making ready to fire again—which I prevented by striking up their firelocks with my hand. Immediately after, a townsman came and told me that 4 or 5000 people
were assembled in the next street, and had sworn to take my

VIEW OF STATE STREET & OLD STATE HOUSE.

life with every man's with me ; on which I judged it unsafe
to remain there any longer, and therefore sent the party and
sentry to the *main guard*, where the street is narrow and
short, then telling them off into street firings, divided and
planted them at each end of the street to secure their rear,
expecting an attack, as there was a constant cry of the inhabitants, ' To arms, to arms, turn out with your guns,' and the
town drums beating to arms. I ordered my drum to beat to
arms, and being soon after joined by the several companies
of the 29th regiment, I formed them, as the guard, into street
firings. The 14th regiment also got under arms, but remained at their barracks. I immediately sent a serjeant with a
party to Col. Dalrymple, the commanding officer, to acquaint
him with every particular. Several officers going to join
their regiment were knocked down by the mob, one very
much wounded and his sword taken from him. The Lieut.
Gov. and Col. Carr soon after met at the head of the 29th
regt. and agreed that the regiment should retire to their barracks, and the people to their houses : but I kept the piquet
to strengthen the guard. It was with great difficulty that the
Lieut. Gov. prevailed on the people to be quiet and retire :
at last they all went off except about a hundred.' This hundred was composed of some of the most distinguished inhabitants, who volunteered to form a citizens' guard.

A justices' court was forthwith held, and Capt. Preston
surrendered himself, and was committed to prison at three, the
next morning : the eight soldiers also were committed early
in the forenoon.

At eleven o'clock a town meeting was held. Various persons related to the assembly, what they had witnessed of the
events of the preceding day. A committee of fifteen was appointed to wait on the Lieut. Governour and Col. Dalrymple,
and express to them the sentiment of the town, that it was
impossible for the soldiers and inhabitants to live in safety together, and their fervent prayer for the immediate removal of
the former. The answer received to this application was not
such as was wished ; and in the afternoon, seven of the first
committee (viz. John Hancock, Samuel Adams, Wm. Molineux, Wm. Phillips, Jos. Warren, Joshua Henshaw, and
Samuel Pemberton) were again deputed with the following
message : ' It is the unanimous opinion of this meeting, that
the reply made to a vote of the inhabitants presented His
Honour, this morning, is by no means satisfactory ; and that
nothing less will satisfy them, than a total and immediate removal of the troops.' Samuel Adams acted as ' chairman of
this delegation, and discharged its duties with an ability com-
mensurate to the occasion. Col. Dalrymple was by the side
36

of Hutchinson, who at the head of the Council received them.
He at first denied that he had power to grant the request.
Adams plainly, in few words, proved to him that he had the
power by the charter.   Hutchinson then consulted with Dalrymple in a whisper, the result of which was, a repetition of
the offer to remove one of the regiments, the 14th, which had
had no part in the massacre.   At that critical moment Adams
showed the most admirable presence of mind.   Seeming not
to represent, but to personify, the universal feeling, he stretched forth his arm, as if it were upheld by the strength of thousands, and with unhesitating promptness and dignified firmness replied, " *If the Lieutenant-Governour, or Colonel Dalrymple, or both together, have authority to remove one regiment, they have authority to remove two : and nothing short
of the total evacuation of the town, by all the regular troops,
will satisfy the publick mind or preserve the peace of the province.*"   The officers, civil and military, were in reality abash-
ed, before this plain committee of a democratick assembly.
They knew the imminent danger that impended : the very
air was filled with the breathings of compressed indignation.
They shrunk, fortunately shrunk, from all the arrogance,
which they had hitherto maintained.   Their reliance on a
standing army faltered before the undaunted, irresistible resolution of free unarmed citizens.'

Hutchinson consulted the Council, and they gave him their
unqualified advice, that the troops should be sent out of the
town.   The commanding officer then pledged his word of
honour, that the demand of the town should be complied
with, as soon as practicable ; and both regiments were removed to the Castle in less than fourteen days.

The funeral solemnities, which took place on Thursday, the
8th, brought together the greatest concourse, that probably
had ever assembled in America on one occasion.   Attucks,
who was a friendless mulatto, and Caldwell, who also was a
stranger, were borne from Faneuil-Hall ; Maverick, who was
about 17 years old, from his mother's house in Union-street,
and Gray from his brother's in Royal Exchange lane.
The four hearses formed a junction in King-street, and thence
the procession marched in columns of six deep through the
main street to the middle burial ground, where the four victims
were deposited in one sgrave.

The trial of Richardson and Wilmot for the murder of
Snider came on in April. Wilmot was cleared, but Richardson was brought in guilty of murder.   The Lieut. Gov. considered it so clear a case of justifiable manslaughter, that he
refused to sign the warrant for his execution, and after two

years' confinement, he was ultimately pardoned by the king.*

The traders and people had generally adhered in good faith to the agreement not to import or use imported goods. In the session of parliament this spring, a proposition was sustained for repealing the duties on all the articles except tea. Some London traders, supposing this would break up the compact, ventured to send quantities of the proscribed merchandize, and it arrived in the latter part of April.† There was no willingness in Boston to admit of a compromise. On the first intimation of the design of the ministry, new resolutions had been formed, and agreements signed by the ladies throughout the town, that they would drink no more of the obnoxious beverage (except in case of sickness) until *all the acts* were repealed. There was some tea in the cargoes that had just arrived, and nothing would satisfy the publick mind short of its all being returned. Mr. Hancock offered one of of his vessels, freight free, for the purpose, and she was loaded with great despatch and arrived safe in London, to the amazement and chagrin of those concerned in the consignment.

At the time of the May election, the health of Mr. Otis had so far declined, in consequence of the injury he had received, and of the constant excitement, which his devotion to publick business had occasioned, that the town was therefore obliged to dispense with his services in the General Court, this year, and elected in his stead the Hon. James Bowdoin. This gentleman was a descendant of the French Protestants, and inherited from his father a large estate, to which he did honour by his talents, his sound principles, and generous views. He had represented the town three years, previous to 1756, when he was chosen into the council, where he retained a seat till Gov. Bernard negatived him in 1769. At that board he had been a leading member, and ever stood in the front of opposition to what were considered the arbitrary measures of government.‡

The last Wednesday in May, 1770, exhibited a novel scene. The Court was ordered to meet at the College in Cambridge, and the Lieut. Gov. could not be persuaded to adjourn them to Boston. ' A number of gentlemen, friends to the rights of North America,' anticipating this state of things,

---

* On the 18th of April, there was a Liberty Tree celebration in honour of John Wilkes, Esq.

† In six cargoes, there was about half a common vessel's lading of various proscribed articles. B. Gaz. Ap. 23, and News Letter, Sept. 13, 1770.

‡ Mr. Bowdoin was again chosen counsellor, and, unexpectedly, Mr. Hutchinson suffered him to go into that board : Mr. John Adams was chosen to supply his place as a representative.

made preparations for celebrating this annual festival of our
fathers in its ancient seat.   In the morning, the attention of
people was attracted to the Common, by the roasting of an
ox, which had been carried through the town, the day before,
dressed with garlands of ribbons and flowers.   Religious services were performed at noon : Mr. Samuel Mather, ' a worthy descendant of those christian patriots, Increase and
Cotton,' made the prayers, and Dr. Chauncy, ' that inflexi-
ble assertor of our civil and religious rights,' preached the
sermon.   A dinner at Faneuil-Hall, and the distribution of
the ox among the poor concluded the day.

The melancholy result of the affray at Lillie's did not deter
the violent part of the town from attacking another of the
Importers.   Two or three brothers, by the name of M'Masters,
kept shop in King-street, at the corner of Pudding-lane, (late
Abiel Smith, esq.'s house,) where they made bold to sell teas
or broadcloth to the tories, and arms and ammunition to
the whigs, as best suited their interest.   But their good services in the last did not screen them from vengeance for their
offence in the first.   One of them was taken on the 19th of
June, and carted, in the heat of the day, from the South-end,
with a bag of feathers and some tar in a barrel at his side,
towards King-street, where it was intended to expose him to
publick view, besmeared with the one and coated with the
other.   But as he drew near to the spot, his colour forsook
his lips, his eye sunk, and he was about to fall lifeless in the
cart, when some gentlemen compassionated his case, so far as
to beg permission to take him into a house.   Cordials were
exhibited, and M'Masters revived ; and on a solemn promise
never to return, he was excused from ' this new-invented
mode of punishment,' and carted, sitting in a chair, to the
Roxbury line, where he was dismissed with hearty cheers.

The trial of Capt. Preston and the soldiers seemed to be
unnecessarily delayed, and some apprehensions were mur-
mured, that they might be rescued by government from the
hand of the law.   In September, the Castle, which had hitherto been in charge of a province garrison, was by order
from England delivered by the Lieut. Gov. into the command
of Col. Dalrymple, and the absence of troops from the town
was compensated by the presence of six ships of war and
two schooners in the harbour.   At length the trial of Capt.
Preston was commenced in October.   He was defended with
masterly ability, by *John Adams and Josiah Quincy jr.* esqrs.[*]
who, to use the words of Tudor, ' in so doing, gave a proof
of that elevated genuine courage, which ennobles human na-

---

[*] Assisted by Sampson Salter Blowers, esq. in the case of the soldiers.

ture. For leaders on the patriotick side, the attempt, while the publick were in a state of such high exasperation, to defend an officer who was accused of murdering their fellow citizens, required an effort of no ordinary mind : it was made successfully, and will ever hold a distinguished rank among those causes that adorn the profession of the law ; in which a magnanimous, fearless advocate boldly espouses the side of the unfortunate, against the passions of the people, and hazards his own safety or fortune in the exertion.' Capt. P. was acquitted and discharged October 29th.

The soldiers were afterwards tried, and on the 8th of December, six of them were found *Not Guilty*, and the verdict against the other two, Matthew Killroy and Hugh Montgomery, was ' Not guilty of murder. but guilty of manslaughter.' These two were slightly branded, and all of them liberated and sent to the Castle.

At this distance of time, we can look back and rejoice in this result, which was an honourable triumph of law and mercy over violence and revenge. But in that day of irritation there were many who believed the soldiers worthy of death, and regarded their acquittal as the effect of legal chicanery. Those who still bore in their own limbs the scars of wounds received on the fatal fifth of March, and those who were still mourning for the loss of their friends, could not suffer its anniversary day to pass unnoticed. It was proposed to substitute the celebration of the Boston Massacre for that of the Gunpowder plot. Accordingly when the evening arrived, in 1771, an address was delivered by Dr. Thomas Young to a collection of people at the Manufactory House.* At the north part of the town, Mr. Paul Revere (afterwards Col.) who lived in North square, had his house illuminated, and at one window exhibited a representation of Snider's ghost, at another a view of the massacre, and at a third the Genius of America in tears. The whole exhibition was so well executed, that it produced a melancholy gloom and solemn silence in several thousand spectators, which was deepened by the

---

* This building stood where Hamilton place now does. It was selected for this occasion, because the first opposition to the soldiers had been made here in October, 1768. Mr. John Brown, having possession of the building as a tenant under the province, refused admission to the military.—The Sheriff was sent by Gov. Bernard to take possession and was refused admittance. On a third attempt he found a window open, and entered by that : upon which, the people gathered about him and made him prisoner. Notice of this being given to an officer of the regiment on the Common, a party of soldiers came and took possession of the yard and relieved the sheriff from his confinement. Mr. Brown continued obstinate : the soldiers stood guard all that day and the best part of the next, when the council declared to the governour, that they would not justify the use of force to dispossess him, and the soldiers were withdrawn.

dismal sound of the bells tolling from nine to ten o'clock.
These were the acts of private individuals, but they probably occasioned the resolution to commemorate the fifth of
March in a publick way.   Master James Lovell was this year
appointed and delivered the first of the ' Boston Orations' on
the 2d of April, and provision was made for a similar celebration, by the timely appointment of Dr. Joseph Warren for
the orator of the next year.*

CHAPTER XLIX.

" For that he has,
As much as in him lies, from time to time
Envied against the people, seeking means
To pluck away their power."

Mr. Hutchinson had received a commission promoting him
to the office of Governour on the 8th of March, 1771, and been
proclaimed in customary form on the fifteenth.   On the third
of April, he met the General Court at Cambridge.   As soon
as they had opportunity, they appointed a committee to present him a verbal message requesting him to ' remove the
court to its ancient and legal seat, the town of Boston.'   This
he declined to do, while the House denied the King's right to
order the court to be held where he thought proper.   A controversy was maintained for a long time on this subject, which
served to make the governour an object of publick odium.
This was not decreased by his proclamation for aid and assistance to a recruiting party, which arrived here on the 29th
of April to enlist for His Majesty's service.†   People could not
misunderstand this movement, or consider it in any other
light than that of a pretext for keeping a guard in the town,
to be in readiness to protect the crown officers.   And they
found it employed for that purpose, on occasion of a ball at
Concert-hall, given by Mrs. Gambier, wife of the commander of
the naval forces on this station, on the king's birth day (June 4,)

* The anniversary was observed every year till 1783, inclusive.   The orators in order
were, Mr. Lovell, Dr. Warren, Dr. Benja. Church, John Hancock, Dr. Warren, Rev. Peter
Thacher (of Malden, at Watertown, 1776,) Benja. Hichborn, Jona. W. Austin, Wm. Tudor,
Jona. Mason Jr. Thomas Dawes Jr. Geo. R. Minot, Dr. Thomas Welsh.   The orations
are published in a separate volume.

† From an advertisement of Mr. Hancock's in the B. Gazette of April 15th, it appears
that the agreement not to import, had before that time become null, except as to the article
of *Tea* on which the duty of three pence per pound was still demanded.

which was attended by the Governour and other friends to government.

The General Court,* which was obliged again to assemble at Cambridge, found other causes of complaint. It had been decided in England that the Governour's salary should be paid by the crown, and thus he was made independent of the people. The alarm which this step occasioned was very ex- tensive, and the indignation expressed against it was couched in no equivocal terms. The language of the whigs became every day more high-toned: ' *We know,*' say the H. of. R. on one occasion, ' *we know of no commissioners of His Majesty's customs, nor of any revenue His Majesty has a right to establish in North America.*' Heretofore the complaint had been against the ministry and parliament; we find it here against the King himself. But this increased determination in favour of liberty produced no popular tumult: Boston remained as quiet throughout the year, as it had ever been before the ar- rival of the troops, and entirely free from those petty broils, which the soldiers were always creating. The greatest agi- tation was occasioned, by an abortive attempt to procure an indictment against Mr. Isaiah Thomas, for an article which appeared in his Massachusetts Spy, November 14th, signed *Mucius Scævola,* which was said to be the most daring produc- tion ever published in America. The Spy had been estab- lished about a year in Boston, and had taken a very decided stand in favour of liberty, in a stile calculated to engage the middling class of society.†

Early in 1772,‡ a prominent writer made the declaration, ' the dispute between the kingdom and colonies has ceased every where except in this province—We are now left in the lurch—every other colony has made its peace.' On this ground he exhorted the Massachusetts to lay aside their animosities, and submit like dutiful children to parental au- thority. Governour H. intimated the same in his messages to the General Court. This drew, from the partizans on the other side, rejoinders equally positive of the contrary. 'They (the colonies) will soon put in practise their *meditated plan* of the United Provinces, and form an independent common-

---

* Mr. Otis was returned this year (1771) from Boston instead of Mr. John Adams : but his infirmities had now increased so much that he could no longer give a close and continued attention to business : he withdrew soon after from publick life, and was bereft of his rea- son, except at very short intervals, for several years before his death, which happened at Andover, May 23, 1783.

† See News Letter, Feb. 6, 1772. Bost. Gaz. March 2, May 11, July 17. *Thomas'* H. of P. ii. 249.

The Boston representatives, in 1772, were S. Adams, Hancock, Cushing, and William Phillips, who also served in '73 and '74.

wealth.—That the colonies will in some future time be an
independent state is morally certain—it is very near—'tis not
probable that it is at the distance of fifteen years.' Again, in
May, on a rumour that war was to be expected between England and some European power, the people are exhorted to
establish a correspondence between the several colonies and
unitedly refuse supplies, unless a redress of grievances can
be obtained.*

Such a war did not take place, but the people of Boston
found an opportunity for commencing a union on a smaller
scale, which probably led to the general union of all the colonies. People had remonstrated firmly against the Governour's receiving his salary from the crown, but they were
answered only by the further indignity of putting the judges
on the same footing. As soon as the news of this design
reached Boston, a petition was circulated to procure a town
meeting, to consult on the measures required at this critical
juncture. Several meetings were held, and continued by ad-
journments to Nov. 2d, when, after ineffectual application to
the Governour for information on this important subject, and
having obtained from him a refusal to call together the General Court, the following proceedings took place.

' *Nov.* 1772.   *Proceedings of Town Meeting.*

' *It was then moved by Mr. Samuel Adams, that a Committee of Correspondence be appointed, to consist of twenty-one
persons---to state the Right of these Colonists, and of this Province in particular, as men, as christians, and as subjects : to
communicate and publish the same to the several towns in this
province and to the world, as the sense of this town, with the
infringements and violations thereof, that have been, or from
time to time may be made. Also requesting of each town a free
communication of their sentiments on this subject ; and the
question being accordingly put, passed in the affirmative,*
nem. con.

'*Also voted, that James Otis, S. Adams, Joseph Warren, Dr.
B. Church, Wm. Dennie, Wm. Greenleaf, Jos. Greenleaf,
Thomas Young, Wm. Powell, Nath. Appleton, Oliver Wendell, John Sweetser, Josiah Quincy jr. John Bradford, Richard Boynton, Wm. Mackay, Nath. Barber, Caleb Davis, Alex.
Hill, Wm. Molineux, and Robert Pierpont, be and hereby are
appointed a Committee for the purpose aforesaid, and that they
be desired to report to the town as soon as may be.*'

The committee reported on the 19th of November an elaborate declaration of rights, and a lucid statement of the

---

* June 13, 1772. The Governour removed the Court to Boston, on the opinion of the
Council that he could do it consistently with his instructions.

violations of them, of which the town ordered 600 copies to be printed and distributed, together with a circular letter to every town in the province. These town meetings were rather thinly attended, and the tories improved that circumstance to represent the whole in a ludicrous light. But their smiles were changed to sadness when they found that almost every town adopted the measures proposed by Boston ; and the Governour considered it so serious a subject as to be worthy of mention to the general court in his message, Jan. 6, 1773. His condemnation of the towns drew from the representatives a justification, in which they were emboldened to say to him, ' Notwithstanding all the terrours which Your Ex. has depicted to us as the effects of a *total independence*, there is more reason to dread the consequences of absolute, uncontrolled power, whether of a nation or a monarch, than those of a total independence.'

Following up the plan of union, the town, in their instructions to their representatives, chosen in May, thus express their approbation of it :

' We recommend to your serious consideration, whether an application to the English colonies on this continent, correspondent to the plan proposed by our noble patriotick sister colony of Virginia (which in our opinion is a wise and salutary proposal,) will not secure our threatened liberties, and restore that mutual harmony and confidence between the British nation and the English colonies, so important to both, especially the former, which, if rescinded from her connexion with this continent, must eventually fall a prey to her numerous and jealous neighbours.'

The Virginia proposal, to which these instructions referred, was contained in Resolves, passed by the House of Burgesses in that colony, on the twelfth of March ; and in accordance with that, the Massachusetts House of Representatives, on motion of Samuel Adams, appointed a committee of correspondence and inquiry, to consist of 15 members, ' whose business it should be to obtain the most early and authentick intelligence of all such acts and resolutions of the British parliament, or proceedings of administrations, as may relate to, or affect the British colonies in America ; and to keep up and maintain a correspondence and communication with our sister colonies, respecting these important considerations : and the result of such their proceedings, from time to time, to lay before the House.' This was adopted (110 to 4) on the 28th of May.

On the 2d of June, (the galleries of the house being cleared,) a disclosure was made by Mr. Adams, relative to the discovery of certain letters written by Messrs. Hutchinson and Oliver, Paxton, Auchmuty, and others, in which it appeared that they had long maintained and favoured the design of in-

37

troducing arbitrary power into this country.* In consequence of this discovery, the House adopted resolutions of
censure, which concluded with a petition to the king for the
removal of Hutchinson and Oliver from their offices.

CHAPTER L.

> " I do believe
> (Statist though I am none, nor like to be)
> That this will prove a war, and you shall hear
> The legions, now in Gallia, sooner landed
> In our not-fearing Britain, than have tidings
> Of any penny tribute paid."   *Shakspeare.*

ALTHOUGH the resolution of the Americans not to pay the
duty on tea, imported from England, continued firm, there
was still a considerable quantity of the article consumed. It
could be obtained in Holland. at a less price than the English
merchants demanded, and there was no difficulty in smuggling
it, on its arrival here. Not one chest in 500 had been seized
for the three years past, and the custom-house officers seemed
unwilling to run any risk to make a seizure. The English
East India Company ascertained by very accurate information, that the annual consumption in the colonies was not less
than 3,264,000 pounds, and that the net profit, which they
might reasonably calculate on realizing from that quantity,
after paying the duties themselves, and deducting incidental
charges, would amount to £39,320 sterling. They were,
therefore, induced to apply for and obtained licence (Aug. 20,
1773) to export a quantity of tea to America, not exceeding
600,000 pounds wt. 'discharged from the payment of any customs or duties whatsoever' in the kingdom, on the understanding,
that they were to pay the three pence per pound duty, at the
custom-houses in America.†

As soon as this determination of the Company was known,
a number of American merchants, then in London, petitioned

---

* These letters were originals, which had been obtained in England through the instru-
mentality of Dr. Franklin, as it afterwards appeared, (News-Letter, March, 1774,) and forwarded to Mr. Bowdoin.

† MS. account of the proceedings of the E. I. Co. relative to the exportation of tea to
America, 1773. pp. 262.

The first tea that paid the American duty arrived in 1768 : from that time to Nov. 1773,
there had been entered at Boston, 3092 chests. A chest was estimated 340 pounds wt.

very greedily for the privilege of receiving the consignments or furnishing vessels to convey the tea. Jona. Clarke, of the firm of Richard Clarke and Sons, of Boston, obtained the favour for his house, and the friends of Benja. Faneuil jr. and Joshua Winslow, and those of Elisha and Th. Hutchinson jr. obtained similar privileges for them.

All these facts became known in Boston early in October, and several caucus meetings were held, ' in various parts of the town, of a large number of persons, to consult and conclude on some method to prevent the execution of the Company's plan.' About one o'clock on the morning of Tuesday, the 2d of November, the Messrs. Clarkes were roused out of sleep by a violent knocking at their door, when a letter was delivered to them, purporting to be from the freemen of this province, requiring them to appear at Liberty Tree, at 12 o'clock on Wednesday, to make a publick resignation of their commission as consignees of the tea. On Tuesday, there was a notification to the freemen of this and the other towns, to attend to witness this resignation. On Wednesday the bells began to ring at 11, and continued ringing till 12 o'clock, and the town crier went through the streets summoning the people to assemble. About 500 collected ; (the selectmen were present to prevent disorder ;) but the gentlemen consignees did not appear. A committee was therefore appointed, consisting of Mr. Molineux, Mr. Wm. Dennie, Dr. Warren, Dr. Church, Major Barber, Mr. Gabriel Johonnot, Mr. Proctor, and Mr. Ezekiel Cheever, to expostulate with them on the high insult they had cast upon the people, and demand their signature to a paper, obligating themselves not to land or pay duty on any tea sent by the E. I. C. The assembly then accompanied the committee to the store of Messrs. C. & Sons, at the lower end of King-street, where all the consignees were assembled, and waited for their answer ; which not being satisfactory, some little indignity was offered to them, but the people were soon persuaded to disperse, without doing any essential injury.

The next day a town meeting was notified, to be held on the 5th, when the consignees were called upon by the Town to resign their appointments ; but they still refused to do it, on the ground ' that they knew not on what terms the tea would be sent to them, nor what obligations of a moral or pecuniary nature they might be under to fulfil the trust.' The meeting was adjourned to the 6th, when these answers were voted to be daringly affrontive to the town, and the meeting immediately dissolved. On the 17th, Mr. Jonathan Clarke arrived, and at night the town was disturbed by an assemblage around his father's house, in School-street. A pistol was fired from the windows, which in return were saluted

with stones, but no personal injury appears to have been
done to any one.

The consignees threw themselves upon the Gov. and Council for protection ; and, after having the subject under discussion for ten days, the Council could only advise His Ex.
to order the justices, sheriff, and other officers of the law, to
exert themselves to the utmost for the preservation of the publick peace. The consignees and custom-house officers thereupon took refuge in the Castle.

During this time all was expectation. At length, on Sunday, Nov. 28, the ship Dartmouth, Capt. James Hall, arrived,
with 112 chests of the tea. The next morning, the following
notice was widely circulated :

Friends, Brethren, Countrymen !
That worst of plagues, the detested TEA, shipped for this
port by the East India Company, is now arrived in this har-
bour. The hour of destruction, or manly opposition to the
machinations of Tyranny, stares you in the face. Every friend
to his country, to himself and to posterity, is now called upon
to meet at Faneuil-Hall, at nine o'clock, this day (at which
time the bells will ring) to make a united and successful re-
sistance to this last, worst, and most destructive measure of
administration.
Boston, Nov. 29, 1773.

This notification brought together a vast concourse of
' THE PEOPLE of Boston and the neighbouring towns,' at
the time and place appointed. Jona. Williams of B. was chosen moderator. The first step of this meeting was to confirm
the resolve of the town, that the tea should ' be returned to
the place from whence it came, at all events.' It then appearing, that the Hall could not contain the people assembled, it
was voted to adjourn to the Old South (leave having been
obtained for this purpose.) There it was further resolved,
that ' the tea should not only be sent back, but no duty should
be paid thereon.' Then, to give time to the consignees to
prepare a communication to this body, the meeting was adjourned to 3 P. M. In the afternoon, Capt. Hall, and Mr.
Francis Rotch, the owner of the Dartmouth, were convented
and charged not to land the tea at their peril. A watch of
25 persons, under direction of Capt. Edw. Proctor, was appointed to prevent the landing of the tea in the night. Censure was passed on the Governour for an order he had issued
to the law officers. An excuse was then offered by Mr.
Hancock, in the name of a friend of the consignees, for their
delay ; and, ' out of great tenderness' to them, the meeting
was adjourned to nine o'clock the next morning.

Tuesday, Nov. 30th, the Body met, according to adjournment, and received a letter from the consignees, informing that their orders had arrived from the E. I. C. and stating, that it was entirely out of their power to send the tea back, but that they were willing to store it, until they could send to England for further advice. Before the assembly had time to express their indignation at this communication, Mr. Sheriff Greenleaf came into the meeting, and ' begged leave to read a letter he had received from the Governour,' requiring him to read a proclamation to the people here assembled ; which was granted and done. ' Whereupon it was moved and the question put, whether the sheriff should be permitted to read the proclamation, which passed in the affirmative, *nem. con.*' It was an order ' forthwith to disperse and surcease all further unlawful proceedings, at their utmost peril. And the same being read by the sheriff, there was immediately after a loud and very general hiss.'—And the question being put, whether the assembly would disperse, &c. according to the Governour's requirement, it passed in the negative, *nem. con.*

There was another meeting in the afternoon, when, after ineffectual conference with Mr. Copley, the friend of the consignees, Captain Hall, and the owners and factors of the Dartmouth and the other vessels expected, were put under solemn injunction not to land a particle of the Tea. Captain Ezekiel Cheever was appointed to command the watch this night, and provision was made for a watch ' the following nights, *until the vessels leave the harbour.*' If the watch should be molested in the night, the bells were to be tolled, or rung if any thing happened in the day time. Six persons were appointed ' to give notice to the country towns, when they shall be required so to do, on any important occasion.'

Resolutions of gentle censure were then passed against those who had inadvertently imported tea from G. B. while subject to a duty, and followed by another, which declared whoever should hereafter import, until the said unrighteous act shall be repealed, an enemy to this country. Then it was ' *Voted,* that it is the determination of this Body to carry their votes and resolutions into execution, at the risk of their lives and property.' Provision then being made for the disposal of the expected vessels, and thanks from those of the Body belonging to Boston to their brethren from the neighbouring towns, and to the moderator for his good services, the meeting was dissolved.

On the first of December, Capt. James Bruce, in the ship Eleanor, arrived with another portion of the tea. On the 3d he was ordered to attend the next day, on a committee of the people, in Faneuil-Hall, where he was commanded by Samuel Adams and Jonathan Williams, assembled with John Rowe,

John Hancock, Wm. Phillips, and John Pitts, esqrs. and a great number of others, not to land any of the said tea, but to proceed to Griffin's whf. and there discharge the rest of his cargo. Capt. Hez. Coffin arrived in the brig Beaver, near the same time, and was ordered to pursue the same course.

It being perceived, that Mr. Rotch rather lingered in his preparations to return the Dartmouth to London, and the twenty days being nearly expired, after which the collector might seize the ship and cargo, Mr. R. was summoned before the committee, and stated to them, that it would prove his entire ruin, if he should comply with the resolutions of the 29th and 30th of November, and therefore he should not do it. A meeting of the people was assembled at the Old South, on Tuesday p. m. Dec. 14th, when Mr. R. appeared, and was enjoined forthwith to demand a clearance. It was ascertained, that one could not be obtained till the next day, and therefore the meeting was adjourned to Thursday at the same place.

On Thursday, there was the fullest meeting ever known : 2000 men at least were present from the country. Samuel Phillips Savage, esq. of Weston, was appointed moderator. Mr. Rotch reported, that the collector would not give him a clearance. He was then ordered upon his peril to get his ship ready for sea *this day*, enter a protest *immediately* against the Custom-house, and proceed *directly* to the Governour, (then at Milton, 7 miles distant,) and demand a pass for his ship to go by the Castle. An adjournment to 3 P. M. then took place. At three having met, they waited very patiently till five o'clock, when finding that Mr. Rotch did not return, they began to be very uneasy, called for a dissolution of the meeting, and finally obtained a vote for it. But the more judicious, fearing what would be the consequences, begged for a re-consideration of that vote, ' for this reason, that they ought to do every thing in their power to send the tea back, *according to their resolves.*' This touched the pride of the assembly, and they agreed to remain together one hour.

This interval was improved by Josiah Quincy jr. to apprize his fellow citizens of the importance of the crisis, and direct their attention to the probable results of this controversy. He succeeded in holding them in attentive silence, till Mr. Rotch's return, at three quarters past five o'clock. The answer which he brought from the governour was, ' that, for the honour of the laws, and from duty towards the king, he could not grant the permit, until the vessel was regularly cleared.' A violent commotion immediately ensued. A person who was in the gallery, disguised after the manner of the Indians, shouted at this juncture the cry of war : it was answered by about thirty persons, disguised in like manner, at the door. The meeting was dissolved in the twinkling of an eye. The multitude rushed to Griffin's wharf. The disguised In-

dians went on board the ships laden with the tea. In less than
2 hours, 240 chests and 100 half chests were staved and empti-
ed into the dock. The affair was conducted without any tumult : no damage was done to the vessels or to any other
effects whatever.

This was executed in the presence of several ships of war
lying in the harbour, and almost under the guns of the castle,
where there was a large body of troops at the command of
the commissioners. We are left to conjecture for the reasons
why no opposition was made to this bold adventure. The
names of the men, who dared to engage in it, have never been
made publick. Three or four of them are yet living. They
had the honour of a part in the act, which brought the king
and parliament to a decision that America must be subdued
by force of arms.

CHAPTER LI.

" Well, let them come,
And to the fire-eyed maid of smoky war
All hot and bleeding we will offer them."

THE reception, which the news of this transaction met in England,may readily be anticipated. It produced an instantaneous
determination, that ' as the people of Boston had notoriously
struck the first blow,' it should be returned with the full force
of ministerial vengeance. ' *Delenda est Carthago*,' said one
member of the House of Commons, ' the town of Boston
ought to be knocked about their ears and destroyed. I am of
opinion, you never will meet with that proper obedience to
the laws of this country, until you have destroyed that nest
of locusts.'

A vast majority of parliament was of the same mind, and the
king, on the 31st of March, 1774, gave his assent to the *Boston
Port Bill* ; by which it was enacted, that, from and after the
first of June, the landing and discharging, lading or shipping
of goods at the town, and within the harbour of Boston, should
be discontinued. Information of the passage of this bill was
received on the 10th of May. On the 13th, the town was
called together upon the subject, and passed the following
vote :

VOTED, *That it is the opinion of this town that if the other
colonies come into a joint resolution to stop all importations
from G. B. and exportations to G.B. the same will prove the*

salvation of N. America and her liberties. On the other hand, if they continue their exports and imports, there is high reason to fear that fraud, power, and the most odious oppression will rise triumphant over right, justice, social happiness, and freedom. And ordered, That this vote be transmitted by the Moderator to all our sister colonies in the name and behalf of this town.

It happened that Gen. Gage arrived here on the same day from England, with the commission of Governour and Vice-Admiral of the Province, Mr. Hutchinson having received permission, at his own request, to come to England.* Gov. Gage stopped a day or two at the castle, and provision was made by the Council that he should be received with military honours ' at the end of Long-wharf, and thence escorted to the State-house,† and a publick dinner be prepared on the occasion.' H. E. met the two houses in assembly on the 26th of May, and in his speech advised them to despatch the business of the session as speedily as possible, because it was made his duty to remove the court to Salem on the first of June. When that day arrived, the court was accordingly adjourned ; and at twelve o'clock, at noon, all business ceased in the Custom-house of Boston, and the port was shut against every vessel that offered to enter. The next day, an arrival from England brought the intelligence, that the bills were before the parliament, which immediately after became acts, whereby the charter of the province was completely subverted, and the administration of justice to criminal offenders transferred from the province courts to courts in England.

These things bore heavily upon Massachusetts, and particularly upon Boston, but her citizens did not sink under the weight of them. Confiding in the sympathy of their countrymen, already loudly expressed, the Boston Committee of Correspondence framed a *Solemn League and Covenant,* whereby all that signed it bound themselves from henceforth to suspend all commercial intercourse with G. Britain, until a restoration of their charter rights. This League was sent to every part of the province ; and, in despite of a proclamation from Gov. Gage, denouncing the authors of it, and cautioning all persons to beware of entering into this traitorous combination, thousands put their names to it, and faithfully complied with its obligations.

The air of Salem was no less propitious to Liberty than that of Boston. The Court, after entering a protest against their

* The Privy Council had acted on the petition against Hutchinson and Oliver, and pronounced a judgment of acquittal.

† It is observable, that this building has been variously called, the Town-house, Court-house, State-house, old State house, or old Town-house. It belongs now to the city.

removal, proceeded to make arrangements for the choice of Delegates to the Continental Congress, to be held on the first of September at Philadelphia. On the 17th of June, they elected for this purpose Messrs. Bowdoin, Cushing, S. and J. Adams, and Robert Treat Paine. Gov. Gage could suffer this spirit to progress no farther : on that day he dissolved the court by proclamation.

Boston soon began to suffer under the operation of the Port Bill : all business was at a stand, the poor were thrown out of employment, and the means of subsistence became enhanced in price, from the rigour with which the Commissioners executed the act. The town could hardly have supported the affliction, if assistance and encouragement had not been afforded her from all quarters. Donations of all sorts of provisions were forwarded for the use of the poor, and employment was found for many of them at the town's expence.

The solemnity of these sad times was heightened by the occurrence of a Fire, on Wednesday, Aug. 10th. It broke out between 10 and 11, P.M. in a large brick dwelling-house, belonging to Mr. Milliken and Mrs. Campbell, in Fish-street, five or six doors north of Mountfort's corner, at the foot of North-square. The lower part of the house was in flames before the distressed tenants were apprized of it. Several escaped out of the windows, some naked and much burnt, and five others perished in the flames, three women and two small children. The house was entirely consumed with part of a bake-house. The inhabitants speedily assembling, with their usual dexterous management happily put a stop to the further progress of the flames. Earl Percy politely offered the services of some soldiers, who could be depended upon, but was informed that the regulations of the town rendered their assistance unnecessary.

In the course of June, July, and August, troops had been constantly arriving, and the Governour had them employed in the construction of barracks, and the erection of fortifications on the neck. The town's people would afford no assistance in these works, and H. E. was obliged to send to other places for suitable persons to perform that part of the work, which the soldiers did not understand. On the first of September, 200 troops in 13 boats went from Long-wharf up the Mystick river, landed at Temple's farm, and took from the powder-house on Quarry-hill, 212 half-barrels of powder, belonging to the province. A detachment from the same corps went to Cambridge and brought off two field-pieces. This excursion caused a great alarm, and by the next day, several thousand people were assembled in arms, in the vicinity of Cambridge. Finding no armed foe to combat, they laid aside their muskets, and went in a body to the houses of several

38

individuals, who had taken part on the side of government, and compelled them to recant and forswear all concern in any offices under the law for altering the charter. The same thing was done so effectually in all the other counties, that Gov. Gage had scarcely a mandamus counsellor left to give him advice, except the few that resided in Boston under his protection. The jurors also refused to serve under judges subservient to the crown, or paid by salary from the king, and the province was thus left almost in a state of anarchy.

The new Charter, so to call it, made it unlawful that any town meetings should be held, except the March and May meetings, without the previous approbation of the Governour, and H. E. had informed the selectmen of Boston, that he should insist on a compliance with this regulation. Instead, therefore, of meeting in Boston, the people of the county of Suffolk assembled at Dedham, on the sixth of September, and thence adjourned to Milton, where, on the 9th, they passed a set of spirited resolutions, which were forwarded to the Congress then sitting in Philadelphia. Congress unanimously approved them and recommended them for universal adoption.*

Gov. Gage was pleased to issue His Majesty's writs for convening a General Assembly at Salem, on the fifth of October. But finding from the many tumults and disorders that were taking place, and ' the instructions given by the town of Boston and some other towns to their representatives,' that it would be highly inexpedient to convene a general court at that time, he prorogued the same indefinitely by proclamation, on the 28th of September. The representatives, however, appeared, and after waiting a day for the Governour's notice, on the 7th of October they resolved themselves into a Provincial Congress, and chose a chairman and clerk, John Hancock and Benjamin Lincoln, and adjourned to meet at Concord, on the 11th of the month. Dr. Warren, Dr.Church, and Mr. Nath'l Appleton, together with the representatives, composed the Boston delegation to this assembly.

The Provincial Congress continued in session to the 29th of October, during which time they proposed to the people to take measures for an efficient organization of the militia and the supply of the town stores with ammunition. They also appointed a treasurer and receiver general, in the room of Mr. Gray, and advised all persons to refrain from paying the publick monies to the latter. They also denounced the man-

* The law against town-meetings was obviated in Boston by adjournment of the May meeting and the Boston Port-bill meeting from time to time. In this way, meetings were continually held, until the next March meeting in 1775.

damus counsellors as *rebels against the state.* For these and other offensive acts, Gov. Gage denounced the congress by proclamation, as an unlawful assembly, with whose recommendations it would be dangerous for any person to comply. This, however, did not deter the same persons from meeting again in December, and pursuing similar measures of preparation for defence, and also for the execution of the plans of the Continental Congress. They created a body, termed the Committee of Safety, which became the real executive of Massachusetts. These were elected anew at every session, and were empowered generally to watch over the safety of the commonwealth, and advise the Congress of such measures as they thought beneficial, and especially to assemble such of the militia as they judged necessary, and station them where they deemed it most conducive to the defence and service of the colony.

On the 19th of December, the people of Boston were somewhat enlivened by news from Portsmouth, N. H. that a party of the people of that province, on the 15th, attacked the fort at Newcastle, scaled the walls, disarmed the captain and his men, took possession of 97 barrels of powder, with upwards of 60 stands of small arms, and 16 pieces of cannon, and conveyed them to a safe place in the country. The acquisition made a partial offset to the loss at Cambridge. Gov. Wentworth, with some propriety, proclaimed the act to be ' in open hostility and direct oppugnation of His Majesty's government.' Affairs were evidently approaching to a crisis in the vicinity of Boston. Exertions were made with the utmost solicitude to procure the arms and ammunition, recommended by the provincial congress. As these articles were principally held in Boston, the inhabitants employed all their address to transport them to places of safety in the country, by deceiving the guard stationed upon the neck. Cannon, balls, and other implements of war, were carried through the fortification gates, in carts apparently loaded with manure ; powder in the baskets or panniers of the market men ; and cartridges were concealed in candle boxes.

At the close of the year 1774, Gov. Gage had under his command, in Boston, eleven regiments, besides four companies of artillery. Five hundred men were on duty every day. The behaviour of the troops was generally peaceable : some of the officers were gentlemen of the first standing in society, and there appears hitherto to have been no disposition on their part to countenance any licentiousness.

CHAPTER LII.

The army broken,
And but the backs of Britons seen, all flying,
Through a strait lane, the enemy full hearted,
Chickens the way which they stooped eagles.
Shakspeare.

THE soldiery did not maintain their good character through the winter. Several riotous acts were committed, in which both officers and men bore a part, in the course of January, 1775. On the 23d of that month, a detachment of above a hundred men was sent by water to Marshfield, for the protection of some of His Majesty's loyal subjects there, from the fury of the whigs. They found nothing to do, and of course met with no resistance. Another detachment sent to Salem was received with less complaisance. Gen. Gage had information that some brass cannon were deposited in or near Salem, and H. E. sent an officer to discover where they were lodged, and at the same time ordered a transport to take on board a part of the 64th regiment, under the command of Lieut. Col. Leslie, from the Castle, and convey them to Marblehead. This was on Sunday, Feb. 20th. They landed at M. met the officers, and immediately began their march for Salem ; but some of the Marblehead people, suspecting their object, despatched messengers to give warning at S. and before the regiment arrived at the North river, which it was necessary for them to cross, the Salem people had possession of the bridge, and raised the draw. The colonel ' desired it might be immediately let down ; but they refused, saying it was a private road, and he had no authority to demand a passage that way. On this he determined to ferry a few men over in a gondola,' of which craft there were two on the bank of the river, but the people scuttled both of them before he could effect his intention. ' Finally the colonel said he must go over, and if the drawbridge was let down so that he might pass, he pledged his honour he would pass not above 30 rods beyond it, and then immediately return. The regiment had now been on the bridge about an hour and a half, and every thing being secured, the people directed the drawbridge to be let down. The regiment passed over, marched a few rods, leaving a party in possession of the bridge till they returned, which they soon did, it being dark, and with great expedition went back again to Marblehead, where they re-embarked on board the transport, between eight and nine o'clock, and reached Boston the next day.' The result of this expedition afforded merriment for the wits of the day, and gave the royalists no little chagrin.

The soldiery seem to have wreaked their vengeance for this defeat, by tarring and feathering Thomas Ditson, an inhabitant of Billerica, who had come to town (March 8th) for the purpose of purchasing a gun. Supposing, very honestly, that a soldier was a likely person to inform him where he could most advantageously procure the article, he accosted one in the street, who conducted him to his own quarters, and there, having beguiled him out of five dollars on pretence of selling him a gun and equipments, set up a hue and cry, that here was a rebel purchasing king's arms of a king's soldier. and enticing him to desert. On this, Ditson was seized by a serjeant and a party, and hurried to the barracks. There they tarred and feathered him from head to foot, and escorted him, with their colonel (Nesbit) at their head, to Liberty-tree. where they let him go. The selectmen of Billerica demanded satisfaction of Gen. Gage, for this outrage, giving him the assurance, that, if the intercourse with Boston must be thus interrupted, they should ' hereafter use a different style from that of petition and complaint.'*

The Provincial Congress held their sessions in February, March, and April, without molestation. They appointed general officers for the command of the minute-men who should be detached, subject to the orders of the Committee of Safety, and appropriated funds for the purchase of warlike stores. In April, intelligence reached the congress, that Massachusetts had been declared in a state of rebellion, and that Gov. Gage would receive orders to transport certain of the popular leaders to England for trial. On the 10th, there was an arrival which brought the official information to Governour Gage. On the 15th, the congress adjourned, having during their session addressed the people with confidence, and urged them ' effectually to oppose and resist such attempt or attempts as shall be made' for carrying into execution the offensive acts of parliament.

For several months past there had been an association in Boston of upwards of thirty persons, chiefly mechanicks, who formed themselves into a committee for the purpose of watching the movements of the British.† Towards the spring they

* The Act for tarring and feathering, as it was humorously called, had often been held up, in terrorem, against obnoxious tories, but never absolutely executed upon more than one. John Malcom, a renowned informer, suffered its penalty in January, 1774, and was most cruelly abused.

† See Col. Revere's letter, Mass. H. C. 1. v. 106.

frequently took turns, two and two, to watch the soldiers, by patrolling the streets all night. About twelve o'clock on Saturday night (April the 15th) they discovered that the boats belonging to the transports were all launched and carried under the sterns of the men-of-war. The grenadiers and light infantry were also observed to be all taken off duty. This movement alarmed Dr. Warren, who despatched Mr. Revere to Lexington to give notice of the same to S. Adams and Hancock, who had been persuaded not to return to Boston, lest they should be exposed to seizure by the Governour.

On Tuesday, the 18th, there were strong indications of a speedy movement. The light infantry and grenadiers were concentrated at the Common. About half-past 10 at night, Lieut. Col. Francis Smith of the 10th regt. embarked in the boats, with about 800 men, and landed at Lechmere's point, in Cambridge. Here the troops received a day's provision, and began their march about 12 o'clock.

The object of this expedition was the destruction of the stores collected at Concord. Profound secrecy had been observed in the camp, and it was supposed nobody in Boston suspected the movements. But the vigilance of Warren had anticipated the slow processes of regular troops. He had again despatched Revere and another messenger, in different directions, to give the alarm to Hancock and Adams, and they forwarded the intelligence to Concord.

Lexington is about 12 miles N. W. from Boston, and Concord six miles farther in the same direction. The road, which the British took, lay through West Cambridge. The moon, which rose upon them as they disembarked, shone clearly, and their progress was undisturbed : their own drums were mute, and all nature was quiet around them. In this solemn silence they stole their march, and arrived about dawn of day at Lexington. But there the stillness of the night was changed. The drum was heard beating to arms, and they soon came in sight of an American company, paraded in posture of defiance.

The British troops were halted. at about 100 rods distance, ordered to charge their guns, double their ranks, and then to march at double quick time. The Lexington company, previously ordered to load with ball, were now commanded to stand their ground and no man leave his post without orders, and not to fire unless they were attacked. There were about sixty of these brave men, who presented their bodies a living sacrifice to the cause of their country. In the face of 800 troops then supposed to be 1500, they maintained their position in two ranks, heard the order from the British Major to disperse, and disobeyed it : heard his command to fire, received the first discharge unhurt, and maintained their ground till another discharge from the enemy proved fatal to several of their number. Upon this, part of the company, if not all, returned the fire, and then dispersed in various directions. The British drew up on the common, fired a volley, and gave three huzzas in token of victory ; and after a very short halt, marched for Concord, where they arrived without further opposition.

LEXINGTON MONUMENT.

They reached Concord about nine o'clock. The main body was immediately employed in searching for powder and other warlike stores : a detachment was sent forward to get command of a bridge north of the town. The alarm had reached Concord early in the morning, and many of the militia had assembled, but not having heard of the events at Lexington, they made no attack on the troops, lest they should be the aggressors. They however approached the party stationed at the bridge, and when they had advanced sufficiently near, the British opened a fire upon them, by which several were killed and wounded. The Americans returned the fire, and several of the king's officers and troops fell. The detachment soon after joined the main body, and all prepared, having

---

* Erected in 1799, in memory of those who fell there on the 19th of April, 1775.

partially effected their object in the destruction of some stores
and provisions, to return to Boston, about noon.

But ' in place of the high and insulting confidence with
which the troops had wheeled into the streets of Concord,
they left them, when the order was given to march, with faces bent anxiously on the surrounding heights, and with looks
that bespoke a consciousness of the dangers that were likely
to beset the long road which lay before them. Their apprehensions were not groundless. The troops had hardly commenced their march before a volley was fired upon them from
the protection of a barn, and as they advanced, volley succeeded volley, and musket answered musket from behind
every cover that offered to their assailants. At first these
desultory and feeble attacks were but little regarded ; a brisk
charge, and a smart fire of a few moments never failing to
disperse their enemies, when the troops again proceeded for
a short distance unmolested. But the alarm of the preceding night had gathered the people over an immense extent of
country ; and, having waited for information, those nearest to
the scene of action were already pressing forward to the assistance of their friends. There was but little order, and no
concert among the Americans ; but each party, as it arrived,
pushed into the fray, hanging on the skirts of their enemies,
or making spirited though ineffectual efforts to stop their
progress. On either side of the highway, along the skirts
of every wood or orchard, in the open fields and from every
house, or barn, or cover in sight, the flash of fire arms was to
be seen, while the shouts of the British grew at each instant
feebler and less inspirited.'* The utmost confusion seized
their ranks : they began to run rather than to retreat in order : the officers attempted to stop the men and form them,
but to no purpose ; the confusion increased : at last, after they
had passed Lexington village, the officers gained the front,
presented their bayonets, and told the men if they advanced
they should die. Upon this they began to form, under a very
heavy fire. But they must, no doubt, have soon surrendered, had they not been met, about a mile from the meeting-
house, by a reinforcement under Brig. Gen. Lord Percy, of a
thousand men, with two field pieces. The Americans gave
way as the two detachments joined, and the artillery being
opened upon them, kept them at some distance, while the
British halted about half an hour to rest. But the instant the
guns were limbered and the files had once more opened for
room, the attacks were renewed from every quarter with
redoubled fury. At every step of the retreating army, they
met a new cluster of enemies, that constantly annoyed them

* Lionel Lincoln.

till they reached Charlestown neck, at about seven o'clock in the evening. Lord Percy took his station at Bunker-hill; the men-of-war boats were employed first in getting over the wounded, and afterward the rest of the troops. Fresh soldiers were sent to stand guard during the night, and the next day all were removed to Boston. The loss of the British was 73 killed, 26 missing, besides 174 wounded. The American loss was 49 killed, 3 missing, and 36 wounded.

The news of this transaction spread with the rapidity of the wind, and in the course of two days so great a number of the provincial militia was collected in the vicinity, that the British officers acknowledged themselves ' fairly blocked up in Boston.'

CHAPTER LIII.

" Advance our waving colours on the walls,
Rescued is Orleans from the English wolves."

THIS state of things rendering the situation of the inhabitants of Boston very undesirable, a town-meeting was held on Saturday, the 22d of April, and a conference had with Gov. Gage, in which he proposed to permit such of the citizens as would surrender their arms, to depart from the town with their families and effects. This proposition was considered and adopted by the town, at an adjournment on the Sabbath day following, and many people immediately deposited their arms in the place appointed. But the Governour perceiving that, by letting the people go, he deprived himself of a security from destruction, which their presence might prevent, found a pretext to detain the greatest part of them, and compelled the few, who were permitted to retire, to leave their most valuable effects behind. All intercourse between town and country ceased, and the inhabitants and the troops were reduced to the necessity of subsisting on the provisions that happened to have been laid up in store.* On the 5th of May, the Provincial Congress resolved, that Gen. Gage had by the late transactions and many others ' utterly disqualified him-

---

* " 1775, May 17th. On the evening of this day, a store on the south side of the Town-dock, occupied as a barrack by British troops, took fire by the bursting of some cartridges, imprudently handled by the soldiers. About thirty warehouses and buildings were destroyed, with great part of the effects, contained in them, some of which were donations to the town, for relief of the inhabitants, suffering under the oppressive Port Bill."—Shaw.

39

self from serving the colony as governour, or in any other capacity, and that therefore no obedience was in future due to him.'

Towards the end of May, considerable reinforcements arrived at Boston from England, and on the 25th, Generals Howe, Clinton, and Burgoyne arrived. General Gage prepared to act with more decision. His troops had had several skirmishes on the islands in the harbour, and the provincials had in every case been victorious. The latter were also animated with news from Ticonderoga and Crown Point, that the American parties, which had attacked those posts, had been completely successful. The British army burned for what they termed a fair trial of their prowess against the rebels in open fight : the officers demanded more ' elbow room.' Gen. Gage renewed the campaign on his side by issuing a proclamation on the 12th of June, in which he offered pardon to all persons, *except Samuel Adams and John Hancock*, and proclaimed martial law throughout the province. The congress was about replying by a counter declaration, but were diverted from that design by a movement of more importance.

The American army consisted of about 15,000 men, under Gen. Artemas Ward. Information found its way to the commanders, that the British contemplated posting themselves on Bunker's Hill, and it was immediately determined to make an effort to defeat their design. ' Accordingly on the 16th of June, orders were issued, that a detachment of 1000 men should that evening march to Charlestown, and entrench upon that Hill. Just before 9 o'clock they left Cambridge, and proceeded to Breed's Hill, situated on the further part of the peninsula next to Boston, (for by some mistake this hill was marked out for the entrenchment instead of the other.) Many things being necessary to be done preparatory to the entrenchments being thrown up, which could not be done before, lest the enemy should discover and defeat the design, it was nearly twelve o'clock before the works were entered upon. They were then carried on with the utmost diligence and alacrity ; so that by the dawn of the day they had thrown up a small redoubt, about eight rods square. At this time a heavy fire began from the enemy's ships, a number of floating batteries, and from a fortification of the enemy's upon Copp's Hill in Boston, directly opposite to our little redoubt. An incessant shower of shot and bombs was rained by these upon our works. The Provincials continued to labour indefatigably till they had thrown up a small breast-work, extending from the east side of the redoubt to the bottom of the Hill, but were prevented completing it by the intolerable fire of the enemy.

' Between twelve and one o'clock a number of boats and barges, filled with the regular troops from Boston, were observed approaching towards Charlestown ; these troops landed at a place called Moreton's Point, situated a little to the eastward of our works. This brigade formed upon their landing, and stood thus formed till a second detachment arrived from Boston to join them ; having sent out large flank guards, they began a very slow march towards our lines. At this instant smoke and flames were seen to arise from the town of Charlestown, which had been set on fire by the enemy.

' The Provincials within their entrenchments impatiently waited the attack of the enemy, and reserved their fire till they came within 10 or 12 rods, and then began a furious discharge of small arms. This fire arrested the enemy, which they for some time returned, without advancing a step, and then retreated in disorder and with great precipitation to the place of landing, and some of them sought refuge even within their boats. Here the officers were observed, by the spectators on the opposite shore, to run down to them, using the most passionate gestures, and pushing the men forward with their swords. At length they were rallied, and marched up with apparent reluctance towards the entrenchment ; the Americans again reserved their fire until the enemy came within five or six rods, and a second time put the Regulars to flight, who ran in great confusion towards their boats. Similar and superior exertions were now necessarily made by the officers, which, notwithstanding the men discovered an almost insuperable reluctance to fighting in this cause, were again successful. They formed once more, and having brought some cannon to bear in such a manner as to rake the inside of the breast-work from one end of it to the other, the Provincials retreated within their little fort. The ministerial army now made a decisive effort. The fire from the ships and batteries, as well as from the cannon in the front of their army, was redoubled. The officers in the rear of their army were observed to goad forward the men with renewed exertions, and they attacked the redoubt on three sides at once. The breast-work on the outside of the fort was abandoned ; the ammunition of the Provincials was expended, and few of their arms were fixed with bayonets. Can it then be wondered that the word was given by the commander of the party to retreat ? But this he delayed till the redoubt was half filled with Regulars, and the Provincials had kept the enemy at bay some time, confronting them with the butt ends of their muskets.

' The retreat of this little handful of brave men would have been effectually cut off, had it not happened that the flanking party of the enemy, which was to have come upon

the back of the redoubt, was checked by a party of the
Provincials, who fought with the utmost bravery, and kept
them from advancing farther than the beach ; the engagement of these two parties was kept up with the utmost vigour ;
and it must be acknowledged that this party of the ministerial
troops evidenced a courage worthy of a better cause ; all
their efforts, however, were insufficient to compel the Provincials to retreat till their main body had left the Hill; perceiving
this was done, they then gave ground, but with more regularity than could be expected of troops who had no longer been
under discipline, and many of whom never before saw an engagement. In this retreat, the Americans had to pass over
the Neck, which joins the Peninsula of Charlestown to the
main land. This Neck was commanded by the Glasgow
man-of-war, and two floating batteries, placed in such a manner, as that their shot raked every part of it. The incessant
fire kept up across this Neck had, from the beginning of the
engagement, prevented any considerable reinforcements from
getting to the Provincials on the Hill, and it was feared it
would cut off their retreat, but they retired over it with little
or no loss. With a ridiculous parade of triumph, the ministerial generals again took possession of the Hill which had
served them as a retreat in flight from the battle of Concord.

' The loss of the New-England army amounted, according
to an exact return, to 145 killed and missing, and 304 wounded ; 30 of the first were wounded and taken prisoners by
the enemy. Among the dead was Maj. Gen. Joseph Warren,
a man whose memory will be endeared to his countrymen,
and to the worthy in every part and age of the world, so long
as virtue and valour shall be esteemed among mankind.* The
heroick Col. Gardner, of Cambridge, has since died of his
wounds ; and the brave Lieut. Col. Parker, of Chelmsford,
who was wounded and taken prisoner, perished in Boston gaol.'

The British loss was 1054, according to the official return.
Of these 226 were killed, including 19 officers, and 828 wounded, including 70 officers.

The destruction of Charlestown was regarded by the A-
mericans as an act of wanton barbarity : the British justified
it, on account of the annoyance their troops received from the
Provincials stationed in some of the houses. Many of the
buildings were valuable. ' The meeting-house, a court-house,
prison, county house, two school-houses, and a work-house,

---

* Gen. Warren was Grand Master of Free-Masons for North America, at the time of his
death. Near the spot on which he fell, the members of that fraternity in Charlestown erected a monument, which they dedicated to his memory (Dec. 2, 1794). It was a Tuscan
pillar, 18 feet high, on a brick foundation 10 feet from the ground, eight feet square, and

with upwards of 380 other buildings were totally consumed, together with the furniture and effects of the occupants, besides much property that belonged to the unhappy sufferers in Boston, who had removed their goods into Charlestown.'

The main body of the British troops was stationed, after the battle, in Charlestown, upon Bunker's Hill : the other division of it was deeply intrenched and strongly fortified on

---

enclosed by posts. On the top was a gilt urn, with the letters ' J. W. aged 35,' entwined in masonick emblems. The subjoined view was taken a few weeks before the monument was destroyed. On the south side of the pedestal was the following inscription :

' Erected, A. D. MDCCXCIV. by King Solomon's Lodge of Free-Masons, constituted in Charlestown, 1783, in memory of Major-General JOSEPH WARREN, and his Associates, who were slain on this memorable spot, June 17, 1775.

' None but they who set a just value upon the blessings of Liberty are worthy to enjoy her. In vain we toiled ; in vain we fought ; we bled in vain ; if you, our offspring, want valour to repel the assaults of her invaders.'

' Charlestown settled 1628.   Burnt 1775.   Rebuilt 1776.

' The enclosed land was given by the Hon. James Russell.'

Boston Neck, leading to Roxbury. The American army lay on both sides of Charles river. Its right occupied the high ground about Roxbury, whence it extended towards Dorchester, and its left was covered by Mystick river, a space of at least twelve miles. Every pass was effectually guarded, and Boston was absolutely in a state of siege.* No provision of any kind for man or beast was allowed to enter : the troops and inhabitants were together reduced to great necessities : succours which had been ordered from other parts had been intercepted or lost at sea, and the small-pox broke out among the soldiers and spread among the people.

General Washington had taken command of the American forces July 2d, and Gen. Gage had resigned the British to Gen. Howe, and sailed for England about the first of October. As the winter approached, the scarcity of fuel began to be sensibly felt. The Old North meeting-house and above 100 other large wooden buildings were taken down and distributed for firewood. Some of the wharves also at the north end were broken up for the same purpose. The British officers found little to amuse them, except the occasional performance of a farce, in Faneuil Hall, where they themselves were the actors. Their soldiers had enjoyed a single day of mirth, in which they were employed in felling Liberty Tree and cutting it up for fuel. A squadron of cavalry, attached to the army, occasionally exhibited feats of horsemanship in that sanctuary of freedom, the Old South church, which was transformed into a riding-school. Hollis-street, Brattle-street, the West, and the First Baptist meeting-houses were occupied as hospitals or barracks for the troops.

Both parties were dissatisfied with so inactive a service. Washington ' had been some time contemplating an attack on Boston, as soon as he could be justified in attempting the execution of so bold a design. About the middle of February, 1776,† the severe cold setting in, and the ice becoming sufficiently firm to bear the troops, he was disposed to make the attempt ; but a council of war, summoned on the occasion, being almost unanimous against the measure, he reluctantly abandoned it.

' The effective regular force of the Americans now amounted to upwards of fourteen thousand men ; in addition to which the commander in chief called out about six thousand of the militia of Massachusetts. With these troops he determined to take possession of the heights of Dorchester, whence it would be in his power greatly to annoy the ships in the harbour and the soldiers in the town. By taking this position,

---

* See an account of the Forts around Boston, in Silliman's Journal, viii. 338.
† Holmes' Annals.

from which the enemy would inevitably attempt to drive him, he expected to bring on a general action, during which he intended to cross over from Cambridge side with four thousand chosen men, and attack the town of Boston. To conceal his design, and to divert the attention of the garrison, a heavy bombardment of the town and lines of the enemy was begun on the evening of the 2d of March, and repeated the two succeeding nights. On the night of the 4th, immediately after the firing began, a considerable detachment, under the command of Gen. Thomas, passing from Roxbury, took silent possession of Dorchester heights. The ground was almost impenetrably hard, but the night was mild, and by labouring with great diligence, their works were so far advanced by morning, as to cover them in a great measure from the shot of the enemy. When the British after day break discovered these works, which were magnified to the view by a hazy atmosphere, nothing could exceed their astonishment. No alternative now remained, but to abandon the town, or to dislodge the provincials. General Howe, with his usual spirit, chose the latter part of the alternative, and took measures for the embarkation on that very evening of five regiments with the light infantry and grenadiers, on the important but most hazardous service. The transports fell down in the evening towards the castle, with the troops, amounting to about two thousand men ; but a tremendous storm at night rendered the execution of the design absolutely impracticable. A council of war was called the next morning, and agreed to evacuate the town as soon as possible. A fortnight elapsed before that measure was effected. Meanwhile the Americans strengthened and extended their works ; and on the morning of the seventeenth of March the British discovered a breast work, that had been thrown up in the night at Nook's Hill, on Dorchester peninsula, which perfectly commanded Boston Neck, and the south part of the town. Delay was no longer safe. By four in the morning, the king's troops, with those Americans, who were attached to the royal cause, began to embark ; and before ten all of them were under sail. As the rear embarked, general Washington marched triumphantly into Boston, where he was joyfully received, as a deliverer.'*

---

* 'The British fleet, after a detention of nine days in Nantasket roads, set sail for Halifax. The number of the British, who evacuated Boston, exclusive of the staff, was 7575 ; and the addition of the marines and sailors is supposed to have rendered Howe 10,000 strong. They left their barracks standing, and a number of pieces of cannon spiked, 4 large iron sea mortars, and stores, to the value of 30,000*l.* They demolished the castle, and knocked off the trunnions of the cannon.'

A detachment of the fleet remained to execute the Port Bill, by blockading the harbour, until the 14th of June, when a strong force went down from Boston, and made so effectual

CHAPTER LIV.

" The laws, the rights,
The generous plan of power delivered down
From age to age, by your renown'd forefathers,
So dearly bought, the price of so much blood."

THE inhabitants of Boston speedily returned to their homes, and on the 29th of March they held a regular meeting for the choice of town officers, in the Old Brick church.* May meeting for the choice of representatives was held on the 23d of that month, and the following step was taken relative to a declaration of independence :

' The article in the warrant, viz :—To consider whether the town will, in conformity to a Resolve of the late Honourable House of Representatives for this Colony [on the 10th of May] advise their Representatives, " That if the Honourable Continental Congress should, for the safety of the Colonies, declare them *independent* of the Kingdom of Great Britain they, the inhabitants, will solemnly engage with their lives and fortunes, to support them in the measure," was read, and duly considered, and the question being accordingly put, passed in the affirmative unanimously.'

The instructions to the representatives expressed the same sentiments, and contained also many very judicious remarks concerning the establishment of a regular government for the people of Massachusetts. The declaration of Independence, bearing the signature of the proscribed HANCOCK, as President of the Congress that issued it, on the 4th of July,1776,was made publick at Boston on the 18th with great parade and exultation.†

The subject of a state constitution was taken into consideration by the general court, without delay : but it was not till the year 1780 that our present form was adopted, after the rejection of a previous plan. Several meetings were held in

---

an attack upon them as to compel them to leave their station, and take the advantage of a westerly wind to sail for Halifax. Had the wind continued from the east, they must inevitably have surrendered.

Several transports arrived at different dates some weeks after the evacuation of the town, not having received information of the fact, and were taken. The number of prisoners amounted to about 500.

* The people of Boston had assembled twice or three times at Watertown, for the transaction of town affairs, during the siege. Thursday lecture had been continued by Dr. Andrew Eliot until about the 23d of Dec. and was renewed immediately after the evacuation of the town, on the 28th of March, when Washington attended.

† Bradford, Hist. of Mass. ii. 104, 116, 186, 320, 326.

Boston on the occasion, and the debates were very animated. The town finally agreed to the adoption of the constitution, recommending some amendments. A majority of the people accepting the plan as it stood, the 4th of Sept. was appointed for the election of the state officers. The votes for governour in Boston were 923, of which Hancock had 858, Bowdoin 64, S. Adams 1. The Gen. Court met on the 25th of October, when it was ascertained that Hancock was elected governour by a great majority. There was no choice of Lt. Gov. by the people; Mr. Bowdoin was chosen by the court, but declined; so likewise did James Warren Esq. of Plymouth; Thomas Cushing Esq. of Boston accepted the office.

The joy, which the people of Boston could not suppress on this occasion, from ' having a Governour who proceeded out of the midst of us,' was signified to Gov. Hancock in an address from the selectmen, to which he returned an answer, concluding with the assurance that in whatever situation his country should please to place him, the metropolis of this commonwealth might ever depend upon his particular attention to its interests.

From the time of the evacuation of the town and the rout of the British fleet from the lower harbour, Boston and its vicinity had ceased to be the seat of the war. The citizens however bore their full portion in its burdens, and took part in its fatigues and duties by sea and land, as well as in the councils of the Congress and embassies to foreign parts. They maintained throughout the contest that no terms should be made with Britain, unaccompanied with the unconditional acknowledgment of independence. They were not however desirous to prolong the warfare, and received as joyfully as any of their countrymen the intelligence of peace. The proclamation of Congress announcing this event, reached Boston by express, on the 23d of April, 1783, and ' the sheriff of the co. of Suffolk, Jos. Henderson Esq. announced the same from the balcony of the State-house, at one o'clock, before which a large concourse of the most respectable inhabitants of the town were assembled, who demonstrated by three loud huzzas their joy upon this occasion: after which 13 cannon from the fortresses at the castle, and the same number at Fort-hill were fired.'

The adoption of the Federal Constitution was an event of equal importance. The Massachusetts convention, which assembled on this subject, in January 1788, consisted of 360 members, of whom a great portion came with strong prejudices against the constitution : but after a discussion of several weeks, when the question of acceptance was finally decided, there were found to be 187 for, and 168 against it, giving a

40

majority of 19.   This decision was declared ' on the 6th of
Feb. in a manner too impressive to be forgotten by any who
were present.'*   The citizens of Boston expressed great joy on
the occasion, which was manifested by a numerous procession
composed of all classes and trades, with their respective and
appropriate badges.   Many farmers and others attended from
the country and joined the procession, with the plough and
other implements of husbandry.   They formed at Faneuil-
hall, and thence proceeded to the houses of the gentlemen,
who had represented the town in the convention, and saluted
them with cheers and from the guns of a small ship, which
made part of the procession.   Afterwards, as many as could
find seats partook of an entertainment at the hall; but multitudes we are told went away empty.

The principal events of the revolutionary war and other
important dates having been preserved in the inscriptions on
the monument, which was erected on Beacon Hill, we insert
the same here, with a drawing of the monument and of the
beacon whose place it occupied.   The beacon was blown
down (Nov. 26, 1789) and the monument was commenced in
the next year, but not finished till the spring of 1791.   It was
' a plain column of the Dorick order, raised on its proper pedestal, substantially built of brick and stone.   It was encrust-
ed with a white cement, and had a large eagle of wood, gilt,
at the top, supporting the American arms.   The height, including the eagle, was 60 feet ; the diameter of the column
was 4 feet, the pedestal was 8 feet.'   The beacon was about
the same height.

INSCRIPTION ON THE SOUTH SIDE OF THE MONUMENT.

TO COMMEMORATE THAT TRAIN OF EVENTS WHICH LED TO THE AMERICAN
REVOLUTION, AND FINALLY SECURED LIBERTY AND INDEPENDENCE TO THE
UNITED STATES,   THIS COLUMN IS ERECTED BY THE VOLUNTARY CONTRIBU-
TION OF THE CITIZENS OF BOSTON,

MDCCXC.

ON THE WEST SIDE :

Stamp Act passed, 1765, repealed, 1766.—Board of customs established, 1767.—British troops
fired on the inhabitants of Boston, March 5, 1770.—Tea act passed, 1773.—Tea destroyed in
Boston, Decem. 16.—Port of Boston shut and guarded, June 1, 1774.—General Congress
at Philadelphia, Sep. 4.—Provincial Congress at Concord, Oct. 11.—Battle of Lexington,
April 19, 1775.—Battle of Bunker Hill, June 17.—Washington took command of the
army, July 2.—Boston evacuated, March 17, 1776.—Independance declared by Congress,
July 4, 1776 ; Hancock President.

---

* The session of the convention on that day was held in the meeting house, in *Long-lane,*
which afterwards received the name of *Federal-Street,* from this circumstance.

ON THE NORTH SIDE:

Capture of Hessians at Trenton, Dec. 26, 1776.—Capture of Hessians at Bennington, Aug. 16, 1777.—Capture of British army at Saratoga, Oct. 17.—Alliance with France, Feb. 6, 1778.—Confederation of the United States formed, July 9.—Constitution of Massachusetts formed, 1780; Bowdoin President of Convention.—Capture of British army at York, Oct. 19, 1781.—Preliminaries of Peace, Nov. 30, 1782.—Definitive treaty of Peace, Sept. 10, 1783.—Federal Constitution formed, Sept. 17, 1787, and ratified by the United States, 1787 to 1790.—New Congress assembled at New-York, April 6, 1789.—Washington inaugurated President, April 30.—Publick debts funded, Aug. 4, 1790.

ON THE EAST SIDE:

AMERICANS

WHILE FROM THIS EMINENCE, SCENES OF LUXURIANT FERTILITY, OF FLOURISHING COMMERCE, AND THE ABODES OF SOCIAL HAPPINESS MEET YOUR VIEW, FORGET NOT THOSE, WHO BY THEIR EXERTIONS HAVE SECURED TO YOU THESE BLESSINGS.

VIEW OF THE BEACON AND MONUMENT ON BEACON-HILL.*

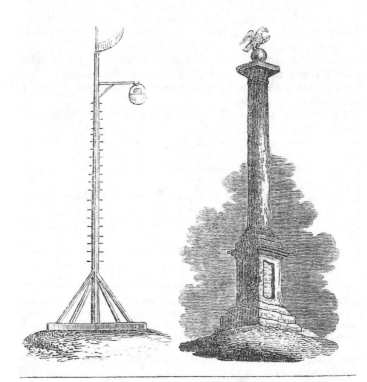

* The stones bearing the inscriptions, (which we have copied literally) with the eagle which surmounted the column, may be seen in the new State House.

CHAPTER LV.

Famed as the Appian way,
The world's first bridge to day
All nations shall convey
From shore to shore.—*Dawes.*

HAVING thus noticed the principal publick events of general interest, we shall devote the remainder of our work to accounts of the various improvements, institutions, and undertakings, which have engaged the attention of the people of Boston, since the revolution.

The first great undertaking, (which at the time was considered the greatest that had ever been projected in America,*) was the erection of ' a bridge over Charles river in the place where the ferry between Boston and Charlestown was kept.' The Act, which incorporated Messrs. John Hancock, Thomas Russell, Nath. Gorham, and Eben Parsons and others, who had subscribed to a fund for executing and completing this purpose, was passed March 9, 1785, and the bridge was so far completed that the last pier was ready to be put down on the 31st of May, 1786.

On the 17th of June, the bridge was opened for passengers. Preparations had been made for great festivity on the occasion. Salutes of 13 guns were fired at sunrise from Bunker and Copps' hills, and the bells of Christ church rang repeated peals. This salute formed a contrast so striking, compared with the hostile and bloody one of the same day, of the same month, and of the week, in '75, as to excite in every breast emotions of the happiest kind. At one, P. M. the proprietors ' assembled in the [Old] State-house, for the purpose of waiting on the different branches of the legislature over the bridge. The procession consisted of almost every respectable character in publick and private life ; as they moved from

---

* In a pamphlet on ' the distressed state of Boston,' 1720, we find the following remark : 'if there was a bridge built over Charles River, if 50,000*l.* were expended to make it durable, and so a moderate toll laid on all carts, coaches, horses, &c. this would help us by employing the poor, and the circulation of the bills would be of great service, and other things of this nature might be thought on.' On the town records, we find, April 27, 1720, ' Voted that it be given as an instruction to the representatives of this town, now chosen, to promote the building a bridge over Charles River, at the place where the ferry hath been usually kept, viz. between Mr. Gee's and Mr. Hudson's point, and at no other place.'

In 1726, Town Rec. p. 467, there is mention of a proposed bridge from Winnessimet ferry to Noddle's Island, by John Yeamans, Esq.

State-street, a salute was fired from the Castle; and upon
their arrival at the entrance of the bridge, the attendant companies of artillery and artificers, formed two lines on the right
and left of the proprietors, and moved on to the centre of the
bridge, when the President of the proprietary advanced
alone, and gave orders to Mr. Cox, the master workman, to
fix the draw for the passage of the company, which was immediately done.   At this moment 13 cannon were fired from
Copps' hill, and the procession passed forward, attended by
the loudest shouts of acclamation, from a concourse of at
least 20,000 spectators.   As the company ascended Breed's
hill, 13 cannon were discharged.   The gentlemen took their
seats at two tables of 320 feet, united at each end by a semi-
circular one, which accommodated 800 persons, who spent
the day in sober festivity, and separated at 6 o'clock.'

The following description of Charles-river bridge was published at the time, as taken from actual survey. ' The abutment at Charlestown, from the old landing, is 100 feet ; space
to the first pier 16½ feet ; 36 piers at equal distances to the
draw 622½ feet; width of the draw 30 feet ; 39 piers at equal
distances from the draw 672 feet ; space to the abutment at
Boston 16½ feet ; abutment at Boston to the old landing 45¼
feet ; whole length1503 feet.

' The 75 piers total, upon which this elegant structure
stands, are each composed of 7 sticks of oak timber, united
by a cap piece, strong braces and girts, and afterwards driv-
en into the bed of the river, and firmly secured by a single
pile on each side, driven obliquely to a solid bottom.   The
piers are connected to each other by large string-pieces,
which are covered with 4 inch plank.   The Bridge is 42
feet in width, and on each side is accommodated with a passage 6 feet wide, railed in for the safety of people on foot.
The Bridge has a gradual rise from each end, so as to be two
feet higher in the middle than at the extremities.   Forty elegant lamps are erected at suitable distances, to illuminate it
when necessary.   There are four strong stone wharves connected with three piers each, sunk in various parts of the
river.

' The floor of the Bridge at the highest tides, is 4 feet above
the water, which generally rises about 12 or 14 feet.   The
distance where the longest pier is erected, from the floor of
the Bridge to the bed of the river, is 46¾ feet.'

The cost of this bridge has been stated at £15,000, lawful,
and the property was divided into 150 shares of £100 each.
Rates of toll. to be double on Lord's days, were established,
by the act of incorporation, which the proprietors were to enjoy for forty years, paying to the college at Cambridge an
annuity of £200, in consideration of their loss of income from

the ferry. This period was extended to 70 years, and the double toll repealed, when the charter was granted for West Boston Bridge, at the expiration of which period the property reverts to the state.

There had been considerable effort to have the first bridge carried from West Boston to Cambridge, but the expediency of making the experiment across the narrower part of the river was so apparent, that the town of Boston had expressed an opinion almost unanimous (1238 to 2) in favour of it.

West Boston Bridge is a conveyance from the late Pest-house point, at the west end of Cambridge-street, over Charles river, to the opposite shore in Cambridge. A number of gentlemen, (Francis Dana, Oliver Wendell, James Sullivan, Henry Jackson, Mungo Mackay, Wm. Wetmore,) were incorporated for the purpose of erecting this bridge, March 9th, 1792.

'The causeway to W. Boston bridge was begun July 15th, 1792, and suspended after the 26th of December, till the 20th of March 1793, when the work was resumed. The wood work of the bridge was begun the 8th of April, 1793, and the bridge and causeway opened for passengers the 23d of November following, being seven months and an half from laying the first pier. The sides of the causeway are stoned, capstand, and railed ; on each side of which is a canal about thirty feet wide.

'The bridge stands on 180 piers, is - - - - - -	3483 feet long.
Bridge over the gore, 14 do. - - - - - - - -	275 do.
Abutment Boston side, - - - - - - - - -	87 1-2
Causeway, - - - - - - - - - - -	3344
Distance from end of the causeway to Cambridge Meeting-house, -	7810
Width of the bridge, - - - - - - - - -	40

Railed on each side for foot passengers.

' To the proprietors a toll was granted for 70 years from the opening of the bridge,* which together with the causeway was estimated to have cost about £23,000, l. m. The principal undertaker for building the bridge, was Mr. Whiting.'

Those two bridges and the neck continued to be the only avenues to the town, landward, until the opening of South Boston Bridge. This grew out of the project for annexing Dorchester Neck (so called) to Boston, as a part of the same town. In the latter end of 1803, there were but ten families on that peninsula, which comprised an extent of 560 acres of land. These families united with several citizens of Boston in a petition to the town (Dec. 27) for the privilege of being

---

* This term has since been extended to 70 years from the opening of Craigie's bridge. West Boston to pay the College 200l. annually, and Craigie's to pay West Boston 100l. during their joint existence.

annexed thereto, ' upon the single condition that the inhabitants [of B.] will procure a bridge to be erected between Boston and Dorchester neck.' On the 31st of Jan. 1804, after several confused meetings on .the subject, the town agreed to the proposition, on condition ' that the place from which and the terms on which the bridge should be built shall be left entirely to the Legislature.' Application was made to the General Court, and measures were in train for authorising a bridge from South-Street to the point. The inhabitants of the South-end of the town, having opposed this measure in vain thus far in its progress, formed a plan at this juncture, in which they proposed to erect a bridge where the present bridge stands, and, to obviate the objection that such a bridge would not lessen the distance from the point so much as the South-street bridge would, they offered to construct a commodious street, across the flats from Rainsford's lane to the head of the proposed bridge. They presented a petition to the Court to be incorporated for these purposes ' upon the presumption that no liberty will be granted for the erection of any other bridge,' to the northward of their bridge, ' unless at some future period the increased settlement of this part of the country should be such, that the publick exigencies should require the same.' This plan and petition met with so favourable a reception, that the Dorchester point proprietors were induced to make a compromise with the South-end petitioners, in which it was agreed, that the South-Street bridge should be abandoned, and that the South-end bridge should be transferred to the Dorchester company, and the proposed street be carried forward by the petitioners. A joint committee made a report on the bases of this compromise, which was accepted in concurrence, Feb. 23d ; and on the 6th of March. bills were passed for the three objects, the annexation of Dorchester neck to Boston, the incorporation of the Proprietors of Boston South Bridge, and also of the Front-Street Corporation in the town of Boston.

Messrs. William Tudor, Gardiner Green, Jona. Mason, and Harrison Gray Otis, were the proprietors named in Boston South Bridge act.* Seventy years' improvement was allowed, from the date of the first opening of said bridge for passengers, which took place ' in the summer of 1805.' On the first of October, it was the scene of a military display and sham fight. This bridge is 1551 feet in length, and cost the proprietors about 56,000 dollars.

---

* The proprietors of Roxbury canal (incorporated Feb. 7, 1796) procured the insertion of a clause in the act, requiring the South Boston bridge proprietors to pay a certain sum to vessels passing above the draw.

Canal or Craigie's Bridge was opened on Commencement-
day, August 30, 1809. It runs from Barton's pt. in Boston, to
Lechmere's pt. in Cambridge. Its length is 2796 ft.; its width,
40 ft. This bridge on the Cambridge side is united toCharles-
town by Prison-point bridge, which is 1821 ft. long, and 35
ft. broad, having but one side railed for foot passengers.

All these bridges are well lighted by lamps when the even-
ings are dark, and the lights, placed at regular distances,
have a splendid and romantic appearance. The rates of toll
are the same on Charlestown, Craigie's and W. Boston. Passengers to and from Cambridge over Prison-point bridge
are not subject to toll. Foot passengers are not taxed on
South-Boston bridge, but the rates for vehicles, &c. are rather
higher. The construction of all these bridges is said to be
similar, excepting that Craigie's is covered with a layer of
gravel, and some part of it has been recently Macadamized.*

The Western Avenue, or Mill Dam, erected by the Boston
and Roxbury Mill Corporation, from Beacon-street in Boston
to Sewall's point in Brookline, constitutes a sixth avenue into
the city. The project for this great work was brought before
the town in a petition from Isaac P. Davis and others, June
11, 1813, and the inhabitants having given their assent to its
execution, on certain conditions, Messrs. I. P. Davis, Uriah
Cotting, Wm. Brown, and their associates, were incorporated
for the purpose, June 14, 1814. Very little was done towards
the accomplishment of this object before January 1818, when
Mr. Cotting issued an address to the publick, setting forth the
advantages to be derived to Boston from the contemplated
improvement. Subscription papers were not long after opened, and all the shares were immediately taken on one day,
and the next day were on sale at an advanced price. The
work was commenced under the eye of Mr. Cotting, but he
did not live to witness its completion : his place was supplied
by Col. Loammi Baldwin, and the road was opened for passengers, July 2, 1821. There was a splendid ceremony on
the occasion : a cavalcade of citizens, under the direction of
Adj. Gen. Wm. H. Sumner, at an early hour entered the
town over the dam, and were welcomed on this side by the
inhabitants, who waited to receive them.

The main Dam is composed of solid materials, water-tight :
its surface is three or four feet above high-water mark : it is
fifty feet in width in the narrowest part, and 100 in the widest,
and one mile and a half in length. The rates of toll are the
same as at West-Boston bridge.

---

* Persons named in act incorporating the Canal Bridge, Feb. 27, 1807. John C. Jones,
Loammi Baldwin, Aaron Dexter, Benjamin Wild, Jos. Coolidge jun. Benja. Joy, Gorham
Parsons, Jona. Ingersoll, John Beach, Abijah Cheever, Wm. B. Hutchins, Stephen Howard,
and Andrew Craigie.

CHAPTER LVI.

"Then Commerce brought into the publick walk
The busy merchant ; the big warehouse built ;
Then, too, the pillar'd dome, magnifick, heav'd
Its ample roof."

In noticing the changes which took place in various parts of the town, after the peace, prior to the establishment of the city government, we have occasion first to mention an extensive fire, which occurred on Friday, April 20, 1787. It commenced about sunset, in a malt-house belonging to William Patten, in Beach-street. The wind at N. E. blowing hard carried the flakes to a great distance, so that many houses were on fire at the same moment. In less than fifteen minutes the spire of the Hollis-street meeting-house, nearly 50 rods from where the fire began, was seen to catch, and the whole edifice was in a short time burnt to the ground. The buildings consumed were about 100, of which 60 were dwelling-houses, some elegant and costly. Both sides of the main street were laid waste : the east from Mr. Knapp's to Mr. Bradford's, and from Mrs. Inches' to Mr. Osborne's on the west : that is, from Elliot to Nassau-street on the west side of the main street, and on the east side from Beach-street to the corner opposite Nassau-street. The buildings which were erected on the ruins were mostly of wood, three stories high, some of them neat and very elegant.

The *first block* of brick buildings was the range called the *Tontine,* in Franklin-street. Until the year 1792, that street had lain in an unimproved state. There was a slough or quagmire at the lower part of it, and the project to build in its neighbourhood was deemed almost quixotick. A plan was brought forward for erecting a block there, on the principles of the tontine, as practised in other parts of the world.* Subscribers were to furnish stipulated sums towards the accomplishment of the object, to be invested in a capital stock, which was to be improved to the best advantage, and at the expiration of a term of years to be divided among the surviving subscribers. The Legislature discouraged this plan by

---

* The slough was first drained by Jos. Barrell, esq. who connected it with his land in Summer-street, and laid it out as a garden : he afterwards sunk a large fish-pond on the same spot, and stored it with gold and silver fish, and ornamented it with a handsome fountain.

41

refusing an act of incorporation : but the work proceeded under a different arrangement, and the foundation of the buildings on the south side was laid August 8, 1793. These formed a Crescent of sixteen dwelling-houses, extending 480 feet
in length, three stories high, finished in the modern style. The
general appearance is simple and uniform. The outline is
varied by a large arch, having publick rooms over it, with an
attick in the centre, and two houses at each end, which project in advance and are decorated with pilasters and a balustrade. The open space in front of these buildings is 100 feet
wide in the centre and 50 ft. at the ends. A grass plat 300 ft.
long occupies the middle of that space : it is inclosed, and contains a monumental urn, in memory of Dr. Franklin. The
opposite side, which is built on a straight line, in a varied style
of architecture, consists of eight houses, in four blocks, which
constitute what is called Franklin-place. Messrs. William
Scollay, Charles Bulfinch, and Charles Vaughan, were the
principal agents in this great improvement.

A very distressing fire occurred on the morning of July 30,
1794, which laid waste the extensive square between Pearl-
street, Milk, Atkinson, and Purchase streets, to the sea. It
commenced about 4 A. M. in the rope-walk of Mr. Edward
Howe, and communicated to six other walks adjacent,
of which one was two stories high, and all 600 feet in length,
well stored with hemp and other materials adapted to the
trade. The wind holding N.N.E. till near the close of the fire,
prevented the devastation from extending so far, as almost
any other wind would inevitably have carried it. Ninety-six
buildings, of which 43 were dwelling-houses, were consumed.
The amount of losses, rendered to a committee of the town,
was $209,861 50, exclusive of several large sums not ex-
hibited.

Great interest was at this time excited in favour of removing the ropewalks from the heart of the town. Lechmere's
point was proposed by some as a suitable location for them,
but the town ' in a moment of sympathy and feeling for the
sufferings of particular individuals,' voluntarily gave them the
right of using the land at the bottom of the Common.* By
this disposition a very fine square was left open, capable of
making many valuable building lots ; it is now covered by
some of the most eligible houses in the city.

---

* Six ropewalks were erected at the bottom of the Common : they were all destroyed by
fire, Feb. 18, 1806 : five being rebuilt, four of them were again burnt in the fall of
1819, and in the course of the year 1824, the city purchased the rights of the ropewalk
owners, by which the property has reverted to the inhabitants, and the walks are removed
to the neck and mill-dam.

J. Echtert del.

Entered according to Act of Congress, by J. Bowen

A. Bowen &c.

NEW STATE HOUSE.

In the month of May, 1795, the town purchased of Gov. Hancock's heirs the spot of land on which the State-house stands, and transferred it to the Commonwealth. On the 4th of July the corner-stone of this edifice, which makes so striking a figure in every view of Boston, was laid with great ceremony. The stone was drawn to the spot by 15 white horses, (then the number of States in the Union,) and laid by the Governour, assisted by the Grand Masters of masonick lodges. A silver plate, bearing the name of the depositors, and many pieces of current money, were placed beneath the stone.*

This building is of an oblong form, ' 173 ft. front and 61 deep. It consists externally of a basement story, twenty feet high, and a principal story thirty feet. This, in the centre of the front, is covered with an attic sixty feet wide, twenty feet high, which is covered with a pediment. Immediately above this rises a dome. fifty feet diameter, and thirty high ; the whole terminates with an elegant circular lantern supporting an elegant pine cone. The basement story is finished plain on the wings with square windows. The centre is 94 feet in length, and formed of arches which project 14 feet ; they form a covered walk below ; and support a colonnade of Corinthian columns of the same extent above. The outside walls are of large patent bricks, with white marble fascias, imposts, and keystones.' The body of the building is painted of a Portland-stone colour ; the dome of a bronze.

The foundation of this edifice is about 100 feet above the level of the harbour, and its elevation and size make it a very conspicuous object. Two flights of stairs lead to the top of the outer dome, 170 steps from the foundation. The view from this dome affords one of the most interesting and beautiful spectacles. The eye embraces at once every avenue and every publick building in the city, and overlooks the towns adjacent ' all speckled with white houses and country seats amidst groves and luxuriant fields.' At our feet, on the right, we see the mansion house of Hancock, (a venerable stone building of eighty years standing) and in front is spread the common, like a splendid carpet of green, bounded on all sides by the malls closely shaded by trees of various growth, over which the great elm in the middle of the common, (near to an old redoubt and beside a small artificial pond,) seems to com-

* The inscription was as follows : *This Corner Stone of a building intended for the use of the Legislative and Executive branches of Government of the Commonwealth of Massachusetts, was laid by His Excellency Samuel Adams Esq. Governour of said Commonwealth, assisted by the most Worshipful Paul Revere, Grand Master and the Right Worshipful William Sedley, Deputy Grand Master, the Grand Wardens and brethren of the Grand Lodge of Massachusetts on the fourth day of July An. Dom. 1795. A. L. 5795 being the XXth anniversary of American Independence.*

mand the whole, with the majestick waving of his huge branches, the growth of a century.* East, lies in full view, the sight
unobstructed in its farthest reach, the ocean and the harbour,
bespangled with islands, almost as numerous and said to be
equally as charming as those which beautify the bay of Na-
ples : all together combining to make this view one of the
most delightful panoramas that the world affords.†

'The New Alms-house, so called,‡ (which stood till May,
1825, in Leverett-Street) was built in the year 1800 : the
Overseers of the poor held their first meeting in it, Dec.
3d. It was an oblong building, pleasantly situated on the
bank of Charles river, measuring 270 feet front, and 56 deep.
It consisted of a basement story, divided into three large kitch-
ens, and a number of commodious rooms, which were improved for work-shops and other purposes. Above were three
upright stories, which gave forty-eight rooms, 24 by 22 feet ;
four staircases, 10 feet in width, leading through the several
stories. In the centre was a hall 40 by 50, and a chapel
above of the same dimensions ; each of them being about 15
feet in height. The large arched windows were finished with
fluted pilasters of the Ionic order. The outside walls were
of large bricks, with white marble fascias, imposts and keystones, and the roof covered with slate. Four brick partitions ran through the building, in which stood the chimnies,
containing a funnel for every room. The whole building
was enclosed with brick walls and handsome gates. The
front and rear yards were 80 by 280 feet.'

West Row, the next oldest range of brick buildings, on the
west side of Court street, between Hanover street and Bow-

---

* The height of the Great Tree on the Common is 65 feet ; the girth, at 30 inches from the
ground, is 21 ft. 8 inches. The extent of the branches is 86 feet.

† The new State house was first occupied by the Legislature on the 11th of January, 1798.
The several branches of the Gen. Court marched in procession from the old state house, and
the new building was solemnly dedicated ' to the honour of God and the people's good.'
Rev. Dr. Thacher offered the dedicatory prayer.

‡ The old Alms house, Work house and Bridewell, together with the Granary were situated on Park Street. The *Granary* was a long wooden building at the corner of Common
st. capable of containing 12000 bushels of grain, which it was customary for a committee,
annually appointed by the town, to have stored in it for the accommodation of the poor and
others who wished to purchase in small quantities, at an advance on the wholesale price not
exceeding ten per cent. The *Alms house* was a two story brick building, in the form of an L,
with a gable roof, appropriated to the aged and infirm poor. The *Work house* was a large
brick building, 120 feet long, two stories high with a gable roof for the reception of vagrant,
idle and dissolute persons. *Bridewell* was contiguous to the workhouse, and was a sort of
prison for the disorderly a part of the house was assigned to the insane.

The first proposal for an Alms house on the Town records occurs in Nov. 1660. In Feb.
1665, a person is admitted into the Alms house. Dec. 18, 1682, the Alms house being burnt a
new one is proposed it was building June 2, 1686. The Work-house was built in 1738.

doin square, was erected in 1800. South Row, a handsome
block of stores belonging to the Old South church, and situate
on the land adjoining it, was completed about the same time.

On the 16th of December,1801, a destructive fire happened
in Fish and Ann streets. It commenced in a large wooden
building in the rear of [now] No. 95, Ann st. and immediately
communicated to the houses in front. Thence it extended
north on the east side of Fish street to Swett's wharf, consuming every house. On the west side of Ann street no house
was burnt, although the street was then ten feet narrower
than it is at present; but every building from Cross street to
the one opposite Swett's wharf was burnt, or pulled down to
arrest the progress of the flames. The next year, 1802, several brick buildings were erected on the ruins, and the block
on the west side of Fish street received the name of North
Row.

The law to prevent the erection of wooden buildings more
than ten feet high was passed Feb. 9, 1803. It was an act in
addition to an act to secure the town of Boston from damage
by fire, and its provisions were so faithfully executed that
none other than brick or stone buildings were raised from
that time, until the recent modification of the law.

The town land, on which the old Alms house &c. stood, had
been sold to individuals some time before the removal of the
inmates took place, and very shortly after that, the block of
four buildings on Park Street, adjoining the meeting house
was put up. So far as we can ascertain this was the first of
the improvements near the State house and common. By the
fall of 1804,the houses on Beacon street at the corner of Park
street were erected. Hamilton place was finished in 1806,
and Bumstead place not long after. Pinckney street, Myrtle
street, Hancock street and the whole extent of Mount Vernon, which in 1799 presented a dreary waste on which only
three decent houses were to be seen, began to present the appearance of improvement, and in a very little time were covered with extensive ranges of some of the best houses in the
town. By the year 1806, they became the resort of wealth
and fashion, and subsequent improvements have made that
neighbourhood the most eligible of any part of the city.

Beacon hill and the eminences west of it were levelled, and
their materials served to fill up the millpond, which the mill
proprietors (the successors of Henry Simons, &c. see *p.* 124)
obtained the consent of the town to do, May 14, 1804. The
proprietors had been incorporated, by the name of the Boston
Mill Corporation, March, 9, 1804 ; and on March 11th,1806,
certain associates were incorporated under the name of the
Pond Street Corporation ' for the purpose of making a street
from the Boston side of Charles River Bridge, across the Mill

Pond, in the most convenient route to connect with Middle street,' to be laid out by the Selectmen as a publick street and to be at least 60 ft. wide. That street, which by admeasurement is 1980 ft. in length was commenced without delay. The proprietors having made arrangements for the accommodation of the Baptist churches abutting on the pond, they came to a definite agreement with the town July 24, 1807, that the town, ' waive and release the conditions and obligations annexed to the said original grant, for a just and valuable consideration, and that the premises should be filled up and made fit for building by excluding the water; and the said Proprietors are content in exchange for such release to fill up and convert the premises into solid land, and to grant and confirm to the town of Boston forever an estate in fee simple, in and to one eighth lot so filled up, of every tract or portion of the premises, which shall, within twenty years from this date, be filled up and converted into solid land, within and without the present existing causeway, and one undivided moiety of every lot or portion of the premises, which at the expiration of said term shall not be filled up and converted into solid land, or boxed out in a manner equivalent to filling up.' The principal part of the pond is already filled up, and the whole superficies is laid out into squares and streets of convenient breadth. Several brick buildings were early erected on the made land, at the bottom of Friend street and of Cross street. The New street (as Mill-pond-street, G. d. 35, is yet familiarly called) considerably shortens the distance between Charlestown and the centre of Boston.* A canal passing through the mill-creek unites the river with the harbour, and receives the boats from Middlesex canal with their cargoes of wood, stone and produce. When the pond is wholly filled up, the area of the peninsula will have been increased about 43 acres.

It was about this time that Copps' hill began to be dug away, and a few brick buildings were erected in Lynn-street, in 1806, about Hon. Wm. Gray's whf. and on the opposite side of the street. These were the principal improvements at the north part of the town. A fire which happened, Aug. 18th destroyed six houses, between Ann (then Fish) st. and the North square. It commenced at nine o'clock in the evening, in the third house from Mountfort's corner. Very great exertions were necessary to prevent its extending across the street and communicating to many of the neighbouring houses, which at that time were all of wood and very near each other. A few brick buildings have risen slowly on this spot, and

---

* Another street (Charlestown st. G. d. 34,) is now almost completed, by which that distance will be yet more diminished.

the width of the street has been greatly improved. But the the prospect of gain from exertions in other parts of the town has hitherto been so much brighter, that very little improvement has yet been made north of the creek. Here and there an individual has erected a substantial house, and not a few have done their part towards rendering the general appearance of buildings in that quarter more agreeable, so far as that could be effected by a coat of paint.

' Sundry persons, proprietors of the ship yard, and of certain wharves and flats, lying on the harbour of Boston, between Battery March street and State st. associated for the purpose of improving said land and laying out a spacious street near the harbour through their estates,' and were incorporated for that purpose, Feb. 11, 1805, by the name of the *Broad Street Association.* While the plans of this Association were progressing, another company was carrying forward India Wharf, which was finished before Broad Street was completed. India Street extending from India Wharf to the head of Long Wharf was the next improvement, and the stores and houses on them all were ready to be occupied in the course of 1807, '08, and '09. The range of four-story brick stores and dwelling-houses, in Broad-street, measures on the west side, from State-street to Purchase-street, 1373 feet, in a line somewhat circular. Broad-street is 70 ft. in width. Custom-House street, in which the Custom-House stands, measures 194 ft. from Broad to India street, and this last measures 989 feet from Long-wharf to India-whf. These admeasurements give an idea of the extent of space rescued from the water, and converted into commodious stores and dwellings.

To these great improvements we must add, in the same quarter, that of Central-wharf, which was completed in the year 1816. It extends into the harbour, from India-street about midway between Long and India wharves, and is 1240 feet in length, and 150 in width. There are 54 stores on this wharf, four stories high. There is a spacious hall in the centre, over which is erected an elegant observatory. The stores are fifty feet in width, and stand in the middle of the wharf, so that there is, on either side, the best of accommodation for the landing and delivery of merchandize. It has been remarked, that for extent, convenience, and elegance combined, Central-wharf is not exceeded by any in the commercial world.

While these undertakings were going forward, the same great projector of the whole, Mr. Cotting, had his mind employed on another. Between the foot of Cornhill and the northerly end of Tremont-street, in a straight course, there was considerable vacant land and many old buildings of little value. Possession was obtained of these estates by pur-

chase, and a street 48 ft. in width was laid out, in as direct a
coarse as the unevenness of the ground would permit. In
1817, a block of stores was erected on each side, which, between Cornhill and Court st. measure 432 ft. in length on the
north side, and 436 on the south. They are all four stories high
and have uniform fronts. The stores on the north side are
marked with the odd numbers (1 to 91) and those on the
south with the even numbers, (2 to 76) the chambers in each
building bearing one number, and the store, below, the odd or
even number next in order. It was at first proposed to call
this avenue New Cornhill, from the circumstance of its being
devoted to the same kinds of business for which Cornhill had
so long been celebrated : to what fancy the present name is
to be attributed we know not.*

Immediately on the completion of Market-street, part of
the building at the east end of Scollay's buildings, (long
famous as Master Carter's school, but which became private
property, March 4, 1793) was taken down, to make the passage free from Tremont street into Market-street. In the
next year, Brattle street leading E. from Court st. to Dock
square by the rear of the stores on Market st. was opened, and
an elegant block of 14 houses built on the north side, presenting a front of hammered stone, 312 ft. in extent and four stories high. This was the first stone block erected in the town.

While these changes were making mostly for commercial
purposes, extensive improvements were going forward in other parts of the town, to accommodate a population increasing
in wealth and numbers, with dwelling houses suited to their
fancies and wants. Fort hill was put into repair and the lots
adjacent sold by the town to individuals,† who erected the
brick block called Washington place, around the mall, or circular green which is a walk about 200 ft. in diameter, lined with
double rows of poplars. North-Russell, Vine, and Poplar streets,
and the neighbourhood of the Massachusetts Hospital to the
Alms-house in Leverett st. which had recently been marsh and
pasture ground, or improved only for Ropewalks, were converted into building lots and covered with fashionable and
substantial houses. Beacon street on the west side of the

---

* The stores in Market Street were the first erected on granite pillars, a thing now so
common. Mr. Tuckerman's store at the corner of Dock sq. and Market Row, was about
the first in which the improvement was attempted (1820) of substituting those pillars for the
original brick walls. Extreme caution was deemed necessary, and the work occupied almost
a whole summer. Market Row, which is a continuation of similar buildings from Market
street to Dock sq. measures 118 feet, making the whole block on the north side 550 feet.

† The town empowered the Selectmen to dispose of the Fort hill lots, May 23, 1805, and
sales were made to Messrs. Wells, Bradbury, Tuck, Howland and others, in the month of
June, 1806.

Common, and Colonnade row on the east, (mostly built in 1811,) presented, the one an elegant uniform range of 24 brick dwellings four stories high, and the other an irregular series of single buildings finished in a varied style, according to the taste of the individual owners. Besides these there were numerous other courts, rows, squares, and places, comprising from six to twelve or more modern brick houses, erected prior to the year 1822, which is the period within which we confine our observations in this chapter.

There were also erected prior to this period several edifices devoted to publick purposes, which are worthy to be noted in this connection.

The Custom-House stands on the north side of Custom-house street, near the head of Central wharf. ' It is 60 feet square and two stories in height exclusive of the basement, which is divided by brick walls and brick arches supporting the different passages above. The lower part of the front is built of stone and the upper part of brick, with a colonnade 60 feet long and 10 ft. wide, supported by 10 stone columns of the Doric order, 14 feet in length. The floor is paved with stone, and a broad flight of stone steps with iron railings leads to the several offices. It is finished with a stone frieze and cornice, and the windows ornamented with marble dressings. The front is crowned by a pediment, on the top of which is a spread eagle. The basement and first story is calculated for the storing of goods, and contains a number of compartments occupied by the house-keeper, and some of the under officers. The upper story contains 6 rooms 20 feet high. in which the business of the office is transacted. The building is remarkably well contrived for the convenience of business, and exhibits a chaste and elegant specimen of architecture. It cost about thirty thousand dollars.'

The Boston Exchange Coffee-House, whose name designates the purposes to which it was appropriated, was the most capacious building and most extensive establishment of its kind in the U. S. The early history of this structure is that of an unsuccessful speculation, which involved individuals in ruin, and seriously injured a large portion of the community. It cost the projector, and through him the publick, upwards of $500,000, and was unfinished when he failed. In other hands it was completed so far as to be tenantable, and went into operation in 1808, two years and a half from the time it was commenced.*

---

* ' This grand edifice was destroyed by fire, on Tuesday, Nov. 3, 1818. It was first discovered near the southwest corner of the attick story, about seven in the evening, and before ten o'clock the whole building was reduced to a melancholy heap of ruins. The most spir-

‘ The E. C. H. was an immense pile of building, 7 stories
in height, with a cellar under the whole, and covering 12,753
square feet of ground. Its shape was an irregular square, or
that of an irregular triangle cut off at the acute angle, measuring 132 feet in its broadest front, and only 94 feet on its
narrowest, from which the line of the sides diverged nearly
equally. The base of the building was of hammered granite
and the basement of white marble.

‘ The front in Congress-street was highly ornamented. Six
marble pilasters, of the Ionic order, upon a rustic basement
supported an architrave and cornice of the same ; and the
whole front, which had an arched door way, was crowned
with a Corinthian pediment.’ On this side there were 48
superb Venetian windows. There was another entrance towards State-street, through an Ionick porch or vestibule. and
this front was ornamented with ten Ionick pilasters, and lighted by 58 windows. There was also an entrance, for the
lodgers in the hotel, on Salter's court. having a passage for
the ingress and egress of carriages. From this door there
was a circular stair-case, elegantly decorated, which led
without interruption to the attick story. There was also a
communication from Devonshire-street, through an adjoining
house.

‘ Upon entering the house, you stood on an interior area 70
feet in length and 40 ft. wide, in the form of a parallelogram,
which was lighted from the top by means of a magnificent
dome, 100 ft. 10 inches in diameter. Around this area was
extended a portico, or rather several porticos, each consisting
of 20 columns, which reached from the ground floor to the
roof, and supported five galleries leading to the different apartments. The height of the top of the dome from the floor was
83 feet. Here was an assemblage of the different orders of
architecture, from the ornamental Doric to the Corinthian,
which produced a very agreeable impression upon the eyes
of the spectator, as he passed from the dome which surmount-

---

ited and judicious efforts could only give a temporary check to the flames, which were has-
tily working their way behind the partition walls and round the cornices, in places beyond
reach. In a very short time, the greater part of the 210 halls, rooms, chambers, &c. exhibited a mass of intense fire seldom witnessed. About 9 o'clock the noble dome came down
with a frightful crash, and, soon after, nearly all the north and part of the south walls, each
more than 80 feet in height, fell, and damaged many of the neighbouring buildings. Several
houses were much damaged, but none wholly burnt out, except the one on Devonshire-street, adjoining the Exchange. On Wednesday morning, the whole isolated front wall of the ruin, 90
feet high by 80 ft. wide, with its marble columns and chimnies, appeared to stand tottering
over the people's heads, and threatened in its fall to overwhelm the buildings opposite, which
stood at the distance of 28 feet only from the wall. But in the course of that and the succeeding day they were levelled, without the least damage to the neighbourhood or to the
thousands of spectators, who were witnesses to this sublime wreck of matter.’

BOSTON EXCHANGE COFFEE HOUSE, BUILT 1808...BURNT 1818.

A Bowen Sc

ed the whole, to the floor upon which he stood. The interior space was as nearly as possible equi-distant from the sides of the structure ; and the apartments, which surrounded it upon the various stories, amounted to about 210.

' The house was divided into two species of rooms ; those which belonged to the hotel, and those which were rented for offices and shops to individuals. The basement story consisted chiefly of an extensive kitchen, private lodging rooms, larder, and the cellars, with some offices that were entered from the street. The principal floor was originally intended for a public Exchange, which design never was executed, as the merchants from long habit, prefer to stand in the street, even during the inclement winter months. A publick reading room, with a very large list of subscribers, was also upon this floor, where the lodgers in the hotel had the privilege ot resorting, and in which was regularly kept a journal of the most interesting occurrences of the times, whether of a political or commercial nature. A convenient Coffee room, a Bar and withdrawing-room for boarders, were also on this floor ; besides various apartments occupied by publick incorporations and private individuals. On the second floor chiefly devoted to the hotel, upon the southern side, there was a dining room sufficiently spacious to admit tables for three hundred persons ; about fourteen other apartments comprised the whole of the second story.

' The third and fourth floors belonged to the tavern. An arched ball-room, finished with great taste in the Corinthian order of architecture, extended through both stories, and was placed immediately over the large dining hall. The other apartments on these floors were either connected with the ball room, or were lodging chambers.

' Upon the northern side of the fifth and sixth floors, a large Masonick Hall was formed from a large number of lodging rooms, which were included in the apartments which we have just enumerated. The other rooms were appropriated for lodging chambers, with the exception of an observatory on the sixth floor, connected with the news room below.*

THE STONE COURT-HOUSE in Court-square, to which for distinction's sake we have given the name of *Johnson Hall* on our plate, (with reference to the memory of Isaac Johnson esq. whom we have mentioned as a chief patron of the first settlers of Boston, *see p.* 37,) was built in 1810. It is described as consisting of an octagon centre, 55 ft. wide, with two wings, 26 by 40 feet, connected by the entrance and passages to the centre. The length of the whole building is 140

---

* For a more particular account of the E.C.H. see *Omnium Gatherum*, Nov. 1809.

ft.   The lower story of the centre is improved by the Register of Deeds, and Clerk of the C. C. P.—the second story by
the County Courts, and the upper by the Common Council of
the city.   The Mayor and Aldermen's room is in the upper
story of the western wing ; under that are the offices of the
Auditor and City Marshal, and on the lower floor the Probate
Office.   In the eastern wing are the offices of the Clerk of the
S. J. Court, rooms for the judges and for the juries, and one
occupied by the Law Library.

BOYLSTON HALL, situated at the corner of Washington and
Boylston st. was so named in honour of Ward Nicholas
Boylston esq.   It was opened in 1810.   It is in length 120 ft.
and in width 50 feet, of three stories, with a deep cellar.   On
the first floor are twelve stalls for the sale of provisions.   The
second is separated by an avenue running lengthwise, on the
sides of which are four spacious rooms.   The third story consists of a hall 100 feet in length with the entire width of the
building.   The central height of the ceiling is 24 feet.   It
contains an orchestra, and two convenient withdrawing-rooms
adjoining.*

PARKMAN'S MARKET, so called, is a large brick building at
the corner of Grove and Cambridge-streets, distinguished by
a cupola.   It was erected by the late Samuel Parkman, esq.
for the purpose of a market to accommodate the population in
that neighbourhood.   It was built in the fall of 1810.

THE CITY MARKET, so called, at the end of Brattle-street
next to Dock-square, is also an extensive brick building, three
stories high.   The lower story and cellars were appropriated
to the sale of provisions.   The Gallery of Fine Arts was kept in
the rooms above.   This building was erected by private citizens in the year 1819: the town had opposed their wish to
be incorporated and their application to the General Court
was in consequence unsuccessful.   The city has since refused
to accept the building as a donation. and a furniture warehouse is now kept in the part formerly occupied as a market.

We have thus endeavoured to give a general view of the
principal local changes, which took place under the town government.   It will be our aim to render that view more definite,
as we proceed to the edifices which have been devoted to fashionable amusements, or to the more sober purposes of religious worship, education, and charity.

---

* ' The proprietors were incorporated Feb. 27, 1809, and the foundation of the building
was commenced in the April following.   The land belonging to the corporation was formerly owned by Sam'l Welles esq. of whose heirs it was purchased by Mr. Jos. C. Dyer,
and by him conveyed to the present proprietors for $20,560.   The cost of the building was
about $39,000, beside the cupola, which was built by subscription.   The clock was a dona
tion of Mr. Boylston

CHAPTER LVII.

This is the place as well as I may guess
Whence even now the tumult of loud mirth
Was rife, and perfect in my listening ear:
a thousand fantasies
Begin to throng into my memory,
Of calling shapes and beckoning shadows dire.

Comus, A Mask.

THE puritan spirit of our ancestors was transfused into the first and second generations which succeeded them : nothing like the fashionable amusements of our day found any countenance with them. A third and fourth generation became by degrees a little more lax in manners and sentiments, and the fifth had so far thrown off restraint as to look upon balls and assemblies without much abhorrence. Probably, the intercourse, which under the royal government was constantly taking place between our people and officers of the army and navy from England, may have tended to introduce this change. ' In the year 1756, *Concert Hall*, a handsome building at the head of Hanover-street, was erected by Mr. Stephen Deblois, a musician, for the purposes of concerts, dancing, and other entertainments. A few years ago the building was enlarged, and improved at a great expense. The front hall is about 60 feet by 30, in the second story, and is justly admired for its correct proportions and the richness of its architecture. It is highly finished in the Corinthian style, with an orchestra, and the walls are ornamented with superb mirrors. In the rear is another hall on the same story, finished in a plainer style, and well calculated for publick entertainments, and large parties.'

FEDERAL-STREET THEATRE was erected about the same time with the Tontine buildings. Strenuous opposition had been made to the introduction of theatrical exhibitions into Boston. The first attempt of the kind, in 1750 (see Minot, Hist. of Mass. i. 142) was followed by a law of the Province prohibiting them under penalties. During the siege the British officers entertained themselves with amusements of a theatrical sort. From that time we discover no traces of a theatre in Boston till 1789, when the newspapers contain intimations of a design to establish one. While the prohibitory laws remained in force, it was unsafe to proceed openly : an effort was made to repeal them in the winter session of 1792, which failed, and the expedient of exhibiting plays under the title of *Moral Lectures,* was therefore adopted in the fall of that year.   The place of performance was ' the New Exhibition Room in Board-alley,' (now Hawley-street.)   A majority of the town had favoured the petition for a repeal of the prohibitory laws, ' as unconstitutional, inexpedient, and absurd,' and the patronage of the Exhibition Room was so liberal, that the plan of erecting a commodious brick building, purposely for a theatre, was easily carried into execution.   A lofty and spacious edifice was built on Federal and Franklin streets, 140 feet long, 61 wide, and 40 feet in height.*   It was opened on the 3d of February, 1794, with the tragedy of Gustavus Vasa Erickson, the deliverer of Sweden.   Mr. Charles Stuart Powell was manager. ' In consequence of a misunderstanding between Mr. P. and

---

* This summer (1825) an addition has been made to the west end of the building, of about 12 feet, and corresponding improvements in the interior.

The following memoranda may be gratifying to the lovers of the Drama.

1797.—Mr. Williamson having failed as Manager of the Federal street Theatre, it was taken by Messrs. Barrett and Harper.   During the season this Theatre was destroyed by fire, on the afternoon of Feb. 2, 1798.   Messrs B. and H. applied for the use of the Haymarket Theatre and were refused.

Oct. 29th, 1798.—The Theatre, having been rebuilt, was opened under the management of Mr. Hodgkinson.   The pieces performed were a Prelude, called ' The First Night's Apology, or All in a Bustle,' ' Wives as they Were,' and the ' Purse.'

April 29th, 1799.—Mr. Hodgkinson, having failed in the Federal street concern, removed the Company to the Haymarket Theatre, which he opened with the ' Stranger,' and ' Plymouth Rock.'   This was the last season Mr. Hodgkinson performed in Boston.

Oct. 1799.—Theatre opened under the management of Mr. G. L. Barrett, with the Comedy of ' Laugh when you Can.'   Mr. B. failed before the season expired.

Oct. 27th, 1800.—Theatre opened under the management of Mr. Whitlock, who, after experiencing a loss of about $4000, relinquished the concern.   This season introduced to a Boston audience the celebrated Mrs. Jones.

Nov. 30th, 1801.—The Theatre was opened under the joint management of Messrs. Powell and Harper.   ' The School for Scandal,' and ' Poor Soldier,' were the entertainments.

Oct. 27th, 1802.—The Theatre opened under the management of Mr. Snelling Powell, with the ' Poor Gentleman,' and ' Purse.'

The Theatre continued under the sole management of Mr. Snelling Powell, until Oct. 1806, when it was opened under the joint management of Messrs. Powell, Bernard, and Dickson who continued it till 1811, when Mr. Bernard relinquished his part, and Messrs. Powell and Dickson retained the management of it for 11 years.   In 1816-17, Mr. D. retired from the stage, and has performed only twice since; in April, 1819, he appeared in the character of Hardy, in the ' Belle's Stratagem,' and Oglow, in ' Timour the Tartar,' for Mrs. Powell's benefit: and in May, 1821, he performed Sir Robert Bramble, in the ' Poor Gentleman,' Will Steady, in the ' Purse,' and Tag, in the ' Spoil'd Child :' this was likewise for the benefit of Mrs. Powell, who was prevented from appearing before her friends on that occasion, in consequence of the decease of Mr. Powell, which occurred the previous month.

Mr. Dickson, although he retired from the stage, continued in the management.   The season of 1817 commenced under the joint direction of Messrs. Powell, Dickson, and Duff: this connexion continued for three years, when Mr. Duff relinquished his share in the concern.

After the lamented decease of Mr. Powell, (April 8, 1821,) the management devolved upon Mr. D. (for Mrs. Powell, who was principally interested, and himself,) aided by

BOSTON THEATRE.

Federal Street.

Entered according to Act of Congress by J. Stimson

the proprietors, Col. J. S. Tyler was appointed to the management, but not succeeding, he relinquished and was succeeded by John Brown Williamson.

In the mean time, the friends of Mr. Powell raised by subscription a sum sufficient to build of wood the *Haymarket Theatre*, which was one of the most spacious and convenient ever erected in America.' It was located near the foot of the Mall, on the spot now occupied by the three-story buildings, next south of Colonnade-row. The house was opened, Dec. 26, 1796, with an Occasional Address, written and delivered by Mr. C. S. Powell, which was followed by the Comedy of the Belle's Stratagem, in which Mr. Dickinson, (since J. A. Dickson, the late Manager,) appeared upon the stage for the first time. The afterpiece was a grand pantomime called Mirza and Lindor, performed by a French Corps du Ballet. It was at this time that Mrs. Darley made her debut as Narcissa in ' Inkle and Yarico.'

Haymarket Theatre was discontinued in the course of a few years, and no other was established until the year 1819, when the entertainments at Washington Gardens were commenced. At first the managers of the Federal-street house were interested in the performances at *the Amphitheatre*, but in a short time the control over it passed into the hands of of several amateurs, and the two institutions became in some sort rivals to each other. The Amphitheatre was so constructed as to answer the purposes of a Circus,† and was on that account better adapted to the performance of such plays as required the introduction of troops and caravans, a happy invention for supplying the defects to which the best selected companies may sometimes be liable, not unknown in Addison's day, but not demanded till recently to please a Boston audience.

THE MUSEUM was commenced in Boston by the exhibition of a few specimens of wax-work, at the American Coffee-house, opposite the Bunch-of-Grapes in State-street. The proprie-

---

Mr. Kilner, as Acting Manager ; this continued until the expiration of their lease from the proprietors, in May, 1824.

The next season, in Sept. 1824, Messrs. Kilner and Finn undertook the management, for themselves and Mrs. Powell, on a lease of three years.

It is a fact, worthy of record, and highly creditable to the Managers, that, from the time of Mr. Powell's undertaking the management, until the present date, there never has been an instance known of a performer's salary, a tradesman's bill, or any other demand against the Theatre being refused payment. This punctuality has given a respectability and credit to the establishment, that is not surpassed by any other in this country or in England.

† Messrs. Pepin and Breschard had established a regular Circus in Charlestown in 1809 : and the Circus at the Washington Gardens has been occasionally used for that specifick object. There was also a Circus by Lailson in 1796, and ten years before that, the Selectmen had granted a licence for the exhibition of feats of horsemanship.

tor was Mr. Daniel Bowen, whose collection received very
handsome notice in the papers of June, 1791. It was soon
removed to ' the hall over the New School-house near the
Rev. Mr. West's meeting :' additions of natural and artificial
curiosities, paintings, &c. were constantly made to the collection till 1795, when it assumed the name of *Columbian Museum*,
and was established ' at the head of the Mall [on the corner
of Bromfield's lane], in the longest and perhaps the most elegant hall in the United States.' This establishment rose in
value and in publick estimation, and became a fashionable resort, till Jan. 15, 1803, when it was destroyed by fire.

The liberality of the publick and the aid of private friends
enabled Mr. Bowen to commence another museum, at the
corner of Milk and Oliver streets, in the succeeding May. In
1806, Mr. B. in connexion with Mr. Wm. M. S. Doyle erected a costly brick edifice, five stories high, on the lot north of
the Chapel burial ground, and removed the collection, which
had now become splendid, to that place, which was opened
for company, on Thanksgiving evening, Nov. 27th. Here
they were doomed again to suffer disappointment. On the
morning of Jan. 16, 1807, a fire was discovered in the hall
over the Museum, and in a very short time all its valuable
contents were consumed.* The proprietors, however, were
not wholly disheartened. With some encouragement from
the publick they rebuilt the house to the height of two stories,
and opened it on the 2d of June, 1807. Mr. B. some time after removed from Boston, and Mr. Doyle continued the sole
manager, until the collection was sold to the proprietors of
the New England Museum, (Jan. 1, 1825.)

The Boston Museum was advertised as ' just opened,' by
Ph. Woods, at the large five-story building over No. 6, north
side of the market, Feb. 28, 1804. A considerable number
of interesting curiosities were collected in this Museum, but it
never became so fashionable a place of resort as the Columbian. It was removed for a short time to a building on the
west side of Dock-square, but was returned to its original
stand, where it was sold at auction in the summer of 1822.
Chief of the articles were transferred to the New England
Museum.

A collection called the Washington Museum was for a
short time exhibited here in 1804.

The New York Museum, was opened in Boylston Hall, in
1812. This latter was the commencement of the New England,
which is now the only establishment of the kind in Boston.

---

* This building was 103 feet long, and 34 ft. wide. The height was 62 feet from the
basement floor to the top of the observatory, which was surmounted by a figure of Minerva.

It is situated on Court street, occupying the chambers over several stores, extending from Market to Brattle street. The collection is the most extensive ever brought together here, both in point of excellence and variety. Mr. E. A. Greenwood has had the superintendance of it, since it assumed its present appellation, under which it was opened, July 4, 1818. Mr. Mix's New Haven Museum was added to it, in 1821.

It is not foreign from our purpose to state, that this museum contains, besides its curiosities of a general character, a plan of Boston, engraved by Price in 1743 ; likenesses of the following persons ,whose names occur in this book : viz. Gov. Winthrop, Endicot, Leverett, Bradstreet (from the paintings in the State-house), Hancock, S. Adams, Bowdoin, Gen. Warren, Franklin, Gen. Ward, R. T. Paine, John Adams, J. Q. Adams,—and of the following distinguished citizens ; Rev.Drs. Cooper, Stillman, Lathrop. Baldwin, Holley, and Griffin,— Messrs. Ballou, Buckminster, Huntington, Frothingham, Winchell, and Dean ; Dr. Jeffries, Benjamin Austin, Isaiah Thomas ; William Cooper, Mr. John Tileston, Miss Hannah Adams, together with prints of many other eminent persons.

CHAPTER LVIII.

How all religions should enjoy their liberty, justice its due regularity, civil cohabitation moral honesty, in one and the same jurisdiction, is beyond the artique of my comprehension.—*Simple Cobler*, A. D. 1647.

THE churches of Boston had been thrown into great confusion by the events of the war. Five of their houses of worship had been transformed into barracks or hospitals, or in some way* appropriated to the use of the British troops. All their pastors who were friendly to the American cause (except Dr. Samuel Mather and Dr. Andrew Eliot) had deemed it prudent to leave the town during the siege. The clergymen of the three Episcopal churches fled with Gen. Howe on the memorable 17th of March, 1776, and Dr. Byles of Hollisstreet was dismissed, in 1777, by his people, on account of his supposed predilection for the royal cause. Mr. Moorhead's church was vacant, and Mr. Croswell's meeting-house was

----

* *The desecration* of the Old South excited universal indignation. To fit it for the purposes of a circus for the dragoons, 'every moveable part within the walls (except the sounding board over the pulpit, and the east gallery, which was left to accommodate spectators) was taken down, pillars, pews, galleries, and pulpit. About 1 and a half or 2 feet of earth was spread upon the floor, for the horses to exercise upon.'

untenantable during the winter season. The Old North, we know, had been entirely destroyed. and Dr. Ebenezer Pemberton, the pastor of the New Brick, had deceased, Sept. 15, 1777.

The first change consequent on this state of things was the union of the Old North and New Brick churches. under the name of the Second Church. This event took place June 27, 1779 ; Rev. John Lathrop then became pastor of both societies.

The Old South church were accommodated in King's chapel, until they were ready to remove to their own house.* At length the remaining proprietors of the Chapel determined to restore their former mode of worship, and invited Rev. James Freeman to perform divine services in their desk. Mr. F. accepted their invitation, and commenced Reader, Oct. 20, 1782. The society adopted the Unitarian liturgy, altered from the common prayer book of the Church of England, after the plan of Dr. Samuel Clarke. On Lord's-day, Nov. 18, 1787. after evening service, Mr. Freeman was ordained as Rector, Priest, &c. by the wardens, vestry, proprietors, and congregation of the Chapel, ' by virtue of the third article in the declaration of rights,' which provides that religious societies shall at all times have the exclusive right of electing their publick teachers. A minority protested against this measure, because the new proprietors had 'introduced a liturgy different from any now used in the Episcopal churches in the United States, and articles of faith which,' say they, ' in our opinion, are unscriptural and heretical.' Another ' protest or excommunication' was also issued on the same subject, by the rectors of Episcopal churches in Boston, Salem, Marblehead, Newburyport, and Portsmouth, who pronounced the mode of ordination ' diametrically opposite to every principle adopted in any Episcopal church.'† The society, however, has pursued the course of its own choosing, and though discountenanced by the Episcopal churches, its rectors hold ministerial intercourse with the members of the Boston Association.

The origin of the denomination of Universalists in America was in the year 1770. Mr. John Murray commenced preaching near New York ; visited Philadelphia, and several parts of New Jersey ; came in 1773 to Newport and thence to Boston, where he arrived on the 26th of October. He delivered his first discourse on the 30th, in the hall over the Factory. In September 1774, Mr. Murray made another visit, and preached sometimes at a private house, sometimes in Faneuil-hall, at the

* From Nov. 9, 1777, to Feb. 23, 1783.
† See Centinel, Nov. 24, 1787, and Jan. 2, 1788.

Factory, or at Masons'-hall, and at length was admitted into Mr. Croswell's pulpit, not, however, without strenuous opposition from Mr. C. A society was gradually gathered under the preaching of Mr. Murray and Mr. Adam Streeter, ' and other preachers of the universal gospel of salvation to all mankind ;' and on the 29th of Dec. 1785, Messrs. Shippie Townsend, James Prentiss, Jona. Stoddard, John Page, and Josiah Snelling, (' being a committee appointed by a Christian congregation commonly called Universalists, now meeting in the said house') purchased the meeting-house then recently vacated by the death of Dr. Sam'l Mather. Mr. Murray was installed over this society, Oct. 24. 1793. The solemnities of the occasion were introduced by Dea. Oliver W.Lane, who addressed the brethren of the church and congregation. Mr. M. prayed. Then Dea. L. asked of each party a publick recognition of their acceptance of each other as pastor and people, which being signified, the deacon proceeded thus : ' I therefore, in the name and behalf of this church and congregation, supported by the constitution of this commonwealth, declare you, John Murray, to be the pastor and teacher of this first Universal church in Boston.' Dea. L. then presented a bible to Mr. M. with the pledge that, so long as he continued to preach the gospel as therein delineated, he should be considered their pastor and teacher, and no longer ; and concluded with the charge of Paul to Timothy, usually introduced on such occasions. Mr. M. made an affectionate reply ; then followed singing accompanied by the organ. Mr. Murray gave a sermon from 1 Cor. ix. 16. *Woe is unto me if I preach not the gospel*, and the services were concluded with an anthem.

The society, known as the Presbyterian church, which had been under the pastoral care of Rev. Robert Annan, from 1783 to 1786, embraced the Congregational order, and thus became the Twelfth Congregational church. We have discovered no record of this fact, but it probably was made known in a formal manner on the day of the installation of their first pastor, Rev. Jeremy Belknap, April, 4, 1787, concerning which we find the following account. ' After a large and respectable council of churches, assembled on the occasion, had taken the steps usually previous to such solemnity, they proceeded to the meeting house. An anthem excellently performed, began the service. Rev. Mr. Eckley then made the first prayer : Rev. Mr. McClintock of Greenland, (N. H.) delivered a sermon well adapted to the occasion : Rev. Dr. Lathrop made the installation prayer: Rev. Mr. Jackson or Brookline gave the charge ; Rev. Mr. Eliot prayed after it, and Rev. Mr. Thacher gave the right hand of fellowship, and another anthem concluded the service.'

The first Roman Catholick congregation was assembled in Boston, in the year 1784, from the few French and Irish then resident here, by the Abbe La Poitrie, a chaplain in the French navy. In the year 1788 they obtained possession of the old French church in School street, which had become vacant on the death of Mr. Croswell : mass was first performed in it Nov. 2, 1788. M. La Poitrie was succeeded by M. Louis de Rousselet, and Mr. John Thayer, a native of Boston, who had renounced the Protestant faith and taken orders under the Romish see, as Catholick Missionary of Boston. Mr. T. began his mission here, June 10th, 1790, and exhibited great zeal in the cause he had espoused.* The Rt. Rev. Bp. Carroll (late of Baltimore) visited Boston, in May, 1791, and administered confirmation to a number who had received baptism here. In 1792, the Rev. Dr. Francis A. Matignon arrived in Boston, and by his prudence, judgment, and conciliating disposition, considerably softened and removed the prejudices which had impeded the advancement and progress of the Roman Catholick religion. Dr. Matignon was joined by the Rev. John Cheverus, (afterwards R.C. Bishop of this city and at present Bishop of Montauban,) in the year 1796. These two gentlemen made applications to the Protestants, who generously contributed ; a lot was purchased in Franklin Place, and the Roman Catholick church, a neat and well proportioned edifice, was dedicated to the worship of God, under the name of " The Church of the Holy Cross," by the late Bishop Carroll, on the 29th day of September, 1803.†— Under Dr. Matignon and Bp. Cheverus the congregation increased in numbers and respectability, by accessions not only from the foreign population of the town, but from native citizens. Dr. Matignon was removed by death, and the bishop has been called to his native country to the enjoyment of higher honours in the church. The departure of both was deeply lamented, not only by catholicks, but by all who knew them either personally or by character.

The origin of the Methodist Society in Boston was attended with some circumstances of discouragement. Rev.Wm.Black, from Halifax, was the first minister of that denomination who preached here. He arrived in October, 1784, and was allowed to appear in the pulpit of the Second Baptist church. He was here but a short time, yet many persons became con-

---

* Mass. His. Col. 1. iii. 264. Col. Centinel, Nov. 24, 1790—Jan. 26, June 24, July 30. 1791.

† The Rev. Mr. Thayer, by a disposition in his will, bequeathed money for the erection of an Ursuline Convent, which has been since erected contiguous to the Church, and in which the female children of the R. Catholick communion are educated.

verted under his preaching : most of them joined the Baptist churches. In 1790, Rev. Jesse Lee visited Boston and the vicinity : he preached, as Whitfield had done before him, on the Common. A considerable number adopted his sentiments, and met together for worship at the house of Samuel Burrill, in Sheafe-street, till June 1792,* when they obtained the use of the North School-house. At that time, Mr. Jeremiah Cosden was their preacher. In August, 1792, twelve persons ' were joined into a society, under the denomination of the Methodist Episcopal church.' After the old school-house was pulled down, this society met once at the Green Dragon : thence they removed to Mr. Conner's in Ship-street, and thence to Mr. John Ruddock's house, opposite Clark's (since Ballard & Hartt's) ship-yard, in the same street ; a room in this last house was formally dedicated Aug. 17, 1793. Finding themselves very unpleasantly situated for the want of a commodious place for their meetings. the society made an effort to obtain subscriptions towards a proper house of worship. On the 5th of Sept. 1795, Messrs. Sam. Burrill, Elijah Lewis, Uriah Tufts, Joseph Snelling, Sam'l Mills, and Abraham Ingersoll, as a committee of the society, purchased a lot of land in Methodist alley (now so called), and a house was built thereon, measuring 46 feet by 36, and 22 ft. post. It was first occupied and dedicated May 15, 1796 ; Rev. Geo. Pickering being the officiating clergyman. The church at that time consisted of 50 members.

In the year 1803, a religious society was commenced, of the denomination of Freewill Baptists. It was at first composed of persons who seceded from the other Baptist churches in town, and adhered to the doctrines at that time promulgated by Messrs. Thomas Jones and Elias Smith. They have since been known under the distinctive appellation of CHRISTians. Their first meetings were held in a large wooden building in Friend-street, then adjoining the Mill-pond. They have since occupied the hall in Bedford-street, and now (Oct. 1825) have a brick meeting-house erecting at the corner of Summer and Sea streets. They have had a number of preachers, who have continued with them a short time. " When they have no Elders to preach, they often exhort each other, both male and female. The same privilege is granted to all pious people, when assembled with them, of whatever denomination they may be. They hold to the six principles of the doctrine

---

* *Records of the Society.*—In Selectmen's minutes, Sept. 16, 1785, permission is granted to the hearers of Mr. William Black to occupy the North Grammar School until further order. The new School-house was finished, Oct. 1792.

of Christ, viz. ' Repentance from dead works, faith towards God, of baptisms, of laying on of hands, of resurrection of the dead, and of eternal judgment : urging frequently upon their hearers the necessity of the two first principles above in order for sinners to become ' born again,' or become ' new creatures,' or have the ' divine nature,' or ' holiness,' without which no man shall see the Lord. The safety of those who ' endure to the end,' is firmly believed by them, and that none but such shall have eternal life."

In the year 1805, a church was gathered from among the coloured people of this town, which when formed was denominated the African Baptist church. Their number at first was twenty, most of whom were fruits of the ministry of Rev. Thomas Paul, an ordained clergyman of their own colour, who commenced preaching in Franklin Hall, an apartment in the school-house in Nassau street. The year after this church was formed, they began to make exertions towards building them a place of worship. They chose a committee to make collections, among whom was Cato Gardiner, a native of Africa, who had long been one of Dr. Stillman's respectable members. At his importunity Dr. Stillman drew a subscription paper, which Cato circulated in different places, and obtained about 1500 dollars. Others of the church made collections to a considerable amount, and having received encouragement to go forward in their design, they chose a committee of white men to superintend the building, which was finished and dedicated, Dec. 4, 1806. Mr. Paul was installed at the same time. Rev. Drs. Stillman and Baldwin, Mr. Grafton [of Newton,] Mr. Briggs [of Randolph,] Mr. Stone [of New Boston, N. H.] all of the Baptist denomination, officiated on the occasion. This house is built of brick forty feet by forty-eight, three stories high. The lower story is fitted up for a school-room for coloured children, and has been occupied for that purpose from the time it was finished. The two upper stories are well finished with pews, pulpit, galleries, &c. The lot is small, and with the house cost 8,000 dollars.

In the year 1806, the Methodist society, on the 3d of March, ' resolved that it was expedient to build another chapel for the worship of Almighty God.' On the 15th of April, the corner stone of the house in Bromfield's lane was laid by Rev. Peter Jayne, and it was completed and dedicated on the 19th of November following. Rev. Samuel Merwin preached on the occasion. This chapel is built of brick, its dimensions are 84 by 54 ft. Near the N. E. corner, in the middle course of hammered stone, in the foundation, is a block taken from the celebrated rock on which our forefathers landed at Plymouth.

Proposals for building another Baptist meeting-house were issued in August, 1806. A lot of land had been previously procured on Charles-street, part of which was given by the Mount Vernon Company, and the greater part purchased by the subscribers to the undertaking. Five members from the First, and nineteen from the Second Baptist church, united on the 5th of Aug. 1807, and were regularly constituted ' as a separate church of Christ, by the name of the Third Baptist church in Boston.' On the same day the house was dedicated. Rev. Dr. Baldwin preached on the occasion. On the 5th of October, Rev. Caleb Blood accepted the office of pastor. The sentiments of this church are expressed in the subjoined ' declaration of their views of divine truth.'*

The formation of *Park-Street Church* was first proposed in the latter part of the year 1808, when a subscription was opened for the erection of a place of publick worship. On the 6th of Feb. 1809, ten of the subscribers had a meeting, and it was resolved to proceed in the important undertaking. Articles of faith and a church covenant were adopted, and a council called to assist in forming the church. The number of persons who first associated (Feb. 27) was twenty-six, of

---

* *Third Baptist church Articles of faith.*

We believe the Holy Bible was written by men divinely inspired, and is a perfect rule of faith and practice ; and that, among others, it teaches the following all important truths : I. The existence of one only living and true God, infinite in every natural and moral perfection. II. That he has made himself known to his people under the name of the Father, and of the Son, and of the Holy Ghost, the same in essence, and equal in every divine perfection. III. That man was created holy; but by wilfully violating the law of his Maker, he fell from that state, and from all communion with God ; and as, by divine appointment, Adam was the representative of all his posterity, we in him became wholly defiled, and dead in trespasses and sins : So that by nature we are indisposed to all good, and inclined to all evil, and are children of wrath, and subjects of death, and of all other miseries, temporal, spiritual and eternal. IV. That the only way of salvation from this state of guilt and condemnation is through the righteousness and atonement of Jesus Christ, who, as the Good Shepherd, laid down his life for his sheep ; and that those only, who receive the gift of repentance, and faith in him, will be finally saved by his atonement. V. That all who ever have been, or will be, brought to repentance, and faith in the gospel, were chosen in Christ to salvation before the foundation of the world ; and that in consequence of the eternal love of God to them, through the atonement, the Holy Ghost is sent to effect the work of regeneration in their hearts, without which regenerating influence, none would ever repent or believe. VI. That nothing can separate true believers from the love of God, but they will be kept by his power, through faith, unto salvation. VII. That the only proper subjects of the ordinances of baptism and the Lord's Supper are professed believers ; and that baptism is properly adminstered only by immersion, and is, by scriptural example, a pre-requisite to communion at the Lord's table. VIII. That there will be a resurrection, both of the just and unjust ; and that Christ will come a second time to judge both the quick and the dead ; when those who die impenitent, and unreconciled to God, will be sentenced to endless misery, as the just desert of their sins ; and those who have been renewed by grace, and washed their robes in the blood of the Lamb, will be completely delivered from the dominion of sin, and admitted into the holy and heavenly Jerusalem, with songs and everlasting joy. So shall they be ever with the Lord.

whom 21 were dismissed from other churches, and 5 received
by the council on profession of faith. The corner-stone of
their meeting-house was laid on the first of May. A plate,
bearing the following inscription, was deposited in the south-
east corner : sc. " *Jesus Christ the chief corner stone, in whom
all the building, fitly framed together, groweth unto an holy
temple in the Lord. This church formed February 27th, and
this foundation laid May 1st*, 1809." The house was dedicated to the service of God, Jan. 10, 1810. Rev. Edward Dorr
Griffin, D. D. (then Bartlett Professor of Pulpit Eloquence at
Andover) preached on the occasion.

There had been hopes with the founders of this church
that they should be able to obtain the services of Dr. Henry
Kollock of Savannah, but they were disappointed. The
church continued without a settled pastor until July 31, 1811,
when Dr. Griffin, (who had constantly supplied their pulpit,)
was installed over them.

This church professes a ' decided attachment to that system of the Christian religion which is distinguishingly denominated Evangelical, more particularly to those doctrines
which in a proper sense are styled the doctrines of
grace,' and adopts the Congregational form of government, as
contained in the Cambridge Platform framed by the synod of
sixteen hundred and forty-eight.

The erection of a meeting-house for the *Second Society of
Universalists* was proposed ' at a meeting of a number of members of the First Universal Society,' holden on Thursday,
November 14, 1816. Preparatory measures were adopted,
and they were incorporated Dec. 13, 1816, ' by the name of
the Second Society of Universalists in the town of Boston.'*
On Monday morning, May 19, 1817, the corner-stone of the

---

* A church was formed in this society, Dec. 3, 1817. Their *Uniting Compact* is as follows:

Uniting Compact of the Second Universalist church in Boston.

1st. Being persuaded of the truth of the gospel of the grace of God, and feeling truly
grateful for such a revelation of divine favour, we, whose names are undersigned, with a
view to promote the cause of the Redeemer, to edify and comfort each other, and in obedience to the command of Christ, who directs us to ' let our light shine before men,' do hereby
unite in the solemn and important relation of a Christian church. 2d. We mutually agree
to celebrate the unspeakably glorious event of the death and resurrection of Jesus, in the
sacrament of the Lord's supper, as often as a majority of the chh. may think proper. 3d.
Claiming no right to fix a creed, which might in any way impede our progress in the grace
and knowledge of our L.J.C. or operate as a mean to prevent any sincere lover of truth
from uniting with us in the Christian communion and fellowship, we accept no other rule
of faith, practice, or discipline than the S. Scriptures. 4th. Disclaiming any right to examine or judge another's faith, and adhering to the Apostle's directions to ' let a man examine himself, and so let him eat of that bread and drink of that cup,' we consider the table
of the Lord free for the communion of all, whose moral conduct would not bring a reproach.
5th. We furthermore mutually agree to pay all expenses which may be deemed necessary
according to any distribution which a majority may see fit to make.

new meeting-house, in School-street, was laid and a silver plate deposited, being the gift of Dr. David Townsend, bearing the following inscription : " *The Second Universal church, devoted to the worship of the True God, Jesus Christ being the chief corner-stone. May 19th, 1817.*" This house is a plain building of brick, without a steeple, 75 ft. long and 67 broad. The dedication took place on Thursday, Oct. 16th : Rev. Thomas Jones, of Gloucester, preached on the occasion. October 21st, Rev. Hosea Ballou was unanimously invited to the ministry over this society, and his installation took place on Christmas-day, Dec. 25th 1817. Rev. Paul Dean preached from John xx. 24, and gave the fellowship of the churches ; Rev. Edw. Turner, of Charlestown, made the installation prayer and gave the charge ; and Rev. Mr. Flagg, of Salem, made the concluding prayer.

The services of the Protestant Episcopal church were celebrated, for the first time, in that part of the town called South Boston, on Sunday, March 31, 1816. For more than two years the congregation met in a school-house, and services were conducted by different clergymen and lay-readers. *St. Matthew's church* was consecrated on the 24th of June, 1818, by the Right Rev. Dr. Griswold, Bishop of the Eastern diocese. It is situated on Broad-way, and is a neat and commodious brick building. The expences of its erection were chiefly defrayed by benevolent members of Trinity and Christ churches, with a view to the future wants of that section of the city. A service of plate for the use of the altar was presented by the ladies of Christ church, and the pulpit, desk, and chancel were furnished with appropriate dressings by the ladies of Trinity church. The late Mrs. Elizabeth Bowdoin Winthrop was a most liberal benefactor. Religious services were maintained in this church, by occasional supplies, but it was not till June, 1824, that the parish enjoyed the stated labours of a minister in full orders, when the Rev. John L. Blake became Rector. The wardens are Messrs. Abraham Gould and Robert P. Williams.

In August, 1818, there was a church formed that adopts the sentiments of Baron Emanuel Swedenborg. They first associated on Saturday, the 15th of August, and on the next day held a publick meeting at Boylston Hall. The number of their first associates was eleven, six of whom were gentlemen, and five ladies. Their first preacher was Mr. Samuel Worcester : he is not ordained, but administers the sacrament of baptism. The society was incorporated, Feb. 11, 1823, by the name of ' *the Boston Society of the New Jerusalem.*' They have held meetings at different periods at Boylston Hall, Bedford st. hall, and the Pantheon. Their present place of worship is in Pantheon Hall.

44

ESSEX-STREET CHURCH was organized on the 27th of January, 1819. It was gathered under the preaching of the Rev. James Sabine, who came to Boston in July, 1818, from St. John's, Newfoundland, where he had been settled about two years over a society, which became reduced in numbers, and in the means of giving him support, after the desolating fires that occurred at that place in November. 1817. Upon his arrival in Boston, Mr. Sabine commenced preaching in Boylston hall, and when the church was organized, he was publickly recognized as its pastor. Seventeen members, of whom 10 were brethren, constituted the church. The congregation increasing, arrangements were made for building a meeting-house in Essex st. The corner-stone was laid, June 26, 1819, and the new house was dedicated, on the 15th of December.*

The members of the Romish communion at South Boston are accommodated in a neat Gothick church, which bears the name of *St. Augustine's Chapel.* A tablet wrought into the front of the building bears the following inscription : " *Erected by the Catholic Congregation of Boston, with the approbation and assistance of Right Reverend Bishop Cheverus, A.D.* 1819."

ST. PAUL'S CHURCH was proposed to be erected by a subscription which was commenced in March, 1819. The corner-stone was laid, Sept. 4th, with appropriate solemnities. The church was consecrated, June 30, 1820, by the Rt. Rev. Bp. Alex. Viets Griswold, bishop of the Eastern diocese, assisted by the Rt. Rev. Bp. Thos. C. Brownell, of Connecticut, with many of the clergy. Dr. Samuel Farmar Jarvis was instituted rector, Friday, July 7, 1820.

This edifice is situated on Common st. between Winter and West streets, and fronts towards the Common. It is built of fine gray granite, and is an imitation, so far as respects the architecture, of a Grecian model of the Ionick order. The body of the church is about 112 ft. long by 72 ft. wide, and 40 ft. high from the platform to the top of the cornice. The portico projects about 14 feet, and has six Ionick columns, 3 ft. 5 in. diameter, and 32 ft. high, of Potomac sandstone, laid in courses. The base of the building rises four

---

* In the course of two years, some difficulties arose, which resulted in a vote, March 6, 1822, ' that this chh. think it necessary to withdraw from the house of worship in Essex st. and that after this date they do meet for worship and communion in Boylston hall.' Accordingly on the following sabbath they assembled there.

This body retained the name of Essex st. church, until Nov. 26, 1823, when they were acknowledged and received by the Londonderry Presbytery, and organized into their body. Thus they became the second Presbyterian church in Boston, (Mr. Moorhead's having been the first,) but they are ' known by the name of the *First Presbyterian church in the City of Boston.*'

feet, and there is a flight of steps to the portico, extending the whole width of the front. The interior is lighted by ten long windows, and has a chancel and organ gallery. The ceiling is a cylindrical vault, with pannels which span the whole width of the church. Beneath the principal floor, there are commodious and well constructed tombs, secured in a manner to obviate any objection which fear, or experience, or observation may have suggested.*

Under the patronage and influence of benevolent individuals associated as a society for the moral and religious instruction of the poor, a MEETING FOR SEAMEN was opened at the hall on Central wharf, on Lord's day, Aug. 9, 1818 : and through the exertions of the same body, another meeting was established at Parkman's market, Jan. 31, 1819. At these places, publick worship was regularly maintained, half a day at each ; and besides the particular classes, for which the meetings were instituted, it was found that a considerable number of persons assembled, whose circumstances rendered their attendance at the more frequented houses of worship inconvenient. Further exertions were therefore made for their accommodation, and a house has been erected on the west side of Butolph-street, known by the name of the MISSION HOUSE. It was dedicated, July 5, 1821, and a church, consisting of 17 members, was constituted, Dec. 30, 1823. The Rev. Dr. William Jenks officiates as their minister.

This was the forty-ninth house, built for the worship of God in Boston. Since the organization of the city government, several other religious societies have been formed, of which we shall speak in a subsequent chapter.

---

* The interior of *St. Paul's* is remarkable for its simplicity and beauty, and the materials of which the building has been constructed give it an intrinsick value and an effect, which have not been produced by any imitations of the classick models, that have been attempted of bricks and plaster in other cities. The erection of this church may be considered the commencement of an era in the art, in Boston ; and although from its situation it is somewhat obscured, the beauties it displays have already had a sensible influence on taste in architecture : and those who are aware of the importance of this art, in giving form to our city, will consider themselves under the highest obligations to the disinterested and high-minded individuals of the committee, by whom this church has been designed and erected, and will not withhold the meed of praise from the architect and artists, who supriented the construction of it.

CHAPTER LIX.

" Whate'er the humanizing Muses teach ;
The godlike wisdom of the temper'd breast ;
Progressive truth ; the patient force of thought ;
Investigation calm, whose silent powers
Command the world ;—these all are theirs."

THE earliest trace of our system of free schools is to be found on the Boston records, under date of April 13, 1635, where it is stated to have been ' agreed upon that our brother Philemon Purmont shall be intreated to become schoolmaster, for the teaching and nurturing of children with us.' Whether Mr. P. consented to serve the town, does not appear :* but another person, Mr. Daniel Maude, was ' also chosen' to the office of ' free-school master' in August, 1636.

The first provision for the support of schools seems to have been made by voluntary contribution. There is a subscription recorded, on the last leaf of the oldest volume of town records, which, though the first line is illegible, is plainly discerned to be ' *towards the maintenance of — free Schoolmaster.*' It is headed by ' the Gov. Mr. Henry Vane, Esq.' who puts down £10, as do also the Dep. Gov. Mr. John Winthrop, and Mr. Richard Bellingham. Forty-two other persons subscribe according to their ability, some 30s. and some as low as 4s. making in all about the sum of forty pounds. In 1641, the income from Deer Island was appropriated for the school's use ; and in other years the rents of that and other islands were devoted to the same purpose. Under date of 1645, Gov. Winthrop notes in his Journal, that ' divers free schools were erected,' and observes that, at Boston, they made an order to allow forever £50 per ann. for the master, and a house,— and £30 to an usher, who should also teach to read, write, and cipher—and the charge was to be defrayed ' by yearly contribution, either by voluntary allowance or by rate of such as refused.'

Mr. Maude was a minister, and soon removed to Dover, N. H. His successors in the school were probably a Mr. Woodbridge (mentioned Dec. 2, 1644.) and Mr. Robert Woodmansey, whose name appears on the records, April 11, 1650. On the 12th of March, 1666, Mr. Daniel Henchman was employ-

---

* *First Church rec.* Jan. 6, 1639, Philemon Purmont was dismissed to join Mr. Wheelwright and others at Piscataqua.

ed ' to assist Mr. Woodmansey in the grammar school and teach children to write.' Mr. Woodmansey was succeeded by Mr. Benjamin Thomson, 'a man of great learning and wit, well acquainted with the Roman and Greek writers, and a good poet.' He was chosen Aug. 26, 1667, to officiate for one year, and appears to have continued in the service of the town, together with Mr. Henchman, until Jan. 3, 1671, when he resigned, and Mr. Ezekiel Cheever took the principal charge of the school. Mr. C. had been a distinguished instructer, in various parts of New England, and his reputation was not diminished by his career in this place : under him the Grammar-school of Boston attained the rank of ' the principal school of the British colonies, if not in all America.'

Several persons had been licensed to keep private schools ' to teach children to write and keep accounts ;' but there is no reason to suppose that there had been more than one publick school, prior to 1684. In April, 1683, the town voted to provide two schools, and to allow £25 per ann. for the support of each, with the understanding ' that such persons as send their children to the school, that are able, should pay something to the master for his better encouragement.' And, Nov. 22, 1684, ' Dea. Henry Allen and Capt. Frarye made a return, that, ' according to a former order they had agreed with John Cole to keep a free school, to teach the children of the town to read and write, for one year from the first of this instant November, for which the town is to pay him £10 in money, and £20 in country pay as money, or at money price.' This was the first of the *free writing schools*, and Mr. Cole seems to have been as much respected and beloved in his department, as Mr. Cheever was in his.

The original Latin school-house was located on the North side of School-street, at the south-east corner of the Chapel burying-ground, nearly opposite to the present school-house. One of the writing schools was kept in Court-street, and the other, we suppose, at the north part of the town.*

A Grammar school was opened at the North end, in 1713, agreeably to a vote of March 11, 1712. It was located on Bennet-street, on the lot now occupied by the Eliot school,

---

* In the Hutchinson MSS. we find the following order of Gov. Andros, dated Boston, the 24th of May, 1687. " *By his Ex.'s command. Upon the petition of Joshua Natstock, and recommendation of many of the inh. of the N. part of the town of B. I do hereby appoint the said Joshua to be master of the publick school there, and to have and enjoy such profits and benefits and advantages as have been heretofore paid and allowed to his predecessors.*" It was a favourite object with Randolph to have all the schools supplied with masters of the persuasion of the Church of England. When Andros's power ceased, the town lost no time in voting, (Records, June 24, 1689,) that the custom and practice of managing free schools be restored and continued.

which the town purchased of Mrs. Susanna Love. The house was built by Capt. Thos. Hutchinson (father of Gov. Hutchinson,) at his own charge. Recompense Wadsworth was the first master.

A free writing-school was built, in 1718, on the same lot, on Love-lane, by Thos. and Edw. Hutchinson, as executors of the will of Foster Hutchinson, and went into operation the next year. Mr. Jeremiah Condy was appointed master.

In 1717, a south writing-school was established, and located ' on the Common over against Mr. Wainwright's,' that is, near the corner of West and Common streets. The first master's name appears to have been Amos Angier.

These two Grammar and three Writing Schools were the only publick schools in Boston, before the Revolution. They were under the inspection of the selectmen and ' a certain number of gentlemen of liberal education, together with some of the reverend ministers,' whose custom it was to make an annual report to the town of the state of the schools. In 1742, when the population of the town was 16,382, there were reported (as present June 23, 1741,)

At the South Writing-school	73	At the South Latin-school	94
Queen-st.	73	North	65
North	230	Total	—535

At the visitation, July 1, 1772, there were present 823 scholars. During the siege, the town schools were suspended : a few children attended the instructions of Mr. Elias Dupee, who remained in Boston, and gratuitously devoted himself to his employment of a teacher, in which he took peculiar delight. November 8, 1776, there was a vote of the town, that the schools should be opened under the direction of the selectmen ; and we soon find them all in successful operation. In March, 1785, a writing school, to be located farther south than that in the Common, was established, and Mr. Samuel Cheney was formally inducted into the office of master, on the 26th of April following. He was charged to hear the children read the scriptures occasionally, and teach them the catechism once a week, besides instructing them in writing and arithmetick. The number of children reported present, May 23, 1785, was only 564 : both the Latin schools having together but 64 pupils ; Queen st. and the North W. each, 150 ; Common, 119 ; Cheney's, 81. At this time the rule was adopted, that no children be admitted to the writing schools, under seven years of age.

The concerns of the schools were conducted in the usual train until the year 1789. On the 23d of Sept. that year, a committee was appointed, of one from each ward, to draft a new system of education. Their report, which was made and accepted, Oct. 16th, recommended the plan, which has since been pursued and improved. They proposed to continue but one (the south) Latin Grammar school, and to establish three reading schools, in apartments separate from the three writing schools. Candidates for admission were required to be 7 years of age, ' having previously received the instruction usual at women's schools.' Children of both sexes were to be admitted, boys for the year round, and girls from April to October, ' to be taught to spell, accent, and read prose and verse, and also to be instructed in English grammar and composition.' A committee of twelve, was proposed to be chosen annually ; who, in conjunction with the selectmen, should exercise all the powers which the laws of the state or votes of the town had delegated to selectmen or school committees. The execution of the system was immediately commenced, by the appointment of the *First School Committee*, Oct. 20, 1789.

The elements of geography and astronomy were soon added to the studies of the English grammar schools ; and the increase of population and the rising reputation of these seminaries in a little time demanded more ample accommodations for the numerous pupils who resorted to them. In 1790, a wooden building of two stories was erected on the north side of School street (now Court square) calculated for the accommodation of 200 scholars in each story. In 1792, the old school houses at the North were taken down and a two story brick building erected on the same spot. These two buildings were occupied by the Centre and North reading and writing schools. The South reading school was accommodated in Nassau (now Common) street, and the South writing at the corner of West and Common streets.

In 1800, there were seven publick schools in operation, in which seven masters were employed on salaries of $666 66 cts. and an allowance of $200, together with seven ushers at $333 33 cts. with an allowance of $100. The town tax in that year was $61489,25 and the charge for schools $11100,85. In the spring of 1804 another reading and writing school were opened in the new brick school house at the corner of Hawkins and Chardon street. In 1806, the number of scholars belonging to all the schools was 1760 : boys 1030, girls 730.

In process of time it had been found that the rule requiring applicants for admission to be able " to read the English language by spelling the same," had operated to the exclusion of a large class of children, whose parents were unable or unwilling either to instruct them, or to give them a private education. Sunday schools were revived in the town, in the year 1816, in which it was the object of the managers, besides

conveying religious instruction, to fit their charge for the
English grammar schools: but the number, which needed to
be thus fitted, proved to be so great, that many citizens became desirous that something should be done by the town towards the same object. A petition was presented, that free
schools might be established for children between the age of
four and seven years. A committee was appointed to ascertain the number of children, throughout the town, who did
not attend any school, and the number that attended private
schools, and this examination resulted in the establishment of
the Board of Primary Schools, by a vote passed June, 11,
1818. This board was at first composed of three gentlemen,
from each ward, chosen by the school committee, with powers to establish a suitable number of schools, appoint teachers, and have the general superintendence : the increase
of the schools has rendered it necessary to increase the number of the committee, which now consists of one member for
each school, together with a standing committee of seven and
a treasurer. The board is subdivided into district committees. It is the duty of each member frequently to visit his
particular school and to report its state to the district committee, to which he is attached, and they report the state of all
the schools in their district to the standing committee, whose
duty it is to visit all the schools, semiannually, and make a
general report, which is sent, after its acceptance by the
Primary Board, to the school committee. The effect of this
system, which has been executed with untiring assiduity and
unvarying regularity. never perhaps excelled, has been to
raise the tone of general instruction and moral improvement
in the great mass of our population. The children are here
committed to the care of female instructers, who are selected
from the worthiest in point of moral and literary qualifications ; and the poorest receive the same attention as is bestowed upon the more wealthy, of whom many are sent to the
primary, in preference to the private schools : and the whole
may be ' fairly said to be more carefully taught, and more
effectually watched and guarded in their characters and conduct, than the same number of children of the same age ever
were before.'
   The complete success, which immediately attended the institution of primary schools, produced a very strong feeling in
favour of publick education, and created a seasonable opportunity for gratifying the wishes of those who had been long
calling for a school, in which such as have not a desire, or
lack the means to pursue a collegiate education, might receive
instruction in some branches of great practical importance,
usually taught only at colleges. The plan for the establishment of the English Classical school (now called the English

High school) was brought forward in the School Committee, June 17, 1820; the town adopted it in the course of that year, and the school went into operation, in May, 1821. The principal instructer was Mr. Geo. B. Emerson. The higher branches of mathematicks, natural and moral philosophy, natural and civil history, natural theology and evidences of christianity, composition, declamation, and instruction in the French language, constitute the course pursued at this school. No boy may be admitted under 12 years of age, and none remain more than three years. By the present regulations of the school committee, there is to be at least one instructer to every forty pupils.*

In the autumn of 1821, the basement room in the Fort-hill school was fitted up for an experiment on the plan of *mutual instruction*, and about 150 children, (who with few exceptions were too old for the primary schools, and unqualified to enter the E. grammar schools) were admitted. Full liberty was allowed the instructer to adopt such parts of the system as were suitable to our state of society, and to make such improvements as circumstances might suggest. The number of boys that attended was seldom less than 90, nor that of the girls less than 70.

This school was kept in operation about two years, and fully justified all reasonable expectation. One hundred and sixty children were taught the same branches by one master, as are taught in the grammar and writing schools by two. The inspection and direction of this school was at first confided to a sub-committee of the Primary Board, by whom the experiment was originally proposed. In 1823, it was assumed by the School Committee, in whose hands it died, on the resignation of the enlightened gentleman, who consented to assist in organizing the school, and to take charge of it for the first year or two.

The people of the north part of the town were disappointed that a school had not been built for their accommodation in 1818; at the close of the year 1821, they renewed their petition, and one of the last acts of the town of Boston, as such, was a provision for the erection of the English grammar and writing school, now called Hancock school, in Hanover-street, which went into operation, June, 1823.†

---

* The English Classical school was commenced in Derne-street school-house : in 1824 it was removed to the new building at the corner of Pinckney and Centre streets.

† The Adams school was opened in 1817 : Boylston school, April 20th, 1819 : Bowdoin school, in 1821 : South Boston, in 1822. There had been a publick school at S. Boston some time previous.

Under the city charter the care and superintendence of the publick schools devolves on the School Committee, which body is composed of one member chosen in each ward, together with the Mayor and Aldermen. A course of study for the various schools is marked out, and rules established for the government of the scholars,and instructers,and committee. The system, if closely pursued, must insure a rigid attention to all the interests of the schools. In addition to regular visits to each school by the sub-committee who have it in charge, all the schools are visited semi-annually by the general committee, accompanied by the authorities of the city, the parents and friends of the pupils, and other persons interested or invited. The summer visitation has been aptly called the City Commencement. The ambition of the children is excited to display their several acquirements to the best advantage, and the exhibitions at the Latin and High schools may be truly said to fall little short of similar exercises at College. Three of the best boys in each of the schools annually receive, on these occasions, a silver medal, " the gift of Franklin," as " a reward of merit." The girls also receive rewards at the expense of the city. The emulation excited in the contest for these marks of distinction is confined to a laudable ambition, and, by its happy effects on the discipline of the schools and on the character of the scholars, evinces the wisdom of the great man, who bequeathed these memorials of his love to his native town.*

---

* The amount of compensation to all the instructers, from June 1, 1824, to June 1, 1825, was 50,953 *dols.* 35 *cts.* Other expenditures for schools 3,665 *d.* 47 *c.* Total amount 54,618 *dols.* 82 *c.* The estimates for the same purposes and the erection of a new school-house, for the current year, amount to 73,000 dollars.

The number of pupils in all the schools in Aug. 1823, was 5863. In this summer of 1825 it has been ascertained to be

In the Eng. Gram. Schools - - - -	1763 boys, - - - - -	1382 girls.
50 Primary „ - - - -	1361 „	- - - - - 1300 „
	3124	2682
African - - - - - - -	53 „	- - - - - 41 „
	3177	2723
Latin - - - - - - - -	175 „	- - - - -
E. High - - - - - - -	145 „	- - - - -
Total - - - - - - - -	3497 boys, - - - - -	2723 girls = 6,220

CHAPTER LX.

" Only add
Deeds to thy Knowledge answerable, add faith,
Add virtue, patience, temperance, add love,
By name to come call'd Charity."

THE formation of a society in Boston for promoting useful knowledge had been in contemplation for many years, but the design was never vigorously pursued till the end of the year 1779, when many gentlemen in various parts of the commonwealth determined to use their endeavours to have one formed upon a liberal and extensive plan, and at the same time to have it established upon a firm basis by the sanction of the legislature. And, to the honour of our political fathers be it spoken, although the country was engaged in a distressing war, they immediately adverted to the usefulness of the design, and incorporated the society by the name of *The American Academy of Arts and Sciences.* The charter was granted May 4, 1780. The design of this institution was declared to be ' the promotion and encouragement of the knowledge of the antiquities of America, and of the natural history of the country, and to determine the uses to which the various productions of the country may be applied ; to promote and encourage medical discoveries, mathematical disquisitions, philosophical inquiries and experiments ; astronomical, meteorological, and geographical observations ; improvements in agriculture, arts, manufactures, and commerce ; and, in fine, to cultivate every art and science, which may tend to advance the interest, honour, dignity, and happiness of a free, independent, and virtuous people.' The Academy has published memoirs of its transactions, in four 4to volumes, of which the last appeared in 1821. Its sessions are held in Boston, and its valuable library is deposited in the Athenæum.

Since the institution of the American Academy, numerous societies have been formed, which have confined their attention to some of the particular objects embraced in the Academy's plan, such as, the American Antiquarian, the Massachusetts Medical, the Historical, and the Agricultural Societies.

The *Massachusetts Historical Society* was incorporated, Feb. 19, 1794. The design of this institution is to collect, preserve, and communicate materials for a complete history of this country, and of all valuable efforts of the ingenuity and industry of its inhabitants. In pursuance of this design, they have already amassed a large collection of books, pamphlets, and manuscripts. The library and museum of the society are deposited in a spacious apartment over the arch in Franklin-street. They have published their Collections in twenty-one 8vo. volumes, which include Hubbard's History of New England, and Johnson's Wonder-Working Providence. The foundation of this society was originally suggested by the late Rev. Jeremy Belknap and Mr. Thomas Wallcut : it was at first supported by the labours of a few, and not sufficiently favoured by the publick : it has since enrolled among its members many of our first scholars, and now claims a very considerable reputation among the literary institutions of America.

The Boston Library Society was incorporated, June 17, 1794. The object of the associates was to make a collection of books in the sciences and general literature, for popular use ; more particularly of those works, which, from their costliness or peculiar value, are not generally found in private collections, and cannot conveniently be obtained by individuals of moderate fortune. The plan has been diligently and successfully pursued, and with the aid of occasional donations, the Library is now as complete in works of general utility, as any similar institution in this part of the country. The books amount to about 6500 volumes, and their number is continually increasing. To gratify the increasing taste for foreign literature, a collection of the best French authors has been added : many recent and valuable English works have been imported the present season. For some years after the Library was founded, the shares were not transferable, and subscribers had only the use of the library for their lives ; consequently, by the death of original proprietors, many shares have fallen into the common stock, which has given to the shares of present proprietors a value far beyond their cost. It is computed, that a share at the present price gives a property in the common stock greatly exceeding the cost of a share, exclusive of the value of the Hall, which is the property of the corporation. The price of a share is $25, subject usually to an annual tax of $2, for the increase of the Library and the charges of maintaining it. This assessment is determined by the major vote of the proprietors. Shares are now transferable, and do not cease at the death of the proprietor. The Library is open at the Hall over the arch in Franklin-street, on the afternoon of Thursdays, and the forenoon and afternoon of Saturdays, for the delivery of books.

The Columbian Library, kept in Boylston-Hall, is established on principles somewhat similar, and contains 4500 volumes.*

* There are also in Boston about six *Circulating Libraries*, containing extensive assortments of modern literature, open to publick use at very moderate charges.

THE ATHENÆUM. For several years, individuals in this metropolis had expressed their wishes that there might be established here a publick reading room, to be kept constantly open, and to contain all the valuable journals, foreign and domestick periodical publications, books of general reference, and other works adapted to such a place of resort. It was thought that an establishment of this kind would receive liberal support. Having these impressions, a society of gentlemen, who conducted a literary publication, (the Monthly Anthology,*) in the year 1806, issued proposals, in which they engaged to provide a room of the forementioned description, open at ten dollars annually to each subscriber. The subscription list was soon filled with a large number of respectable names. In consequence of this success, it was determined to extend the plan by adding a library to the foundation.

By the time the journals and periodical publications were received, more than a thousand volumes of valuable works, principally donations, were collected. At this stage of the undertaking, the gentlemen who had commenced and so far conducted it, in order more effectually to secure and diffuse the benefit of their past labour and expense, and realize their wishes of a respectable establishment, transferred their right and title in the Anthology Reading Room and Library to Trustees, with power to supply vacancies in their number, and to hold and manage said Reading Room and Library as a trust under their then present name. At the winter session of the Legislature in 1807, the proprietors were incorporated under the name of the Boston Athenæum.

The rooms of this institution were first opened in Congress street, from whence they removed to Scollay's buildings, and, in 1810, to the building on Common street, north of the Chapel burial ground. Here they remained until 1822, when they removed to the spacious edifice in Pearl street. The better half of this elegant and commodious building was presented to the institution by the late James Perkins Esq: the other half they purchased at the price of $15,300. The requisite alterations have been made in its interior, and the rooms have been so disposed, and the library so arranged, as to furnish every desirable facility and accommodation to those who visit the establishment.

On entering the Athenæum the visiter finds himself surrounded with the busts and statues of heroes and learned men of antiquity, who seem to bid him, in the SALVETO on the tablet before him, *Welcome* ! At his left, on the first floor, is the Reading room, in which are found the newspapers

---

* Monthly Anthology, for May, 1807.

and journals of the present day, with complete files of periodical publications for many years back. On the right is the Room of the American Academy, in which is deposited their library of 2000 volumes, principally works of science and philosophical transactions of foreign societies. The librarian's room and a conversation room, complete the apartments on the lower story.

On the second floor are found in the 1st Room, Works relative to American History ; in the 2d, Political and Military Works ; in the 3d, Metaphysicks and Theology, which includes ' the Theological Library,' belonging to another association and containing 2000 volumes ; in the 4th, Belles Lettres, and Miscellaneous Works ; in the 5th, Encyclopædias ; in the 6th, History, Geography, Travels, Biography. Ascending into the third story, we find in room No. 7 a collection of tracts amounting to near 10,000, collected principally by the indefatigable perseverance of Mr. Wm. S. Shaw. Room No. 8 contains the publications of Learned Societies ; No. 9, works on Agriculture, Natural History and Botany ; No. 10, Works in the Arts and Sciences, Architecture, Chemistry,&c. No. 11, the Greek and Roman Classics, and translations. No. 12, Engravings,&c. Whole No. of vols. 17,500.

The price of a share in this institution is $300, which entitles a proprietor to to three tickets of admission. A life subscriber pays $100. Annual subscribers are admitted at $10 per annum. A proprietor or life subscriber may introduce company to view the Athenæum.

Omitting some minor literary associations, we proceed to notice a few of our charitable institutions. Besides the publick provision for the destitute of all descriptions, which is so ample that no one need to suffer any privation, who is able to make known his case to an overseer of the poor, there are numerous societies established in Boston, whose object is the alleviation of human misery.

The *Massachusetts Humane Society* was established by law Feb. 23, 1791. The design of their institution is ' the recovery of persons who meet with such accidents as produce in them the appearance of death, and for promoting the cause of humanity, by pursuing such means, from time to time, as shall have for their object the preservation of human life, and the alleviation of its miseries.'

The *Mass. Charitable Fire Society*, incorporated, June 25, 1794, was instituted to provide means to relieve such of the inhabitants of the commonwealth as may unfortunately suffer by fire, and to reward the industry and ingenuity of those who may invent useful machines for extinguishing fires, or make extraordinary personal exertion in the time of such calamity, or make such discoveries for preventing its devastation as shall be thought worthy of their patronage.

The *Massachusetts Charitable Mechanick Association* was instituted March 15, 1795, by a number of publick spirited individuals, of the most industrious and respectable of the mechanick interest ; of various occupations, residing in different parts of the town ; who styled themselves the ' Boston Association of Mechanicks.' In a few months the society increased much in numbers, resources, and usefulness. With the increase of its numbers, and means, its views became enlarged, its utility more apparent, and a laudable emulation pervaded a considerable part of the community to raise the mechanick interest and character to its just grade in society. The associates, in order to extend the benefits of the institution, altered the original appellation, and voted to assume the title of ' The Association of Mechanicks of the commonwealth of Massachusetts,' which gave opportunity for qualified citizens throughout the commonwealth to offer themselves as candidates for membership ; and some few embraced this privilege and became members, besides those residing in Boston. But the society laboured under many disadvantages previous to its incorporation, March 8, 1806, eleven years from its institution ;—when its fair claims became acknowledged, the characters and conduct of its founders, officers, and members, were deemed sufficient pledges of the purity of their intentions ; and one of its primary principles being ingrafted in its title, it was, by an act of the legislature, incorporated by its present name.*

---

* Among other objects of publick utility, connected with this institution, are the Apprentices' Library, and the encouragement of ingenuity and excellence of workmanship among the mechanicks and manufacturers of this commonwealth, by an annual exhibition of premium articles ; for the best of which, suitable premiums are awarded, by judges selected for that purpose ; in awarding which, all other things being equal, preference is first given to an apprentice, then to a journeyman, before the master-workman. The first publick exhibition of premium articles was on July 4, 1818.

The Apprentices' Library, established in this city in 1820, and which is under the supervision of this Association, is an institution, which, if judiciously managed, is calculated to have a beneficial effect on the minds and morals of those who enjoy its privileges. As a proof of the high estimation in which Apprentices' Libraries are held, we have only to notice the increasing popularity of them throughout our country : and even England, in this instance, has not disdained to copy from her descendants. To Boston belongs the honour of having been the first to establish this valuable institution.—*Wells' and Cary's Addresses.*

In connection with this society we should also notice the *Donation of Franklin*, who by his last will bequeathed a thousand pounds sterling to the town of Boston, ' to be let out upon interest at five per cent. per ann. to such young married artificers as have served an apprenticeship in said town, and faithfully fulfilled the duties required by their indentures, so as to obtain a good moral character from at least two respectable citizens, who are willing to become their sureties.' The amount of this fund, by the last annual report, was 14,451 *dols.* 83 *cts.*

The *Boston Dispensary* was instituted in 1795, and incorporated, Feb. 26, 1801.   At the expence of this institution the poor are supplied with medicines, and they are gratuitously attended by physicians appointed yearly by the managers.   A subscriber of five dollars is entitled to tickets for two patients, which number he may keep constantly on the list of the Dispensary.

The *Boston Female Asylum* was instituted Sept. 25, 1800, by a number of ladies, who associated for the charitable purpose of relieving, instructing, employing, and assisting female orphan children.   They were incorporated Feb. 26, 1803. The success which has attended this institution has equalled the most benevolent expectations.   The society has rescued from ruin and distress a great number of fatherless and motherless girls, who have, under its protection, been nourished and brought up to habits of industry and piety.   The asylum-house is situated in Essex st. corner of Lincoln st.

The *Howard Benevolent Society* was organized, June 1,1812, and incorporated Feb. 16, 1818.   Their object is to search out and administer to the wants of the sick and the infirm ; ' more especially of that class of our fellow-citizens, who, not being connected with any religious society, are in no way benefitted by the provisions made in most of them for the relief of their poor.'

The *Boston Asylum for Indigent Boys* was incorporated Feb. 25, 1814.   Its object is to make similar provision for orphan boys, to that which has been so usefully made for girls by the Female Asylum.   This institution occupies the large house on the corner of Salem and Charter streets, formerly the residence of Sir William Phips.

The *Provident Institution for Savings* was incorporated Dec. 13, 1816.   This society is intended to encourage industry and prudence in the poorer classes, and to induce them to save and lay by something of their earnings for a period of life when they will be less able to earn a support.   Deposits are received as low as one dollar, and when any person's deposits amount to five dollars, it is put on interest.   The deposits may be withdrawn on stated days, if desired.   The office of this institution is open every Wednesday, in Scollay's buildings.

The *Boston Society for the Religious and Moral Instruction of the Poor* was incorporated in the year 1820.   Through the exertions of this society, schools for the poor have been instituted in various parts of the town, the gospel has been preach-to them, and pains have been taken to raise the standard of moral character among them.

INSANE HOSPITAL.

London, published &c. &c. Engraved by J. Brown.

The *Penitent Females' Refuge* is an institution formed with the hope of reclaiming, from the paths of vice and ruin, a portion of those unhappy women, whose false steps have blasted their prospects of enjoying a reputable standing in life. A house of refuge is opened by this society, for such as are sincerely desirous of returning to the paths of virtue. This house, which is large and commodious, is under the care of a matron and assistants : a committee of ladies visit it every week, and the pecuniary concerns are under the management of a Board of Directors, chosen annually from the gentlemen who are subscribers to the funds of the institution—Constitution adopted April 14, 1819 : incorporated Jan. 21, 1823.

Some account of the *Massachusetts General Hospital* will conclude our notices on this head. Towards the close of the last century a gentleman died in this town, leaving a bequest in his will of $5000 towards the building of a hospital. This circumstance was attended with the beneficial effect of awakening the attention of the publick to the subject. Nothing, however, was effected before August, 1810, when two physicians living in this town addressed a circular, in which the advantages of a hospital were stated, to several gentlemen of Boston possessed of ample fortunes, and disposed to contribute to institutions in which the publick good was concerned. In the beginning of 1811 (Feb. 25) fifty-six gentlemen, living in different parts of the commonwealth, were incorporated by the name of the Mass. General Hospital. Their charter allowed the corporation to hold property to the amount of $30,000 yearly income. It also granted to the Hospital a fee simple in the estate of the old Province House, on the condition that $100,000 should be raised by subscription within ten years. Little exertion was made before the autumn of 1816, when a subscription was commenced that was attended with uncommon success. In the towns of Boston, Salem, Plymouth, Charlestown, Hingham and Chelsea (including a few subscriptions in some other towns) 1047 individuals subscribed either to the Hospital or the Asylum for the insane. More than 200 of these contributed $100 or more, and several from 1000 to 5000, and one $20,000. Donations of equal and larger amounts have since been made, which have increased the funds of this institution, for immediate use and permanent stock, to a greater sum than any other among us has realized, excepting the University at Cambridge.

In 1816, the Trustees purchased the estate at Charlestown, belonging to the late Mr. Barrell, commonly called Poplar Grove, and have there built two brick houses, besides the requisite out houses. In 1817, they purchased four acres in a field at the west end of Boston, called Prince's Pasture, and

46

on the 4th day of July, 1818, the corner stone of the present Hospital was there laid, in the presence of many persons of great dignity in publick life, and of a numerous assemblage of citizens.   The civil, religious and masonick services were performed with such impressive pomp as rendered the whole scene truly solemn and interesting.   This building was so far completed on the first of Sept. 1821, as to be in a fit condition to receive patients.   The Asylum for the Insane had been opened for the reception of boarders, October 1, 1818.*

Besides these institutions whose views extend to society at large, we ought to name many others, whose efforts in the cause of benevolence are equally ardent, though the objects of their charity are more limited ; such as the Female Samaritan and the Fragment Societies. (supported by ladies for the relief of necessitous women and children ; the Fatherless and Widows' society ; the Society for employment of the poor ; Society for the relief of the distressed ; the Episcopal charitable society, the British charitable, the Irish charitable, the Mass. charitable, and the Fuel Societies, &c.   These institutions embrace among their members almost every individual who maintains a respectable standing in the community.   And if we add to these the numerous religious associations for missionary and benevolent purposes, we may, without vanity, adopt concerning Boston the language of Increase Mather, when he said, that " for charity, he might indeed speak it without flattery, this town hath not many equals on the face of the earth."

---

* The Massachusetts General Hospital has been pronounced the finest building in the State. It stands on a small eminence *(B c)* open to the south, east, and west. It is 168 ft. in length and 54 in its greatest breadth, having a portico of eight Ionick columns in front. It is built of Chelmsford granite, the columns and their capitals being of the same material. In the centre of the two principal stories are the rooms of the officers of the institution. Above these is the operating theatre which is lighted from the dome. The wings of the building are divided into wards and sick rooms. The stair cases and floorings of the entries are of stone. The whole house is supplied with heat by air-flues from furnaces, and with water by pipes and a forcing pump. The beautiful hills which surround Boston are seen from every part of the building, and the grounds on the south west are washed by the waters of the bay.

J. R. Penniman del.

Entered according to Act of Congress by A. Bowen

A. Bowen Sc.

MASSACHUSETTS GENERAL HOSPITAL.

CHAPTER LXI.

O, sir, you are old ;
Nature in you stands on the very verge
Of her confine; you should be rul'd and led
By some discretion, that discerns your state
Better than you yourself.   *King Lear.*

We have already noticed three ineffectual attempts to obtain for the town of Boston the name and privileges of a city.
That in 1651 (see *p.* 137) was probably made in accordance
with the wishes of a majority ; that in 1708, we have seen,
was accounted as an experiment fraught with mischief; and in
1762, the proposition was unanimously rejected. From that
period we hear nothing more of the project until 1784 ; in
which year, on the 11th of May, the town was called to consider the expediency of an application for an act of incorporation. The subject produced ' a long debate, which was very
masterly handled by the several speakers, though not without
a small degree of tartness ; but concluded in the appointment
of a committee of 13, to report whether there were defects in
the existing mode of government, and, if necessary, to report a
plan for the better regulation of the police.' The Committee
reported, on the 4th of June, two distinct plans, one of which
proposed to vest the government in a Mayor, Recorder, and
12 Aldermen, and 24 Common council men ; the other, to
delegate nearly the same powers to 12 Selectmen (one from
each ward) joined with a President and six selectmen chosen
at large. The discussion on this report was ' lengthy, but
displayed the greatest candour and liberality of sentiment ;' it
closed with a motion to print the report and adjourn to the
17th of June. The adjourned meeting proved a very tumultuous one. Several gentlemen endeavoured to ' fix the attention of the town to the subject before them, but their arguments
were drowned in the incessant shouts for the *question.* Dr.
Charles Jarvis, peculiarly a man of the people, though now
on the unpopular side, caught their attention for a few moments : he concluded his remarks with a hope ' that every
man, rich and poor, might be heard in his turn ; that the confusion that had commenced might subside ; that love, friendship and urbanity might pervade the hall.' The momentary
quietude was succeeded by a general cry of *No corporation—
No Mayor and Aldermen,—No innovations,* all echoed with un-
abated roaring. Many gentlemen of character left the hall.
As soon as the honourable moderator (Thos. Dawes Esq.) had

it in his power, the motion was put, and the vote was carried against the proposed alterations.'

This repulse did not dishearten the friends of a reform. They renewed their petition the next year (Nov. 1, 1785) but were received with less attention by the town, who immediately gave leave for them to withdraw. In 1792, another plan was brought forward, which simply proposed to create a town council, to be composed of the Selectmen, chosen as theretofore, and of three persons to be chosen from each of the wards (of which the town should be divided into nine.) This council was to be invested with the powers of the town in its corporate capacity, to make by-laws and appoint inferior officers. The principal effect of the change would have been to render frequent town-meetings unnecessary. It was also proposed to petition the court for the establishment of a municipal judge, who should have cognizance of all minor prosecutions for causes arising within the town. Several meetings were held, and the debates, which in the early stage were simply eloquent and warm, at last became turbulent and agitated, and the question was put to rest (Jan. 26th) by a vote of 701 against 517.   Persons of both the great political parties, which began by this time to be distinctly marked, were found on each side. The name of Mr. Benjamin Austin is prominent among the opponents, and that of Mr. Sullivan (since Governour) among the friends of the measure.

In 1804, Jan 12, two persons were chosen by each ward to compose a committee to devise a new system of government. A plan was matured, and being taken into consideration by the town, April 9th, after some debate it also was rejected. 'A very great number of our citizens,' however, retained the 'wish that the name of *City* should be adopted; being of opinion that this name has an effect to raise the rank of a place in the estimation of foreigners, and is better adapted than the name of *Town* to express our real standing compared with the other cities of the Union.' This with other considerations occasioned another application to the town, in 1815, to obtain their consent to the adoption of 'the discriminating appellation, universally given to their most distinguished places, by the practice of all European powers.' Under the proposed system, said a committee, 'town-meetings will continue to be held and all questions relative to our political rights and interests to be discussed in them ; a course of proceeding happily as inseparable from the genius of our constitution as it is justly dear to the affections of our citizens.'* Yet even with this reservation, the people could not be persuaded to adopt the improvements recommended. Here it

* Report of Committee, Oct. 16, 1815.

was thought the question was 'put to rest for some years :' but various causes conspired to revive it in 1821, and in 1822 it was determined by the establishment of the City Government.

Experience had proved that there was no real obstacle to the passage of a long code of excellent by-laws, adapted to every imaginable contingency. Officers too were not wanting, whose duty and interest it was to carry them into execution. There were nine Selectmen (whose chairman had been customarily superintendant of Police) 12 overseers of the poor, 30 Firewards and a School Committee of 12, annually chosen at March meeting.* A Board of Health, consisting of 12 members (one chosen by each ward) had the regulation of Quarantine, and all such affairs, as concerned the health of the inhabitants. The town in publick meeting voted the amount of its annual taxes, and these were assessed by a board composed of 24 members (two for each ward) called Assistant Assessors, and three others, selected by the assistants to be Permanent Assessors. A Town Treasurer and Town Clerk completed the list of municipal officers. Each of these boards performed their duties with alacrity and fidelity, yet there was a universal complaint that every by-law was infringed with impunity, and the want of ' one efficient responsible head,' to take the lead in the affairs of the town and maintain a general oversight, was extensively felt.

There were serious complaints too of the expense attending the Justices' courts. As the judicial concerns of the county stood regulated by law, many petty suits were constantly brought by parties unable to pay the costs, and the justices of the peace whose duty it was to sit in judgment, had no alternative but to charge the same to the county, or in other words to the town.† Some abuses were thought to exist in this system, and a committee was appointed, July 2, 1821, to consider and report thereon.

The report of this committee was laid before the town, Oct. 22d ; and the consideration of it resulted in the appointment of another committee, who were authorized to report ' a complete system relating to the administration of the town and county, which shall remedy the present evils, and to recommend any other measures calculated to create a more efficient, responsible, and acceptable system for Town and County Government.' This committee consisted of Messrs.

---

* The town also chose at March meetings, 20 surveyors of boards, 6 fence viewers, 6 cullers of hoops, 9 cullers of dry fish, 4 field drivers, 3 inspectors of lime, 2 surveyors of hemp, 2 surveyors of wheat, and 2 assay masters.

† Of the County tax, 1820, which was 30,000 *dols.* Chelsea paid 231,60. In 1821, of 25,332,52, Chelsea paid 187,63.

John Phillips, Wm. Sullivan, Charles Jackson, Wm. Prescott, Wm. Tudor, Geo. Blake, Henry Orne, Daniel Webster, Isaac Winslow, Lemuel Shaw, Stephen Codman, Joseph Tilden. Their report made on the 10th of Dec. was not sufficiently strong in favour of a city government : people were ready to enjoy the satisfaction of accepting or refusing something better. The committee was enlarged, with directions to report such a system as was 'contemplated by the amendment of the constitution, authorizing the General Court to constitute city governments.' Accordingly, on Monday the 31st day of Dec. the town was called together to consider and act upon such a system. The first step at this meeting was the determination to take a final question on the subject, by written vote, on the Monday following : then the report was taken up by paragraphs. A motion to retain the name of Town of Boston was made, and warmly advocated, but was negatived. The committee had proposed to call the chief officer of the city by the name of ' Intendant :' this was changed to ' Mayor.' The committee proposed a board of ' seven selectmen ;' the town voted a board of eight Aldermen, and instead of a ' Board of Assistants,' recommended by the committee, a board of Common Councilmen was determined upon. The Mayor and Aldermen were to be chosen by general ticket, by the qualified voters of the city voting in wards : each ward was to choose four Common Councilmen. The Mayor and Aldermen, sitting and acting together, were to compose one body ; and the board of Common Council to compose a separate body ; and both together (each having a negative upon the other) constitute the City Council. These provisions were accepted. The committee proposed to give the City Council power to choose Overseers of the Poor, Firewards and the School Committee, but the vote prevailed, that those officers should be chosen in wards. All other corporate powers, possessed by the town, were delegated to the City Council. except the right to sell or lease the Common and Faneuil Hall, which was reserved. The organization of the wards, which became necessary as a part of the proposed system, was arranged by a provision for the choice of a warden, clerk, and five inspectors of elections in each ward. The plan was completed by the proposal of one Police Court, which should have cognizance of all offences against the by-laws of the city, and of all minor causes usually decided by Justices of the peace.

The discussions on this subject occupied three successive days, and called some of the first talents of the town into exercise. Faneuil-Hall was thronged, yet every thing proceeded very orderly. Several questions arising, which were thought too important to be decided by hand vote, they were postponed to be determined by the ballot on the final question. Every thing being matured, the meeting adjourned on Wednesday, to meet again on Monday, Jan. 7, 1822, to decide on the report as amended, when the result of the balloting was as follows :

Whole No. of votes 4839.

1st Resolve.—Shall there be a City Government ?　　　Yeas....2805
　　　　　　　　　　　　　　　　　　　　　　　　　Nays....2006

2d Resolve.—Shall the elective United States and State Officers
be chosen in Wards ?　..　..　..　..　..　..　..　..　Yeas....2611
　　　　　　　　　　　　　　　　　　　　　　　　　Nays....2195

3d Resolve.—Shall the City Council decide the number of Representatives　..　..　..　..　..　..　..　..　..　..　Yeas....2690
　　　　　　　　　　　　　　　　　　　　　　　　　Nays....2128

4th Resolve.—Shall the Town be a County, and have a Police Court?　Yeas....4557
　　　　　　　　　　　　　　　　　　　　　　　　　Nays.....257

5th Resolve.—Shall the name be altered from Town of Boston to City of Boston ?　..　..　..　..　..　..　..　..　Yeas....2727
　　　　　　　　　　　　　　　　　　　　　　　　　Nays....2087

There was no little disappointment occasioned by this result : the warm friends of a city had hoped for a larger majority in their favour on the first question, and for a strong negative against the second : the opponents of the reform would not believe, till they had the demonstration, that the people of Boston would yield up their birth-right of self government and self protection, for what some considered the mere tinsel of a name. The feature in the system, which more than any other circumstance saved it from being rejected, was that part which gave to the wards the right to choose overseers, school committee, and firewards. As those boards had heretofore been chosen, it had happened for the most part that all the members were selected from the political party, which for many years had been the majority of the town. Some of the minority thought the present offered them a favourable opportunity to secure a portion of those boards to their own party : and that, together with the general desire to effect a reform in the justices' courts, and the belief that such a reform could not be effected, otherwise than in connection with the establishment of a city government, probably turned the scale.

The subject was forthwith presented to the legislature, and a law, framed on the principles of the report, received the signature of Governour Brooks, Feb. 23, 1822. The act reserved to the General Court the right to alter or amend the charter whenever they should deem it expedient : it also provided that the charter should be void, unless the inhabitants of Boston should accept it by written vote within 12 days. The former of these provisions was thought by some to be very exceptionable ; others considered it perfectly nugatory. The latter was in accordance with a proposition which had been offered to the town and rejected ; but those, who were gratified by this opportunity once more to attempt the defeat of the whole plan, were obliged also to submit again their favourite feature (the choice of national and state officers by election in wards) to the hazard of a rejection. The final meeting took place on the fourth of March, when a decision was obtained in favour of the charter by a majority of 916, (2797 to 1881,) and in favour of election in wards by a vote of 2813 to 1887. The result was forthwith made known to the Governour, and he announced the fact by proclamation on the seventh of March.

CHAPTER LXII.

" - - - The patriot Council met, the full,
The free, and fairly represented whole;
For all they plann'd the holy guardian laws,
Distinguish'd orders, animated arts,
And with joint force oppression chaining, set
Imperial justice at the helm."

PURSUANT to the direction of the charter, the Selectmen made a new division of the town into twelve wards, in such manner as to include an equal number of inhabitants in each ward, as nearly as conveniently might be, taking the last census made under the authority of the United States as a basis for such computation.* This was done on the 13th of March, and the various parties immediately proceeded to take the steps preparatory to an organization of the wards. There was no difficulty in finding candidates for all the offices, together with large quotas of rallying-committees and vote-distributors. When the second Monday of April arrived, there was little doubt respecting the result of any of the elections, except that of the Mayor. A ticket for the board of aldermen had been framed on such principles as were calculated to ensure its success : the various parties had each received a pledge that all should share the honours of that office. But in regard to the chief magistracy of the City, it was an honour which could not be divided, and the contest

---

* The Act places it ' in the power of the City council—from time to time, not oftener than once in ten years, to alter such divisions of wards, in such a manner as to preserve, as nearly as may be, an equal number of inhabitants in each ward.'

was warm between the friends of several eminent individuals. It was soon ascertained that the board of Aldermen would be filled by Messrs. *Ephraim Eliot, Joseph Head, Bryant P. Tilden, Nath'l P. Russell, Joseph Lovering, Samuel Billings, Joseph Jenkins,* and *Jacob Hall.* It was also ascertained that there would be no choice of Mayor, and it appeared from the official canvass that the votes were principally divided between Messrs. H. G. Otis and Josiah Quincy.* The friends of the former gentleman immediately withdrew his name from the list of candidates for the mayoralty, and Mr. Quincy, in his own name, publickly declined the honour. The excitement on this occasion was excessive, but it rapidly subsided, and in the course of four days, the eyes of all parties were fixed on the Hon. John Phillips, as the man whose character would command a universal suffrage. He consented to the nomination, and at the next election ('Tuesday, April 16th) received an almost unanimous vote.†

The first of May was appointed by the charter as the day for the commencement of the municipal year.‡ Suitable preparations were made in Faneuil Hall for the ceremonies of inducting the Mayor and other officers into their new stations. A platform, raised about two feet from the floor, was thrown from the selectmen's box to nearly the extent of the hall. On this the Selectmen of the past year, the Aldermen, and Common Council elect were accommodated with chairs and settees, the floor being covered with carpets. Two of the galleries were filled with ladies and the Hall was crowded to excess. The Rev. Dr. Baldwin (as senior in age of the clergymen of the metropolis) addressed the throne of grace in prayer. Chief Justice Parker administered the oaths of allegiance and office to the Mayor elect, who in turn administered similar oaths to the Aldermen and members of the Common Council. The Chairman of the selectmen (Mr. Eliphalet Williams) then rose, and, after an appropriate address, delivered the city charter to the Mayor, contained in a superb silver case, and the ancient act incorporating the town nearly two centuries past, together with all the books of records, title deeds, and documents belonging to the inhabitants. He concluded with a compliment to the wisdom and judgment, which had selected the gentlemen composing the present boards, for the purpose of putting into operation the new and untried system of city government.

---

* The whole number of votes was 3708, of which Mr. Q. had 1736—Mr. O. 1384—Thomas L. Winthrop, 361—Others 227.

† Mr. Phillips had 2500 votes: whole number was 2650.

‡ An amendment, made Jan. 27, 1825, makes the municipal year to commence with the calendar year from and after Jan. 1, 1826.

The address of the Mayor commenced with ample testimony to the wisdom of those institutions, which our ancestors established for the management of their municipal concerns, and to the intelligence and experience of our citizens, who had for so long a period meditated a change and exerted their influence to effect it. He spoke in full terms of the ability, diligence and integrity of the boards of Selectmen, justly denominated the fathers of the Town, and acknowledged particular obligations to the board now retiring from office. His concluding observations give a fair view of the merits of the city charter, and at the same time exhibit, in strong light, the traits in the publick and private character of their author, which endeared him to men of all parties.

'Difference of opinion must be expected, and mutual concessions made, in all cases where the interest of a large community is to be accommodated. The precise form in which this charter is presented may not be acceptable to all, but its provisions have met the approbation of a large majority, and it will receive the support of every good citizen. Those who encourage hopes that can never be realized, and those who indulge unreasonable apprehensions, because this instrument is not framed agreeably to their wishes, will be benefitted by reflecting how much more our social happiness depends upon other causes, than the provisions of a charter. Purity of manners, general diffusion of knowledge, and strict attention to the education of the young, and above all a firm practical belief of that divine revelation, which has affixed the penalty of unceasing anguish to vice, and promised to virtue rewards of interminable duration, will counteract the evils of any form of government. While the love of order, benevolent affections and christian piety, distinguish as they have done the inhabitants of this city, they may enjoy the highest blessings under a charter with so few imperfections, as that which the wisdom of our Legislature has sanctioned.—In my official intercourse I shall not encumber you with unnecessary forms, or encroach upon your time by prolix dissertations. In all the communications which the charter requires me to make, conciseness and brevity will be carefully studied. I will detain you no longer—than to invite you to unite in beseeching the Father of lights, without whose blessing all exertion is fruitless, and whose grace alone can give efficacy to the councils of human wisdom, to enlighten and guide our deliberations, with the influence of his holy spirit, and then we cannot fail to promote the best interests of our fellow citizens.'

After the address, the boards withdrew. The Common Council was organized by the choice of Hon. William Prescott for President, and Mr. Thomas Clark (late town clerk) for Clerk of the Common Council, and the two boards in Convention elected Samuel F. McCleary, Esq. City Clerk.*

The first year of the city government passed away without producing any events of a striking character. There was no

* The Police Court was organized by the Governour by the appointment of Messrs. Benjamin Whitman, Henry Orne, and William Simmons, esquires, as Justices, and Thomas Power, Esq. Clerk. Its first session was held on the 20th of June, 1822.

The Police Act, so called, gives to this court jurisdiction in all cases theretofore triable by Justices of Peace; makes all warrants issued by any J. of P. returnable before the Police court; and provides that no fees shall be paid for warrants issued by a J. P. unless this court shall decide that there was just and reasonable cause for the issuing thereof, &c. &c.

cause of special complaint, and nothing occurred to excite special admiration. At its close, the Mayor together with the board of Aldermen (one member excepted) declined a re-election. Mr. Quincy was again solicited to consent to being a candidate for the mayoralty, and was elected on the second Monday of April, 1823. An entire new board of Aldermen was chosen, and a majority of the members of the Common council were also new members.*

The Mayor's inaugural addresss paid the merited compliment to the services of that high and honourable individual, who had preceded him in the office,† and the wise, prudent, and faithful citizens who composed the first City Council.

' Their labours,' said he, ' have been indeed, in a measure, unobtrusive, but they have been various, useful, and well considered. They have laid the foundations of the prosperity of our city, deep and on right principles.—A task was committed to the first administration to perform, in no common degree arduous and delicate.—In the outset of a new form of government, among variously affected passions and interests, and among indistinct expectations, impossible to realize, it was apparently wise to shape the course of the first administration, rather by the spirit of the long experienced constitution of the town than by that of the unsettled charter of the city. It was natural for prudent men, first entrusted with city authorities, to apprehend that measures partaking of the mild, domestick character of our ancient institutions, might be as useful and would be likely to be more acceptable than those which should develop the entire powers of the new government. It is yet to be proved whether, in these measures, our predecessors were not right.————

' In executing the trust,' he proceeds, ' which my fellow citizens have confided to me, I shall yield entirely to the influences and be guided exclusively by the principles of the city charter ; striving to give prudent efficiency to all its powers, endeavouring to perform all its duties, in forms and modes, at once the most useful and most acceptable to my fellow citizens. If at any time, however, through any intrinsick incompatibility, it is impracticable to unite both these objects, I shall in such case, follow duty ; and leave the event to the decision of a just, wise and generous people. In every exigency, it will be my endeavour to imbibe and to exhibit, in purpose and act, the spirit of the city charter.'

The new boards entered with alacrity upon the duties of their various offices. The course they pursued was such as to excite a general expression of admiration. The Mayor and Aldermen were re-elected in 1824, without any considerable opposition; some extracts from the Mayor's inaugural address will furnish us with the best view of the transactions of the first year of his administration.

' The acts of the administration of the past year had reference to morals ; to comfort ; and convenience ; and ornament.—With respect to morals, there

---

* The votes, for Mr. Quincy, 2504 : for Geo. Blake, Esq. 2179 : others, 81.

The Aldermen were Messrs. Caleb Eddy, Daniel Baxter, David W. Child, Stephen Hooper, Joseph H. Dorr, George Odiorne, Enoch Patterson and Ashur Benjamin.

† Mr. Phillips lived only a few weeks after his retirement from the office of Mayor. He was seized with an attack of angina pectoris while attending his publick duties on the day of General Election, May 28, 1823, and his death took place on the following morning. He was in the 53d year of his age.

had existed in one section of the city an audacious obtrusiveness of vice, notorious and lamentable ; setting at defiance not only the decencies of life but the authority of the laws. The evil was met in the face.—In spite of clamour, of threat, of insult ;--a determined course was pursued. The whole section was put under the ban of authority. All licenses in it were denied, a vigorous police was organized, which, aided by the courts of justice and the House of correction, effected its purpose.—These measures did not originate in any theories or visions of ideal purity, attainable in the existing state of human society, but in a single sense of duty and respect for the character of the city.—The expense, by which this effect has been produced, has been somewhat less than one thousand dollars ; an amount already, perhaps, saved to the community in the diminution of those prosecutions and of their costs, which the continuance of the former unobstructed course of predominating vice, in that section would have occasioned.

'The next object of attention of the City government was the cleansing of the streets. In cities as well as among individuals, cleanliness has reference to morals as well as to comfort. Sense of dignity and self-respect are essentially connected with purity, physical and moral. And a city is as much elevated as an individual by self-respect. To remove from our streets whatever might offend the sense or endanger the health was the first duty. To do it as economically as was consistent with doing it well, was the second.——

'The widening of our streets as occasions offered was the next object, to which the attention of the city administration was directed ; and the one involving the greatest expense. The circumstances of the times, and the enterprize of private individuals opened opportunities, in this respect, unexampled, in point of number and importance.——The administration availed themselves of those opportunities, as a matter of duty, in the actual condition of a city so extremely irregular and inconvenient as is Boston, in the original plan and projection of its streets. Important improvements have been made in Lynn, Ship, Thacher, and Mill Pond Streets ; in Hanover, Elm, Brattle, Court and Union Streets ; in Temple, Lynde, Summer, and Milk Streets ; in Federal, Orange, Eliot, and Warren Streets.'——

' Another object of attention during the past year has been the drains.—— The principle adopted was to take all new drains into the hands of the city ;— to divide the expense as equally as possible among those estates immediately benefitted ; upon principles applicable to the particular nature of this subject, and retain in the city the whole property both as it respects control and assessment.'——

'A new Mall has been nearly completed on Charles Street, and all the missing and dead trees of the old Malls, the Common and Fort Hill, have been replaced with a care and protection, which almost insure success to these ornaments of the city.'——

'Two objects of very great interest to which the proceedings of last year have reference, remain to be elucidated. The purchase of the interest of the proprietors of the Rope Walks, west of the Common ; and the projected improvements about Faneuil Hall Market.——In consequence of the exclusion of the water by the Mill Dam, a tract of land has been opened either for sale, as an object of profit, or for use, as an object of ornament, with which the rights of these proprietors absolutely interfered. It was thought that no moment could be more favourable than the present to secure a relinquishment of those rights. An agreement of reference has been entered into, with those proprietors, and the amount to be paid by the city for such relinquishment, has been left to the decision of five of our most intelligent, independent and confidential citizens.'——

'Touching the projected improvements, in the vicinity of Faneuil Hall Market, not only the extreme necessities of the city, in relation to space for a market, have led to this project, but also the particular relations of that vicinity have indicated the wisdom and policy, even at some risque and sacrifice, of bringing together in one compact, efficient, and commodious connexion, the northern and central sections of our city, so as to facilitate the intercourse of business and enterprize between them, and bring into market, and into use, and into improvement, parts of the city, at present old, sightless, inconvenient, and in comparison with that competency, which must result from a judicious arrangement, at present absolutely useless. Both these measures of the City

Government, relative to the Rope Walks and to Faneuil Hall Market, will necessarily lead to what, to many of our citizens, is an object of great dread, a
city debt.'——'To create a debt is a power, vested by our charter, in the City
Council. Now this, like every other power, is to be characterized by its use.
  'The destinies of the City of Boston, are of a nature too plain to be denied,
or misconceived. The prognosticks of its future greatness are written on the
face of nature, too legibly, and too indelibly to be mistaken. These indications
are apparent from the location of our city, from its harbour, and its relative
position among rival towns and cities ; above all, from the character of its
inhabitants, and the singular degree of enterprize, and intelligence, which are
diffused through every class of its citizens. Already capital and population
is determined towards it, from other places, by a certain and irresistible power of attraction. It remains then, for the citizens of Boston to be true to their
own destinies ; to be willing to meet wise expenditures and temporary sacri-
fices, and thus to co-operate with nature and providence in their apparent ten-
dencies to promote their greatness and prosperity ; thereby not only improving the general condition of the city, elevating its character, multiplying its
accommodations and strengthening the predilections, which exist already in
its favour ; but also patronizing and finding employment for its labourers and
mechanicks. It is true the power of credit, like every other power, is subject
to abuse. But to improve the general convenience of the city, to augment its
facilities for business, to add to the comfort of its inhabitants, and in this way
to augment its resources, are among the most obvious and legitimate uses of
that power, which doubtless, for these purposes, was entrusted to the City
Council.'——

  The labours of the city government during the year, which
commenced with May, 1824, were chiefly devoted to the
completion of the plan, and the accomplishment of the improvements in the vicinity of the market. An effort was also
made to advance a project for an improvement of the flats at
the bottom of the Common (which the city obtained at the
price of 50,000 dollars,) but it was discouraged by a vote of
the inhabitants in town-meeting. Publick attention was also
excited to a difference of opinion between the city council and the board of overseers of the poor, relative to the
powers of each, in the government of the Alms-House and
House of Industry. A plan was submitted to the people proposing that the choice of that board should be vested in the
City Council, but a vote could not be obtained for an alteration of the charter for that purpose.* A new organization of
the Health department took place, by which the duties heretofore performed by 12 persons, one resident in each ward,
are transferred to one Health-officer, and the regulations of

* The alterations, that have been made in the charter, are by Acts of the legislature, Jan.
30, 1823, authorizing the Mayor and Aldermen to increase the number of engine men ; Feb.
28d, authorizing City Council to choose nine directors of the House of Industry,&c.—June 10,
1823, authorizing Council to elect the Mayor and Aldermen surveyors of high ways.—June
12, 1824, an act regulating the house of correction and the form of actions under the by-laws,
and to provide for the filling of vacancies in the board of Aldermen.—Jan. 27, 1825, act to
alter the time of commencing the municipal year. June session, to abolish the board of firewards and organize a fire department : and by an order of the City Council, March, 22, 1824,
the charter is so amended that vacancies in the office of Ward clerk may be filled whenever
they occur.

quarantine made more conformable to the views of enlightened experience and less burdensome to the commercial community.

Previous to the expiration of this year, one of the aldermen, Mr.Hooper, had deceased, and two others, Messrs. Eddy
and Benjamin, had ceased to officiate : the remaining
members of the board it was understood would decline a re-
election.   A Union ticket was however formed, which bore
the names of two of them.   All the gentlemen named on it
were elected by large majorities : five of them declined the
service, and the vacancies were filled at a subsequent election.* Mr. Quincy was re-elected to the mayoralty by a
vote almost unanimous.   More than half of the common council were new members.   These boards will continue in office
until the first Monday of January next.

CHAPTER LXIII.

"The city rear'd
In beauteous pride her sky-encircled head."

It was anticipated with much certainty by the advocates
for a city government, that the change would produce a favourable effect on the interests of the city, in relation to publick improvements.   That anticipation has not been disappointed.   Individuals have been more active in putting their
private estates into better repair, several companies have associated to make extensive alterations in adjoining lots,† and
the city has undertaken a magnificent project in the neighbourhood of Faneuil Hall market.

A fire which destroyed six houses and stores with out houses in Union street (July 14, 1821) made way for the improvement, which has been made by the erection of the block of
brick stores and dwellings on the north side of that street, and
led to the completion of the range of brick buildings on the

* The gentlemen chosen at the annual meeting, Ap. 11, 1825, were Messrs. Daniel Baxter
and Joseph H. Dorr, (of the former board) N. P. Russell, (of the first board) Redford Webster and Thomas B. Wales, who declined ; and Messrs. *George Blake, Thomas Welsh jr. Henry J. Oliver,* who accepted the office.   At the second choice Messrs. *John D. Dyer, Daniel
Carney, Josiah Marshall, John Bellows, John Bryant* were elected.

† In the summer of 1824, a memorandum was taken of 194 new buildings then in a state of
forwardness.

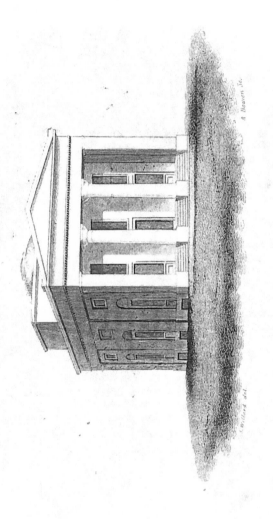

UNITED STATES BRANCH BANK.

south side. Winthrop place in Summer street, Hayward place, St. Paul's Row and Phillips' Row on Common street, Bowdoin row in Court street, Crescent court on Green street, the elegant block of stone stores on Water street, and of stone houses in Washington street, are each examples of enterprize, which have added to the comfort and convenience of the inhabitants.

State street has shared in the general improvements. A number of the old buildings have been demolished and elegant stone ones erected in their stead. The United States Branch Bank demands a particular description. It is situated at the head of Wilson's lane and constitutes a chief ornament of our Exchange.* The building is about 44 ft. in front and 96 ft. deep. The portico is an imitation from the primitive form of the Grecian Temple, with little variation, excepting what was necessary in order to adapt it to the location, and to the refractory material (Chelmsford granite) of which it was to be built. The columns are of the Grecian Dorick, 4 ft. in diameter and 24 ft. high, the shaft being a single piece.

Ground Plan of the United States Bank.

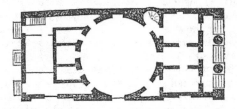

In the front part of the building, on the first floor, there is an entry, and two rooms for the President and Cashier; and in the second story over them, a large room for the use of the Directors. The centre of the building is occupied for the Banking room, which is a rotunda, 36 feet in diameter, and 44

---

* The first outline of a plan for this building was made for the situation which is occupied by the Old State house, and was intended to be an imitation of the purest example of the Grecian Dorick order with two porticos; but the scite, which was finally obtained, required a different arrangement. One of the porticos was dispensed with, and Antae at the angles introduced, according to the primitive form of the Grecian Temple. The shafts of the columns are frustums of cones, the sides being right lines, which, being the most severe and simple form, seemed the best adapted to the occasion. The corner stone of this edifice was laid on Monday, July 5, 1824. Mr. Solomon Willard was the designer and architect; Mr. Gridley Bryant the master mason, and Mr. James McAllaster, master carpenter.

The capital stock of this bank, employed in Boston, is 1,500,000 dls. There are 15 other Banks which employ a capital of 11,050,000 dls and 21 Insurance Companies whose capital is 6,300,000 dollars.

ft. high to the top of the curb stone. The rear of the building contains the vaults, which open into the Banking room, and a number of other apartments which are to serve for the various purposes of the institution.

The destructive fire, which occurred on the 7th of April last,* laid in ruins almost the whole of the square between Doane-st. Broad, Battery march and Kilby streets. The buildings on the square between Adams-st. Milk, Battery M. street and Liberty square had just been demolished for the purpose of erecting on the spot a large block of stores. Both these squares are now covered with new and convenient buildings, nearly finished. One of the stores on Central street was occupied in August.

The House of Industry and House of Correction at South Boston, which are two similar buildings, of rough dimension stone, 220 ft. long, 43 ft. wide, and 29 ft. high, have been mostly erected by the city government. The establishment of the H. of C. was authorized by a vote of the town on the 7th of May, 1821. It was designed 'for the restraint and employment of the idle and vicious poor, for habitual drunkards, beggars and those condemned for petty offences, in the inferior courts of justice. The House of Industry is destined for the comfort, support, and relief, and as far as they are competent, for the employment of the virtuous poor, and of those alone who are reduced to seek this refuge, from misfortune or age or infancy.'

The County Gaol in Leverett street and the House of Correction connected with it, and the Municipal Court house, all which are handsome stone buildings, were commenced several years since, but were not finished and occupied till the year 1822. In 1823, the old gaol was taken down, and its materials were partly used in constructing the Gun house and Ward Room on Thacher street.†

The history of Boston furnishes us with many instances of enterprize, which have excited admiration. The construc-

---

* It commenced in Doane street. Five buildings were destroyed on State-st. 6 in Doane, 6 in Kilby, 19 in Central street (every building) 4 on Broad-st. and 13 on Liberty square. Most of them were fire proof brick stores, filled with valuable goods, foreign products and American manufactures.

The great fire, at noon-day, July, 7, 1824, destroyed fifteen brick dwelling houses, besides out houses, on Chesnut, Charles and Beacon streets.

† *The Old Court House* on the south side of Court-street, is a handsome building of brick, three stories high, and has on the roof an octagon cupola. On the lower floor are the offices of the United States District Marshall, and several private offices. In the second story, the floor of which is supported by pillars of the Tuscan order, are held the Circuit and District Courts of the U. S. for the Massachusetts District, and the office of the District Clerk. In the third story are convenient rooms for jurors, &c. This building, before the erection of the New Court House, described at page 351, was used by all the courts of law held in the county

HOUSE OF INDUSTRY AND HOUSE OF CORRECTION.

tion of the sea-wall or out-wharves, in 1673, was a stupendous undertaking, for that period ; it proved however to be an object of less utility, than was at first supposed. The building of Long wharf was a great and useful work. These and the partial filling up of the town dock were the principal efforts, made previous to the revolution, for the improvement of the natural advantages which the town possessed. Concerning the immense and costly works which have been accomplished since that era, we have spoken at large. But the project, which exceeds them all in boldness of design, in promise of publick benefit, and in energy of execution, is that which is now approaching to its accomplishment in the vicinity of Faneuil Hall Market.

Such an undertaking, involving such an amount of property, and affecting so many private rights, was too great to be prosecuted without the express sanction of the people. This was obtained by a very full vote, in city meeting, Jan. 16, 1824, when the following questions were proposed and decided in the affirmative. 1. *Is it expedient* that Faneuil Hall market should be extended towards the harbour, between Ann-street and the street leading to Bray's wharf, in such direction as the City Council, upon a view of all the circumstances of that vicinity, shall deem most for the publick interest ; and that they be requested to cause the same to be effected accordingly ?—2. *Is it expedient* for the City Council to apply to the legislature for such an extension of the powers of the surveyors of highways as the circumstances of the contemplated project, above mentioned, may make necessary, under such limitations and restrictions as the constitution requires, and as respect for private rights may dictate ?'

The legislature granted the proposed power, but there has been little occasion to exercise it : most, if not all the estates required, have been obtained with the consent of the parties interested. The old buildings were taken down in August ; the lots on the north side of the dock were sold at auction, Sept. 29th, 1824. The highest price obtained was $20,83 per square foot : the lowest $7. There were 36 lots, covering 30,037¼ feet, and the amount of sales was $303,495 44 cts. The lots on the south side of the intended market-house were sold, March 31, 1825. The highest price $21 per sq. foot, lowest $10. There were 22 lots covering 33,865 ft. and the amount of sales was $403,848 13 cts. The stores on the north side are already finished, as to the exterior, and the one which stands on the corner of the Roebuck passage, where

---

The Police Court holds its sessions here daily for the trial of criminal cases, and twice a week, at least, for that of ' civil suits and actions.'

the triangular warehouse formerly stood, was occupied by a
tenant, Sept. 12, 1825.   The stores on the south side, and
the Market-house also, are rapidly progressing.*

The New Market-house stands between these two ranges
of stores, at the distance of 102 ft. from those on the south
side, and 65 ft. from the north.   The centre part of the building is 74 ft. 6 in. by 55 ft. having a hall in the second story.
The wings are 231 ft. long by 50 wide, and two stories high.
There is a cellar under the whole.   The wings have each a
portico of 4 columns, 3 ft. 7 in. diameter and 23 ft. high ; the
shafts are of granite in a single piece.   The first story has
arched windows, and those in the second story are square.
The construction of the whole is of hammered granite of a
uniform colour.

The corner stone of this building was laid with much ceremony.   The plate deposited beneath it bears the names of
the Mayor, Aldermen and Common Council, Building Committee and Principal Architect, and Engraver, besides the
following inscription :

Faneuil Hall Market,

*Established by the City of Boston.   This stone was laid April
27, Anno Domini* MDCCCXXV. *In the forty-ninth year of American Independence and in the third of the Incorporation of the
city.*   John Quincy Adams, *President of the United States.*
Marcus Morton, *Lt. Gov. and Commander in chief of the Commonwealth of Massachusetts.*

*Memoranda.   The population of the city estimated at 50,000 :
that of the United States* 11,000,000.†

---

* The height and form of the stores were regulated by the conditions of sale. The pur-
chaser was required to erect, within a limited time, a brick store with hammered stone front,
(granite piers) in strict conformity with a plan drawn by Mr. Alex. Parris.   This plan required that the stores should be four stories high, with a slated roof, and a cellar water-
tight. The height of the first and second story is 8 ft. 6 inches : the 3d story is 8 ft. 9 in. and
the 4th is 6 ft. 6 inches, in the clear. The windows in the 2d story are arched : the others
are square. The blocks measure about 530 ft. in length, from Merchants-row to the street at
the east end of the Market-house.

† The population of Boston, according to the census of 1820, stood thus

Persons.	Under 10 years.	10 to 16.	White males from 16 to 18.	18 to 26.	26 to 45.	Over 45.	Total.
Whites	10590	5349	877	7832	12991	4037	41,676
Blacks	of both sexes, under 26 yrs.			689	727	285	1,701

Add for the Islands, 675 ; Persons not taxed, 61 ; Omitted, 31 — 767

Total, Males, 21,687—Females, 22,365 — 92 = 44,144

By the Census of 1810, the population was - - - 33,250

"   "   1800   -   -   -   -   -   -   24,937

"   "   1790   -   -   -   -   -   18,038

EAST VIEW OF FANEUIL HALL MARKET.

Entered according to Act Congress by J Brown.

CHAPTER LXIV.

"The Hero hath come in the eve of his day,
To the land where he planted the tree of his glory."

WE have omitted to notice the display of pomp and ceremony, in which the people of Boston exhibited their devotion
to President WASHINGTON, when he visited the town in 1789,
(Oct. 24,) and the similar display which took place on the
visit of President Monroe, July 2, 1817. Both these events
called forth a burst of patriotick feeling, of which it is pleasant
to cherish the recollection. But the splendour of that display
has been surpassed, and the height of that feeling has been, if
possible, more than equalled by the reception of General La
Fayette, and the ceremony of laying the corner-stone of the
monument on Bunker Hill.

LAFAYETTE arrived at New York on the 16th of August,
1824, where he was welcomed in a manner becoming his own
character and that of the people whom he had come to visit :
and the people of Boston gladly heard of his determination to
proceed immediately hither, in season to attend the exercises
of commencement, at Cambridge. On the evening of Monday, August 24th, he reached the residence of Gov. Eustis, in
Roxbury, and the next morning entered the city.

At an early hour, a cavalcade of 800 citizens waited to escort him to the town line, where the Mayor and Aldermen and
Common Council, with a committee of arrangements, were in
readiness to receive him. A military escort consisting of a
corps of Light Dragoons and a battalion of Light Infantry
were also stationed there. On the arrival of General Lafayette at the line, the Mayor of the City, in the name of the City
Government and of the citizens of Boston, bade him welcome,
in an appropriate address, to which the General replied, as
follows :

To the Mayor and People of Boston :

' The emotions of love and gratitude, which I have been accustomed to feel
on my entering this city, have ever mingled with a sense of religious reve-

---

The number of polls rated in 1824, was 10,897 : in 1810, it was 7764 : in 1793 it was 3631 :
in 1784, it was 1143 : in 1741—2972 ; in 1738—3395; in 1687—1457. See pp. 218, 254.

The town of Chelsea contains 642 inhabitants; Charlestown, 6591 ; Medford, 1474; Malden, 1719 ; Watertown, 1518; Cambridge, 3295 ; Brighton, 702 ; Brookline, 900 ; Roxbury,
4135 ; Dorchester, 3684: these towns constitute the environs of Boston. Their population
24,660 added to that of Boston, as above, makes a total of 68,804.

rence for the Cradle of American, and, let us hope it will be hereafter said, of universal liberty.

' What must be, sir, my feelings at the blessed moment when after so long an absence, I feel myself again surrounded by the good citizens of Boston, where I am so affectionately, so honourably welcomed, not only by old friends, but by several successive generations ; where I can witness the prosperity, the immense improvement, that have been the just reward of a noble struggle, virtuous morals, and truly republican institutions.

' I beg of you, Mr. Mayor, gentlemen of the City Council, and all of you, beloved citizens of Boston, to accept the respectful and warm thanks of a heart which has for nearly half a century been particularly devoted to your *Illustrious City.'*

The Mayor then entered the barouche of the General, which was drawn by four white horses, and the procession began to move towards the town about 11 o'clock. It passed through Washington, Milk, Broad, State, Court and Common streets to Boylston street, and entered the Common near the south end of the Mall. From this point towards Park street, the children of the publick schools of both sexes were extended in two lines, neatly clad and under the direction of their instructers. Between these lines the procession of carriages passed to Park street mall, where the military part of the escort was drawn up and the General passed them in review, as he went towards the State House. Here he was received and again welcomed, in the name of the State, by His Excellency Gov. Eustis. He was thence conducted to the residence provided for him, at the corner of Beacon and Park streets.

' The appearance of the entire of this truly grand procession was august and imposing. As it passed, *Lafayette ! Lafayette !* sprang from the voice of multitudes that rolled on, and on, like wave after wave of the ocean. *Lafayette* beat in every heart ; *Lafayette* glowed on every cheek ; *Lafayette* glistened in every swimming eye ; every tongue vibrated LAFAYETTE. The whole city and country appeared to have arrayed themselves in all their glory, and beauty, and strength, at once to witness and adorn the majesty of the spectacle.'

During the General's stay the popular excitement was constant and increasing ; every thing gave way to the desire of seeing Lafayette, and every means was taken to demonstrate the joy which his arrival had produced, and to manifest the respect which every individual cherished towards him. He left Boston, with the intention, if possible, to prolong his stay in America, until the seventeenth day of the succeeding June, in order to be present at the laying of the corner stone of the Bunker Hill monument ; and he was here on that day : ' it is not necessary to say, indeed it cannot be said, how much his presence added to the interest and pleasure of the occasion.'

The day was temperate and fair, and all the arrangements made to honour it were executed with punctuality and good order. A procession was formed, about half past 10 A. M. near the State house under the direction of Brig. Gen. Theodore Lyman Jr. The military escort was composed of 16 companies, and a corps of cavalry, all volunteers and in full uniform. Next to them followed the *Survivors of the Battle*, about 40 in number, and after them about 200 other Revolutionary officers and soldiers each wearing an appropriate badge : then the subscribers to the Monument, in columns six deep, all wearing the badge of the B. H. M. Association. The Masonick fraternity succeeded. This section of the procession was very splendid, and numbered at least 2000 members, all with their jewels and regalia. The President and officers of the Association, the chaplains and committees followed. General Lafayette in a coach and four came next, accompanied by Gen. Lallemand, and followed by a carriage in which were the General's son and suite. The Governour and State officers, distinguished persons from the different states, officers of the army, navy and militia, in uniform, and a large body of private citizens closed the procession.

In this order the whole moved through Park, Common, School, Washington, Union, Hanover and Prince streets to Charles River Bridge, and thence through the Main, Green, and High streets, in Charlestown, to the Monumental square. The front of the procession had nearly reached the bridge when the rear of it left the Common. Arrived at the spot intended for the monument, (which is a little to the east of the site of the monument to Warren,) the procession formed in squares around it ; and the stone, being squared, levelled and plumbed by the Grand Master, the General, and the Hon. Daniel Webster, (president of the association,) was declared in due form to be true and proper, and the ceremonies closed with the customary religious services. Cheers from the multitude of witnesses, and salutes from Bunker's and Copp's hills announced the moment of the fact to the thousands who could not be gratified with the sight of it.

'The procession then moved to an amphitheatrical area, where preparations had been made, on a most ample scale, for the accommodation of the auditors of the Address of the President of the Association. They included a large portion of the north-eastern declivity of the battle hill. On each side of the bower, seats with awnings had been prepared, and were filled by over one thousand ladies, from all parts of the Union. In the centre of the base, a rural arch and bower, surmounted by the American Eagle, was formed for the government of the Association and some of the guests, in front of which, after the venerable Mr. Thaxter had addressed the Throne of Grace, the Orator, *sub cœlo*, pronounced an Address, which none but its author is capable of doing justice to in a summary, and which will be read with a pleasure equalled only by that which electrified the vast assemblage who listened to it for nearly one hour and a quarter. It is enough for us to say, that it was in every particular worthy of the celebrity of the orator, and that his address to the silver-headed worthies of the Revolution, and to the distinguished Guest of the Nation, filled every heart with transport.'

After the close of the Address the company repaired to Bunker's Hill, where a sumptuous entertainment was provided, at which more than four thousand persons partook. The guests separated at a seasonable hour, and the festivities of the occasion terminated with a private party at the residence of a distinguished citizen.

CHAPTER LXV.

Sicut patribus sit Deus nobis.—*City Seal.*
And as thou wast our fathers' God, be ours.

SEVERAL religious societies have been organized in Boston, since the acceptance of the city charter. After the Essex street church, first so called, removed to Boylston hall, (p. 346) a minority of that body continued to maintain worship in the Essex st. house. On the 22d of March, 1822, they requested 'a regular dismission from the majority' for the purpose of being formed into a regular church. This they received on the 5th of April, and on the 10th of June following, ten of their number, with two members of another church, were embodied according to the custom of Congregational churches. Having received an accession of members from the Old South and Park st. churches and one from Braintree, this body adopted the name by which it is now known, of *Union Church*, on the 26th of August, 1822, and on the 26th of March, 1823, the Rev. Samuel Green was installed as their pastor.

The Corner stone of the Third Universalist meeting house was laid October, 7, 1822. A silver plate was as usual deposited beneath it, on which the following was the principal inscription :

" *He that built and sustains all things is Jehovah*—This House devoted to the worship of Almighty God, and to the promulgation of his great salvation through Jesus Christ, the chief corner stone, was commenced and this stone laid, October 7th, in the year of our Lord, 1822, of the independence of the United States the 46th, and of the Institution of the City of Boston the First."

The house was dedicated in the forenoon of the 7th of May, 1823, and in the afternoon, the Rev. Paul Dean, having recently dissolved his connection with the First Universalist church, was installed as pastor of the new society. This edifice is situated at the corner of Bulfinch street and Bulfinch place. Its dimensions are 74 by 70 feet, and 35 high above the base. It is a brick building and has two towers, one for the accommodation of the bell and the other for symmetry.

In February, 1823, the Rev. Prince Hawes commenced preaching to a small congregation at South Boston. In the spring of that year, one of the members at his own expense erected a hall for their accommodation. On the 10th of December a church was organized by the name of the Evangelical Congregational Church, consisting of 13 members. Mr. Hawes was installed pastor of this church April 28, 1824. The hall in which this society assembled became so crowded that it was desirable they should be provided with a more convenient place for publick worship. Benevolent individuals subscribed for the purpose, and they have built a house of brick, 70 ft. by 50, every way commodious, but without galleries, except at one of the ends. The house was dedicated on the 9th of March, 1825.

The church that worships in the house in Chambers st. was the sixteenth Congregational church formed in Boston, and is the thirteenth in order of those now existing, but the proprietors are incorporated under the title of 'The Twelfth Congregational Society in the City of Boston.' The following statement of the leading facts connected with its early history is gathered from a memoir appended to Rev. Dr. Lowell's sermon at the ordination of the first pastor. In the year 1823, several gentlemen conferred together on the apparent want of a new house of worship for the accommodation of the increasing population of the western section of the city. It was ascertained that the Rev. Dr. Lowell's, the only Congregational society in that part of the city, comprised at that time about 350 families, and that many in the neighbourhood could not obtain suitable accommodations within a convenient distance. In view of these circumstances, a plan was originated for the erection of a new church, and in the course of a few weeks, 230 shares were subscribed by ninety persons. In January, 1824, an act of incorporation was obtained. The corner stone of the new house was laid on the 10th of May. The dedication took place October 13th : Rev. Jno. G. Palfrey preached on the occasion, from Matt. xvi. 3. On the 19th of December, Mr. Samuel Barrett, from the Theological school at Cambridge, was invited by the society to become their pastor. January 28, 1825, a church was constituted

from the members of the society, and on the 9th of February
Mr. Barrett was ordained.

The Methodist society erected a house of worship at South
Boston in the course of the year 1824. It was dedicated
January 22, 1825. By the regulations of this denomination
their clergymen are stationed in Boston, only for two successive years : this arrangement has given to the societies here
the labours of about 35 different clergymen in the course of
thirty-five years.

The Trinitarian church in Hanover street was brought
forward by members of the Old South, Park street and Union
churches. The corner stone of their edifice was laid June
20, 1825, in the presence of numerous spectators. A church
was organized July 18th, consisting of thirty-three members, part from each of the abovenamed churches. They
were formally recognized by the name of Hanover Church
at a publick meeting in Park street on the succeeding day. The
walls of this building are of rough granite, 70 feet on the
street by 71 in depth, and about 40 ft. high : tower 28 ft.
square and about 68 high. The height of walls will be accounted for, when it is remarked that a basement story, 10
feet in the clear, will occupy the whole extent of the ground :
the front part being designed for the Missionary rooms of the
American Board, and the rest for a spacious vestry. The
meeting house in Sea street is built on a similar plan, the lower story being designed for tenants.

A new Unitarian meeting house is also in a state of forwardness. It is to be built of stone, and is situated in Purchase
street. The corner stone was laid, September 7th, 1825, with
appropriate services, in the presence of about 300 persons.
An account of the origin of this undertaking was read by
Rev. ALEXANDER YOUNG. A fervent prayer was next offered
by Rev. Dr. LOWELL.—The inscription on the silver plate
to be deposited under the Stone, was read by Mr. YOUNG.—
The Chairman of the Building Committee, JOHN COTTON, Esq.
then deposited the box containing the plate, and other articles ; and the stone being duly laid, Rev. HENRY WARE Jr.
delivered an impressive address commencing with these words,
" Except the Lord build the House, they labour in vain that
build it."

There are also three other meetings regularly maintained
at the present time ; one in Charter street by Trinitarian congregationalists ; one in Purchase street by Baptists : and the
other by Methodists at the corner of Castle and Washington
streets ; so that the present number of worshipping assemblies
in the city is thirty-five.

TABLE

SHOWING

THE DATE OF THE DEDICATION OF CHURCHES,

AND OF THE

SETTLEMENT OF MINISTERS.

Meeting-houses.			Dedication.	Ministers.	Settlement.
1. New Brick.	Brick.	Steeple.	May 10, 1721.	Henry Ware jun.	Jan. 1, 1817
2. Christ Church.	Brick.	Steeple.	Dec. 29, 1723.	Asa Eaton,	Oct. 23, 1803
3. Old South.	Brick.	Steeple.	Apr. 26, 1730.	B. B. Wisner,	Feb. 21, 1821
4. Trinity.	Wood.	Plain.	Aug. 15, 1735.	J. S. J. Gardiner,	Apr. 12, 1792
5. 1. Universal.	Wood.	Plain.	1742.	S. Streeter,	May 13, 1824
6. King's Chapel.	Stone.	Tower.	Aug. 21, 1754.	{ James Freeman, F.W.P.Greenwood,	Oct. 20, 1782 Aug.29, 1824
7. 1. Baptist.	Wood.	Plain.	Dec. 22, 1771.	F. Wayland jun.	Aug. 22, 1821
8. Brattle-street.	Brick.	Tower.	July 25, 1773.	J. G. Palfrey,	June 17, 1818
9. 1. Methodist.	Wood.	Plain.	May 15, 1796.	Isaac Bonney,	1824
10. 1. Catholick.	Brick.	Cupola.	Sep. 29, 1803.	William Taylor,	1821
11. New North.	Brick.	Cupola.	May 2, 1804.	F. Parkman,	Dec. 8, 1813
12. 2. Methodist.	Brick.	Plain.	Nov. 19, 1806.	Timo. Merritt,	1825
13. Lynde-street.	Brick.	Cupola.	Nov. 27, 1806.	Charles Lowell,	Jan. 1, 1806
14. African.	Brick.	Plain.	Dec. 4, 1806.	Thomas Paul,	Dec. 4, 1806
15. 3. Baptist.	Brick.	Cupola.	Aug. 5, 1807.	Daniel Sharp,	April 29,1812
16. Chauncy-place.	Brick.	Cupola.	July 21, 1808.	N. L. Frothingham,	Mar. 15,1815
17. Federal-street.	Brick.	Steeple.	Nov. 23, 1809.	{ W. E. Channing, E. S. Gannett,	June 1, 1803 June 30,1824
18. Park-street.	Brick.	Steeple.	Jan. 10, 1810.	S. E. Dwight,	Sept. 3, 1817
19. 2. Baptist.	Brick.	Tower.	Jan. 1, 1811.	Vacant,	
20. Hollis-street.	Brick.	Steeple.	Jan. 31, 1811.	John Pierpont,	Apr. 14, 1819
21. New South.	Stone.	Steeple.	Dec. 29, 1814.	Alex. Young jun.	Jan. 19, 1825
22. 2. Universal.	Brick.	Plain.	Oct. 16, 1817.	Hosea Ballou,	Dec. 25, 1817
23. St. Matthew's.	Brick.	Cupola.	June 24, 1818.	J. L. Blake,	June, 1824
24. 2. Roman C.	Brick.	Gothick.	1819.	Patrick Byrne	
25. Essex-street.	Brick.	Steeple.	Dec. 15, 1819.	S. Green,	Mar. 27, 1823
26. St. Paul's.	Stone.	Plain.	June 30, 1820.	Vacant,	
27. Butolph-street.	Brick.	Plain.	July 5, 1821.	William Jenks,	
28. 3. Universal.	Brick.	2 Cupolas.	May 7, 1823.	Paul Dean,	May 7, 1823
29. Chambers-st.	Brick.	Plain.	Oct. 13, 1824.	Samuel Barrett,	Feb. 9, 1825
30. S. Boston Meth.	Brick.	Plain.	Jan. 22, 1825.	Solomon Sias,	1824
31. —— Evangel.	Brick.	Cupola.	Mar. 9, 1825.	Prince Hawes,	April 28,1824
32. Sea-street.	Brick.	Plain.	Unfinished.		
33. Hanover-street.	Stone.	Tower.	do.		
34. Purchase-street.	Stone.	Cupola.	do.		

Rev. Mr. Dean previous to his installation over the third Universalist church had been settled 10 years over the First: Rev.Mr. Greenwood officiated as pastor of the New South from
1818 to 1820: Rev. Mr. Merritt was located in Boston in the year 1818: Methodist clergymen officiate interchangeably: Rev. Mr. Sabine, of the Presbyterian church, was settled, Jan.
27, 1819 : the 2d Roman Catholick is under the charge of the same officers as the first.

CHAPTER LXVI.

"Lo! vales that teem with fruits, romantick hills,
(Oh! and these hills uphold a freeborn race)
Whereon to gaze the eye with joyaunce fills."

WE include in our map of Boston and its environs, some
part of each of the towns of Dorchester, Roxbury, Brookline,
Brighton, Cambridge, Watertown, Charlestown, and Chelsea.

DORCHESTER is a very pleasant town about 4½ miles south
from Boston, measuring from the centre of each town. At
present it contains about 8000 acres, including Thompson's
Island and Moon Island. The soil is generally rich and highly cultivated. The roads are numerous and crooked, but
mostly level and kept in good repair. Many fine country
seats and substantial farm-houses are thickly arranged on
their sides. The population amounts to 3684. They have a
town house, 3 congregational meeting houses, and one for
methodists. Savin Hill in this town is a place of considerable resort, and the peninsula of Squantum is famous for its
yearly Feast of Shells.

ROXBURY, adjoining Dorchester on the west, has a population of 4135. The portion of the town next to Boston is
thickly settled and forms a handsome village. Here are three
meeting houses, within a few rods of each other. There are
two other churches in different parts of the town. The west
part of the town, Jamaica plains, is a delightful spot, ornamented with elegant country seats and well cultivated gardens.
The pond which supplies the Boston aqueduct lies in that
quarter.*

BROOKLINE, next to Roxbury on the west, was formerly
considered part of Boston. This town contains about 4400
acres of land. Several gentlemen of Boston have their country seats here. The number of inhabitants by the last census was 900. This town lies on the west of the bay, and its
hills and wood lands form a pleasing portion of the scenery
in the view from Boston common. In a direct line, Brookline is four miles from the city.

---

* The proprietors of the Boston Aqueduct were incorporated to bring water in subterra-
neous pipes from Jamaica Pond in Roxbury, to the town of Boston, by an Act of the Legislature, passed February, 27, 1795. Said Pond is about four miles from Boston, and there
are four main logs from the pond, to and through most of the principal streets. The four
main logs, and all the branches connected with them, amount to about forty miles in length.
There are generally about eight hundred families supplied with water from the Aqueduct.

BRIGHTON was formerly part of the town of Cambridge and known by the name of Little Cambridge. It lies between C. and Brookline. A cattle fair was commenced here during the revolutionary war and has been increasing in importance ever since. Most of the cattle for the supply of Boston market are brought in droves to this place; often from 2 to 8000 a week : every Monday is the fair day, when the dealers in provisions resort thither to make their purchases. Once a year, in the month of October, the Mass. Agricultural Society encourage a Cattle Show and exhibition of Manufactures, by the offer and award of premiums, for the best animals, products or articles of specified descriptions, produced in any part of this state. Brighton numbers 702 inhabitants.

WATERTOWN. The village of Watertown is a flourishing neighbourhood : it is the seat of several extensive manufactories. The United States have an arsenal established in this town. *Fresh Pond*, a place of genteel resort, five miles from Boston, lies partly within this town and partly in Cambridge.

CAMBRIDGE is celebrated as the seat of Harvard College. This institution was founded in the year 1636,* and received its name from the Rev. John Harvard of Charlestown, who made the first great donation to its funds. Since that the benefactors of this institution have been numerous and liberal. The income of the College for the year 1824, arising from various permanent sources (i. e. exclusive of receipts from students and graduates) amounted to $22244, 74 cts. The expenditures during the same year amounted to $44841, 36 cts. principally in payment of salaries. The College buildings are situated on a delightful plain, three miles from Boston.† They are, University Hall, which is built of granite, 140 by 50 ft. on the ground, and 42 ft. high : Harvard, Massachusetts, Hollis, Stoughton and Holworthy halls, and Holden chapel are all of brick : these buildings all stand within the enclosure of the College fence. (See plate, p. 81.) Besides these there are a new stone building lately erected and 3 College-houses occupied by students, the President's house, and

---

* Colony Records, Oct. 25, 1636, contain the first notice of the College, towards which the Court makes a grant of 400*l.* to be paid when the work is finished—the Court to regulate the place and building.—Nov. 2, 1637, it is ordered that the College be at Newtown.—May, 1638, the name of Newtown was altered and it was called Cambridge.—First Commencement, 1642.

† *The Massachusetts Medical College* is situated in Mason street, near the Boston Common and Mall. The building is brick, 88 feet in length, and 43 in its greatest breadth. Its figure is oblong with a pediment in front, and an octagonal centre rising above the roof, and also forming a three sided projection in the rear of the building. This is surmounted by a dome, with a skylight and balustrade, giving an appearance of elegance to the neatness and fit proportions of the building.

those of several of the professors, and the Medical College in
Boston, all which belong to the University. The number
of alumni, down to the last Wednesday of August, 1825, has
been 4828. The present number of undergraduates is 234.

Cambridge contains 3295 inhabitants : it has a court house,
jail, state arsenal, and 5 houses of publick worship. There
are three principal villages, Lechmere's point, Cambridge-
port, and the neighbourhood of the Colleges.

CHARLESTOWN is a town of singular shape extending in a
northwesterly direction from Boston harbour, about nine miles
in length and not averaging a breadth of one mile, and in
some parts it is not a quarter of a mile in width. The compact or thickly settled part of the town is situated on a peninsula next to Boston, which is about 1¼ mile in length, and ¾ of
a mile in breadth, and is laid out in regular streets.

Charlestown contains a population of 6591. It has 5
houses of publick worship, a spacious alms house, and a handsome market house. It is a port of entry in conjunction with
Boston : Bunker Hill Bank is recently established here.
Besides Charlestown and Prison point bridges, which connect this town with Boston, there is Chelsea Bridge on the
Salem turnpike, and Malden Bridge, both over the Mystick
river. Breed's hill, and Bunker hill lie within this peninsula :
the former is 62 feet in height, the latter 110 feet. The
U. S. Navy-yard consists of about 60 acres of land, on
which are built a large brick warehouse, several arsenals,
magazines for various kinds of stores, a large brick mansion
house for the superintending officer, and a marine hospital.
The State Prison is at the west end of the town, and is built
of granite, 200 feet by 44, of 5 stories. The prison yard is
50⁰ feet by 400, enclosed by a wall 15 feet high. The Massachusetts Insane Hospital is delightfully situated upon Pleasant hill, on the west side of the town. It has an elegant house
for the superintendant, with 2 buildings, one on each side,
handsomely built of brick, 3 stories high.

CHELSEA is situated on the north side of Boston harbour
and Mystick river, and on the west of Lynn bay: much of
the land is low marsh or fen. The surface of the body of
the town is broken into small eminences, the highest of which
is Powder-Horn Hill, 220 feet above the sea. The settlements are thinly scattered over the town : the number of
inhabitants is 642. Chelsea anciently was considered a part
of Boston, and has always been connected with it as part of
the county of Suffolk. By the law which established the
City Police Court, the people of Chelsea are exempted from
county taxes and deprived of their voice in county concerns.
They have one meeting house occupied by a congregational
church.

APPENDIX.

No. I. Page 49.

INDIAN QUITCLAIM.

To all to whom these presents shall come,

I, Charles Josias, alias Josias Wampatuck, son and heir of Josias Wampatuck Sachem of the Indians inhabiting the Massachusetts in New-England, and grandson of Chickatabut, the former Sachem, send greeting. FORASMUCH as I am informed, and well assured from several antient Indians, as well those of my council as others, that upon the first coming of the English to sit down and settle in these parts of New England, my above named grandfather, Chickatabut, by and with the advice of his council, for encouragement thereof moving, did give, grant, sell, alienate, and confirm unto the English planters and settlers, respectively and to their several and respective heirs and assigns forever all that neck, tract or parcel of land, lying and being within the Massachusetts colony, in order to their settling and building a town there, now known by the name of Boston, as it is environed and compassed by the sea, or salt water, on the northerly, easterly, and westerly sides, and by the line of the town of Roxbury on the southerly side, with all the rivers, harbours, bays, creeks, coves, flats and appurtenances thereunto belonging, as also several other outlands belonging to the said town on the northerly and easterly sides of Charles river, and the Island called Deer Island lying about two leagues easterly from the said town of Boston between Pudding point Gut and the Broad Sound, so called, said island containing one hundred and sixty or 200 acres of land, more or less, with the privileges and appurtenances thereunto belonging, which said neck and land have since been distributed and granted out among themselves into particular allotments and other conveniences, and given, alienated, and transferred to and from one another, having been peaceably and quietly possessed, used, occupied and enjoyed, for the space of about fifty and five years last past, by the said first grantees, their heirs, successors and assigns, and now stand quietly and peaceably possessed thereof at this day. *Wherefore,* I Charles Josias, alias Josias Wampatuck. Sachem, and William Hahatou, Robert Momentauge, and Ahawton, senior, my counsellors, (by and with the allowance and advice of William Stoughton and Joseph Dudley, Esquires, my prochain amys and guardians) as well for the reasons and considerations abovementioned as for and in consideration of a valuable sum of money to me and them in hand paid by Elisha Cook, Elisha Hutchinson, Esquires, Messrs. Samuel Shrimpton, John Joyliffe, Simon Lynde, John Saffin, Edward Willis, Daniel Turell, senior, Henry Allen, John Fayerweather, Timothy Prout, senior, and Theophilus Frarey, of Boston aforesaid, for and in be-

half of themselves and the rest of the proprietated inhabitants of the town of
Boston abovesaid, the receipt of which said sum of money as full and lawful
consideration we do hereby acknowledge to have received, and thereof, and
of every part and parcel thereof, do fully acquit and discharge the said Elisha
Cooke, Elisha Hutchinson, Samuel Shrimpton, John Joyliffe, Simon Lynde,
John Saffin, Edward Willis, Daniel Turell, senior, Henry Allen, John Fayerweather, Timo. Prout, senior, and Theophilus Fraryc, and every of them, their
and every of their heirs, executors, administrators, and assigns forever, by
these presents have and hereby do for the further confirmation and ratification
of the said gift, grant, bargain or sale of the said grand Sachem, Chickatabut,
fully freely and willingly approve, ratify, establish, enfeoff and confirm the
same and do also fully and absolutely remise, release and forever quitclaim
unto the said Elisha Cooke, Elisha Hutchinson, Samuel Shrimpton, John Joyliffe, Simon Lynde, John Saffin, Edward Willis, Daniel Turell, senior, Henry
Allen, John Fayerweather, Timo. Prout, senior, and Theophilus Frarye, their
heirs and assigns respectively forever, so far as their own several and respective rights and interests are or may be: And further for and in behalf of the rest
of the proprietated inhabitants of said town of Boston and precincts thereof,
severally and their several and respective heirs and assigns forever, according
to the several interests, rights, titles and property, which each person respectively hath right unto and standeth now seized and possessed of all the aforesaid neck and tract of land now called and known by the name of the town of
Boston, and all other lands whatsoever with the said township and precincts
thereof easterly and southerly of and from Charles River, with all and every
the housing, buildings and improvements thereupon and on every part and
parcel thereof, and the Island aforesaid called Deer Island and the buildings
thereon, with all harbours, streams, coves, flats, waters, rivers, immunities,
rights, benefits, advantages, liberties, privileges, hereditaments and appurtenances whatsoever to all and every the aforementioned premises belonging, or
in any manner or wise appertaining, or therewith heretofore or now used, occupied or enjoyed, also all the estate, right, title, interest, property, claim and
demand of me the said Charles Josias, alias Wampatuck, and of all and every
my beforenamed counsellors, of, in and to the same and every part, parcel or
member thereof :

To have and to hold all and singular the abovementioned land, premises and
appurtenances and every part and parcel thereof unto them the said Elisha
Cooke, Elisha Hutchinson, Samuel Shrimpton, John Joyliffe, Simon Lynde,
John Saffin, Edward Willis, Daniel Turell, senior, Henry Allen, John Fayerweather, Timo. Prout, senior, and Theophilus Frarye, their heirs and assigns
respectively forever, for and in behalf of themselves so far as their own several
and respective rights are or may be therein. And further for and in behalf of
the several and respective proprietated inhabitants of the said town and precincts thereof, their several and respective heirs and assigns forever according
to their interest, title and propriety, which each person hath or may have just
right unto and standeth now seized and possessed of, and to their only proper
use and benefit and behoof forever, freely, peaceably and quietly, without any
manner of reclaim, challenge or contradiction of me, the said Charles Josias,
alias Wampatuck, and my above named counsellors or either or any of us,
or either or any of our heirs, executors, administrators or assigns, and without
any accompt, reckoning, answer, sum or sums of money in time to come to be
made, yielded, paid or done, so that neither I, the said Charles Josias, alias

Wampatuck,my counsellors, our or either of our heirs, executors nor any others
by, from or under me, us or them or any of them, shall or will by any ways or
means hereafter have, ask, or claim, challenge or demand any estate, right,
title or interest, of, in or to the premises or any part or parcel thereof, but are
and shall be utterly excluded and for ever debarred from the same by virtue
of these presents; and I the said Charles Josias alias Wampatuck and counsellors aforesaid for us and every of us, our and every of our heirs, executors, administrators and successors respectively do hereby covenant, promise, grant
and oblige unto the aforenamed grantees, their heirs, executors, administrators and assigns by these presents to warrant, maintain and defend the aforementioned premises and all and every part and parcel thereof unto them the
said grantees, their heirs and assigns forever as aforesaid, for and in behalf of
themselves and others the proprietated inhabitants according to their respective
rights and interest, against all and every person and persons whomsoever law-
fully claiming or demanding the same or any part or parcel thereof, and at
any time or times hereafter, upon demand, to give and pass more full and ample release, confirmation and assurance of all and every the said premises unto the said grantees, their heirs and assigns to the uses aforesaid, and to do
and perform any other act or acts, device or devices in the law necessary or
requisite thereunto, as in law or equity can or may be devised, advised or required. *In witness whereof,* I said Charles Josias alias Wampatuck, William
Hahaton, Robert Momentauge and Ahawton, senior   my counsellors,
have hereunto set our hands and seals the 19th day of March A. D. 1684—5
Annoque Ri. Ris. Caroli Secundi Angliae, &c. xxxvii.

Charles Josias **A**   (L. S.)
Ahawton Senr. **M**   (L. S.)
Willm. Hahaton   (L. S.)
Robert **8** *Momentauge.* (L. S.)

Signed, sealed and delivered in presence of us,
William Williams, E. Lyde.

Charles Josias and Wm. Ahawton jr. in behalf of himself and his father
Ahawton, *Indians,* acknowledged the abovesaid writing to be their voluntary
act and deed, March 19th, 1684—5.   Coram *James Russell,* Assistant.

We underwritten prochain amys and guardians to Charles Josias sachem of
the Massachusetts,do consent and approve of the abovesaid confirmation of title
and release of claim.   *William Stoughton, Joseph Dudley.*

David, Son and heir of Sagamore George and in his right having some claim
to Deer Island, doth hereby for just consideration relinquish his right to the
town of Boston of all his right and claim thereto, and consents to the abovesaid
deed of sale, as witness his hand and seal **Ö**. In presence of us
William Williams, Benja. Dowse.

Feb. 1. 1708. Received and accordingly entered and examined per
Addington Davenport, Register.

No. II. Page 78.

From Welde's Short Story of the Antinomians, &c.—Ed. 1692, *p.* 23.

'We whose names are under written (have diligently observed this honourable Court's proceedings against our dear and reverend brother in Christ, Mr.
Wheel. now *under censure of the Court for the truth of Christ*) we do humbly

beseech this honourable Court to accept this remonstrance and petition of ours, in all due submission tendered to your worships. For first, whereas our beloved brother Mr. W. is censured for contempt, by the greater part of this honoured Court, we desire your worships to consider the sincere intention of our brother to promote your end in the day of fast : for whereas we do perceive your principal intention the day of fast looked chiefly at the public peace of the churches, our reverend brother did to his best strength and as the Lord assisted him labour to promote your end, and therefore endeavoured to draw us nearer unto Christ the head of our union, that so we might be established in peace, which we conceive to be the true way, sanctified of God, to obtain your end, *and therefore deserves no such censure, as we conceive.*

Secondly, Whereas our dear brother is censured of sedition, we beseech your worships to consider that either the person condemned must be culpable of some seditious fact, or his doctrine must be seditious, or must breed sedition in the hearts of his hearers, or else we know not upon what grounds he could be censured. Now to the first, we have not heard any that have witnessed against our brother for any seditious fact. Secondly, neither was the doctrine itself, being no other but *the very expressions of the Holy Ghost himself*, and therefore cannot justly be branded with sedition. Thirdly, if you look at the effects of his doctrine upon the hearers, it hath not stirred up sedition in us, not so much as by accident : we have not drawn the sword, as sometimes Peter did rashly, neither have we rescued *our innocent brother*, as sometimes the Israelites did Jonathan, and yet they did not seditiously. The covenant of free grace, held forth by our brother, hath taught us rather to become humble suppliants to your Worships, and if we should not prevail, we would rather with patience give *our cheeks to the smiters.* Since therefore the teacher, the doctrine and the hearers be most free from sedition (as we conceive) we humbly beseech you in the name of the L. J. C. your Judge and ours, and for the honour of this Court and the proceedings thereof, that you will be pleased either to make it appear to us and all the world, to whom the knowledge of all these things will come, *wherein the sedition lies,* or else acquit our brother of such a censure.

Farther we beseech you remember the old method of Satan, the ancient enemy of free grace, in all ages of the churches, who hath raised up such calumnies against the faithful prophets of God; Elija was called the troubler of Israel, 1 *Kings*, xviii. 17,18. Amos was charged for conspiracy, *Amos,* vii. 10. Paul was counted a pestilent fellow, or mover of sedition, and a ringleader of a sect, *Acts*, xxiv. 5. and Christ himself as well as Paul was charged to be a teacher of new doctrine, *Mark*, i. 27. *Acts*, xvii. 19. Now we beseech you consider, whether that old Serpent work not after his old method, even in our days.

Farther we beseech you consider *the danger of meddling* against the prophets of God. *Ps.* cv. 14, 15. for what ye do unto them, the L. J. takes as done unto himself : if you hurt any of his members the head is very sensible of it, for so saith the Lord of Hosts, *He that toucheth you, toucheth the apple of mine eye, Zech.* ii. 8. And better a mill stone were hanged about our necks, and that we were cast into the sea, than that we should offend any of these little ones which believe on him, *Matt.* xviii. 6.

And lastly we beseech you consider, how you should stand in relation to us, as nursing fathers, which give us encouragement to promote our humble requests to you, or else we would say with the prophet, *Isa.* xxii. 4. *Look from*

me that I may weep bitterly, Labour not to comfort me, &c. or as *Jer* ix. 2.
Oh that I had in the wilderness a lodging place of a way-faring man.

And thus have we made known our griefs and desires to your worships, and
leave them upon record with the Lord and with you, knowing that if we should
receive repulse from you, with the Lord we shall find grace.

Signed by *Wm. Aspinwall, Thos. Marshall, Richard Gridley* and many others.'

No. III.   Page 93.

*Immediately following the words " accept thereof" in the agreement respecting
the incorporation of Braintree, the Boston records, Jan.* 27, 1640, *read thus :*

' Provided that this order shall not extend to any more or other land than
such as shall make payment of the said rates so agreed upon of 4s and 3s an
acre, and upon the former consideration there is granted to the mount all the
rocky ground lying between the fresh brooke and Mr. Coddington's brook adjoining to Mr. Haulghes farme and from the west corner of that farm to the
southermost corner of Mr. Hutchinsons farm, to be reserved and used in common forever by the inhabitants and landholders there together with one other
parcel of rocky ground near to the Knighte neck which was left out by the
third company of Lotte, excepting all such ground lying among or neere the
sd rocky ground formerly granted out in Lotte to pticular persons.

Also there is granted to Mr. William Thompson, pastor of the church at the
Mount, 120 acre of land there free from the forsd. rate of 3s per acre.

Also there is granted to Mr. Henry Flint 80 acre of land there in like sort
free from the sd rate of 3s. per acre.

Also there is granted to John Lugg a great lot for 9 head at the mount upon
the usual terms.'

No. IV.   Page 212.*

Original Covenant of the New North Church.

We, whose names are subscribed, apprehending ourselves called of God
into the chh. state of the gospel, do, first of all, confess ourselves unworthy to
be so highly favoured of the Lord, and admire that free and rich grace of his,
which triumphs over so great unworthiness ; and then, with a humble reliance
upon the aids of grace therein promised to them, that in a sense of their own
inability to do any good thing, do humbly wait upon him for all, we do thankfully lay hold on his covenant, and would do the things that please him. We
declare our serious belief of the chr. religion, contained in the S. S. and as exhibited in the confession of faith received in our chhs. ; heartily resolving to
conform our lives to the rules of that holy religion, so long as we live in this
world. We give ourselves to the Lord Jehovah, who is the Father, Son and
Holy Ghost ; and avouch him to be our God, our Father, our Saviour and
Leader, and receive him as our portion. We give up ourselves unto the bles-

---

* P. 204. The Manifesto of the Brattle-street Society is printed at large, in Rev. Mr. Palfrey's Historical Discourse, published recently.

51

sed Jesus, who is the Lord Jehovah, and adhere to him as the head of his people in the cov. of God, and rely on him as our Prophet, our Priest and our King, to bring us into eternal blessedness. We acknowledge our everlasting and indispensable obligations to glorify God in all the duties of a godly, sober, righteous life ; and very particularly in the duties of a church state, and a body of people associated for an obedience to him, and enjoyment of him, in all the ordinances of the gospel. And we therefore depend upon his gracious assistance for the faithful discharge of the duties thus incumbent upon us. We desire and intend, and with dependence upon promised and powerful grace, we engage to walk together as a church of our L. J. C. in the faith and order of the gospel, so far as we shall have the same revealed unto us, and will conscientiously attend the worship of God, the sacraments of the N. T. and the discipline of his kingdom and all his holy instructions, in communion with one another ;—and that we will lovingly watch over one another, carefully avoid stumbling blocks and contentions, as becomes a people whom the Lord has bound up together in the bundle of life. At the same time, we also present our offspring with us unto the Lord, purposing with his help to do our part in the methods of a religious education, that they may be the Lord's. And all this we do, flying to the blood of the everlasting covenant for the pardon of our many errours, and praying that the glorious Lord, who is the great Shepherd, would prepare and strengthen us for every good work, to do his will, working in us that which is well pleasing in his sight, to whom be glory forever. Amen.

FINIS.

INDEX.

ERRATA.

Page 20, *line* 44, for *now* read *since.* P. 42, *l.* 34, for 151 *were brethren,* r. 94 *were men and 57 women.* P. 51, *l.* 26. for *March,* 9, 1638, r. *Feb.* 27, 1643. P. 56, *l.* 6, dele *number.* and after *deceased* insert *and Robert Harding, now in Virginia. l.* 10, for 1645 r. 1642. P. 84, *l.* 4,* for *Burton's* read *Barton's.* P. 93, *l.* 14, for 17*th.* r. 27*th.* P. 119, *l.* 4, for *Makepeace,* r. *Wm. Wilson.* P. 120, *l.* 15, for *north* r. *south.* P. 173,*l.* 7, after *Randolph* insert *is.* P. 135,* for *reduced* r. *altered.* P. 214. *l.* 1, and P. 217* for *sixth* r. *seventh* P. 221, *l.* 47. for *David* r. *Robert.* P. 226, *l.* 43, for 1736 r. 1737. P. 264,* for *an &c.* r. *the Stamp Act Congress.* P. 282, *l.* 6, after *regiments,* insert *the* 29*th, but to retain.* P. 286, *l.* 4, for *Master* r. *Mr.* P. 313, *l.* 11, for *Plymouth* r. *Milton.* P. 360, *l.* 5, for *two* r. *four.* P. 379, note, *l.* 2. for 1143 r. 2613.

INDEX

BOSTON:
Printed by Munroe & Francis.

CPSIA information can be obtained
at www.ICGtesting.com
Printed in the USA
LVHW101851010722
722567LV00001B/2

9 781429 021913